GROWING VEGETABLES

WEST OF THE
CASCADES

35th Anniversary Edition

GROWING VEGETABLES
WEST OF THE CASCADES 35th Anniversary Edition

the complete guide to

ORGANIC GARDENING

STEVE SOLOMON
& MARINA MCSHANE

SASQUATCH BOOKS
SEATTLE

Copyright © 2015 by Steve Solomon and Marina McShane
Illustrations copyright © 2000 by Muriel Brown

Printed in the United States of America
Published by Sasquatch Books
SASQUATCH BOOKS with colophon is a registered trademark of Penguin Random House LLC

23 22 21 20 19   9 8 7 6 5 4 3 2

Editors: Gary Luke and Christy Cox | Production editor: Emma Reh | Illustrations: Muriel Brown
Cover design: Anna Goldstein | Cover photos: © iStock.com/ Innershadows/ Radishes
   © Alloy Photography/ Veer/ Tomatoes | © Zidi/ Veer/ Artichokes
   © Collage Photography/ Veer/ Eggplants
Interior design: Rebecca Shapiro | Interior composition: Scott Taylor | Copyeditor: Carrie Wicks

Library of Congress Cataloging-in-Publication Data
Solomon, Steve, 1942- author.
 Growing vegetables west of the Cascades : the complete guide to organic
growing / Steve Solomon and Marina McShane. -- 35th anniversary edition [7th edition]
     pages cm
Includes bibliographical references and index.
ISBN 978-1-57061-972-4 (alk. paper)
I. Vegetable gardening--Northwest Coast of North America. 2. Organic gardening--Northwest Coast of North America. I. McShane, Marina, author. II. Title.
SB324.3.S67 2015
635--dc23
                           2015006731

ISBN: 978-1-57061-972-4

Sasquatch Books
1904 Third Avenue, Suite 710
Seattle, WA 98101
(206) 467-4300
SasquatchBooks.com

Certified Chain of Custody
SUSTAINABLE FORESTRY INITIATIVE
Promoting Sustainable Forestry
www.sfiprogram.org
SFI-01268

SFI label applies to the text stock

CONTENTS

Introduction

The cheapest experience you can get comes
secondhand . . . if you'll only buy it.

—Sidney Solomon, my father, in private conversation

IN YOUR HANDS is a food gardening guide for the Cascadia bioregion. Most people call it the maritime Northwest.

Cascadia needs its own food gardening book. West of the mountains, summer days are rarely hot except for a few days during most summers, when they get *really* hot; rarely do summer nights feel warm enough for short-sleeved shirts. Heat-demanding vegetable varieties that perform excellently in the Midwest grow poorly in Cascadia. Cascadian gardens can provide vegetables during the winter when soils east of the Rocky Mountains are frozen solid several feet deep; eastern books say nothing about this possibility. Cascadia has a perverse rainfall pattern; lots of moisture in winter when crops don't need it, but little or none in summer when they do. Heavy winter rains combined with a unique geology have leached Cascadian soils into a pattern of infertility far different than the soils of the eastern United States. The East contends with different pests; traditional eastern techniques that evade those difficulties do not apply to Cascadia.

Had the indigenous Cascadians been food gardeners, then the first Anglo-Americans arriving in the Oregon Territory might have learned regionally appropriate agriculture from them. But the tribes along the West Coast did not grow food. So the invaders farmed and gardened as though they were still in Ohio (where the largest fraction of them came from). As I learned more about Cascadian soils, I came to think the local tribes intelligently avoided food gardening. I also strongly suspect, without evidence, that the first Cascadians knew other Native Americans raised crops, and probably tried it themselves in natural meadows. And failed.

When I arrived in the late 1970s, Cascadia resembled a Third World country exporting wood products and farm crops. Like other poor countries, Cascadia imported technology. We used gardening books published in New York City or Emmaus, Pennsylvania, and we bought seeds from mail-order catalogs east of the Rockies and from national picture-packet distributors' racks that offered varieties not suited to Cascadia. I settled in Oregon one year before the publication of Binda Colebrook's *Winter Gardening in the Maritime Northwest*. Binda's book opened my eyes to this possibility. Thanks to Binda, I started Territorial Seed Company because seeds for varieties crucial to winter gardening were difficult to obtain.

These days many Cascadian gardeners take advantage of their climate's possibilities.

Reputable regional garden/homestead seed businesses and seedling growers now supply appropriate varieties. I feel proud to have helped this transformation along. I consider *Growing Vegetables West of the Cascades* to be a valuable regional resource that I am responsible for, so I have kept this book in print by steadily improving it as I learned more. The last major upgrades were made for the fifth edition, published over 15 years ago. This, the seventh, has been broadly improved by 15 more years of growing experience and the great deal I've learned about soil fertility in that time.

Marina McShane, an old and dear friend who lives near Eugene, Oregon, and has been gardening nearly as many years as I have, helped me write this edition because in 1994 I moved to Nelson, British Columbia, and soon thereafter was led to Tasmania, the smallest and least-known state of Australia. Tassie is a remote, uncrowded temperate South Pacific island, slightly smaller than western Oregon, with a noticeably lower population density. I feel blessed to live here. Tassie life these days is a lot like Oregon was when I first settled there. Tasmania is a hardscrabble place of forests, fisheries, and sheep; of people mostly concerned about family; of narrow, twisty roads and slightly untidy homesteads with chickens, vegetable gardens, and sometimes a house cow. Tasmanians who are after material wealth move to the mainland.

Locals consider the part of Tasmania I live in a "banana belt," much like Elkton, Oregon, where I used to live. Where I garden now has a climate like you'd find near the Rogue River, 5 miles inland from Gold Beach, Oregon, so I have not forgotten how to take full advantage of Cascadia's climate. In fact, living in this gentle district has shown me winter gardening possibilities that apply to coastal Northern California. What I have lost touch with are the newest pest control products and some new vegetable varieties because Australia Quarantine makes it awkward to fully evaluate them. In addition to contributing generally, Marina has investigated and written up those specific areas.

Why I Grow Most of My Own Food

Marina and I have long been homesteaders. Homesteading means producing products or services from your own property that earn income or that are personal survival necessities, like food or firewood. I encourage this lifestyle because when people create any part of their necessities, they develop confidence. They're less concerned with pleasing the authority paying their salary; they're less dependent on a government that can't be influenced and often works toward harmful ends. I think life would be better for everyone if more people would produce their own necessities. Many independence-minded Cascadians agree with me. That's why I've sold so many books these past 35 years and why Territorial Seed Company did surprisingly well.

Independence mindedness greatly increases when a person enjoys a high degree of physical well-being, but these days the majority of North Americans are trapped in a dwindling spiral, starting with poor nutrition leading to poor health, leading to dependency on medicines that further lower overall health. The way out is not found by seeking a smarter doctor. The way out requires (1) overcoming unhealthy eating habits and switching to nutrient-dense whole foods while (2) eliminating otherwise decent foods that happen to be inappropriate for your body's genetic makeup or foods it reacts badly to. In my opinion that's all it takes to keep most people healthy, make them energetic and optimistic, and make them live longer. For those who haven't degenerated too far, eating right heals diseases caused by years of wrong feeding.

Upgrading food habits is not easy at best, but this difficult personal transformation has been made even more difficult because the nutritional content of all foods has declined a great deal over the last century. In order to make a profit, farmers have been mining their soil of plant nutrients. They cannot afford to restore what many previous crops have taken. So the basic foods like wheat and corn as well as fruits and vegetables, whether conventionally or organically grown, are not nearly as nutrient dense as they should be. They do not taste as good as they could. *They do not satisfy.* Eating foods that aren't nutrient-dense creates powerful urges to munch out on over-seasoned junk.

Certified organic is nutritionally better than "conventional" but not good enough, partly because it too must be sold into a profit-driven market. Replace conventional foods with the usual certified organic and habitual cravings are still slow to fade. A more effective way to reform eating habits and improve health is to enjoy the wonderful flavors of fresh, nutrient-dense home-garden vegetables. Give it a few years to work on you, and a big veggie garden can effortlessly uplift your food preferences.

Food produced on remineralized, balanced soil tastes enormously better because it contains much more nutrition. I don't mean the insignificant 25 percent increase that the organic farming industry proudly claims for its fruits and vegetables. I'm talking about packing 200 to 300 percent more nutrition into food by going beyond what most people think of as organically grown. Imagine eating a carrot that tastes twice as carroty, with complex undertones of raspberry and ginger, a barely sensed aroma of carnations, a lingering pleasant aftertaste on the back palate, and a sweetness that's so sweet that any sweeter would be disgusting. That's the sort of thing I mean. I mean steamed snap beans that don't *need* butter, salt, or pepper. That sort of thing.

If you want to conveniently learn more about the benefits of taking in several times the amount of vitamins, essential minerals, enzymes, and other nutritional elements than the average person gets today, this is explained in plain talk (and unobtrusively documented with peer-reviewed publications) by Dr. Jana Bogs, a soil-health consultant working in Hawaii. Her book *Beyond Organics* should make you stand up and demand nutrient-dense food. Thomas Pawlick's *The End of Food* will do that too.

If the majority of North American farms grew nutrient-dense crops, the health of North America would improve enormously. But remineralizing exhausted soils is not affordable when

the only way for the grower to make a profit is to reduce the cost of inputs. I think an honest accounting of the cost of food production would include at least two-thirds the current burden of medical care, 90 plus percent of all dental care (there still would be traumatic injuries), and social costs arising from people self-medicating with illegal substances that have ruined so many lives and communities and so wastefully occupied the criminal justice system.

Have you seen those huge tables in the back of how-to-be-healthy books asserting that 100 grams of broccoli contain exactly so many milligrams of vitamin B_6 and so forth? These statistics are not The Truth. They are, in fact, a powerful statistical deception. The numbers are *averages* of a great many samples grown on different soils taken at different times of year. Had you been shown the range of possibilities instead of the averages, you would realize that one sample contains several times more B_6 than the average and another might provide next to none.

Do these differences really matter? Doesn't it all average out? Sorry! No matter how healthy the choices, consuming average nutrient density no longer produces superior health because the overall nutrition in all foods, either organically grown or conventional, has decreased steadily over the last 60 years. This decline regarding conventionally grown foods has been indisputably documented. Comparing the averages in the most recent USDA report with a similar report from the early 1990s shows a 50 percent decline in almost all nutritional elements in all types of fruits and vegetables. Between 1963 and

2000 the average vitamin C content of peppers dropped from 128 milligrams per 100 grams to 89 milligrams per 100 grams. The vitamin A content of apples dropped from 90 milligrams to 53 milligrams. Nearly half the calcium and vitamin A once found in broccoli has disappeared. The potassium content of collards has fallen from 400 milligrams to 170 milligrams and magnesium from 57 milligrams to 9 milligrams. Cauliflower has lost half its vitamin C, thiamine, and riboflavin. Calcium in pineapple has dropped from 17 milligrams per 100 grams to 7 milligrams. Etc. (Source: "Vegetables Without Vitamins," *Life Extension Foundation Magazine*, www.Lef.org, March 2001)

The organic food industry proudly points out that its food contains about 25 percent more nutrition on average than conventionally grown food. But think beyond that statistical deceit: if roughly half the nutrient content of all foods has been lost between 1963 and 2000, then these days organically grown food provides about two-thirds of the nutrition that conventionally grown foods provided in 1963. And in 1963 foods provided much less nutrition than they did before the First World War, when chemical fertilizers began to replace crop rotations, green manure crops, animal manures, and composts.

To grow nutrient-dense food, the soil has to abundantly provide plants with at least 11 chemical elements in amounts that are in balance with each other. Farmers can't afford to bring soil to that degree of fertility. Instead the soil is fertilized to produce the highest-possible bulk yield at the lowest-possible cost of inputs. And this is a typical result: spuds grown on balanced, remineralized soil can contain about 11 percent protein; however, the usual industrial farming product, the supermarket sort, the frozen french fries by the 50-pound-bag sort, can contain about 8 percent protein. The 11 percent protein spud also provides far more minerals, vitamins, and other nutritional factors. The 8 percent protein spuds yield 25 percent more bushels per acre. The grower of calorie-dense food spends much less on fertilizer. The grower of calorie-dense food stays in business.

Suppose you are an ambitious potato farmer with a mortgage and crop loans. Which sort of spud are you going to grow? An indebted organic potato farmer might agonize over the choice, but would he choose differently? It's a rare farmer practicing any agricultural religion who could choose to harvest fewer bushels with a much higher cost of production.

Now suppose Cascadians had to depend on spuds as their staff of life much like Irish cottagers did around 1830—plain spuds; roasted, baked, and boiled spuds—spuds at every meal. We could satisfy our appetites with fine-tasting protein-, mineral-, and vitamin-dense potatoes or we could, by culinary magic, season up our relatively tasteless 8 percent protein demineralized, devitaminized potatoes. If we lived on 8 percent protein potatoes, over a few generations we'd become shorter in height and our life spans would decrease; we'd be less intelligent and, overall, far less healthy. And collectively, socially, we would have to spend far more than any amount of money we saved by not building soil fertility on hospitals and doctors, mental therapists, disability care, and prisons, not to count the cost of all that pain and suffering. That accurately describes what is happening right now.

There is a simple mathematical equation to express this idea:

Health = Nutrition ÷ Calories

The average health of a broad population equals the total nutrition in their dietary intake divided by the total number of calories accompanying these nutrients.

If we receive 2,000 units of nutrition from our daily 2,000 calories, then our health equals "one," but if only 1,000 units of nutrition are in our 2,000 daily calories, then our health equals "one-half" while most people's body size increases from one to two. Perhaps this idea seems too simple to explain such a complex subject, but the truth is actually that simple. If people ate such that their nutritional intake was high compared to the number of calories they were consuming, then they would be slender, far healthier, more intelligent, and naturally longer-lived compared to what is considered normal these days.

For nearly a century, a huge amount of evidence connecting nutrient density to health has been ignored or denigrated by interests controlling how medical doctors are educated. These same interests try to control what the public is told about health. For example, in 1939 an American research dentist named Weston Price published a book called *Nutrition and Physical Degeneration*. It is so straightforward it could be required reading in high school. The book should have transformed how all people grow and process their foods, but it was widely ignored. Price discovered why *every* person living in dozens of extremely remote communities he visited had perfect teeth,

legendary good health, and a long life. Everybody. The reason was extreme isolation. They had little or no money, and nothing to buy in any case. There was no general store. There were no tins of jam or Spam or condensed milk or refined sugar, no white flour. They grew, gathered, fished, or hunted everything they ate. They had no choice but to raise food naturally and prepare it simply. The community was so healthy because, over time, it had learned which foods healed illness and produced the greatest health—and concentrated on those. I consider Price's book one of the most important works of the twentieth century; without this information we would be entirely lost in a stormy sea of illness and suffering, without the slightest idea of how healthy and long-lived properly nourished humans can be.

Weston Price and his wife made three globe-spanning journeys between 1933 and 1936. Their first was to Europe, where they visited healthy communities in extremely remote Swiss highland valleys and the Outer Hebrides off Scotland. They subsequently visited Africa, Peru, Australia, Melanesia, Polynesia, and the Canadian north. In every isolated community most people lived past age 80 and possessed all their teeth in old age with no sign of tooth decay, gum disease, or loss of jawbone. Price provides many photos showing bright, toothy smiles without a toothbrush in the community. There was no sign of the degenerative diseases we consider normal these days—cancer, heart disease, diabetes, etc. Childbirth was rarely difficult; almost all children and mothers survived. Infant mortality was very low, and the birth rate was in balance with that. Death arrived from misadventure or old age. Old people died with all their teeth, without decay and firmly in place. Price also commented on the high moral standards in these healthy communities. The people seemed more intelligent than usual, better poised, and more spiritually aware (without organized religious formalities). Price also analyzed their foods as best he could using the (portable) chemistry of his era. He determined that on average people in these communities received about five times the nutrition compared to the average American of that time. The only major aspect Price missed researching would have required doing soil analyses to compare the local soil with the human health it created.

One lesson I take from Price's book is that no diet is optimal for all humans. The highland Swiss thrived on rye bread and dairy products; the Scots in the Outer Hebrides ate seafood, kale, and oats. The isolated Native Americans of northern Canada ate mostly animal foods (but not only muscle tissue). Healthy highland Africans ate mostly cereals; isolated tropical Africans ate mostly starchy roots. Long-lived remote Pacific Islanders mostly ate garden vegetables and seafood. It is obvious to me that after wandering humans settle in a new region, those who can't handle the local food possibilities fail to run the gauntlet of childhood disease, and a community's genetics comes to match the available foods. People can thrive on almost any reasonable assortment of nutrient-dense foods.

No place remained free of industrial foods after the Second World War. People in these once-remote communities still have the same genes, but their extraordinary health and longevity have disappeared. Price's book provides the best documentation we have of the natural human potential for health and longevity. His research proves to me that a long, healthy life is the God-given entitlement of almost every body, but we have sold our birthright for cheap, industrial food.

I'm not yet done with health equals nutrition divided by calories. Please examine a few foods through the lens of my formula. Take refined sugar. It is all calories and no nutrition. None! Every single calorie we eat as sugar reduces our total nutritional intake because taking in empty calories *prevents* us from eating foods that do contain nutrition. Worse, we now know that eating too much fruit sugar (except when it is part of whole raw fruit) causes deadly metabolic diseases.

Gram for gram, fats contain more calories than sugars. Most fats contain very little nutrition. Every calorie of low-grade fat we take in reduces our ability to consume foods that do contain the nutrients we need. The body does require fats, but ask yourself, please, what proportion of most people's total caloric intake these days comes in the forms of fat and sugar. Half? More than half? When I was a young man, it would have been less than 25 percent.

So if sugar and most fats are the worst, what's at the extreme healthy end of the food spectrum? The best single food I know of, the one that offers the most nutrition for the calories it provides, is an uncooked dark green leaf that was grown on fully mineralized soil. You might have to spend half your entire day chewing in order to take in enough calories from a diet of only raw lettuce, kale, spinach, endive, Swiss chard, etc. Your jaw muscles would become very strong, and you would be slender no matter how much you ate. But you would certainly be a well-nourished, long-lived scarecrow.

I think God makes jokes to enlighten us. Yes, an occasional aged Alaskan bush dweller may seem healthy on a diet of whiskey, coffee with evaporated milk and sugar, overcooked moose meat, and white flour and lard biscuits with tinned jam, but we're probably not looking at the result of superman genes. More likely, that guy had a very good nutritional start, and then supplementing mostly empty industrial foods with wild game and by foraging kept him going. But for most of us to have a long, enjoyable life, we must eat a broad mixture of whole, fresh nutrient-dense foods. Our foods must not have been devitalized (some nutritional elements removed) like white flour is. Our foods must not be adulterated with toxic preservatives or other artificial ingredients. And most importantly, our foods must be grown on soils we have intentionally made as fertile and balanced as they possibly can be so that the food coming from those soils is maximally nutrient dense.

The smallest and easiest-to-comprehend book I know of about the human potential for health and longevity is *The Wheel of Health* by Dr. G. T. Wrench (see Additional Reading, page 339). Dr. Wrench explains that our health began with our "start," our mother's nutrition long before our conception. A person whose body got a good start and who then mostly eats whole nutrient-dense foods can enjoy perfect teeth without ever seeing a dentist, will experience no degenerative disease, and will have to a long and physically pleasant life. The human birthright includes the possibility of an easy death at extreme old age if we are healthy. Alternatively, we may experience a lot of disease, but with medical intervention probably live almost as long, suffering from suboptimum health all the way through. It's our choice.

As things stand now I cannot buy nutrient-dense food at any price. That's why I feel compelled to grow a big food garden. There have been times when I've wished to travel for months or years, to adventure, to not be responsible for my nutrition beyond making healthy choices, but each time I depended on industrial foods for more than a few months, my health suffered. There's much truth in this old saying: If you wish to be happy for a day, buy a new car. If you wish to be happy for a weekend, get married. If you wish to be happy for your lifetime, be a food gardener.

I have always made myself available to help others. If you wish to contact me, send an e-mail to stsolomo@soilandhealth.org or write by snail mail to PO Box 524, Exeter, Tasmania 7275 Australia. To contact Marina McShane, use mcshanemarina@gmail.com.

The best books about improving human health with better farming methods were written between 1930 and 1960. Often not even one used copy of these titles is for sale on the Internet. I have made many of these books available as free downloads from soilandhealth.org. Complete bibliographic information on every book I mention can be found in Additional Reading (page 339). You are invited to study the contents of the Soil and Health Library; it will substantiate everything I have asserted in this introduction.

Chapter One
BASICS

The agriculturalist is the servant of the plant.

—Louise Howard, second wife of Sir Albert Howard

BEFORE THE TWENTIETH century 90 percent of Americans lived on farms or in small towns where residential lots were often a half acre or larger. Growing backyard veggies was the usual. Children learned by helping. People these days grow up with computers, mass-market entertainment, and fast-food restaurants. And much of the veggie gardening information in circulation today is oversimplified, incomplete, or does not apply to Cascadia. This chapter tries to compensate.

Competition

The best way I know to understand another being is to imagine being in its boots and trying to walk in them. So please consider the awareness of a wild plant, and then assume the viewpoint of a vegetable.

Sure, plants are aware! We don't notice because plants aren't concerned about the things humans are. Some people intuitively understand animals. These folks rarely get snapped at by little dogs, nor do they try to pet cats that'll scratch. Some people have green thumbs. For others, every plant they tend sickens and dies. I hope most brown-thumbedness is caused by ignorance.

Plants do not possess individuality. A plant is like one skin cell. Kill a few cells and the skin grows back. I suspect each skin cell considers itself to be the whole skin. Plants similarly participate in a shared consciousness involving all the plants of their species in the region. Their collective interest is survival, usually by domination and occasionally by clever tricks that avoid domination. The spiritual nature of plants can't be easily communicated with words, so I hope you will come to see what plants are up to. One way to entice that insight is to spend some time leaning on your hoe.

When your muscles become a bit tired, rest the working end of the hoe on the soil, hold the handle near the top with both hands, and take some weight off your feet. Then stare into the distance or at some part of your garden, and just *look*—better you don't think. When you inevitably do think, don't give yourself a problem about having resumed thinking when you're supposed

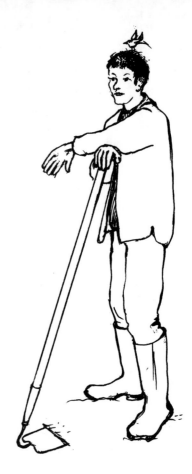

to not be thinking—a mistake that people who try to meditate often make—just resume hoeing. And don't let anyone call this practice laziness! Hoe leaning is every bit as vital a gardening task as hoe sharpening.

Hoe leaning helps to silence mental chatter; to paraphrase the Book on this, be still and ye shall know. My own hoe leaning revealed that plants are focused on a constant life-or-death struggle to access light and soil resources and to dominate space. And that plants are not nice contestants. They steal the other guy's light and poison the other guy's soil.

Each plant family has unique strategies to win the domination game. Young trees make no seeds for some years but initially direct all their energy into growing tall so that they can shade out competition. Once they secure some space, they then make jillions of seeds that can, because of the height they're released at, travel longer distances. Wild lettuce rapidly spreads broad leaves over its low-growing neighbors while its juicy taproot patiently stores up food against the day its seedstalk rapidly overtops everything around.

Cascadia's mild winters support many biennial species that use a strategy similar to lettuce's. Biennials mature their seeds in midsummer while conditions are dry, and then they die. The seeds sprout with the autumn rains and proceed to grow slowly through winter, a season when most competitors go dormant or die. During winter they slowly store up food while the grasses can barely grow. In spring biennials use up their larder to grow so fast that they outdo competitors.

Wild plants are adapted to intense competition; many species thrive on infertile soil. They survive long periods of moisture stress. They tolerate strong wind. When edible wild plants became garden vegetables, they received a protected environment; richer, moister, and looser soil; far less competition; and assisted reproduction. In exchange they transformed themselves into noncompetitive monstrosities: grotesque things that make thick, juicy great-tasting leaves, pods, or stems; larger flowers; bigger, sweeter fruit; and tastier seeds. Vegetables only grow fast in rich garden soil, but weeds in the garden grow several times faster. Gardeners observe that veggies do poorly when competing with weeds,

but most gardeners fail to grasp that vegetables shouldn't be allowed to compete with each other too much.

Intensive gardening is the fashionable system. It aims to achieve the highest-possible yield from the least possible land and water, by making super soil and then packing plants as densely as they can seem to withstand each other's competition. Intensive gardening requires more hand labor but food gardening is small scale. That seems sensible. I started food gardening in 1974 by practicing the intensive method and continued with it until I went into the vegetable seed business in 1980.

To sell vegetable seeds ethically, I had to grow variety trials. A trial requires careful observation of each plant. Are all the plants from that seed packet identical, similar, or variable? Does every plant taste the same (and taste good) and mature at the same time or over a period of time? Are all the plants from that seed packet productive? Because every plant under trial must be given enough growing room to fully reveal itself, I made most of my rows 4 feet apart center to center. Cauliflower and broccoli plants were 2 feet apart in their row; the intensive system would have broccoli plants on a 12-by-12-inch grid. Small vegetables under trial, like carrots, were arranged in pairs of rows about 12 inches apart, with the carrots about 1 inch apart in the row; intensive would have carrots on a 1-by-1-inch grid, 144 carrots per square foot of bed. Vining species like cucumbers had to be given enough in-the-row separation that there was no doubt about which fruit belonged to which plant—4 feet. The amount of work involved to grow a half acre of trials proved to be about the same as growing an intensive ⅛-acre kitchen garden. Soil preparation, planting, and weeding of widely separated rows was a lot easier. I discovered that the trials ground needed watering far less often than my intensive garden did, most species grew larger, seemed healthier, yielded longer and ultimately more. The biggest surprise was that larger-size plants, like broccoli or peppers, produced about as much food per square foot/growing week as my intensive kitchen garden did. And down the drain went all that intensivist propaganda I had blindly accepted about how the method produced enormously increased yields.

Extensive layouts save time because they can be weeded efficiently with a lightweight, sharp, long-handled hoe. Hoeing is not hard on the back or knees, although doing it does develop strong hands and wrists. Intensive beds must be weeded while bent over with dull fingers, but pulling out some weed species by their roots can be nearly impossible if the weed has gotten very large or the soil has become compacted; the top snaps off while leaving the growing point intact so that the weed regrows rapidly. Hoeing efficiently slices the tops off below their growing points; hoeing almost inevitably kills weeds. Sometimes a hoed weed is badly damaged but not killed; when I hoe it again a week later, it is even less likely to survive. Very few weeds are in positions from which they cannot be hoed out.

After the trials ground showed me what a *sharp* hoe can do, I increased interplant spacing in my kitchen garden to allow hoeing there as well. When I did that, everything grew much better

while gardening took less of my time. The yield in my kitchen garden did not decline much if any.

My present food garden occupies about 10,000 square feet because, in addition to our own needs, I provide a weekly food box to a few families and grow seeds for two garden seed merchants. If it were only providing two vegetableatarian adults with about half of the year's entire food supply, our garden would occupy about 5,000 square feet. When I was in the seed business, I learned the average backyard vegetable garden is around 1,000 square feet.

Between midspring and early summer the weeds are growing their fastest for the entire year, so on sunny, pleasant days I spend about an hour working my hoe. I could keep a 1,000-square-foot garden immaculately clean during these weeks in almost no time. Weeding takes much less time after summer arrives. I completely stop cleaning the paths in the last month of summer because weeds reduce erosion during heavy winter rains, and without them the paths will be muddier. I confess, come autumn I indulge my inertia.

It is not necessary to eliminate every weed the instant it is spotted. I have priorities. Grass is the highest.

Grass competition quickly overwhelms or badly stunts vegetables. Many grasses form tough, spreading root masses that aren't easily hoed out, much less hand-pulled without damaging nearby vegetables. So it is best to eliminate grasses before they get well established.

My garden is divided into slightly raised beds with narrow footpaths between them. During spring I repeatedly hoe the paths until they are bare. If I didn't, grasses would soon spread into the beds. The paths become compacted over winter, so initially this is hard work. But once the paths are clean, it takes hardly any time to keep them that way. Of course, because of the way I garden, the paths, as well as the beds, have steadily gotten softer and easier to hoe. Grasses and other self-sown weeds carpet my paths again during autumn, but I don't hoe them out then because end-of-season weeds don't form seeds before I eliminate them next spring. Instead, they create some biomass and prevent my boots from getting so muddy.

Many people lack knowledge of hoe sharpening. The (dull) hoe they bought soon exhausts them, so they try mulching garden paths to keep the weeds down, but unless the mulch is very thick, many weeds come up anyway. Mulched paths are still compacted by foot traffic, so weeds that do manage to come up don't yank easily. But if they are allowed to make seeds, the beds soon become hopelessly weedy.

Some grass species expand rapidly by putting out underground runners, properly termed "stolons." Gardeners call these types witchgrass, twitch, or crab. Or worse names. If stoloniferous grasses get established in the paths, they rapidly invade adjoining beds. Gardeners who weed by hand never seem to be able to get rid of them, but stoloniferous grasses aren't invulnerable. If once a week you cut them off a half inch below the soil line with a sharp hoe, get every blade showing, and significantly damage the roots, the plant's food reserves become depleted. It might take you a month of repeated weekly hoeing to kill some types, but they all die eventually.

You can also get rid of horseradish, blackberries, and comfrey exactly the same way. The key is regular weekly hoeing of the entire garden, which, after the spring cleanup, takes little more effort than sweeping the floor. Some weeds go to seed a few weeks after coming up. These seeds often germinate right away. Included in this group are capeweed (*Arctotheca calendula*) and nightshade. These pernicious species should not be permitted to survive more than a week after sprouting inside or even near the garden fence.

If you use my spacing recommendations, your plants may seem rather far apart at the start, but on the other hand you'll find hoeing in the isles can keep the beds almost weed-free. Only an occasional weed nestled in or immediately against a row of seedlings must be hand-pulled. In their second month vegetables form a leaf canopy that prevents hoeing. The canopy's shade also suppresses weeds that sprout under it. But an occasional weed will still emerge above the canopy and should be hand-pulled when spotted. There won't be many like this, and they'll yank easily because the hoeing that went before loosened the soil while the leaf canopy prevents rain or irrigation from compacting it again.

After September it is only necessary to weed overwintering crops for harvest next spring. Otherwise, from here on you can afford to let weeds make biomass because the vegetables are way ahead. It's also better for the soil to go through the winter covered with as much green as possible. Like an intentionally sown green manure, weeds reduce soil compaction from winter rains, prevent erosion, and leave the soil looser next spring.

NO-WEEDING SYSTEMS

I have been shown a great many gardens. Sometimes the patch is such a catastrophe that I comment as nonjudgmentally as possible, "Seems a bit weedy . . ." And then I inevitably hear many reasons why weeds are a good thing and should be allowed. Clearly, "nonjudgmentally" is not quite the same thing as "without judgment."

Weedy gardens often get justified like this: my soil is too hard, so I couldn't pull the weeds; hoeing doesn't work (usually because the hoe was dull), so I put down mulch. But the mulch was full of weed seeds, or wasn't thick enough, or simply failed to suppress the weeds, so I guess I'll make the mulch even thicker. Besides, there's still more food here than I can use. (Ugh! Behind my best poker face, I think: what a disgusting bunch of gnarly, over–competed with, slug-damaged, nitrogen- and who-knows-what-else-deficient, foul-tasting vegetables!)

I have two further comments:

1. A garden gradually becomes less weedy when no weeds are allowed to form seeds. It takes a few years.
2. If you firmly believe in not weeding, please set apart a few square yards of your garden and keep it weed-free through an entire crop cycle no matter how difficult that is. Seeing the result may adjust your opinion, especially if you also provided enough interplant spacing.

THINNING

I think the word "garden" links to the word "guard." Guard from moisture, stress, insects, wandering deer, wind, and springtime frost.

Protect from strong competition. But eliminating weeds doesn't necessarily end overcompetition. Root vegetables grow more top and less bottom when they are crowded. Densely packed bush bean plants set small, often tough, and frequently misshapen pods that take more time to pick, top, and tail. Tomatoes, zucchini, and cucumbers produce well until their root zone gets crowded; then fruit set greatly slows and quality drops.

If every seed came up and became a desirable plant, there would be no thinning. But this, alas, is not the nature of vegetable seed. Which brings to mind the old American legend about Squanto teaching the Pilgrims how to grow corn: "make a hole, put in a dead fish, cover it, sow four seeds above the fish—one for the worm, one for the crow, one to rot, and one to grow." Squanto should also have rhymed, "If some don't rot or the crow don't come, there's thinnin' to be done."

I've met gardeners who resist thinning as though it were phytological murder. I entreat you, oh gentlest of persons, to reconsider the nature of plants. Thinning seedlings is not like drowning unwanted kittens. Vegetables *don't mind being thinned.* They know that thinning helps them. Your veggies completely accept that you must plant many seeds to end up with one plant; left to their own devices, plants do the very same thing but enormously more so. In order to establish a single offspring, wild plants will strew—"sow" is too refined a term for this—hundreds of times more seeds than a gardener ever will. And wild plants thin themselves in far less merciful ways than you will.

Consider wild cabbage. After overwintering, the plant shoots up sprays of small yellow flowers. Each pollinated flower becomes a skinny seedpod containing half a dozen or so seeds that mature in summer. Some pods split open as the seeds ripen; escaped seeds don't travel far and sprout if there's an unusual summer rain. But these early starters die or become permanently stunted if the rest of the summer proves as rainless as it usually is. Some seeds remain securely within their pod; these are protected from the first rains and sprout only after the seedpod gets thoroughly soaked, by which time soil conditions have become reliably moist. Often all the seeds within a single pod sprout at once and come up as a little cluster. Imagine the intensity, the painful struggle as hundreds of clusters of cabbage seedlings on a few square yards of ground fight it out to the last plant standing.

There's great wisdom in this arrangement. Brassica seedlings are fragile and small, but by coming up in tight bunches, they combine forces so that a cluster may push aside an obstacle and find the light, whereas a single seedling would fail. Then the cluster proceeds to compete for water, nutrients, and light. The most vigorous seedling or the one best adapted to the current circumstance dominates the space. The others die. Do they die in slow agony or peacefully, having fulfilled their function in the Great Scheme of Things? You decide.

A wild cabbage plant may disperse 10,000 seeds over a few square yards of ground so that at least one of them survives to make the next 10,000 seeds. Perhaps all 10,000 embryos in those 10,000 seeds are at peace with the process; perhaps all are entirely unaware; perhaps all are immortal parts of the big cabbage spirit. You choose.

Consider the cucurbits. A wild cucumber or wild melon makes many fruits, each full of seeds. When the dried-out fruit gets wet again, the seeds sprout in a cluster. Like the cabbage, the flowers were fertilized by bees carrying pollen from hither and yon. Consequently, the emerging seedlings will be genetically diverse. Eventually the best-adapted plant dominates; the others die after much struggle. Hundreds of deaths to produce a successful life!

I hope that's sufficient argument to convince you gentlest of readers that thinning agrees with nature's plan. Your way of doing it is, in comparison, merciful. And there's no avoiding thinning. You must sow several seeds to end up with one good plant, because even the highest-quality vegetable seeds occasionally produce the odd weak seedling. Rarely do more than half the seeds you sow actually emerge. And many young seedlings fall over or vanish while running the gauntlet of soil diseases and predators.

Market gardeners use machines that accurately position each seed. Home gardeners improvise and end up with too many seedlings. Within days of emergence, thin any clumps or clusters in the row so that no seedlings touch each other. During their first week some weak seedlings disappear by themselves. By the second week the first pair of true leaves should develop (on dicots)—time to thin small seedlings again so that none are touching each other. And as growth continues, you continue to thin until the desired interplant spacing has been arrived at.

When sowing what will become large plants on positions like 24 inches by 24 inches, several seedlings should come up on each spot. Thin them gradually to prevent light competition. I call this method "progressive thinning."

Seedlings become what I call *well established* once they are large enough to withstand a bit of nibbling, when they are not likely to suddenly disappear overnight as a slug's meal or to wither and fall over dead from a seedling disease. Vegetable seedlings have become well established by the time they have grown three (pairs of) regular leaves. Well-established seedlings may safely be thinned to their final spacing. And promptly should be in most cases.

Seasonal Light Intensity

The word "cultivation" is taken by most to mean hoeing, plowing, or otherwise loosening the soil, but considered broadly the term means improving growing conditions from the plant's viewpoint.

We cultivate plants in a variety of ways. We maintain soil moisture at a high level; we build up and balance soil nutrients, limit competition, and increase the quantity of air and of organic matter in the soil. We raise temperature with cloches and greenhouses. But we can't do much to increase light levels when growing outdoors, except to position a few special plants against a white-painted reflective wall and prevent plants from shading each other too much.

I apologize for belaboring the obvious, but sometimes there is great wisdom to be discovered by reconsidering what everyone already knows. In Cascadia's latitudes, about mid- to late February, a bit of strength returns to the sun; overwintering vegetables that had been almost static since the end of November begin to grow slowly. This is the moment to fertilize them. The first spring bulbs shoot up at this time, indicating that you can sow frost-tolerant crops capable of germinating in cold soil, like peas and broad beans, and in a few more weeks lettuce, mustards, and spinach.

By late March the sun feels warm on the face and provides enough energy for cold-tolerant pasture species to grow rapidly; I sow the vegetable equivalent—beets, carrots, and parsley. Cabbage family plants, semidormant during winter, start going to seed now, and since they can grow, I sow broccoli, cabbage, kohlrabi, and radishes.

Getting the sowing dates right for autumn and winter crops is critical. Start most of them in the first half of July while there remains three months with enough light intensity to make rapid vegetative growth. Autumn/winter crops slow down in October; in November they become almost static and will hold for months in the field awaiting harvest (or until they freeze out). Sow later than mid-July and they'll be disappointingly small at harvest. If you sow autumn/winter crops too early, say in mid-June, they will have been harvested before the end of October.

Start most overwintering crops during August so that they get large enough to survive winter. These crops do most of their growing the following spring. Overwintering brassicas handle winter best at a moderate size. Start too soon and they grow too big in autumn to be maximally winter hardy. Start overwintered bulbing onions a few weeks too early and you end up with a seed crop, not onions. Start them late and the small seedlings are likely to freeze out.

In early September tomatoes don't taste quite as good as they did in mid-August; eggplants and peppers get smaller and less sweet (or less hot) as the month progresses; and melons succumb to powdery mildew for the same reason our suntans start fading. Powdery mildew also attacks the other cucurbits; next the cucumbers go down, and then, even if there is no rain or heavy dew, by the end of September the squash give in too. The causes of powdery mildew *seem* to be colder nights, heavy morning dews, daytime humidity, and exhaustion after such heavy bearing. But lack of light energy is a major cause of lowered disease resistance.

Only a few species can grow (slowly) in winter's weak sunshine. There is not enough light energy to accumulate surplus sugar, so root vegetables do not enlarge. In cloudy periods during winter, plants consume sugar reserves to get through. They also cannibalize their own leaves and go backward. Often, plants that become diseased in winter are actually dying of energy starvation.

Everyone knows this fact of light at gut level, but few know they know it. In the 40-degree latitudes, the rise and fall of average temperature does not quite follow the annual change in day length. Yes, the shortest day is on December 21, and you'd think that from December 22 onward, average conditions would start warming up. Actually, the northern hemisphere loses more heat to outer space than it receives until about January 21, then it starts warming up. And in summer, the average temperature doesn't start declining until the end of July.

Tools

I mentioned that most people these days did not grow up with a vegetable garden. So in this section I hope to make up for the practical education your upbringing probably didn't provide.

THE HOE

Chopping big weeds with a dull hoe is exhausting and then some. Slicing young weeds with a sharp hoe takes no more effort than sweeping the floor, and the work goes quickly.

The weeding hoes I prefer are lightweight tools designed to slide through the soil like a sharp knife, separating the tops of weeds from their roots. Doing this is easy if the soil is soft and the weeds have not grown too large. On hard soil (compacted paths, for example), the common garden hoe can also scrape the tops of small weeds off their roots as you pull the blade toward you while pressing its sharp edge down firmly on hard earth. Slicing and scraping with a sharp hoe doesn't wear me out.

When cutting off small weeds with a common hoe, the blade should rest flat on the ground so that it slides through the soil without pulling itself in deeper or lifting itself out.

Slicing weeds just below the surface.

It should be at the correct angle when you are standing erect and comfortably holding the handle close to your body (see drawing). Hoe blades are almost always attached to their handles by a rod (Tasmanians call it a "swan's neck") made of mild (flexible) steel so that you can adjust the blade's angle of attack to fit your height and natural stance. Bending the swan's neck is best done by striking it with a hammer while it is in a stout bench vise or held against an anvil.

Hoeing with a sharp blade takes little effort *when the weeds are small and the soil is loose.* If you sliced off all the weeds once a week without fail, then, except for the winter's accumulation of weeds that get hoed in spring, all weeds would be small and tender, and the soil's surface would

always be reasonably soft, especially if you take my suggestion to incorporate compost into the surface with a rake instead of digging it in.

The common garden hoe isn't sharp when you buy it. After a few futile chops, the discouraged gardener considers far-less-effective alternatives when the only thing they need is a metal file or a coarse, large sharpening stone or both.

If you use a handheld electric grinder to quickly sharpen new tools but lack experience, go slowly. Take metal off gradually. Rest the grinding wheel lightly on the blade. Keep it moving so that heat doesn't build up at one spot or else you'll burn the edge. Burned spots permanently lose hardness. I suggest sharpening new tools the first time with a *new, sharp* metal file because files do not overheat the metal. Clamp the blade in a stout vise and patiently grind down the outside face until you form a 15-degree one-sided bevel, like the cutting edge of a wood chisel. If you don't have a proper workbench, ask someone to stand on the handle while you file. When the entire bevel is perfect, then remove the inevitable

Scraping weeds in compacted soil.

burr that forms on the opposite face by giving it a few light strokes with the file laid almost flat against the blade; do not grind an angle into this side. Now the edge should almost be able to cut your finger if you press hard.

I'm sorry to inform you that filing an effective edge the first time will make you sweat. You must *concentrate* on holding the file at exactly the same angle through each and every stroke or the edge will never get sharp.

Don't forget that metal files get dull. Files get entirely dull overnight if you let them rust. The only garden chore as painful as weeding with a dull hoe is using a dull file to sharpen it. And don't take what may seem to be the easy way out, making the bevel less acute so that there's less metal to grind off; you'll only end up working many times harder weeding than any effort you saved while filing.

And what is a 15-degree angle? Well, take a *thin* sheet of paper and fold it in quarters. Those are 90-degree angles. Now fold one of those quarters diagonally and you have 45-degree angles.

And one more such fold gives you 22½-degree angles, which are still too blunt for a garden hoe. Better to fold it one more time, 11¼ degrees, and use that angle as your target.

A cheap hoe works against you. Inexpensive blades are usually made of soft (mild) steel because it is the least costly, quick to shape, and easy to weld. If filing the initial bevel goes rapidly, you're working mild steel that won't get very sharp no matter how skillfully you wield a file. And mild steel gets dull very quickly. What you really need is a blade made of tool steel. This is hard, expensive stuff that takes more time and effort to sharpen the first time, but it won't need resharpening for years if your soil is free of stones.

The common garden hoe can be the only hoe you need. It is "common" because the design is so useful and, if made properly, very strong. One tool slices and scrapes weeds, chops hard ground, makes furrows, and can push soil back into those furrows after seeds have been sown.

In the spring the overwintered weeds are large, there are grass clumps to handle, and the paths have been compacted by winter rains. So in this season I mostly use a common garden hoe. But once there are new crops growing and the paths are clean, I prefer to weed with a very sharp, double-edged, thin-bladed hoe that slices off small weeds equally well pushing or pulling. The design I grab the most often for this job is built like a letter *U*. Sometimes this design is called a stirrup hoe or a hula hoe because the *U* wiggles slightly in order to hold the cutting edge at the optimum angle on both the push and the pull stroke. I have several other push-pull hoes with propeller-shaped blades that work nearly as well. Beware of cheap *U* hoes that do not wiggle. These work well only on one stroke (push or pull) and will be at the wrong angle for the other.

Hoes working only on the push-away stroke, sometimes called Dutch hoes, or scuffle hoes, are exhausting to use and hard to control; I don't recommend them.

THE GARDEN KNIFE

A kitchen peeling knife makes a valuable garden tool. Mine has a red composite handle that helps me spot it should I forget where I last put it down. Of course I use it for harvesting, but its most valuable applications are thinning young seedlings and separating leaves from roots if it happens to be in my hand when I spot a weed. When a newly emerged row needs thinning, the

slow way is with fingers. The easy way is cutting surplus seedlings off just below the soil line with a small, pointed knife that is quite sharp at the tip. Running any knife blade through soil rapidly dulls it, which is why a sharpening stone is kept by the wooden gatepost the knife is stuck into.

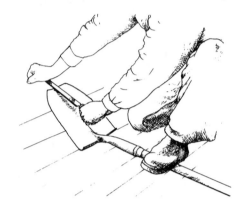

SHOVELS AND SPADES

I find preparing beds a pleasure when using a *sharp* spade or combination shovel. Digging blades are made of tempered, springy steel that gets sharp and holds an edge for a long time. But even high-quality spades are blunt when purchased. To dig stoneless soil, file an acute chisel-like bevel (10 degrees) on the surface facing away from you when you're digging. For a stony garden I'd make the bevel about 15 degrees, so as to avoid damaging the edge.

Shovels and spades have different purposes. Shovels move loose materials effectively but dig poorly, if at all. They have wide spoon-like blades that hold more loose stuff. They're angled to scoop up and shift loose sand, gravel, or compost, and snow. Spades have narrow, flat blades attached to the handle almost straight on. A spade can slice into firm soil and turn over a chunk, but it can't efficiently fill a wheelbarrow or spread what is in that wheelbarrow. Because I'm constantly switching from digging to moving material, and because the soil I dig has already been dug recently and fed compost, my preferred tool is the combination shovel, a design that does both tasks fairly well. It is angled to dig effectively, yet the blade efficiently moves loose soil or compost into or out of a wheelbarrow.

The spade is pushed into the soil with one foot, using leg and core muscles combined with body weight. The larger the person, the wider the blade they can push in and, all things being equal, the faster the digging goes.

I weigh about 170 pounds; to me a soft garden bed feels like cake with a combination shovel. If I weighed 120 pounds, I'd do much better with a 6-inch-wide spade. If I were teaching a child to garden, I'd try to find her a 4-inch spade with a 6-inch-long blade that wasn't made like a toy. Because you're repeatedly pushing the blade down with the sole of your shoe or boot, having its top edge rolled over makes doing that a lot easier on your foot.

Shovels and spades come with either short or long handles. Short-handled tools make my back tired. A short-handled combination shovel carried in the trunk of a car might prove useful in an emergency, but for serious digging I prefer the long-handled tool anytime. Your body may work differently.

When you're moving loose materials, choose the lighter-weight shovel that's honestly strong. When it comes to digging, a bit more metal helps withstand the stresses spades get put through. However, repeatedly lifting a few extra ounces

tires me sooner. That's why I prefer composite handles over wooden ones.

Spading forks can be pushed in to their full depth even easier than a spade. They do not work well in compact, clayey soils. Marina says:

I find a garden fork indispensable. It won't replace a shovel for many jobs, but it will aerate between rows or in unoccupied spaces. I poke it into the areas I want to side-dress so the fertilizers are blended in deeper. I use it to loosen a carrot bed so they pull out cleanly, minimally disrupting the ones still growing nearby. I also use the fork to poke apart and then flatten clods. And a sturdy garden fork turns compost excellently. A tall man might need a long-handled fork, but I like short, the D-handle model.

When buying a digging fork, keep in mind that your foot must push the tines in; make sure your boot can get a good purchase. And beware of cheap or secondhand forks; the tines must be extremely strong or they bend. You can bend one back so that it's straight again, but after being straightened, a tine is more prone to bending again.

ROTARY CULTIVATORS

A garden-size self-propelled rear-tine rotary cultivator (usually around seven horsepower) can pulverize a 100-square-foot bed in under five minutes, but *at very best* only loosens the top 6 inches. A front-end five-horsepower tiller can work the same area in about 20 minutes and may well dig it two honest inches deeper. To put that in better perspective, at age 72, using a sharp combination shovel on a day when I am feeling fit and eager, I can blend fertilizer into a 100-square-foot bed an honest 11 inches deep, then spread a wheelbarrow load of compost over the top and rake out a seedbed, all in about 60 minutes.

If most kinds of soil are loosened immediately before sowing or transplanting, then most kinds of vegetables grow faster during their first six weeks. Digging 1 foot deep gives two more weeks of faster growth compared to loosening the top 6 inches. Deep digging produces longer, straighter carrots and parsnips. So for the first few years of a new garden I suggest "subsoiling" *after* rototilling. As long as you're not working clay, this quick task is easiest done using a long-handled spading fork with 12-inch tines. A spade or combination shovel will handle clay and does almost as well in loam soil but takes somewhat more effort than a fork. It's best to keep most of the organic matter in the top 6 inches. To accomplish that, push the tool down with one foot as you wiggle the tines straight in to their full depth, then pull back on the handle until the subsoil breaks apart. Extract the fork, move it back about 6 inches, press it in again, and repeat. Because my beds are not raised much, I can fork a 4-foot-wide bed while always keeping my weight on the surrounding path.

I abandoned a seven-horsepower Honda tiller in Oregon. Every time I considered getting another (until the year I turned 67), I would recall how much time it took to guide the machine out to the garden and then back into the garage, and the time and effort to clear vegetation tangled around the digging tines. There was the effort to turn it around at the ends of the bed, the smell of engine exhaust, the engine noise, and my hands tingling for several minutes after the engine was shut down. Then I'd recall the pleasure of digging and meditatively raking out a seedbed . . . and I'd conclude I didn't need a tiller. And I'd remind myself that if more gardeners knew how to sharpen their tools, there'd be a lot fewer powered cultivators sold. Then aging made it necessary to buy another rototiller, but this time a front-ender more suited to the size of garden I have now.

I am confident that, as of the year 2015, Honda makes the highest-quality small tillers. A Honda may cost you double the price of a seemingly equivalent advertised special because Honda tillers are not short-lived consumer items; they are designed for market gardeners and small-scale farmers. The self-propelled seven hp Honda I owned in Oregon worked my trials ground for three years. After I sold Territorial Seed Company, it tilled a very large veggie garden for six more years. It also broke old pasture sod by one-sixth acres when I experimented with breeding fava beans and growing chickpeas, wheat, millet, and quinoa. During those nine years I changed the engine oil every 25 running hours and always in early spring. I cleaned the air filter at each oil change. I installed a new spark plug every spring too, needed or not. Once I had to replace a clutch cable. And about year six I had put so many hours on the machine that I had to replace the digging tines because the original set had worn away to nubbins. Had I taken it to Tasmania with me 15 years ago, I am sure that tiller would still be starting on the first pull.

In contrast, I have watched other homesteaders buy other brands of self-propelled walk-behind tillers. And then I watched them take these tillers to be serviced and wait many weeks for parts to arrive while spring planting needed to be done.

Front-end tillers make tighter turns and dig deeper than most rear-end models. Take off the outer pair of tines and their full weight presses on a 12-inch-wide strip, so they go a few more honest inches deeper. Front-enders cost less than half the price of a rear-ender and work one-quarter the area per unit of your time. So they're best for smaller gardens where you're only digging a few hundred square feet at one go.

Front-enders have down points. The bed has to be fairly free of vegetation or else their tines get tangled and then blunted. I wouldn't use one to convert compacted lawn or pasture into a garden—the tines bounce off as it tosses the operator around—but it digs quickly in soil that has been dug before. A new-to-front-ender driver soon tires from using upper-body strength to control the machine. However, apply the poise of a martial artist and you'll soon drive one with little effort. The tricks are controlling forward motion by slightly lifting or pressing down on the drag bar and adjusting forward direction by tilting the handles, much like a bicycle goes around a corner.

Rear-end models are best if you dig 1,000 square feet or more at one time. They demand much less effort to operate—point them in the right direction and the machine does the work as long as you don't set the drag bar too high so that the tines bite off too much at one time. If that happens, it'll leap forward at every hard spot. Honda's counter-rotating tine, self-propelled model is especially fast working and easy to control. I tested one. It did not try to leap out of control when it hit fibrous grass stools. It made a seedbed out of a three-year-old stand of orchard grass in two quick passes.

When I reach age 80, I may have to replace my front-ender with a rear-ender and change my gardening style to single long rows, like gardening author Dick Raymond recommended. Back in the 1970s Raymond published many how-to books in collaboration with Garden Way Publishing and the Troy-Bilt tiller company. Raymond's books suggest making planting beds the width of the tiller's tines (2 feet) and paths between them the same width, using the tiller to weed paths and for chopping old vegetation in, no heap composting necessary. Green manure crops were also chopped in. These methods admirably suit dry gardening.

RAKES

Every time I write about using tools, I wish I could replace words with a demonstration DVD. This is especially so when I attempt to describe the Zen of raking.

Anyone can gather loose vegetation with a garden rake. And it takes little time to discover you can push loose soil around with the back of a rake while pointing the teeth up. Raking can also create a fine seedbed by combing small lumps from just tilled or spaded ground as you blend compost into the surface. Both at once. I suggest you teach yourself how by passing the teeth in slow motion through a bed you already dug up and roughly leveled. The whole trick is controlling how deeply the teeth penetrate. The rake should seem to float just above the soil line, with the teeth penetrating only half their length. Once this trick is learned, you should be able to comb most of the lumps out of a 100-square-foot seedbed in a few minutes.

Your rake's handle should be a foot longer than a common hoe handle in order to counterbalance the working end. That helps you stably control how deep the teeth penetrate. If you try to control the depth the comb goes into the soil by strength of wrist, at best you'll soon exhaust yourself. Instead, one hand loosely grasps the handle about a foot behind the rake's natural balance point in a way that allows the handle to slide forward and back through the hand. This "front" hand supports the tool's weight and acts like a pivot for the sliding handle. The rear hand holds the handle closer to its butt end; this arm does most of the pushing and pulling and mostly controls how deep the comb goes. Both arms move in harmony as you groom the bed's surface. Used this way, the stress on your wrists is minor and endurable for long periods. You'll probably discover why you should bend your knees a bit and assume a poised stance when raking out a seedbed.

The idea is to glide those teeth through loose soil without letting them dig in too deeply so that you can tease out lumps and pull them over the edge of the bed as you simultaneously level the bed's surface. To rake excellently requires your total attention on the soil flowing between the rake's teeth. I cannot think while raking.

There are two designs, the bow rake and the *T*, or level, rake. The comb of a *T* rake is welded to a stout metal strip that usually sticks into a slot cut into the end of the handle. Because of the stresses on that single attachment point, the attachment strip (like a swan's neck on a hoe) must be strong, the comb must be made of thicker, more rigid steel, and the handle is stouter, which means the working end must weigh more. I usually can't reach out as far with a *T* rake because its natural balance point is closer to the working end. Because of its simpler construction, the *T* rake usually costs less than a bow rake. The bow rake's comb is attached to the handle by a pair of thin, curved springy rods welded to its outer-upper corners. This tool is lighter in your hands than a *T* design. I much prefer using a bow rake.

Most rakes have a comb 14 to 16 inches wide. There are unusually wide rakes that might seem to work faster but actually are front heavy and prove exhausting. Similarly, someone with arms and wrists that aren't too strong might look for a rake with a narrower comb.

Chapter Two

SOIL

Only after the supply of organic matter has been adequately provided for, will the full benefit of artificials [chemical fertilizers] be realized. There appears to be a great field for future experiment in the judicious use of artificials to land already in a fair state of fertility.

—Sir Albert Howard, *The Waste Products of Agriculture*, 1931

RECENTLY I RECEIVED this letter from a serious Washingtonian home and market gardener.

Hi Steve,

Winter is different now. My plants do not die as they have done in past years. There is two inches of ice in the bucket of water, but the collards still live with a measured Brix of 15.

Radishes are supposed to die with frost, but look at the Daikon I have. No harm from hard frost! With the mineral augmented organics the plants have produced enough sugars to act as an antifreeze against a short freezing period.

Artichokes established themselves in October with babies and kept growing without dieback so far.

Of course, the Kale is usually bullet proof here and I have plenty for our cooking greens in the Scotch and Russian.

The green onions are sending up 2-3 inch new shoots, and transplants of cauliflower and veronica seem to be doing well and growing slowly, as expected with the sun at 38-40°F. Last year I got my first spring cauliflower by wintering over new starts. When the time is right, about April 15-May 1, the cauliflower throws out a beautiful head untouched by the cabbage worms still shivering in their cocoons. I have about 10 gardens planted in such things so that I can have an early market advantage.

My plants have made a huge response to mineral balancing.

Mineral augmented organics is the answer to our orchard woes in the Maritime NW. I believe we will have a Sir Albert Howard experience with the soil treatment we are giving. After one year, my ancient apple trees are healing canker wounds caused by an infection of Neonectria galligena fungus that overwhelms the tree. In the past I have been trimming off the dead branches and dealing with it by pruning carefully. No treatment except proper soil treatment and the tree's immune system is able to deal with the infection naturally.

Jim Karnofski

What Jim calls "mineral augmented organics," what others have called remineralization or going beyond organic, not only lets your winter garden survive better; it also makes your vegetables taste better because they become much more nutrient dense. We all want that.

Leaching

To produce nutrient-dense vegetables, the soil must provide plants with substantial quantities of copper, zinc, manganese, iron, boron, sulfur, nitrogen, phosphorus, calcium, magnesium, potassium, and sodium as well as slight traces of cobalt, selenium, iodine, chromium, etc. Some soils provide these elements in balanced abundance; people whose food comes from soil like that are usually healthy and long lived. But in Cascadia, heavy winter rains strongly leach essential plant nutrient elements from the soil, lowering the nutritional value of food crops, and not just of vegetables and fruit in your garden, but of cereals, grasses, and other food crops too. For example, the winter wheat grown extensively in the Willamette Valley is a soft white variety with a protein content of 7 to 8 percent. It is used to make instant noodles. The protein content of hard red winter wheat from the highly mineralized Kansas prairies usually exceeds 14 percent; there are prairie districts where bread wheat reaches 18 percent protein. One more example: Cascadians owning thoroughbred horses often import hay from the eastern side of the Cascades, where the unleached soils grow nutrient-dense grass.

CASCADIAN MANURES AND COMPOSTS

Livestock eating grass and hay from demineralized pastures produce manure whose plant nutrient content resembles the soil it derived from. Compost made from Cascadian forest residues is similarly deficient and out of balance. Adding these materials to soil that is already chemically unbalanced in the same direction further distorts the soil. As I discovered, to my sorrow.

In my late 30s I homesteaded in the Oregon Coast Range. Even at that young age I made fresh garden vegetables the majority of my food intake. After five years in Oregon, I experienced loosening teeth that eventually were lost to infections below the gumline. One tooth after another got wobbly because in order to source enough calcium and phosphorus, my body was forced to extract these elements from my jawbone. My homegrown food did not supply enough of these elements. My garden veggies looked good and tasted better than supermarket stuff, but they had not been nutritionally sound.

Bones are made of calcium and phosphorus. Cascadian soils lack calcium because winter rains strongly leach this element. Cascadia's rocks don't contain much phosphorus, and neither do the soils they formed nor the vegetation growing from them. Cascadia's soil-forming rocks provide a great deal of potassium. So do most of the soils deriving from those rocks. Crops fertilized with what I consider excess potassium use it to increase the amount of fiber and starch they produce. They grow larger and contain a higher concentration of calories but provide less protein and a lower concentration of essential nutrients. They also don't have all the flavor they could. The same happens with grass.

Consequently, Cascadian livestock produce manure that lacks most plant nutrients except potassium. Local sawdust and other woody wastes used to make industrial compost also are potassium rich and lack other plant nutrients. Cascadian gardeners of the traditional organic persuasion try to compensate by spreading compost thicker, but doing this further increases the amount of potassium going into food-producing land that probably had more than enough already. So Cascadian gardeners harvest vegetables richer in fiber and carbohydrates than they should be while providing fewer proteins, minerals, vitamins, and enzymes than they could. And should. Maintaining health on such food is like an impoverished athlete training on instant noodle soup packets.

Very few Cascadians these days eat almost entirely from their own land. I hope no one tries that without first bringing their soil into the kind of plant nutrient balance that grows nutrient-dense food, because if they don't fully reminerize, they'll soon find out why the indigenous Cascadians did not garden and ate more seafood than anything else.

To maximize nutritional outcomes, all Cascadian gardeners must import no more organic matter than is needed to maintain the soil ecology. And with the exception of those gardening on Washington's glacial moraines, they should avoid adding any potassium-rich fertilizer unless this element is called for after a complete laboratory (not a home test kit) soil test has been analyzed by someone who knows how to maximize nutritional outcomes.

Building Soil Fertility

The least complicated way I know of for Cascadians to raise nutrient-dense food is by depending upon my complete organic fertilizer (COF) recipe or a similar manufactured product. COF is simple to make for yourself and straightforward to use. The standard recipe grows big, healthy plants in most of Cascadia's soils and circumstances. COF is ideal for novices and for small gardens. COF brings most

Cascadian soils closer to providing a balanced, abundant mineral nutrition, but being a one-size-fits-most method, it cannot perfectly adjust anyone's soil. (See page 29 for the COF recipe.)

In 1984 I published my first COF recipe in this book's third edition. That primitive version grew bountiful crops. Since then the recipe has been adjusted and improved by small increments. Every version of COF has grown excellent food gardens. It works! It's simple and convenient. The approach sparked imitation.

While writing *The Intelligent Gardener* I analyzed soil tests provided by gardeners living all over North America, including more than 20 tests from Cascadia. Cascadian soils that had not been limed recently were acidic because they lacked calcium. Except for glacial moraine sands, Cascadian soils were well endowed with magnesium. Many soils held far too much magnesium because the gardener had spread dolomite lime. Most were severely short of phosphorus and copper. Most Cascadian home gardens had already received so much organic matter that their soils would need no more for years to come.

COF brings Cascadian soils into better balance. It includes a *light dose* of agricultural lime that amounts to around 1 ton per acre per year when COF is spread two times a year. This repeated light liming gently and gradually saturates the soil with calcium. The gypsum in COF ensures that even in never-limed-before soils there still will be plenty of soluble calcium available for any nutritional need the crop has. Gypsum also supplies abundant sulfur. COF gradually brings the soil pH closer to neutral. The small yet safe-in-any-circumstance doses of zinc, boron, and copper prevent gross deficiencies, sort of like the MDR approach to taking vitamins. However, COF cannot bring about a near perfect balance because every soil's existing strengths and weaknesses differ.

The basic theory behind COF was developed in the 1930s by an agricultural scientist and farm adviser named Victor Tiedjens. If you want a full explanation, it's best to get it direct and unfiltered; see Tiedjens's *More Food from Soil Science* and *Olena Farm* (see Additional Reading, page 339).

LIME

Many garden writers assert that to produce a successful garden, all you need is lots of compost and enough lime to bring the pH to the mid-6s. And if that prescription did not grow things well enough, then the solution is "building up the soil" with even more compost. My fellow travelers denigrate this method by naming it the "more-on-it" system.

Here's another often-asserted falsie. If the soil needs lime, use dolomite lime because dolomite provides magnesium as well as calcium. Pound for pound, dolomite raises soil pH about 20 percent more than ordinary agricultural lime. By using dolomite, you put more on it for less money.

Please take this warning seriously: dolomite lime can worsen topsoils that contain much clay. It further tightens clay subsoils. Cascadia's clays already hold enough or, more often, too much magnesium. So dolomite makes them become even more hostile to root penetration. When the amount of magnesium exceeds about one-seventh the amount of calcium, clay particles respond by strongly attracting each other. The whole soil then shrinks and becomes compacted, airless—the opposite of the kind of soil that grows great vegetables. The traditional organic cure for soil compaction puts you on a treadmill of adding ever more compost, causing a potassium excess in Cascadia. To counteract acidity that is caused by decomposing organic matter, dolomite lime is recommended by many garden writers. But bringing in more magnesium tightens the clay even more, creating a vicious cycle of ongoing effort and lowered nutrient density.

Am I describing your treadmill? The way off it is simple—abandon dolomite lime in favor of ordinary aglime. Gardeners are often surprised by how much clayey soil can loosen up and how it can become naturally crumbly. But it can take a few years for calcium released by both aglime and gypsum to replace excess magnesium in topsoil—even longer than that to loosen a sticky clay subsoil enough that vegetable crops can put roots into it.

Low soil pH develops because soil has been leached of alkaline nutrients or extractive farming has mined them out or otherwise caused them to be lost. Four alkaline plant nutrients counteract soil acidity—calcium, magnesium, potassium, and, surprising to most, sodium. Bringing these four soil elements to concentrations that produce the highest nutrient density in foods simultaneously corrects soil acidity *and* makes crops grow excellently.

If the parent rocks that formed most Cascadian soils contained little magnesium, then you could supply more or less the right proportions of calcium, magnesium, and sulfur by blending equal parts of agricultural lime, dolomite lime, and gypsum. A previous version of COF did just that before I learned most soils west of the Cascades already contain plenty of magnesium. Here is a safe and simple way to lime new gardens:

- *If you're starting a new garden where grass or weeds grew before, if you are using land that has never been limed, or if you are ending a many-years-long rest and rebuilding period while an area was in grass, before doing anything else, spread 50 pounds of finely ground (#65 or #100) agricultural lime per 1,000 square feet (1 ton per acre).*
- *And from that point on use COF, or else double the quantity of aglime in COF for the first two years, and then revert to the regular recipe.*
- *If it happens to be a clay soil, first spread a ton of aglime per acre and double the quantities of both aglime and gypsum in COF for the first two years.*

SUPPLYING ESSENTIAL PLANT NUTRIENTS

If all essential plant nutrient elements are present in *adequate* amounts, the crop grows well and yields a lot. This is the degree of soil fertility successful farmers try to achieve. The yield might not be higher if all essential plant nutrients are *abundant* and in close to ideal proportions relative to each other, but the nutritional quality will be far better and there'll be far fewer insect or disease problems. This is the degree of fertility I want in my own garden.

Five elements must be available in quantities ranging from hundreds to thousands of pounds per acre of topsoil. These are nitrate (N, in the form of NO_3), phosphate (P, in the form of P_2O_5), potassium (K), calcium (Ca), and magnesium (Mg). Other elements, sometimes misnamed "trace elements" should be available in quantities ranging from 2 pounds in each acre of topsoil to a few hundred pounds per acre. These include sulfate (S, in the form of SO_4), iron (Fe), manganese (Mn), zinc (Zn), copper (Cu), and boron (B). Micronutrients must be present, but only in ounces per acre of topsoil. These include iodine, selenium, chromium, cobalt, etc. Be very careful if you think to add micros as straight fertilizer; a few excess ounces of selenium per acre and the eater of the food may be poisoned.

Those of the religiously organic persuasion assert *all* synthetic soluble fertilizers damage soil and harm the soil ecology. The truth of the matter is that most soluble plant nutrients strongly encourage all soil life. Feed microbes soluble chemicals in concentrations they are comfortable with and their population mushrooms. Some chemical fertilizers harm soil organisms or otherwise degrade the soil chemically. These include urea, diammonium phosphate (not monoammonium phosphate), gaseous ammonia and muriate of potash (KCl), a natural mined product. Most inexpensive "complete" chemical fertilizers like 16-16-16 use the chloride form of potassium because it is the cheaper option.

Vegetable gardeners have no need for most synthetic fertilizers. They get far better results with unprocessed or slightly processed organic materials and nutrient-rich rock flours. However, the only effective trace element sources are manufactured sulfate salts. That's why sulfates are now approved by organic certification bureaucrats.

GEOLOGY AND SOIL

I am interested in geology because rocks become soil. I have paid close attention when any information about Cascadian rocks came my way but have not intensely studied the subject. I may have made small mistakes in what follows, but I am sure the overall picture is correct.

Soils in Western Oregon and much of Western Washington are chemically similar, because with a few exceptions, Cascadia's soil-forming rocks originated with one extended episode of basalt eruptions that formed the Old Cascades. These mountains were long ago eroded away. A few remnants presently form soil in areas such as the Salem Hills and around Morton, Washington. Old Cascades basalts are especially rich in magnesium and potassium, average in calcium, and poor in phosphorus and copper. You can recognize Old Cascades remnants by their dark black color. The soils above them are usually a deep, free-draining red-brown clay that farmers south of Salem, Oregon, used for growing orchards.

Material eroded from the Old Cascades formed soil that first was leached by rain and then formed sedimentary rocks immediately off the coast. Then plate tectonics subducted these sediments beneath the Old Cascades, where they melted. The resulting lava erupted, covered the Old Cascades, and formed most of the Cascade peaks we see today. However, this younger volcanic material is gray-colored andesite, containing a lower concentration of the same plant nutrient elements found in the original basalt. The alluvial soils along the Willamette, Santiam, Umpqua, and so forth are mainly particles of andesite.

Soils derived from andesite still contain a lot of magnesium and potassium.

The New Cascades started out higher than they are now. Their erosional residues were again deposited in the ocean immediately offshore, where they formed layered mudstones. Two things happened with these twice-demineralized sedimentary rocks: some were uplifted and now form the Oregon Coast Range that starts around Bandon, Oregon, and includes the coastal hills of southwest Washington. Infertile they may be, but Coast Range soils still hold much potassium. Other mudstones were subducted, melted, and erupted in the form of rhyolite, a light-colored rock that is rich in quartz (silicon) and contains very few plant nutrients. The volcanic ash around Crater Lake and the recent eruption of Mount Saint Helens are rhyolite. North of Chehalis the geology becomes more complex and the soils are more varied. In addition, there are thick surface deposits of sand, gravel, and rounded rocks brought down from Canada by the Vashon glaciation. The Olympic Mountains, Vancouver Island, and the islands in the Puget Sound are geologically complex beyond my understanding. COF works on these soils too, although there is a different recipe for the ultrainfertile glacial sands.

Between the Rogue Valley and the coast extending north to south from Northern California to about Bandon is an area of highly complex rocks that generally make very poor, out-of-balance soils. COF may not be as effective in this area, but then again, there are very few people living there.

Complete Organic Fertilizer (COF)

Cascadian gardens routinely produce vegetables with low nutrient density because of soil deficiencies involving nitrogen, calcium, sulfur, phosphorus, boron, and copper. The only effective way I know to remedy these deficiencies is with fertilizer.

The word "fertilizer" means a concentrated source of plant nutrients. Some organic folks growl at the word. For them, compost is the correct way to build up soil while fertilizer equals the words "chemical, synthetic, artificial, harmful." Actually, chemical (synthetic) fertilizers are not the only kind. For example, agricultural lime, finely pulverized limestone rock, is a powerful calcium fertilizer. Oilseed meals are potent, slow-release organic nitrogen fertilizers that come with a phosphate bonus. Soft (colloidal) phosphate rock, guano, and bonemeal are natural materials that release phosphorus gradually instead of all at once. Gypsum is a soft, slowly soluble rock that provides sulfur and calcium. For providing micronutrients, there are rock flours chockablock full of them, and there is kelp meal. Sulfate salts are artificial fertilizers that organic certification bureaucrats now allow because they benefit the soil, not damage it. The only effective way to add much copper, zinc, manganese, and iron to soil is in the form of a sulfate salt.

Working out which plant nutrients a particular soil lacks and how much is needed to balance it is a complex subject that Cascadian gardeners who do not raise a large proportion of their family's food need not worry about, because COF conveniently brings Cascadian soils into better balance and also grows great crops. This edition provides a much improved recipe plus an alternative formulation designed for Western Washington sands left by the Vashon glacier or other deep sand soils anywhere in the region.

New gardeners have so much to learn that there is little reason to add the interpretation of soil testing to their load. I urge newbies with big ambitions to enjoy the simplicity of using my standard COF recipe for their first few years. You'll get great results. Gardeners producing more than a minor part of their total food intake should go beyond COF. My other book, *The Intelligent Gardener: Growing Nutrient-Dense Food*, will teach you how to analyze a soil test and from that information concoct a custom COF that exactly balances a particular soil.

MAKING COMPLETE ORGANIC FERTILIZER

The ideal fertilizer for growing garden vegetables and small fruit would be a dry, odorless powder that when mixed into soil (or even spread over it and not worked in) gradually releases the plant nutrients that soil needs in order to produce a large harvest of nutrient-dense food. It should not harm leaves if a bit gets on them and should not damage plants or soil microlife if spread several times thicker than the recommended rate. It should not interest pets or wildlife. It should be powerful yet not so concentrated that it is hard to spread uniformly. A single application should steadily feed a crop from start to finish. It would be compounded from substances acceptable for certified organic production. This describes COF.

Cascadian gardens need fertilizer that provides nitrogen and phosphorus in abundance but contains as little potassium as possible, because most soils west of the Cascades are already excessively endowed with potassium, and even more potassium is imported by bringing in organic matter. To make vegetables more nutrient dense, COF supplies enough agricultural lime to slightly more than replace the 300 or so pounds of elemental calcium that 40 inches of rainfall leaches from every acre of land every winter. It contains enough gypsum to provide readily available calcium and sulfur to abundantly feed the current crop; enough zinc, copper, and boron to prevent a crop-ruining deficiency should the soil be really short; and a scant whiff of iodine, cobalt, selenium, molybdenum, etc. There is rarely a need to add manganese, iron, or magnesium to any Cascadian soil except the glacial sands of Western Washington, and for this circumstance I provide another recipe.

COF can easily be compounded at home. Measurement of borax, zinc sulfate, and copper sulfate is done with kitchen measuring spoons. Gardeners can buy these ingredients in small quantities from a few regional merchants or through the Internet. I hope in a few years they'll be sold by the one-pound box at most garden centers. The other nutrients are measured by the pint and quart, so it makes sense to buy them by the 50-pound sack.

Enough fertilizer to cover 100 square feet can be mixed in a 3-gallon bucket. Highly accurate measurement is not needed; anything that comes out within 10 percent of the recipe's suggested proportions will work excellently. Thorough mixing is important. The best way I've found is to measure out the ingredients into one bucket and then, when the wind is not blowing hard, pour them from one bucket to another at least eight times.

This recipe makes the right amount of COF for 100 square feet of growing bed:

Nitrogen

4 quarts of oilseed meal. In Cascadia that's usually canola or cottonseed meals (2,800 grams). This is the standard recipe. The two nitrogen variants immediately following will soon be explained.

OR

3 quarts oilseed meal (2,100 grams) and 1 quart feather meal (470 grams).

OR

3 quarts of oilseed meal (2,100 grams) and 1 quart of fish meal (635 grams); or for less odor, instead of fish use 1 pint of blood meal (290 grams). You may use 3 quarts of oilseed meal, 1 quart fish meal, and 1 pint blood meal (290 grams).

Calcium

1 pint agricultural lime (850 grams) best ground finely, #65 or #100, and 1 pint agricultural gypsum (600 grams). Do not use dolomite lime.

Phosphorous

1 quart of any one of these ingredients: colloidal (soft) rock phosphate (1,500 grams), bone meal (ordinary or fishbone) (1,000 grams), or high phosphate guano (1,500 grams)

Trace elements and micronutrients

2 teaspoon laundry borax (10–11 percent purity) (10 grams)

1½ teaspoons zinc sulfate (10 grams)

1 teaspoon copper sulfate (5 grams)

1 pint kelp meal (400 grams) or azomite (400 grams)

ABOUT THE INGREDIENTS IN COF AND HOW IT WORKS

Spreading only oilseed meal, lime, and compost grows a good-*looking* garden. Adding fish meal or blood meal (or better, both) to the recipe causes nitrogen to be released more rapidly in chilly soil, accelerating spring growth. Adding feather meal to the recipe extends nitrogen release. This variant works slightly better on crops that grow through the entire summer, like celery, tomatoes, peppers, zucchini, and winter squash.

Oilseed meal. It is the residue left after extracting vegetable oil from canola, cotton, flax, soybean seeds, etc. Most oilseed meals have a nitrogen-phosphorus-potassium (N-P-K) analysis of about 6-2-1, but you won't find a chemical analysis on the sack label. Instead, you'll be told the protein content, because most oilseed meal is used as animal feed. I buy whichever oilseed meal contains the most protein (protein releases nitrogen as it decomposes in soil) for the least money. Any finely ground material providing over 25 percent protein will act like fertilizer if you use enough of it, but at 40 percent protein or more, it works powerfully. Sometimes you find oilseed meal in the high 40 percents. The quick rule is every 6.2 percent protein releases 1 percent nitrogen as it is eaten by the soil ecology.

Organically grown oilseed meals are available, but these days most oilseed meal comes from genetically modified (GM) crops. I will not eat GM foods as they are now. I might if they were bred for providing greater nutrient density than otherwise would be possible and had been checked for safety with multigenerational animal-feeding studies that should show increased life span and function. Some people object to GM foods so much they resist using the waste products of GM crops as fertilizer. But as fertilizer there seems to be no functional difference between non-GM conventionally grown oilseed meal and GM oilseed meal, except that GM oilseed meal will contain traces of glyphosate, while non-GM oilseed meals carry traces of different herbicides that probably cost the farmer more than glyphosate does and may well be even more toxic than glyphosate is.

I think it's highly unlikely that anything in GM oilseed meal, be it unusual proteins or chemical residues, will harm the soil ecology. I know a large-scale food gardener in Maryland who routinely fertilizes with GM soybean meal and also feeds his worm composting beds with soybean meal during winter. After five years on this regimen, his worms are still thriving, as is his garden. I'd be even more confident about using GM oilseed meal as fertilizer if he would have fed those worms up the food chain, say to frogs, and raised four generations of healthy frogs on worms fed on GM oilseed meal. Still, his result so far suggests that, as fertilizer, the stuff is safe.

Lime. COF includes two calcium sources, agricultural lime, sometimes called aglime, which is finely ground calcium carbonate rock, and gypsum, which is calcium sulfate. Sometimes agricultural gypsum is finely ground naturally occurring rock, and sometimes it is obtained as a residue from chemical processing. The first sort meets the requirements of organic certification bureaucrats. Either sort works fine although the industrial by-product gypsum could contain toxic heavy metals, so be careful. Ordinary agricultural lime is not quite insoluble in soil; depending on the fineness of the grind and the degree of soil acidity, it can take 1 to 10 years to break down. When I specify aglime, I use a hash symbol to indicate grind size. For example, #65 is ground fine enough that all of it passes through a sieve having 65 fine wires per inch, #10 is coarse, #100 is very fine. Do not use quicklime, burnt lime, hydrated lime, or any other hot form of lime. Gypsum is slowly soluble in soil and ensures an abundant supply of plant-available calcium and sulfur. Rock gypsum ground to about #10 is fine enough for COF.

The modest amount of aglime in COF gradually brings soil pH to the right level and then works to keep it there. You won't significantly overlime with COF because as the soil becomes increasingly saturated with calcium, most other plant nutrients become more available. The bottom line is that after using COF for a few years, you'll get a bigger bang out of each bucket of it and will intuitively start using less. Even if your garden has been limed in recent years, I suggest that you include the small quantity of lime.

Phosphorus. There are four natural phosphorus fertilizers: bonemeal (fish or slaughterhouse), guano (fossilized seabird poop), hard or soft (sometimes termed "colloidal") rock phosphates. Soft rock phosphate (SRP) is the most broadly useful and the most economical. Buying phosphorus in the form of guano costs more per each pound of elemental phosphorus, but guano releases faster. I prefer guano for container growing mixes. There is a form of guano made by bats that usually brings more nitrogen than phosphorus. I do not use this type. Bonemeal (fish or slaughterhouse) is spendy and even better than guano in potting mixes. I wouldn't hesitate to use guano or bonemeal in COF. Hard rock phosphate (HRP) is the feedstock used to make chemical phosphate fertilizers. HRP provides more elemental phosphorus per dollar than SRP does, but even when ground to talcum-powder fineness, HRP is so insoluble that it is of limited value. The only way I know to get a noticeable effect from HRP is to include it while building the compost heap, because heat and intense biological activity make some of the phosphorus become available.

Potassium. There is a low concentration of potassium in oilseed meals and in kelp meal. No more than that inescapable small quantity is put into COF. Plenty of potassium will be brought into the garden with compost, industrial organic wastes, or animal manures. In fact, limiting organic matter imports to keep soil potassium levels in balance is essential to producing the highest level of nutrient-density in Cascadia.

Kelp meal. It seems expensive. Kelp as fertilizer usually does nothing that you can directly observe, and for that reason some are tempted to leave it out of COF. However, kelp contains useful amounts of all the micronutrients. Various hormones and growth-regulating substances in kelp boost plant fortitude. Azomite, a highly mineralized ground rock, provides micronutrients too, but lacks kelp's biological magic. If it were my choice, I'd use lesser quantities of both at one time, or alternate years, or switch to the other sort when the bag I was using ran out.

Trace elements. As best I know at present, only the glacial moraines of Western Washington lack iron and manganese, so these elements are not included in the regular recipe. Copper deficiencies are common throughout Cascadia; lack of copper causes serious health problems in plants, animals, and humans. I wish I could include several times more copper in each batch of COF but doing that could be unsafe for some soils. Be careful when handling copper sulfate; avoid breathing any dust coming off of it. Copper is toxic in large amounts. Your garden's need for zinc is less certain. The small quantity of zinc in COF won't harm any soil that already is adequately endowed, but may make a huge difference where it is otherwise deficient. Same story with boron. One precaution needs mentioning about storing zinc sulfate. This salt picks up moisture from the atmosphere. After opening and using part of an airtight container, it's better to store the remainder in something airtight. However, mixing a small quantity of damp zinc sulfate into a gallon of oilseed meal poses no problem. There isn't enough moisture in it to trigger decomposition.

Boron can be purchased at the supermarket as laundry borax, which is a naturally occurring soluble salt mined in Death Valley, California. Borax contains about 10 percent boron.

WHERE TO GET COF INGREDIENTS

Several Cascadian businesses have sold natural fertilizer materials for decades. The largest and the oldest of these is Concentrates Inc. (www.concentratesnw.com) serving Portland, Oregon, and the Pacific Northwest. It distributes a full range. They even offer organically grown oilseed meal.

Black Lake Organic (www.blacklakeorganic .com), from Olympia, Washington, supplies natural fertilizer ingredients and has for many years. They also sell premixed COF compounded to my current recipe, as well as a few other similar concoctions of their own invention. To legally label my COF as "fertilizer," Black Lake Organic had the recipe analyzed. So I can tell you that COF tests 3-4-1 for N-P-K and that Black Lake Organic calls it "BLOOM No. 11." Black Lake Organic also sells potassium, iron, manganese, zinc and copper sulfates, and borax by the pound.

Peaceful Valley Farm and Garden Supply (www.groworganic.com) in Northern California provides a broad assortment of Organic Materials Review Institute (OMRI)–approved fertilizers, and Down to Earth Distributors Inc. (www.downtoearthdistributors.com) a wholesale distributor in Eugene, Oregon, sells most COF ingredients in small and large sizes—5, 20, and 50 pounds—including organically grown oilseed meal, but does not yet offer the sulfates. Retail customers can buy direct from the Down to Earth shop in Eugene or through many Cascadian garden centers and health-food co-ops. Down to Earth also compounds a range of organic fertilizer blends that are similar to COF but do not contain aglime or trace elements. In a pinch you could start with 1½ gallons of Down to Earth's Bio-Fish 7-7-2 and mix in 1 pint of aglime and 1 pint of gypsum. If you also added the amounts of boron, zinc, and copper I recommend for COF, you'd about have COF. I do not recommend doing this with any of Down to Earth's other premixed fertilizers.

Lately several smaller businesses have come to offer the full range of COF ingredients. Grow Organic in Hood River, Oregon (www.groworganics.org), also will analyze a soil test report for you on the spot and compound a custom COF based on the test result. Marion Ag Service in Saint Paul, Oregon (www.marionag.com); Healing Ponds Farm in Beaverton, Oregon (www.healingponds.com); KIS Organics of Redmond, Washington (www.kisorganics.com); and Cultivating Soil Solutions in Coombs, British Columbia (www.cultivatingsoil.com) all do the same. And though not in Cascadia, Seven Springs Farm (www.7springsfarm.com) in Floyd, Virginia, and Alpha Chemicals in Missouri (www.alphachemicals.com) supply trace element fertilizers in small quantities that are shipped by UPS.

Farm supply stores and farmers' co-ops often sell oilseed meals at excellent prices. Kelp meal, too, because it's often fed to livestock. They all sell aglime.

USING COMPLETE ORGANIC FERTILIZER

Initial soil preparation. For the first crop of the year, uniformly spread a full batch of COF over 100 square feet of raised bed, or if you grow in long rows with paths between them, spread a full batch on a 2-foot-wide strip 50 feet long. Because it contains insoluble materials like aglime and soft rock phosphate, it's best to hoe in or spade in the COF before sowing or transplanting. One batch on 100 square feet provides enough nutrients for low-demand species such as carrots, beets, parsley, beans, peas, and leaf lettuce.

Side-dressing complete organic fertilizer.

The growing instructions in Chapter 9 state if the vegetable is a low-, medium-, or high-demand crop. Medium-demand and high-demand crops start out with a full dose of COF like low-demand crops, but are fed more after they're up and growing. This is done by side-dressing fertilizer on the soil's surface near the plants.

Side-dressing. This produces a strong growth response that lasts about one month. I usually side-dress COF at 1 gallon per 100 square feet (half the starting dose) in a narrow band close to the seedlings soon after they emerge and then at 2 gallons per 100 square feet every four to six weeks while a medium- or high-demand crop should be growing fast. Side-dressing is best spread thinly and uniformly, like a ring or doughnut that start just beyond the plant's drip line and covers the ground the roots will expand into during the next few weeks. There is no absolute requirement to hoe in or rake in side-dressed COF because minuscule soil animals come to the surface at night and eat it. It becomes available in the root zone after passing through their digestive tracts. If you can work it in shallowly it'll start releasing a few days sooner, a minor difference.

The growth rate of heat-loving crops slows around the last week of August; slow-growing plants do not need as many soil nutrients. Schedule the last side-dressing on these crops before the end of July. Autumn and winter crops grow rapidly through the end of September; these should be side-dressed for the last time around the end of August. Overwintered crops resume growing when the first spring bulbs emerge; they'll benefit hugely from being side-dressed at this time. There is an exception. Near the southern coast of Oregon and through the redwoods there can be a lot of winter growth that benefits from light side-dressing.

Side-dressing should seem to make the plants grow. If side-dressing shows no noticeable effect within a few days, then even more fertility is not needed. To prevent overdose, please don't put more on it.

Subsequent crops that same year. Since the year's first crop received a full dose of COF and maybe side-dressing as well, a low-demand crop immediately following on that bed might only need a half dose before sowing it. Or none. If the crop doesn't grow fast enough, you can always side-dress. However, a moderate excess of COF does not lower nutrient density or cause other problems, so I usually start the second crop with a full dose. Medium- and high-demand crops should always start with a full dose.

Transplants. First, over the entire bed broadcast and work in a full dose of COF. Then, and only if the seedling will grow into a large plant like broccoli or squash, at each spot where a seedling is to go, scoop out a small hole about 4 inches deep and 8 inches in diameter. Put about half a cup (a handful) of COF into the bottom of the hole. Using your fingertips, blend the COF into the soil at the bottom of the hole. Then transplant. As soon as the seedlings start extending roots, they'll discover a zone of super fertility.

Hills. I make super-fertile low mounds for starting large-size, sprawling species like zucchini, pumpkins, melons, cucumber, rambling indeterminate tomatoes, and sometimes the larger brassicas if this is a new garden whose soil hasn't yet come into balance. First, over the entire area the crop will eventually fill with roots, spread and dig in the usual quantity of COF. Then make an extra-fertile hill for each plant. With shovel or spade, remove two large scoops of loose soil from a spot and set them next to the shallow hole you just made. In the bottom of the hole put ½ to 1 cup of COF and a shovelful of your best compost, and mix it in with the spade. Then push the soil you removed back over the hole, making an 18-inch-diameter low mound with the greatest concentration of fertility starting 3 to 4 inches below the surface.

If seeds are to be sown in that hill, first compress the soil directly below the planting spot to help subsoil moisture move up to that area. I do this by making a fist and gently pressing it into the mound's center. Then sow seeds on the firm earth at the bottom of this depression and cover them to the appropriate depth. Don't press down very hard; your goal is not to make rammed earth.

TWEAKING COF

Adjusted COF for certain circumstances.

New gardens on clay or clayey soil initially need more lime than COF provides. I have already suggested doubling the amount of aglime and gypsum for the first two years and then reverting to the regular recipe.

Sandy soils dry out quickly. Sand may hold more moisture if you make it become denser. Increasing magnesium saturation makes the little bit of clay usually present in sand become stickier. Then the soil holds more moisture and anchors the vegetables better. So if your sandy soil *does not have a clay subsoil, change the recipe. Put in ½ pint aglime, ½ cup of dolomite, and ½ pint of gypsum.*

Glacial moraine sand. The last continental glacier left behind deep deposits of coarse sand and rounded rocks from Olympia northward to Canada. Not all soils in this part of Washington are glacial sand, but many are. You can spot them from a car window by observing the trees. On most Cascadian soils Douglas fir grows between 2 and 4 feet between each ring of branches, depending mostly on the amount of moisture the site provides during the summer, but on glacial moraine soils I observed them gaining only 1 foot a year.

Leached glacial sand provides very little of any plant nutrient and, worse, has little capacity to hold on to fertilizer. Growing veggies on these natural barrens is a lot like practicing outdoor hydroponics—to get a good result, you must repeatedly feed a full balance of plant nutrients in small doses while the amount of available plant nutrients (and the soil pH) cycles from high, immediately after you fertilize, to low, after the crop makes withdrawals for a few weeks. But crops grow much better when balanced nutrients are abundant at all times.

Sand benefits far more from compost and manure than heavy soils do because soil organic matter, like clay, holds moisture, adsorbs plant nutrients, and then releases nutrients as the plants need them. If you're gardening on sand, I suggest spreading at least twice as much compost as I call for on heavier soils.

It is safe to assume there's not enough of any plant nutrient in leached glacial sand. They all must be added frequently and in small quantities.

Following is another COF recipe designed for these circumstances. Mix the ingredients thoroughly. Spread the entire amount on 100 square feet before planting. Be prepared to side-dress close to the row about a week after seeds germinate and then spread another full dose of fertilizer every time plant growth slows. That could be as often as once a month, and on all crops, including low-demand crops.

Here's the recipe:

3 to 4 quarts oilseed meal (2,100 to 2,800 grams)
½ cup dolomite lime, use #65 (200 grams)
1 cup agricultural lime, #100 is best; otherwise use #65 (425 grams)

1 cup gypsum (300 grams)

1 quart soft rock phosphate (750 grams) or bonemeal (520 grams)

½ cup potassium sulfate (125 grams)

2 tablespoons ferrous (iron) sulfate (40 grams)

1½ tablespoons manganese sulfate (not magnesium sulfate) (30 grams)

2 teaspoons zinc sulfate (10 grams)

1 teaspoon copper sulfate (5 grams)

2 teaspoons laundry borax (10 grams)

1 cup kelp meal (200 grams) or azomite (200 grams), or both

Liquid Fertilizers

Organic gardeners fertilize with homemade manure/compost tea or else use concentrates like fish emulsion and liquid kelp. These liquids can be poured over plants (drenching), sprayed on their leaves (foliar feeding), or put deeply into the root zone (fertigation). Liquid fertilizers have advantages. They take effect immediately. When foliar fed, a strong growth response happens from a very small quantity of fertilizer, although that effect lasts only a week at best. A downside of liquid *organic* fertilizers is that it is impossible to dissolve more than a trace of phosphorus or calcium out of natural materials. Any "organic" liquid fertilizer claiming to provide more than 1 percent phosphate probably contains food-grade phosphoric acid. In my opinion, there's great benefit from and no harm at all in fertilizing with dilute phosphoric acid. East Indian farmers spray cola soft drinks as foliar fertilizer because to achieve their sour back-taste, cola drinks contain enough phosphoric acid to put a shine on a copper penny (or stealthily dissolve your teeth). Until recently organic certification bureaucrats dogmatically banned phosphoric acid because it is an artificial substance. Those bureaucrats now reckon phosphoric acid is kosher when it is used to prevent liquid kelp and fish extracts from fermenting. I find it amusing that the quantities used to prevent spoilage are, remarkably, the amount needed for balanced fertilization.

Instantly soluble (dry) chemical fertilizers, like Miracle-Gro or Peters (20-20-20), supply nitrogen and potassium, plenty of phosphorus, and enough trace elements to prevent outright deficiency symptoms, but they still do not provide calcium. In soil that already provides plenty of calcium, one fertigation with these roughly balanced soluble chemicals can make a big difference during the next two to three weeks. They also grow container plants fairly well *if* the growing medium contains aglime or, better, both lime and gypsum.

Canna, a Dutch company specializing in hydroponics, makes a pair of very expensive liquid fertilizers for use in soil or soil-like growing media that provide a full balance of all known essential plant nutrients, including calcium, in a highly available form. Canna's Terra Vega encourages rapid, healthy vegetative growth; Canna's Terra Flores does the same for a blooming cannabis plant, strawberries, and ripening tomatoes. The difference between fertigating with Canna's products and using Miracle-Gro or Peters is . . . well . . . quite noticeable, and to me is well worth the much higher price. You may find

Canna's dilution directions hard to comprehend. For raising seedlings, mix Canna Terra Vega at 2 teaspoons per gallon (2.5 milliliter per liter) in all the water they're given. For foliar application, or occasional fertigating, make the dilution 4 teaspoons per gallon (4.5 milliliter/liter).

Canna's Terra Flores produces terrific results when foliar fed to exhausted hot-weather crops nearing the end of their season. About every 10 days in the last month of summer, early in the morning, when the leaf stomata are open and receptive, spray Terra Flores at 4 teaspoons per gallon on the leaves until the water starts dripping off the tips. The result I get is tomatoes, peppers, eggplants, and zucchini that go on setting fruit longer and do not become so quickly diseased at season's end. Late season pole beans benefit too. Some gardeners attempt to create this same effect with compost tea, but I challenge anyone to make a fair comparison unaffected by preexisting beliefs about the evils of chemicals . . . I think they'll either choose Canna's Terra Flores or use both.

Spray foliars when evaporation rates are low—early morning, or an hour or so before dark. If the species has waxy leaves that repel water, then add just enough water softener (penetrant) to your spray tank so that the droplets spread out on the leaves instead of beading up and running off: I use a few drops of ordinary low-sudsing dishwashing liquid for each gallon of solution. There are penetrants sold that are said to enhance nutrient uptake. To me, these seem unnecessarily expensive and potentially toxic.

LIQUID KELP

Kelp has long been used for food, for fertilizer, and in more recent times for the extraction of alginates, valuable chemicals with a wide range of industrial uses. Kelp also contains natural plant hormones. Kelp extracts that retain these hormones (not all do) make container-grown seedlings develop roots at several times the usual rate, so in addition to complete fertilizer concentrate I add 2 teaspoons of top-quality kelp extract (2 milliliter/liter) to every gallon of their water. Kelp hormones help vegetables resist disease. Because it grows in seawater, kelp extracts provide a broad range of micronutrients. If you use COF but consider the price of kelp meal beyond you, try foliar feeding liquid kelp every few weeks.

Some liquid kelp fertilizers are by-products of alginate extraction. Unfortunately, the hormones and growth regulators were extracted along with the alginates; by-product liquid kelp still contains the minerals. Expect to pay more for the good stuff. And don't expect recyclers of alginate-extraction waste to tell you that's what they are doing.

Wood Ash and Charcoal

Ancient gardens discovered deep in the highly leached Amazon rain forest are still fertile after 500 years of neglect because the soil contains charcoal, lately termed "biochar." In the Amazon's constant heat and humidity, organic matter rots away with enormous speed, and soils are far more thoroughly leached than anywhere in Cascadia except, perhaps, the Olympic rain forests. Archaeologists speculate that the first biochar deposits were formed either by nature or unintentionally by humans, but after observing the benefits from gardening on charcoal-containing soil, biochar was then manufactured.

Charcoal holds on to and then releases plant nutrients in the same way clay and humus do. Biochar reduces leaching in sandy soils and stabilizes nutrient delivery. Biochar also effectively sequesters carbon in the soil for a much greater duration (over 500 years) than humus lasts (100 years at most). Non-humified compost pretty much decomposes within three years.

Biochar activists foresee commercial biochar manufactured out of crop wastes with the side benefit of cogenerated electricity. It is also possible to make charcoal on a homestead scale using primitive methods. Presently, biochar is sold by the cubic foot through Concentrates Inc. Lately I've been allowing my woodstove to burn out during the night and then removing the charcoal. Some mornings there is a half gallon of it.

Putting freshly made biochar into soil creates a shockingly bad result because raw biochar is ravenous for plant nutrients, which it grabs aggressively out of the surrounding soil. Until the biochar has satisfied its hunger, vegetables cannot find enough nutrition. The simplest thing to do with new biochar is to first moisten it to keep the dust down, grind—or crush—it to the size of rice grains, and then mix it into compost heaps as they are being formed. During the composting process biochar saturates itself with plant nutrients and turns itself into a powerful release-on-demand fertilizer. It could also be precharged by soaking it for several weeks in concentrated liquid fertilizer or manure tea and then using it like fertilizer.

Biochar is a new interest. Gardeners are doing experiments; information is appearing on Internet forums. We don't yet know if hardwood versus softwood charcoal matters very much. We don't yet know the best range of temperatures to target while processing the material. We don't yet know the best way to charge biochar before mixing it into soil. We don't yet know how much biochar is too much. We don't know the ideal particle size.

I speculate that people with sandy soil would grow much better gardens by including 5 and possibly up to 10 percent charcoal into the starting volume of every compost heap they build. I speculate that sandy soils would benefit hugely by holding as much as one-quarter by volume of finely crushed biochar in the top foot. This much char would act as though there were a similar proportion of clay in the sand, but unlike clay would not act to reduce soil air. I hope biochar becomes inexpensive enough that people can afford to use it generously.

And what about wood ashes? Many garden books advise using them as fertilizer because they are rich in calcium, potassium, and magnesium. True enough, but Cascadian firewood is potassium-rich like the soils that grow the trees, and on most Cascadian soils more potassium is the last thing you want to bring in. I suggest spreading ashes under trees near your property.

Compost as Nitrogen Fertilizer

As soil nitrogen increases, plants grow faster because they require nitrates to manufacture chlorophyll, which is a protein. Nitrogen forms the core of all proteins, animal or vegetable or microbial, so increasing the amount of nitrogen in soil means more microbes and fungi, which means more plant nutrients of all kinds get released by decomposition. Chemical fertilizer opponents spin it the other way —farming with nitrogen fertilizer depletes soil organic matter. But vegetables demand a lot of nitrogen, which means vegetable gardens *must* burn a lot of organic matter and need to be endlessly resupplied.

The only compost I ever used that provoked a strong nitrogen response in Cascadia was made from chicken manure and sawdust, sold in plastic sacks stacked in the Safeway parking lot. Labeled 4-3-2 N-P-K, it was finely granular with a strong odor. And inexpensive. Before I invented COF, I used this compost in exactly the same ways I now use oilseed meal, but it took considerably larger quantities to produce a similar result. Chicken manure and sawdust become nitrogen- and phosphorus-rich compost because poultry mainly eat high protein (nitrogen-rich) seeds, and plants concentrate almost all their phosphorus uptake into the seeds they make. So chicken manure contains much the same nutrient profile as the seed meal I base COF upon, but with lower nitrogen concentration because the chickens have already had a go at making their own proteins from that seed.

As the concentration of nitrogen in organic fertilizers goes up, the growth response they produce increases even faster. It takes four to six buckets of 4 percent nitrogen chicken manure compost to produce the same amount of growth response as you get from one bucket of 7 percent nitrogen oilseed meal. As the nitrogen concentration in organic fertilizers decreases, the growth response they produce diminishes even faster and soon ceases altogether. The next chapter explains that nitrogen in biomass is released by decomposition and that the speed of decomposition is determined by temperature. You may have read of enormously successful gardens that were only fertilized with compost, so I remind you that Cascadian soils do not get nearly as warm in summer as soils usually do east of the Cascades. Expertly made garden waste compost has about 2.5 percent nitrogen. That's concentrated enough to act like fertilizer during two months of Cascadian high summer, if you spread it thick. It takes most gardeners many attempts at making compost before their own provides more than 2 percent nitrogen.

Cascadian gardens receiving only compost experience very slow growth until the soil properly warms up late in June. About when corn gets knee-high in early July the patch finally turns dark green and gets to growing fast. So do your tomatoes, winter squash, and other heat-loving crops. If the summer vegetables could have grown faster during June, they'd start yielding sooner and produce more. That's one reason why using COF as well as compost makes such a difference.

Municipal waste composts usually contain about 1.5 percent nitrogen. Composts made of mostly tree trimmings and paper, or bark and sawdust, provide as little as 1 percent nitrogen. Composts providing less than 2 percent nitrogen increase soil organic matter and usually make vegetables grow better than had it not been added, but they do not act like fertilizer. When more than a small quantity is mixed into soil, they act like antifertilizer until they decompose somewhat. If I wanted my garden to grow strongly with much of this stuff in the soil, I'd also have to use half again more than the usual amount of COF.

Humus and Tilth

Organic matter fuels the soil's ecosystem, just like humans are energized by carbo(n)hydrate foods. If garden soil receives insufficient organic matter, its microecology, the soil workability, and the health of plants decline.

In most gardening books the terms "humus," "compost," and "soil organic matter" are used interchangeably. Actually, they're quite different. Organic matter decaying in soil feeds plants by releasing its mineral content. If the soil contains no clay, then organic matter rots away to nothing within a few years. In heavier soils a portion of decaying organic matter can combine with clay to form humus, a relatively stable substance that provides great benefits for about one hundred years before it ultimately decomposes. Either way, short-lasting or rather permanent,

decomposing organic matter makes an enormous difference. But the presence of humus makes the greatest difference.

Humus has been studied for over a century, but we still do not know its molecular structure. We cannot synthesize it. All humus is dark-colored (brown or black), spongy (holds a lot of moisture), and has powerful, positive effects when mixed into mineral soil particles. The best practical definition of humus states that it is a portion of organic material remaining after the initial decomposition process has done its work; humus is highly resistant to further decomposition.

Organic matter is transformed into humus by passing through the digestive tracts of animals—sometimes the large ones who deposit their manure on the earth's surface, and always a series of tiny soil-dwelling animals that eat animal manure, plant residues, and each other's wastes as well. Each eater converts some carbon into energy and leaves the rest behind to again be eaten by a complex ecology of even smaller life-forms. After everything has finished dining, most of the carbon has been burned off and much of the mineral content has been released for use as plant nutrients; the indigestible residue remaining has been termed "humus."

N. A. Krasil'nikov, a brilliant Soviet-era soil microbiologist and author of the classic *Soil Microorganisms and Higher Plants* (see Additional Reading, page 339), asserted that "soil fertility is determined by biological factors, mainly by microorganisms." Were this microlife eliminated, the soil would become "an object of geology" (not biology). He gauged soil fertility by counting the number of microorganisms per gram of soil; there is always a close match between this number and the productivity of the soil.

Of the many positive effects accomplished by a healthy soil microecology, these are of the most concern to food growers: improved soil structure, suppression of soil-dwelling plant diseases, enormously better plant nutrition through two main processes—the bacterial creation of what Krasil'nikov named "phytamins," and accelerated release of nutrients from rock particles. Additionally, soil-dwelling fungi help feed many plant species through what is termed "mycorrhizal associations," and much has been made of these in organic farming books. However, once soil has been brought to the degree of fertility that a thriving vegetable garden requires, mycorrhizal fungi become inactive.

Humus makes the biggest difference. Like biochar, humus acts like a plant nutrient storage battery that stably and abundantly dispenses plant nutrients. Unfortunately, compost is not necessarily humus. To form humus during the composting process, the heap must start out holding a few percent clay. If non-humified compost is mixed into soil containing clay, some of it will decompose into long-lasting humus and some of it will decompose completely. When mixed into sandy soil, non-humified compost completely decomposes within a few years. For that reason, sandy gardens should be fed twice as much compost.

PHYTAMINS—PLANT VITAMINS

Hydroponic strawberry and lettuce plants always look and taste incomplete to me because they lack tiny quantities of essential somethings that Krasil'nikov named phytamins—the plant's equivalent of vitamins. Plants need to intake phytamins as much as animals and humans need vitamins. That's why advanced hydroponic growers attempt to supply phytamins by adding brewed organic concoctions to their nutrient tank. I prefer soil.

Plants can't make their own phytamins any more than humans can make vitamin C, so they entice the soil ecology to make them. The plant's root tips and root hairs give off watery substances that soil microbiologists term "exudates." Exudates establish a chemical environment immediately around the root, a culture medium that strongly favors those species of bacteria and fungi the plant wishes to have in its root zone. The same exudates inhibit disease organisms. It's a fair exchange; the cultivated microbes secrete phytamins.

Krasil'nikov says root exudates are not the primary food of these beneficial microorganisms; they mainly eat organic matter. If the soil provides enough food, the cultivated microbes thrive immediately around the plant's roots. It is not necessary to build ultrahigh levels of organic matter to create a healthy, abundant soil ecology. Annually adding a ¼-inch-thick layer of finely divided, completely finished compost to most soils is more than sufficient. So is a ½-inch-thick layer of half-rotted horse or cow manure or of most industrial composts.

TILTH

Soil is composed of tiny particles of rock that have not yet been dissolved by weak soil acids, of clay that formed in the soil out of chemical elements previously dissolved from rock particles, of decomposing organic matter and humus, of microorganisms and other life-forms, of water and air. For plants to grow well, soil particles must form a stable structure containing gaps and spaces that provide air to roots, and allow rain or irrigation to penetrate rapidly and excess moisture to drain out freely. All things being equal, the coarser and more stable the structure, the more air there will be and the better the crops will grow. A soil lacking natural structure may provide enough oxygen to roots for a few weeks after digging, but it soon slumps back into relative airlessness. Reckoned by volume, garden soils should contain about half air or water, 45 percent minerals, and in Cascadia, 7 to 10 percent organic matter.

When soil microorganisms are abundant, the slimy, gluey substances they secrete strongly bind soil particles into irregularly shaped crumbs. Worms create crumbs by combining minerals and organic matter in their digestive systems. Without a crumb structure, the finer bits of silt and clay would sift into the gaps between the larger sand particles and then there would be far less air in the soil. A crumbly soil is said to have good *tilth*. It can be worked easily and forms a finely textured, loose seedbed that doesn't slump quickly after tilling, nor will it readily form a hard crust that prevents seedling emergence.

Good tilth lets heavy rain or excessive irrigation flow through soil. When you see long-lasting puddles form on farm fields after a heavy rain, you are often looking at humus-depleted soil. It is also possible that the wet area has a high water table—possible, but not usually. It is also possible you're looking at the result of a clay subsoil clogged up by excess magnesium. Because this is a regional book, I can tell you that the grass seed fields found between Eugene and Albany, Oregon, become shallow, temporary lakes in winter, because a few feet beneath the surface is a thin layer of very fine clay that greatly slows drainage.

Good tilth prevents surface crusts from forming after rain or irrigation. Crusting does worse harm than stopping fragile vegetable seedlings from emerging. Crust seals the surface, reducing the amount of oxygen in soil. I rake compost into the surface, rather than dig it in deeply. That way crusting is impossible. The compost mixes itself in deeper when soil animals and worms come to the surface to feed on it or the next time I dig the bed.

The information in this paragraph is crucially important. Please read it multiple times and consider its implications on plant spacing and the benefits from opening the subsoil to root penetration. Soil with good tilth facilitates root development. Plants grow no faster aboveground than they can grow new roots. Plants take in most of their nutrition through tender young root tips and the tiny hairs just behind those tips. To remain well nourished, the plant must constantly make new tip cells as the tender young cells, which used to be the tip, toughen up and change into ordinary bark-covered root. Bark greatly reduces the root's ability to assimilate plant nutrients. I suppose that's why a pot-bound seedling soon becomes stressed and looks deficient despite using soluble fertilizer.

There's another benefit to improving tilth: well-oxygenated microorganisms thrive. And burn more carbon. So an airy soil means faster nutrient release from decomposing organic matter. Higher microbial populations also mean more phytamins get manufactured.

So I suggest, in addition to improving tilth by adding organic matter, you temporarily boost the soil's air supply by gently sliding a sharp weeding hoe through the surface inch once a week during the main growing season; you may like the result. If you raked in compost before planting, you'll find hoe cultivation requires little time or effort. The more often you hoe, the easier it will be next time.

SO HOW MUCH ORGANIC MATTER DOES SOIL NEED?

Decomposing organic matter releases plant nutrients. Soil organic matter is the food of microorganisms essential to the health of plants. Decomposing organic matter fuels the creation of good tilth. To the founders of the organic farming and gardening movement, it seemed that soil couldn't hold too much organic matter. Their books and the publications of garden writers belonging to the organic followership suggest that gardeners should make and spread as much compost as possible. Inches thick.

Every year. And that we can measure soil fertility by counting earthworms.

Robert Parnes, author of *Fertile Soil: A Grower's Guide to Organic & Inorganic Fertilizers* (see Additional Reading, page 339), says of this:

[A] garden differs fundamentally from a farm. A farm is a source of nutrients, and a garden is a sink for nutrients. A farm produces hay and straw for mulch, and animal manure, both of which contribute to the garden's fertility. A garden takes all that fertility for producing a high intensity of valuable crops. Moreover, the tillage required to maintain a garden tends to destroy fertility, whereas the tillage on a farm, under ideal conditions, builds fertility.

There are two related questions rarely asked by garden writers, much less ever answered with understanding: (1) How much organic matter do gardens really need? And (2), perhaps more important: Could we put in too much?

About excess soil organic matter I have already explained that compost and manure made from Cascadian raw materials contain a great deal of potassium and that in the interest of our own nutrition, we should avoid creating potassium excesses in food gardens. Still, veggie gardeners must increase organic matter because food gardening accelerates its loss—an interesting problem!

At this point I could provide a cast-in-stone rule that says "Most Cascadian garden soils need 7 to 10 percent soil organic matter as measured by a quick, cheap laboratory test." I could say "When starting a brand-new garden mix a layer of compost about 1 inch thick into the top 6 inches of soil and from that point on, provide an annual addition of ¼ inch thick." But following this principle is not as useful as understanding what's behind the numbers.

There can be no single target for how much soil organic matter should ideally be in a veggie garden; the amount varies according to climate and to a lesser extent, by soil type. Hans Jenny explained how and why this occurs in his readily comprehensible book *Factors in Soil Formation*, 1942 (see Additional Reading, page 339). Jenny said, "Within regions of similar moisture conditions, the organic matter content of soil . . . decreases [traveling] from north to south. For each drop of 18 degrees F in annual average temperature, the average organic matter content of soil increases two or three times, provided that [soil moisture] is kept constant."

Humid climates grow more plant material than semiarid or arid ones. Vegetation becomes soil organic matter. The higher the temperature, the faster soil organic matter rots. In fact, for every 18-degree increase in average annual soil temperature, the speed of decomposition doubles. On an annual basis, cool moist soils grow nearly as much biomass as warm moist ones do, but it rots less rapidly. So soils in warm moist climates contain less humus than cool moist climate soils. Maritime climates like Cascadia develop the highest levels; soils in hot, dry climates will be lowest. Other factors such as natural soil mineralization and soil texture affect the soil organic matter level, but the most powerfully controlling influences are moisture and temperature. Without human intervention, soil

organic matter content stabilizes at an ecological climax. A close approximation of this climax would be an ungrazed pasture that had been mowed once a year for a great many years, but from which nothing had ever been removed.

I was leaning on my hoe one morning, staring at nothing, and . . . Eureka! The Universe suggested a theory: the vegetable garden needs slightly more soil organic matter than what you'd find in a highly productive pasture nearby. Aligning this insight with Hans Jenny's data, I could grow a thriving veggie garden with a mere 2 to 3 percent soil organic matter in a hot, humid climate. I would target a higher level in a cool climate.

The most important thing about soil organic matter is not how much of it there is at present but *how much decomposes every year*. For only by decomposing does organic matter release plant nutrients; only by being consumed does it support the microecology that so markedly contributes phytamins to plant nutrition; only while consuming organic matter do soil microorganisms aggressively break down rock particles and release the plant nutrients they contain. Having a high level of organic matter that does not rot makes a peat bog, not an agricultural soil.

Most Cascadian garden soils need 7 to 10 percent organic matter in order to decompose enough of it each year to support plant and soil health. In southern Oregon and through the redwoods, where soil is warmer, a target of 4 to 6 percent would be correct. Seven to 10 percent is enough for all Cascadian soil types except heavy clays, which are a special case to be discussed separately, a bit later, and at some length.

During one growing year more organic matter rots away in a sultry Southern California garden holding only 2 percent organic matter than rots in an Oregon garden with 10 percent organic matter. California gardeners get a much bigger growing result from compost. And to maintain that 2 percent, they'd have to add twice as much compost every year as the Cascadian would in order to maintain their 10 percent.

Let's very conservatively overestimate that a Cascadian garden holding 10 percent organic matter decomposes 10 percent of its organic matter content each year. What is 10 percent of 10 percent in practical terms?

Start by distinguishing the *furrow-slice acre*. "Furrow slice" means the layer of topsoil between 6 and 7 inches thick that a conventional plow turns over. The furrow slice is where almost all the soil's organic matter resides. Varying somewhat by the type of soil and how much air it holds, an acre of furrow slice weighs about two million pounds (1,000 tons). Ten percent of 1,000 tons, about 100 (dry weight) tons of once-living, partly decomposed material changes an acre of dead dust into an acre of productive garden.

If, as a consequence of one year's vegetable gardening, 10 percent of that 100 tons of soil organic matter decomposes into minerals and carbon dioxide, then the annual loss is 10 dry weight tons per acre, or on a home-garden scale, roughly 50 dry weight pounds lost per year from each 100 square feet of vegetable growing bed.

It is extremely difficult to uniformly cover a 100-square-foot bed with 50 completely dry pounds of compost (or 100 damp pounds).

When you try, it seems as though most of the soil still shows through a thin, random scattering. But for the purpose of *maintaining* soil organic matter in an ongoing vegetable garden, this scant frosting done once a year is a gracious plenty. If I were starting a new garden site on a totally depleted field that had almost no organic matter, and I wanted to quickly convert it to a healthy vegetable garden, then to bring that land up to 10 percent organic matter, I would have to add only 500 pounds (dry weight) of compost per 100 square feet. A dose that heavy covers the soil 2 inches thick.

STEVE'S PRINCIPLE

- When starting a new garden where lawn or pasture now grows, spread and dig into the top 6 inches of soil *no more* than a 1-inch-thick layer of compost or other compost-like industrial waste containing little or no sawdust or distinguishable wood chips or bark. Except on clay soils, which need different handling.

- While maintaining an established garden, once a year spread a ¼-inch-thick layer of top-quality compost. If you can't make that much compost yourself, then spread industrial compost. You'll get the most benefit from compost that is raked into the surface inch where decomposition is the most rapid.

Soil Management

Any biomass the garden produces itself means less need to bring it in from outside. When the soil is thickly covered with actively growing vegetation, it is producing new organic matter about as fast or maybe slightly faster than it is decomposing organic matter. So crimson clover, small seeded favas, or other hardy green manure crops should be overwintered on as much of the garden as conveniently possible. A green manure crop dries out the topsoil faster, allowing you to work it earlier in spring. This topsoil gets thickly interpenetrated with tender delicate quick-to-rot roots, so it naturally crumbles into a fine seedbed. A green crop prevents winter rains from compacting the beds, and erosion is reduced on sloping sites. In spring and early summer fast-growing green crops like buckwheat and rocket (arugula) can be squeezed into any short-term vacancies.

You'll find full information in the Legumes section, page 199.

DOLOMITE INCREASES NEED FOR SOIL ORGANIC MATTER

Dolomite is a type of limestone that contains both calcium and magnesium; usually 13 percent magnesium and 24 percent calcium. Depending on its purity, ordinary agricultural lime contains between 32 and 38 percent calcium and less than 2 percent magnesium. Lime that contains less than 13 percent magnesium but more than 2 percent is termed "dolomitic." You won't find dolomitic lime for sale in garden centers.

One reason the organic farming and gardening movement worships compost and soil organic matter is that the movement's founders did not know that too much magnesium makes clay tighten up, get sticky, and become relatively airless, prone to form clods and stick to your boots. They did not know because William Albrecht discovered it *after* the organic movement had cast its dogma in concrete while the chief opinion leader in the American organic movement, J. I. Rodale, considered Albrecht a wrongheaded user of evil chemical fertilizers and refused to consider his research. And Rodale, always the Brooklyn businessman, considered dolomite such a deal because it provides both magnesium and calcium for the price of calcium. But only some soils lack magnesium, and in some broad districts all the soils have too much.

Enough compost temporarily remedies the harm dolomite can do *in the topsoil*. By enough I'm not talking about achieving the soil's natural ecological peak organic matter level, but considerably more. And since the stuff rots away ever faster as more of it is present, then solving surplus magnesium this way means putting yourself on an endless compost-importing treadmill.

Organic matter worked into the topsoil stays there; it does not change the subsoil's texture, but magnesium added to the topsoil does leach into a clay subsoil, where it lodges. If a clayey subsoil already holds excess magnesium (and a high percentage of Cascadian subsoils are naturally like that), it'll already be airless, dense, and inhospitable to root activity. It probably drains slowly. In other words, surplus magnesium blocks crops from making roots in the subsoil. If you use dolomite, the subsoil never improves.

John Jeavons, a highly influential garden writer I will criticize at greater length in Chapter 4, asserts that the effective root zone of vegetables is only 2 feet deep, which is why he advocates making 2 feet of fertile topsoil by double digging in compost to that depth. For sure 2 feet of root zone grows crops better than when they're limited to the furrow slice, but the truth is most vegetable species would, if they could, send roots 4 to 6 feet down. If you wish to confirm my assertion, please consult John Weaver's classic book *Root Development of Vegetable Crops* (see Additional Reading, page 339).

No matter how much fertilizer or compost goes into the topsoil, vegetables can't grow to their limit when their root development stops at the airless clay starting 12 to 18 inches down. But double digging compost and aglime into more than a few hundred square feet of sticky clay subsoil is a task beyond the endurance of most people. Because few Cascadian soils are short of magnesium and many of its subsoils hold too much, there is no dolomite in COF. Subsoils holding excess magnesium can be improved by leaching enough calcium into them to replace some of that magnesium. COF takes more than a few years to accomplish that task. With guidance from a full laboratory soil test, it is possible to accelerate this process.

MULCHING: THE PLUS AND THE MINUS

Many gardeners mulch, meaning they spread a layer of raw organic matter over the entire garden.

National gardening publications promote the method. Mulchers offer up a lot of good-sounding reasons why. Like not having to dig ever again. Or make compost heaps. Or be concerned about building/maintaining soil fertility because decomposing mulch does that.

Mulching causes as many problems as it solves. A thick mulch rarely suppresses weeds completely. Some emerge through it. Because of the mulch you can't use a hoe, although weeds usually yank fairly easily through mulch. Soil that comes out of winter already covered with mulch will be much slower to warm in spring, greatly retarding plant growth until it finally heats up. Mulching in Cascadia means importing large quantities of potassium.

Mulching has positive aspects. Cucurbits, alliums, and salad radishes do most of their feeding close to the surface. These crops may grow better with mulch. Some sandy soils are reluctant to take up moisture after they have become dry. Irrigation beads up on the surface and runs off. Mulch prevents this. Clay soils often become rock hard when dry. Some clays shrink so much as they dry that they form deep cracks that invite even faster moisture loss; mulching also improves this.

If you feel you must mulch, then spread it *after* the topsoil has warmed, usually about mid-June. Mulch cucurbits after they start running. And when you do spread mulch, spread it thinly. Use only enough to keep the surface damp so that you have a chance to slide a hoe under it. And most importantly, when you are doing the after-frost cleanup, *rake up all the mulch and put it in the compost heap.*

In a climate without severe winter, permanent mulch provokes a steady and unstoppable increase of primary decomposers—slugs and two kinds of insects, sow bugs (pill bugs, wood lice, or slaters) and earwigs (pinch bugs). Mulch probably breeds snails in the warmest parts of Cascadia. Primary decomposers are normally present in all gardens; at the population levels normally found, they rarely cause significant damage. Where winter is mild, primary decomposers encounter an unlimited food supply and excellent cover under mulch. By the second summer of permanent mulching, sow bugs, earwigs, and slugs reach plague proportions. They then start eating everything tender, including lettuce seedlings, ripening tomatoes, etc.

Another problem with mulch comes from how seedy almost all Western Oregon grass hay is. No matter how thick it is laid down, enormous amounts of grass emerge.

If you're using permanent mulching with dismaying results, it is easy and quick to cure the mess. Simply rake up all the mulch, every bit of it, and make compost with it. In a few days there'll be far fewer primary decomposers in the garden; they will mainly be found in and immediately around the compost heap, which, in my opinion, is where sow bugs and earwigs should live, helping to accelerate organic matter decomposition.

ELIMINATING SOD

Digging compacted sod is hard work. So gardeners, always inventive, have worked out avoidance techniques. Permanent mulchers get rid of sod by putting a thick layer of hay flakes on it.

Others spread a sheet of black plastic over the grass until everything below dies. I prefer laying down whole sections of newspaper like overlapping shingles, covered with a thin layer of loose soil to prevent them from blowing away. If the soil holds a fair amount of nitrogen (I'd spread COF before the newspaper goes down), by next spring the sod and (hopefully) the newspaper will have rotted. The soil will dig easily.

I no longer use glyphosate, an herbicide often called Roundup, to eliminate sod. I once did when making a new garden or to terminate a long healing rest in grass and to return the plot to veggies. I had justifications for this transgression—I was spraying it but once in a blue moon, and the garden still grew excellently. I've recently discovered that the chemical *does* accumulate in the soil; the stuff *does not* break down rapidly into harmless by-products. Allow it to accumulate and the nutritional content of the crops being grown drops because glyphosate prevents the uptake of trace elements. And there is now strong evidence that glyphosate itself is far more toxic than we were originally told.

The most environmentally friendly way to convert lawn or pasture to garden is not convenient at all. Nor is it quick. The task is done with a sharp spade, methodically cutting and then inverting chunks of sod, leaving them upside down for a few weeks, then reinverting them while digging deeper and breaking the sod into smaller bits as you do so. Much of the grass will die after being denied sunlight for two weeks, and the chunks will begin to crumble. After a few such turns, and a few more waits between these turns, you've got a deeply dug seedbed.

Still, inverting thick sod growing on compacted soil, even with the sharpest of tools, is a young man's work. And the process can take more than a month from start to seedbed.

I've also broken sod with a rotary cultivator—rear-end, not front-end—and if possible it was a big one pulled by a tractor. If I weigh up the environmental damage caused by constructing a powerful rotary cultivator (iron mining and steel making, metal forming, engine manufacture, plastics, copper wire, paint, transport of same, consumption of petrol when running it, etc.), for the sake of the environment the best choice is the sharp spade.

COMPACTION

The topsoil you're planning to garden may have been compacted years ago and still may be that way. Hooves put far higher pressure on the soil than human feet do; cattle or horses may well have grazed the land before it became a garden. Other causes include the heavy machinery that made your residential lot. Compaction makes digging much more difficult the first time you do it. Rototilling or spading 6 or 7 inches deep repairs surface compaction.

You wouldn't think a long-lasting type of soil compaction could be caused by plowing. Plowing loosens soil and fits it for sowing seeds. The damage is accomplished by the weight of the plow itself resting on its bottom as it slides below the layer of soil the plow flips over. Each successive plowing, done each successive year, further compacts the same layer into what is called a "plow pan." I had one at Elkton, Oregon. It was about 2 inches thick starting about 7 inches down. A plow pan prevents crops from putting roots into the subsoil, reducing access to both moisture and nutrients. Gardeners who only prepare soil with a rototiller may have a plow pan and never realize it.

The easiest way I know of to check for a plow pan is to dig a hole with a fence post auger, because its speed of penetration varies greatly with soil compaction. Drilling the first inch into a pasture or lawn is always difficult because roots and leaves tangle the cutters, and because the surface gets compacted from being walked on. Then as you bore in a bit, progress gets easier. But if when you get down about 7 inches, the going becomes slow, and then when you penetrate a few more inches the soil gets soft again, you'll be certain what your problem is—plow pan.

In a farm field, plow pans are shattered by a powerful tractor pulling a subsoiling "shoe" that rips through the soil about 1 foot below the surface. A recently subsoiled pasture looks as though a giant mole has been at work. The gardener accomplishes the same thing with a long-handled 12-inch spade. A sharp spade can be worked full-length into the soil by pressing down with one foot while wriggling the handle slightly. When the blade has been entirely buried, the handle is then levered back to pop loose the soil. You might not be able to loosen a slice more than an inch thick without breaking the handle, but the task is not extremely hard work when you take small bites. The whole job goes a lot easier if you first rototill the top 6 inches. This laborious task has to be done only once, ever.

Clay Soil: Its Care and Special Handling

Soil forms when running water, wind, freezing, and thawing cause rocks to fragment (weather) into little pieces. Soil particles are classified by size.

Stones are too large to support vegetable crops. Remove stones when they are large enough to interfere with cultivation.

Sand particles are large enough to feel gritty when rubbed between the fingers. When viewed through a 10x magnifying glass, sand usually appears to have sharp corners and flat surfaces as though it had recently fractured out of rocks, which is just what happened. Sand feels gritty when rubbed between the fingers.

Sand-size particles are slowly dissolved away by weak soil acids. It can take thousands of years, but when sand particles have weathered small enough, we call them *silt*. If you had a sample of pure silt and rubbed it between your fingers, it would feel like baby powder. Viewed through a microscope, silt particles are rounded and their sharp edges have been dissolved away. Eventually, silt particles entirely dissolve.

The chemicals dissolved out of rocks go through complex recombinations in the soil and become *clay*. Clay consists of thin flat crystals that stack themselves in layers, like pages in a book. Clay crystals are so small that it takes the most powerful electron microscope to capture an image, yet it is easy to visualize the nature of clays if you remember that slate and shale are formed by subjecting clay to heat and pressure. These layered rocks fracture into thin sheets much like the clay that formed them. Clayey soils make several times more water available to plants than sand or silt soils. Sand and silt particles may be compared to books firmly closed with water adhering to their covers, spines, and sides, but clay is like that book with all the pages fanned open. If sand's ability to hold water were expressed numerically as one, silt would be around two, clay four to six and, interestingly, pure humus six to eight. So clay soils sustain plants better between rains or irrigation, but in spring they are slower to dry down and warm up.

Plant nutrients stick to clay like a balloon charged with static electricity sticks to a wall. Clay's "open book pages" have a lot of surface area so clay can hold a great many plant nutrients. Plant nutrients don't easily leach from clay, but plants are able to use them. So having *some* clay in soil is desirable. Having an open, free-draining, moisture-supplying clay subsoil can be highly desirable if it contains enough air to allow root systems to develop in it and is not chemically hostile to roots. But clay *topsoils* are not so desirable for vegetable gardening because clays resist becoming something that minute vegetable seeds will sprout easily in or that delicate new seedlings will grow rapidly in. Clays provide less soil air. Some vegetables grow okay in clay and others don't.

Some clay soils, like those covering the Salem Hills in Oregon, are open, free draining, and not that hard to work. When brought into proper chemical balance, they form clods less readily and will hold considerable soil air. They will grow vegetables. Still, even the most suitable clays make for difficult gardening and, usually, smaller plants. This soil type must be dug/tilled at exactly the right moisture content. If worked when too moist, clay soil forms rock-hard clods that may not disintegrate until they have gone through another winter. Conversely, clayey soils may fall apart into dust if worked with heavy equipment when too dry. That dust then sags into a thick gooey soup the first time it gets wet and then becomes rock hard and airless when it dries. After irrigation or rain, the surface of a recently loosened-up clayey soil often gets sealed over by a hard crust that prevents the emergence of sprouting seeds and reduces the amount of oxygen below. Clay soils can make excellent pastures; free-draining clays grow commercial orchards.

If you have no choice but to grow your veggie patch in clay, it's best to apply some wisdom and be prepared to spend a bit of money, or you are bound to be disappointed. The first step is to make sure you really do have a clay soil. Any soil that is composed of less than 40 percent clay is not, by definition, a clay soil. In fact, the ideal vegetable soil in Cascadia would be composed of 20 to 25 percent clay. At or above 50 percent clay, working the soil gets significantly more difficult.

TESTING FOR CLAY CONTENT

Someone with experience in classifying soils can roll a small sample of moist soil into a fat noodle and discover approximately what sort of particles it is composed of. Several novice gardeners have brought me a sample of "clay" subsoil only to have me tell them that it was not clay at all; actually it was fine sand cemented into hard reddish-brown chunks by iron compounds leached from the topsoil.

There is a quick at-home test that accurately reveals the percentage of sand to silt to clay in a soil sample. The formal name for this procedure is "soil fractional analysis." Dry about a half pint of soil (no roots or obvious organic material), and crush it to fine powder. Don't dry it to zero moisture, just make it dry enough that you can pulverize it. Put that fine soil into a pint-size glass jar with a tight lid. If you don't have a marking pen that'll write on glass, affix a strip of adhesive tape from top to bottom. Then fill the jar with water, leaving an inch of air at the top, and add a few drops of low-sudsing liquid dishwashing detergent to soften the water. *Do not use so much detergent that shaking makes a jar full of suds.* If that happens, you'll have to drain the jar and refill it with pure water a few times until you have washed out the suds. Now start shaking vigorously. And keep on shaking. And then shake some more. You want to make sure every soil particle has separated from every other soil particle. That's why detergent is used. Usually three or four minutes of hard shaking will do it. If the soil has a strong crumb structure, shake very hard for 10 minutes. Then put the jar down somewhere in bright light where it won't be disturbed for several days, although some tests are finished in less than two minutes.

Exactly two minutes after you stop shaking, make a mark on the side of the jar at the level to which the soil has settled out so far. You may need the help of a powerful flashlight to peer into the murk. That mark shows the amount of sand particles in the soil. Being larger, they settle out of suspension the most rapidly. Then wait exactly two hours, and make another mark at the depth to which the soil has now settled out. That mark shows the amount of silt now resting atop the sand.

If your soil is all sand, the test will end two minutes after shaking stops, and it won't take a long shake because sand soils don't form many crumbs. If your soil is a mixture of sand and silt, or all silt, it'll all settle out within two hours. But if there is much clay, you may have to wait as long as two weeks to get the final result.

When the water has finally cleared, draw another line. That layer holds the clay. On the top you might find a thin layer of jellylike organic matter. Now measure the thickness of each layer. A bit of arithmetic will convert these thicknesses to percentages of sand to silt to clay. If the water doesn't ever seem to clear, the soil is almost certainly all clay of the most minute type.

If your soil is more than half clay, you've got a difficult garden. If your soil is all clay or mostly clay that drains well, and you must grow vegetables in it, not fruit trees, you have obstacles that can be overcome. If your soil is very fine clay that takes weeks to settle back out in a shake test, please accept my condolences.

HANDLING CLAY SOIL

First comes the method most gardeners attempt. Including me before I learned better. Another approach is effective and efficient. Either way costs time and effort. The poor solution can be done on the cheap if you don't mind (ex)spending some sweat and gasoline, and have a pickup or trailer. But the poor solution is never going to result in the finest garden, nor will you harvest maximally nutrient-dense food.

The poor solution

Encouraged by a great many gardening books and magazines, you are going to turn your clay pit into a Garden of Eatin' by incorporating heaps of organic matter, thereby making your clay into synthetic loam.

Start by spreading aglime: Leached clay soil ravenously grabs most of the plant nutrients you put in and will not release much fertility until you thoroughly satisfy its hunger with large quantities of the element calcium, obtained from agricultural lime. If you know from doing a shake test that the soil is about one-half clay, and you also know that the soil hasn't been limed in recent years, then spread and dig in 100 pounds of agricultural lime over each 1,000 square feet. If your soil contains two-thirds clay, make that 150 pounds per 1,000 square feet. If it is all clay, spread 200 pounds per 1,000 square feet. *Do not spread more lime than that unless you or a soil analyst know for sure that more calcium is needed according to the result of a complete soil test!* Do that liming with ordinary agricultural lime. *Do not use dolomite unless you discover a significant magnesium deficiency by soil testing.* From this point onward, the aglime and gypsum in COF will maintain and build upon the improvement.

Tillage: Make mighty sure the soil is at the right moisture for tillage. Don't rush it but don't miss it either. The window of opportunity for working clay is narrow. There's a quick "ready-to-till" test. Holding a small handful of loose soil, make a fist, squeezing the soil into a tight ball. If it won't hold a ball shape at all, it is too dry to till. If it makes a ball but that ball won't crumble easily, it is too moist to till and will form clods if you till it anyway. If it makes a ball but that ball crumbles with moderate pressure from your thumb, it is at the right moisture content to work.

Organic matter: When the moisture content is correct, broadcast aglime and then spread a 2-inch-thick layer of industrial compost. Then dig or rototill it all in. It is best if this happens in autumn because so much aglime and compost needs months to settle in, and while that's happening the soil can grow a green manure.

In the garden's first year you'll probably need to side-dress low-demand crops as though they were high-demand crops, partly because it takes a year or two of fertilization before clay soaks up enough plant nutrients to release them freely and partly because all that organic matter you tilled in makes a gigantic microbial bloom that may tie up huge quantities of soil nitrogen and other nutrients.

Clay gardens are especially good candidates for raised beds because if you avoid stepping on the growing areas, you'll not compact them, so tillage gets easier. In fact, by using only raised beds, by almost always growing green manures over the winter, and by adding compost to the surface inch, you may never need to dig that stiff soil again. Handled this way, clay will grow most types of vegetables to an acceptable standard without loosening it any deeper than needed to make a seedbed—1 inch. This can be done with a hoe, best a stirrup hoe. No matter what you

do, clay will not grow great melons, cauliflower, carrots, parsnip, or celery.

The better way

In humid temperate climates rainwater percolating through the topsoil transports clay particles downward and deposits them in a distinct layer we call the "subsoil." Most (nonalluvial) soils in humid temperate climates have a clay subsoil starting less than 2 feet below the surface. Eventually all the sand and silt in the topsoil dissolves and forms clay (or is removed by erosion), and there remains only clay from the surface down to bedrock. If you encounter clay at the surface, why not consider that you have an old subsoil that has lost its topsoil? Bring in new topsoil and off you go.

Buying topsoil is risky because a lot of what is offered as topsoil is actually a short-lasting synthetic growing medium manufactured from sand and low-grade woody waste compost. If you buy what is represented to be topsoil, before accepting it I suggest doing a one-minute-shake, one-minute-settle soil fractional analysis that'll instantly separate the coarse sand from bits of barky compost that remain floating in the water. People often fill boxed-in raised beds with this sort of stuff, but as the organic matter decomposes, the growing medium shrinks down until only sand remains. If you think to blend this stuff into an existing clay soil, keep in mind that an equal mixture of clay and sand forms something like concrete when it dries out.

The ideal vegetable soil would be around 40 percent sand, 30 percent silt, and 25 percent clay. You already have the clay. If you were to cover the clay with a layer of really sandy loam topsoil 10 inches deep, and if that topsoil contained only 10 percent clay, then when digging deep, you'd inevitably mix in a bit more. Worm activity also does that. It might take a few years, but soon enough your imported soil will contain enough clay that it won't dry out so rapidly.

Initially, a foot-thick layer of genuine loam topsoil will cost you more than a few-inches-thick layer of compost, but as you go on you won't have to bring in nearly as much compost. Your vegetables will come out more nutrient packed, and I guarantee they'll grow a lot bigger and lustier.

BALANCING CALCIUM AND MAGNESIUM

The best first step to convert clay into a garden is to perform a proper laboratory soil test, spread aglime according to the test results, and rototill it in. Then it is possible the clay will serve as an adequate topsoil. Even if topsoil is to be brought in, the existing clay will perform far better as subsoil if it is fully limed first. A soil test shows the amount of calcium and magnesium already attached to the clay and what that clay's capacity is to hold more. Then you spread and till in the quantity of aglime the soil analysis determined—and something marvelous usually happens.

The clay loosens up; "flocculates" is the technical term. Flocculated clay soil may grow good-looking vegetables when given only a little more fertilizer, manure, or compost than a loam soil would require. However, clay never will be loam. You'll always have to take some care not to dig it when it is too wet. It'll always be slow to warm up in spring.

Most gardeners never experience clay flocculation because they do not add enough lime or use the right sort of lime to make it happen. Most advice about liming says plant growth may be hindered for years to come by exceeding 4 tons per acre (200 pounds per 1,000 sq. ft.) *in a single application*—which is good sense unless the lime you're spreading is very coarsely ground stuff that takes many years to break down in the soil. Some clays have an *enormous* capacity to hold plant nutrients. I tested one that had a lime requirement of 7 tons per acre, and that's only enough calcium to saturate the top 6 inches. Given enough years, COF eventually loosens clay soils because it brings with it about 1 ton of aglime per acre per year. You'd have to repeat this many times before the top foot of clay fully responded to the liming. And that's why on clay soils I recommend doubling the quantities of aglime and gypsum in COF for the first two years.

Chapter Three

COMPOSTING

Increasing the amount of soil organic matter . . . is of great importance.
The addition of clay to sandy soil may be as important
as the addition of organic matter itself.
A certain quantity of stable manure or compost or mass of plant residues can
be converted into this type of complex [humus] only when it is composted with
a certain amount of clay before it is applied to the soil.

—Selman Waksman, *Soil Microbiology*, 1952

IN THE EARLY 1990s my friend George Van Patten gardened vegetables in his Portland backyard. He self-published a veggie gardening book and several others about growing cannabis. I opined Van Patten Publishing's garden book department lacked a compost-making guide, so I wrote *Organic Gardener's Composting* (see Additional Reading, page 339) for him. It is a complete, practical beginner's guide not that different than most such books. When it went out of print, I put my composting book online for free download in the Soil and Health Library. If using a free e-book doesn't appeal to you, there must be a dozen composting guides in print right now; the local library probably has most of them as well as a few dozen more on their shelves that are out of print. All these books have similar diagrams for building bins and step-by-step recipes for layer-cake heaps. They have tables listing carbon-to-nitrogen ratios and the average nitrogen contents of manures. They'll introduce you to worm bins, tumblers, and the other usual side paths. If you've never read a basic compost-making book or three, you should. In fact, if you haven't, what I am about to offer in this chapter won't be of much use to you.

Composting Reconsidered

Garden books and compost-making guides give the misimpression that you can go about making compost in a variety of ways, but the end result of all these approaches will be useful. Actually, most Cascadian compost comes out short of nitrogen because it contains too much sawdust, bark, or planer shavings. Mix compost like this into Cascadia's cool soil and you don't get a strong growth response.

Home-garden composting manuals do not address the crucial question of how much organic matter soil actually needs in each particular climatic area as I have done in the previous chapter. Instead, gardeners are advised that there is really no limit to how much compost they might want to make and use. Composting books usually assert that compost should be *the* soil improvement, and if the garden doesn't grow well enough—put on more.

Composting has been the *idée fixe* of the organic tradition. The founder of the American organic movement, J. I. Rodale, observed how high levels of soil organic matter boosted plant nutrients enough to grow vegetables, loosened clay soil, and helped light soils hold more moisture; having discovered that absolute truth, he looked no further. But building extraordinary levels of soil organic matter becomes a tedious treadmill—and worse, in Cascadia adding a lot of compost does not lead to harvesting highly nutrient-dense food.

Rodale repeatedly recommended both dolomite lime and greensand (a potassium-rich rock flour most Cascadian soils definitely do not need) as useful adjuncts to manure and compost. Ironically, both dolomite and greensand contain a great deal of magnesium, so they further tighten the soil the compost is supposed to loosen. Farmers might have known centuries ago that lime from one quarry made clayey soil harder to plow whereas lime from a different quarry made plowing easier, but the effect of excess magnesium on clay was not scientifically known when J. I. Rodale was creating an organic religion in the 1940s.

In my first 10 gardening years I made huge compost heaps because Rodale's *Organic Gardening and Farming* magazine repeatedly reminded its readers there were organic treasures going to waste all around our neighborhood that we could convert into black gold that would grow nutritious food and make us healthy. "Healthy" always inspires me, so I bought a pickup truck and started patrolling on trash day, bringing home bags of the neighbors' grass clippings. I had plenty of space for making compost; even better, my half-acre lot had back-alley access. I made some quick bins out of rigid 3-foot-high fencing wire, then I layered trash-day grass clipping collections with stable manure that actually was mostly sawdust and tried to keep everything moist. My heaps sort of decomposed. By the second turn, the stuff resembled compost, and it grew veggies because Southern California's soil temperature is so high and because I spread enough cottonseed meal to compensate.

In the past five years I have made excellent compost. For the thirty-five years before that most of my own compost came out average to poor. Am I a slow learner? Well, maybe. In any case, it took me 34 years of making very average compost to grasp a few things that aren't in most how-to-make-compost books—*making great compost requires putting a significant quantity of garden soil in the heap, and to make really great compost, that soil must provide clay.*

HEAP SIZE

Composting is a complex natural fermentation done by an ecology of decomposers, most of them microbial or fungal. Their action generates quite a bit of heat. Getting the ferment to an optimum temperature range is essential.

A large heap that still can breathe provides so much insulation that its core temperature may come to exceed what the biology can tolerate. When this happens, the core also dries out; decomposition ceases. A heap that is too small loses heat so rapidly that its core never heats enough. A cold heap takes a long, long time to finish. It's basic arithmetic: heat radiates from surfaces while the surface area of a cube, rectangle, or sphere increases less rapidly than its volume increases. You intuitively understand how that works. A heap of steaming hot mashed potatoes cools off faster when it is spread out on the plate. And the thinner you spread 'em, the quicker they cool. Same with a compost heap. Practically speaking, a roughly cubical heap with a starting volume under 3 cubic yards won't stay hot long enough. And how much larger than 3 cubic yards can a heap usefully be?

The composting ecology breathes oxygen, burns carbon, and exhales carbon dioxide. Insufficient air exchange greatly retards their progress. A heap made only of fallen leaves or of grass hay soon collapses into a soggy mess. There can't be much air present, and decomposition almost stops. A heap that is mostly made from mixed dried vegetable garden wastes and garden soil does not collapse and run out of oxygen. Internal heat makes the carbon dioxide–rich air within it rise and exit the top, thereby pulling in fresh, cooler oxygen-rich air through the bottom. But if the heap is too large, there might not be enough air exchange in its center, and then microorganisms that thrive without oxygen, take over. Anaerobic compost is not desirable; I have a hard time even calling the gooey black stuff that derives from anaerobic conditions "compost."

When I balance all that out, I conclude that a heap made mostly from garden waste should start out 6 to 7 feet across at the base and 5 to 6 feet high. You can extend that into a long windrow. Make it narrower and the heap may not heat up enough and definitely will cool off too soon; make it much wider than 7 feet and it may not breathe well enough.

So how big does a garden have to be to generate enough crop waste to build one minimum-size heap each year? We live on a pair of adjoining ¼-acre suburban lots. One lot is exclusively used for food gardening. On the other block is a modest three-bedroom house and attached garage, a small patio, and no lawn. The rest is in ornamentals, a few espaliered fruit trees, and a chicken yard. Crop waste from the ¼-acre veggie garden—plus the trim and deadheading from roughly ⅛ acre of ornamentals and the manure-rich sawdust from the chicken house—makes two heaps each year. There's a substantial autumn cleanup heap, and because where I live has more sunny winter days and slightly warmer winter temperatures than the Willamette, I've a much smaller spring cleanup heap. From that I estimate a 2,500-square-foot food garden should, by itself, generate enough material to build one heap of sufficient starting volume once a year.

Already-fermenting compost heaps that have new material piled on top as it becomes available do not heat up well, tend to dry out fast, and don't make the best product. Far better that all crop waste gets dried into "hay" when it is collected, and is stored relatively dry until enough has accumulated to form a substantial heap all at once. Start accumulating material by spreading the spring garden cleanup out in full sun. Spread more on top in layers as crop waste becomes available through the summer. Continue that until there's enough in the haystack to make a heap. For most Cascadians, that'll be soon after the first frost.

If your garden is too small to make one good-size heap each year, why not consider composting as a method of conveniently recycling, not as a way to manufacture the best possible quality soil amendment. There are compost tumblers that speed the process. Or you could try worm composting (vermicomposting), which does result in pretty good stuff. You also could import materials to add to your own waste stream and form a proper-size compost heap when you do make one.

CONTAINERS

Because I just mentioned compost tumblers, you're probably wondering: If I do not have enough material for a big heap, can I put a smaller quantity of raw materials into a container that holds in the heat? Your answer, as is usual in this chapter, cuts both ways.

In my experience, enclosures do not make the process run any better. However, bins and composting containers do make your yard look tidier, even if they're crudely made with straw bales. Bins of any sort interfere with turning the heap and, in my opinion, are an unnecessary expense, unless you make them of scrap lumber or recycled materials, or use straw bale enclosures that eventually become compost.

Retaining walls also reduce airflow into the heap. To overcome this, you can lay flexible slotted drainpipes or large-diameter highly perforated plastic pipes under the heap before it is built. Or build it on top of a slightly elevated screen or grid that lets air enter from the bottom. How-to-make-compost books are full of ideas like these. But I don't see the sense in first creating a problem (insufficient air due to solid side walls) and then cleverly solving it, when the problem never had to exist in the first place.

I mentioned I compost waste from about 14,000 square feet of vegetable and ornamental gardens. My composting yard is crowded into a rectangular area about 25 by 20 feet. In that space, I have two working heaps covered with loose straw, and twice a year for a few short weeks there is a third heap of finished compost. Also in that space is an expanding untidy stack of sun-drying garden wastes that will become the next heap.

My working heaps are covered with loose straw that is at least 1 foot thick. Straw not only insulates effectively; it helps retain internal moisture while shedding rain and reducing leaching. A thick straw blanket allows air to freely flow in and out. A loose straw layer a foot and a half thick is not excessive. It is quick and easy to rake loose straw off the heap immediately before you turn it. After straw has insulated for about a year, it loses stiffness and starts getting compact; what remains is now ready to become an ingredient in your next heap. Even if you use composting enclosures, it's wise to thickly cover their tops with loose straw.

COMPOSTABLE MATERIALS

In compostable materials the amount of carbon they contain reckoned against the amount of nitrogen is called the C:N. The ratio varies greatly. Garden writers these days describe material with a low carbon-to-nitrogen ratio as "green," and something with a high ratio as "brown," but this oversimplified distinction leads to confusion. Brown or woody materials provide much carbon and little nitrogen. Green materials are supposed to be nitrogen-rich and perform in the heap much like fresh animal manure. But fresh green lawn clippings at the end of summer are as low in nitrogen as grain straw, while drying spring grass clippings into something like hay turns them light brown but does not significantly lower their nitrogen content. They are still very potent "green" material.

I urge food gardeners not to compost woody materials unless it is minimum sawdust mixed with maximum chicken manure. Make almost all the starting volume mixed-vegetable crop waste and *nonwoody* waste from your ornamental beds, such as annual and biennial flowers and perennials that reshoot from the roots every spring, like peonies. The leafy *new* growth trimmed from some hedge plants may decompose readily as long as it has not yet formed bark. Reject sawdust and ground-up tree bark, especially coniferous bark, needles, sticks, or twigs. Absolutely reject paper. At one time, the glues in cardboard were animal based and contributed enough nitrogen to allow the soft kraft paper they're made of to decompose readily. These days I suggest caution.

If you have woody decomposition-resistant material to dispose of and want to try composting it, I suggest making a separate heap with it, using twice the usual quantity of soil (10 percent by starting volume) and thick sprinklings of COF on each layer. Expect a woody or paper-rich heap to take three or four turns and at least a year to resemble compost, and even so, do not plan to use that compost on vegetable crops. Use it for mulching ornamentals, fruit trees, and woody bushes like currants and gooseberries.

Compost quality hinges on the concentration and balance of plant nutrients in the starting materials, and that depends on the soil they grew in. So I suggest remineralizing your lawn and ornamental beds if you can afford to. If you're a homesteader with deep pockets, remineralize any land making organic matter you transfer to the food garden by way of the compost heap. However, don't spread oilseed meal or other nitrogen fertilizer. When perennials are provoked into making rapid growth like a vegetable garden does, they may freeze out in winter. And you'd wear out your lawn mower in short order if you fed the lawn with as much COF as veggies get. To remineralize orchards, small fruit, ornamentals, and lawns, I suggest using a variant of COF containing all the usual ingredients but one—the quantity of seed meal going into this special mix would be reduced by at least half if not completely; it should be spread every mid-spring.

If the food garden, lawn, and ornamentals combined don't make enough raw material each year to build at least one heap of sufficient starting volume, you can import. Top of my list for this purpose is grain straw. *Straw*, not grass hay. Grain straw doesn't compact into a slimy airless mess; hay and most kinds of straw from grass seed crops do. You can make good compost from a blend of two parts grain straw to one part fresh spring grass clippings, plus soil, COF, and moisture. Alfalfa meal is about equivalent to dried spring grass or pure horse/cow manure.

To make turning the heap easier, corn and sunflower stalks, broccoli plants, and especially brussels sprout and kale stalks should be cut into foot-long pieces. This is easy to do with a machete when they are first brought to the composting area.

Autumn leaves tend to pack tightly. Including too many of them makes a heap airless. Tree leaves should not be concentrated into one layer, but blended throughout. Running a lawn mower with a bagger over fallen leaves reduces their volume by about two-thirds and reduces their tendency to pack tight when wet. Do not include conifer needles.

Spreading out compostable materials to dry on an ever building haystack means they end up layered from bottom to top. When you build the compost heap, it is best to take material from one end of the stack. Thus, every layer of the heap you're building gets roughly the same mix of vegetation. I first learned of this technique in Sir Albert Howard's finest book *The Waste Products of Agriculture* (see Additional Reading, page 339). I urge a thorough study of Howard's book for anyone who wants to make the best-possible compost.

Horse manure—long and short

Before the automobile, horse manure was the most common home-garden fertilizer. There were two basic types, either "long" or "short."

Short manure is nearly pure poo raked out of horse stalls without much bedding. Horse droppings on residential streets were quickly collected for use in the garden. Market gardeners would deliver a horse-drawn wagonload of vegetables or fruit to the central produce market and return home with that wagon heaped with street sweepings.

Compost made of short horse manure and quite a bit of soil will grow excellent high-demand vegetables, but only if the horse has been given hay approaching the quality that these days is usually reserved for thoroughbreds. It may still be possible to source potent short horse manure from a stud farm, but much of what is produced by lifestyle horses grazing exhausted pastures is a sad imitation.

Long manure includes all the urine-soaked stall bedding. Urine contains about half the nutrients exiting the animal, so soggy bedding has great potential value. A century ago that bedding usually was straw, and it still is sometimes. Urine-soaked strawy long manure may be "sheet composted," which means spreading it a few inches thick in autumn and shallowly rototilling it in to decompose over winter.

Unfortunately, Cascadian horses are usually bedded on sawdust. At best raw sawdust takes a few years to decompose in soil when not too much of it is mixed in. While decomposing in soil, it slows vegetable growth, often catastrophically. This effect can be partly reversed by using extra nitrogen fertilizer, if there isn't too much sawdust.

In Cascadia's cool climate, and considering the infertile nature of most of its pastures, properly composted straw-based long horse manure can be expected to supply enough nitrogen to grow low-demand crops such as purple-top turnips, rutabagas, kale, beans, carrots, and beets. If sawdust is the bedding, the result will not be this good. Making very low-grade compost out of sawdusty horse manure requires two years, and that estimate assumes the working heap also contains about 5 percent by starting volume of rich garden soil and a strong dose of complete organic fertilizer, and is given two or three turns a year with a thorough watering each time.

The best use for sawdust-based compost is mulching fruit trees or other woody perennials.

Cow manure

Dairy manure with bedding is similar to long horse manure but not quite as high in nitrogen. If urine-soaked straw bedding, cow manure, and some soil are thoroughly composted, the product grows low-demand crops well when the soil is warm enough. If much undecomposed sawdust is present, the end product acts like the reverse of fertilizer.

Sheep manure

Sheep manure you can buy in sacks comes from shearing sheds. Otherwise, it falls where the animals graze. It inevitably lacks bedding and can be as potent as short horse manure.

Rabbit manure

Rabbits are fed a lot of protein to make them grow fast. Their waste equals the best horse manure. Any bedding under the rabbit cages adsorbs a lot of value. Rabbits fed on pelletized feed piss a lot because (too much) salt is added to the pellets in order to create the illusion of rapid weight gain from retained fluids. I prefer healthier meat that doesn't release a lot of water when cooked. When I raised bunnies, I fed them on the best-obtainable alfalfa hay and vegetable trim and spread enough grain straw to soak up most of the urine. When the odor got objectionable, the bedding was raked up and composted. After learning from Howard's *Waste Products of Agriculture*, if I still raised rabbits, I'd also remove and replace a few inches of urine-soaked soil from beneath the bedding and use that in the heap.

INDUSTRIAL COMPOST

Feedlot manure is a better-than-average material. It feeds worms and enlivens the soil but does not make vegetables grow big and fast. COF will do that. Feedlot cattle are given a high salt diet, so they gain watery weight. Their manure is often rich in sodium. Gardeners using too much steer manure have damaged their plants this way. If you're starting a new garden, do not spread it more than an inch deep.

Mushroom compost is based on grain straw and (usually chicken) manure. It can also include peat moss, grape crushings from wineries, oilseed meals, gypsum, chemical fertilizers, and lime. Each mushroom producer uses a proprietary substrate recipe. Mushroom farmers use fungicides to eliminate wild mushroom species and pesticides against small flying insects whose larvae eat mushrooms. Organic purists reject mushroom compost, fearing poison residues. I depend on the stuff. Some landscape yards will, if you ask, tell you what ingredients were used to grow the product they're selling or provide a lab analysis.

Mushroom compost falls far short of producing balanced soil. In my garden, after digging in both a generous inch-thick layer (what I get is only half-decomposed, fluffy, and loose) and the usual dose of COF, seeds sprout handily, and the crop is slightly more robust than a crop given only COF. I speculate the reason is mass inoculation of meadow mushroom mycelia that temporarily suppresses ever-present disease organisms.

Chicken manure compost is potent because fowl are mainly fed seeds. A seed contains the full range of plant nutrients (and fuel) required to feed an embryo until it has become a viable growing seedling, so chicken manure (and oilseed meal) produces vegetables of higher nutritional quality than those from using manures produced by grass eaters.

Chicken manure has usually been composted with sawdust, but its high nitrogen content overcomes sawdust's growth-retarding effect. I consider chicken manure compost a nitrate/phosphate fertilizer that must be spread several times thicker than oilseed meal to see a similar growth response. Chicken manure compost is so concentrated that if you spread it ¼ inch thick, the vegetables may get overdosed. Repeated applications put so much phosphorus into the soil in a form that remains available for a long time that zinc uptake may be inhibited, but explaining how excessive levels of one element can interfere with access to another element and what to do to remedy that situation makes a long complicated story best not gotten into in a gardening book. It's best not to create excesses in the first place. Better to use COF and avoid the sawdust.

Municipal/industrial compost is sold at landscape yards by the cubic yard and by the sack in shops. It doesn't cost much. It is made from tree trimmings, yard wastes, waste paper, food wastes from restaurants, vegetable trim from supermarkets, and food processing residues. It may contain water-treatment sludge that brings considerable magnesium with it. Better-quality industrial composts have a base of steer, chicken, or dairy manure, plus mint straw, spent mushroom compost, or both. They often contain some screened decomposed fir bark and may be inoculated with beneficial fungi. Some composts are balanced with fertilizers and are lab tested to ensure the material achieves a guaranteed potency. Some aren't.

Because of the low cost, it is tempting to spread them thick and often. Keep in mind that decomposing compost releases plant nutrients. If there is a lab analysis available for the compost you're considering, check that it does not contain more than the following concentrations (ppm = parts per million):

Magnesium: 0.25 percent (2,500 ppm)

Zinc: 350 ppm

Potassium: 0.8 percent (8,000 ppm)

If compost does contain concentrations that exceed these numbers, you should know that repeated applications exceeding ¼ inch per year will soon develop excesses in most Cascadian soils.

Industrial compost can definitely fuel the soil ecology, but for food gardening I urge you to avoid compost mainly derived from woody materials and paper. And test your soil after you use it for several years.

HUMUS FORMATION REQUIRES CLAY

To create humus during composting there must be clay. Without clay, the heap still heats and cools, and what's left at the end is crumbly black decomposed organic matter that resembles soil, but it is not humus. And it'll rot down to much less than another heap with the same starting volume that had clay in it. If you keep non-humified compost moist, the heap will continue to shrink fairly rapidly. Mix this black crumbly organic matter into soil, and it continues rotting fast enough to provoke better plant growth for a few years, and then it's gone. If this kind of compost gets mixed into soil that contains some clay, part of it will become humus. The same holds true of using industrial compost. Mix that stuff into a soil containing some clay, and some of it turns to humus. Some, not most.

MARINA'S EXPERIENCE

I moved to my present home in Eugene in February 2000. I discovered the soil was typical for the area—fairly heavy clay with some areas of really bad drainage.

In my first year I saw less than 10 earthworms! I began trucking in enormous amounts of various manures and compost. I also used the then current version of Steve's COF. I had a local dairy deliver pit-washed composted manure, which I spread thickly. I tried Steer Plus, mint manure, and stable manure, and did some cover cropping—my results were pretty good but did not permanently improve my clay's basic nature. The imported organic matter decomposed rapidly and required annual renewal, but as fast as the structure improved, the population of symphylans (see Chapter 8) increased just as dramatically. My first few years of broccoli crops were catalog-cover worthy; later years' cole crops were puny. If I could do it over again, I would spend more of my money and muscle importing topsoil; this would be a permanent improvement addressing the drainage and structure problems. Had I done that, I would still have to add compost regularly, but in much more manageable quantities. And I might not have bred so many symphylans.

Humus does not rot rapidly; it might take humus 100 years to become minerals, water, and carbon dioxide. A heap of humified compost does not shrink away if it is not used right away. When humus forms during the composting process, you end up with more product from the same starting volume. Humus improves soils in the same way clay does, by increasing their capacity to hold and release nutrients on demand. Humus that formed in a compost heap holds in available form the plant nutrients released during composting. Humus can be the salvation of sandy gardens.

If a gardener has sandy topsoil sitting atop a clay subsoil, the affordable way to include clay in a compost heap is to dig a small pit and mine some. Turn a quarter bucket of clay subsoil into a full bucket of clay soup with an electric drill–driven paint mixer. Dip a small broom or stiff long-bristled brush into the slurry, and whisk sprays of clay over each layer of your heap as it is being built. Maybe there's a roadcut nearby where clay is exposed. How much clay? About 2 percent by starting volume. So each cubic yard of starting volume (135 gallons per cubic yard) needs 4 or 5 gallons of thick clay slurry.

When Sir Albert Howard was learning how to make excellent compost at the Indian Research Institute in Indore, India, he had pits dug in the farm's clay soil that were 10 feet wide by 50 feet long and 3 feet deep. These pits were filled with a thick clay soup made of water and urine-soaked clay soil taken from beneath the oxen's loafing pen. Howard's dollar-a-day laborers then stirred in dry crop wastes, letting the vegetation soak until it was both rehydrated and thinly coated with clay. This material was then used to form the compost heap. The same procedure thoroughly inoculated the material so that the heap heated up right away.

SOIL IN THE HEAP

Topsoil is the home of a microorganism that captures ammonia and converts it to nitrogen fertilizer. These microbes make it possible for farmers to inject ammonia gas into damp soil and have all of it become nitrogen fertilizer. In a compost heap the nitrogen in decomposing proteins first becomes ammonia. If that ammonia is captured by microbes, it remains part of the N in the final carbon-to-nitrogen ratio. Otherwise, it off-gasses. So if a heap smells at all like a horse stall that should have been cleaned out a few days ago, you're losing a lot of value.

Compost books all agree that finished compost should contain about 12 units of carbon for every unit of nitrogen, and to make strong compost the total volume of starting material should have an average carbon-to-nitrogen ratio between 25:1 and 35:1. As yet uncomposted "green" materials contain 15 to 30 parts of carbon to each part of nitrogen. Brown materials range from 30:1 to 200:1. Fresh animal manures have a ratio less than 10:1. Total volume of starting material should have an average carbon-to-nitrogen ratio between 25:1 and 35:1. To end up with effective compost, the heap must burn off carbon until the carbon-to-nitrogen ratio gets down to around 12:1—and not lose much nitrogen in the process. However, if the heap also off-gasses ammonia, then the 12:1 ratio is not achieved until a great deal more carbon is burned off.

You might end up with only 20 percent of the starting volume—or much less than that by the time the heap finally settles at 12:1.

Blending topsoil into a forming compost heap at about 5 percent by starting volume thoroughly inoculates it and provides plenty of habitat for ammonia-capturing bacteria. To achieve that, I spread garden soil about ¼ inch thick over each layer as the heap is being constructed. The same action may also provide sufficient clay.

More than 5 percent soil slows down a compost heap something like the moderating rods act in a uranium nuclear reactor. If a heap starts out with too much nitrogen for the amount of carbon, it'll get too hot. This usually happens when a great deal of animal manure is included. In that case mix in more soil; try 10 percent soil by starting volume.

VERMICOMPOSTING

One of the worst plagues a food garden could suffer is a flock of English sparrows (a.k.a. "flying rats") nesting in the immediate neighborhood or hanging around your yard, because they have previously found easy pickings. People who carelessly feed backyard chickens often attract sparrows. Cereal-based kitchen wastes, such as old rice or stale bread, interest sparrows. Cooked foods of all sorts appeal to rats and mice. Scattering these atop the growing stack of drying vegetable garden waste may not be such a good idea.

One way to keep vermin out of compostable kitchen waste is to put it straight into a covered worm bin. Plastic composting enclosures (holding 1 or 2 cubic yards) are actually vermicomposters. They are not large enough to heat up for long, especially if they are gradually filled with new material as the old stuff settles. If your composting bin is open to the soil at the bottom (some municipalities disallow this), you may not need to import worms to get things started; a few of the right sort of worms (not the common earthworm) will soon enough discover this rich source of food and start breeding prolifically. To get the composter off to a certain fast start, inoculate the first buckets of kitchen scraps with a small tub of red wigglers from a bait shop. Once they get established, it's amazing how quickly food wastes and grass clippings disappear after being tossed on top in thin layers.

People with small gardens that do not generate enough compostable waste to heap compost should use a worm bin. Vermicompost is potent, precious stuff. An entire year's waste from our kitchen (there's a lot of waste because it includes much vegetable trim) makes only two big wheelbarrow loads each year.

The free-to-download compost-making book of mine, *Organic Gardener's Composting*, which I referred to earlier, has a lot more to say about vermicomposting.

ATTITUDE ADJUSTMENT

Making nitrogen-deficient compost is easy. Nearly all organic gardeners do it. The deficiency happens because the heap started out with too little soil or too much woody material (or both). The heap may heat and cool, the material now resembles compost, but the C:N hasn't yet dropped to 12:1. It'll still be more like 20:1.

So when this half-done compost is mixed into soil, it does not rapidly release plant nutrients. I apologize for being negative; celebrity garden writers are smiling, eager arm wavers, making everything seem easy.

I mentioned earlier that the compost heap is a controlled fermentation. Foods and drinks are made by fermentation too. When I was a younger man still possessing a strong liver, I brewed beer in 5-gallon batches. The first batch was undrinkable, but by the time I had made a sixth batch, my homebrew was better 'n Bud—and a lot more potent.

Years later I got into making bread with flour I milled on the kitchen counter the day of baking. My first attempt turned rock hard as soon as it cooled. Fortunately, almost anything made of really fresh whole grain flour and water is delicious when still hot out of the oven, especially if you melt some butter into it. A few weeks later my sixth batch didn't turn hard when it cooled down, and it tasted okay, but it was crumbly, like cake. So was the tenth.

Then I found out a few things about wheat—about its variable protein content, that virtually all wheat protein is gluten, that gluten is what makes the bread flexible (not crumbly like cake) and allows big pore spaces to develop (light texture). I found there was rampant wheat ignorance at my local health-food store. Their wholesale distributors distinguished only two kinds of bread wheat, organically grown and conventional. They had no idea of the protein content of either sort, and the retail people had no interest in doing the hard work required to source wheat berries with enough protein in them. So

I started buying wheat berries from a lady in Eugene who sourced direct from a farmer on the Montana prairies. She also sold flour mills and baking supplies out of her garage. After making a few batches with proper wheat, I had the basics pretty well worked out and could depend on an excellent result.

Thing of it was, I could make a new batch of bread every few days, so I sufficiently mastered the art in a few months. Brewing took longer to learn than baking did because each batch fermented for a few weeks before it was ready for bottling, and to smooth out, the beer needed to rest in the bottle for at least three months. Consequently, my beer making improved rapidly over an entire year and then leveled off. As ferments go, beer and bread are easy to learn because they soon become predictable. Switch to a different lot of wheat berries (with about the same amount of protein in them) or use a different malt extract, and your result will vary, but only a little.

Compost is also a fermented product. However, it may take a gardener 10 years to make and use 10 heaps. The ingredients are different every year, usually whatever was readily available at the time. Bread and beer ferment indoors at stable temperatures. Heaps made in autumn ferment over the winter while heaps made in spring ferment through a warm, dry summer. How this constantly changing stream of ingredients and different ambient conditions interacts with the heap ecology and how they interact with the materials available this year is not predictable without a lot of prior experience and close observation.

But I have accumulated experience at this game; here is a brief summary:

Size. The heap must be large enough to hold heat, but the core must breathe. So the starting volume should be at least 6 feet across at the base and no more than 7 feet; it must be at least 5 feet high at the start, and no higher than 6 feet; it must be at least 6 feet long and may be as long as you like. If you lack materials to make at least one heap that large once a year, I suggest you make vermicompost.

Air supply. The bottom layer of the heap should ideally be crisscrossed foot-long pieces of corn stalks, sunflower stalks, brussels sprout stalks, or the like. These kinds of materials allow more fresh air into the bottom of the heap to replace the warm air rising out the top. If the bottom layer compacts too much, you're probably going to have to turn the heap several times before it is finished. If the heap does not compact too much, one turn may be all that's needed.

Moisture. When building the heap, water each layer well before starting the next. I do this with a hose and nozzle set to spray fine droplets at a moderate rate. Best to have a helper spray water constantly as you stack dry material. If you get the entire heap thoroughly moist while building it and then thickly insulate the heap with loose straw, you probably won't have to turn and remoisten the heap more than once.

Extra nitrogen. To make strong compost, the heap must start with an average carbon-to-nitrogen ratio between 24:1 and 36:1, and close to 24:1 is better. People with livestock, even backyard chickens, use fresh manure to lower the starting C:N. If you do not have fresh manure

to layer into the heap as it is being built, then abundantly sprinkle each layer with seed meal or, better, with about the same thickness of COF you'd spread to prepare a bed for a new crop. Each layer! If you can save up your own urine in the garage or toolshed, I suggest pouring a gallon of aged (stinky) urine over each layer as you build the heap. Most of the aroma stays within the heap, and what escapes only lasts for a day.

Materials. Please believe me! To end up with effective compost, you must not put woody material or paper into the heap. The mixture of materials also must have a starting average C:N not exceeding 36:1.

If you can source nitrogen-rich materials, like alfalfa, pea straw, mint straw, etc., you might make these up to one-third the starting volume in place of animal manure. However, these materials tend to compact and become airless. Don't use too much. Most of the heap's starting volume should come from the garden itself. If you must buy materials, the best one is grain straw. It has slightly more carbon (to nitrogen) than a broad mixture of garden trim and waste. The next best is grass seed straw. The worst are from trees—sawdust, planer shavings, bark—or any twigs and sticks that have developed bark.

Insulation. Covering the heap with a 1-foot-thick (or more) layer of loose grain straw or other form of insulation that still allows air to escape the heap is critically important.

Location. Where your heap is located influences core temperature and moisture loss. In summer it's best to compost in the shade, but under a tree is not a good spot; tree roots steal a lot of value and dry out your heap. But spreading a sheet of black plastic under the heap to keep out roots also prevents worms from entering (and leaving). The cold winter wind lowers core temperature. Factor all that together and it is clear an old shed with a dirt floor and at least three walls to break the wind is an ideal place for a heap; the shade of that roof would help during the high heat of summer. Without the shed a thick straw blanket does this too and provides insulation.

Turning. Industrial composters use big machines that turn, aerate, and remoisten windrowed heaps that start with a very high average carbon-to-nitrogen ratio. Their goal is waste disposal, so they intend to burn off as much carbon as possible as fast as possible. Heaps turned and remoistened every two or three days can be finished in three weeks. Frankly, it might be more useful to burn the material for making electricity, which is often done in Euroland. I have a different goal. I wish to make humus and preserve as much carbon as possible. My location, my materials, and my methods usually require one turn after six months and after another six months a final turnout that loosens the compost and prepares it for spreading. I have started a few heaps in spring that finished by the end of summer without any turns. Most of mine need an entire year and one turn. If a heap dries out, the fermentation stops; it needs turning and spraying with a lot of water while so doing. If the heap smells of ammonia, it needs turning, almost certainly watering, and more soil. If it cools prematurely, turning and remoistening it may cause it to heat up again. But high core heat is not necessary; as long as the heap is moist, even slightly warm, and getting sufficient air, there is

no absolute need to turn, unless you're in a hurry for it to finish.

Temperature (and duration). Core temperature briefly exceeding 155 degrees F makes the organisms of decomposition die off. I say briefly because when the heap's ecology dies back, the heap cools and fermentation usually stops because the high heat also dried out the core. Many garden writers advise imitating the economic rationalism of industrial composting. They say to bring the heap to about 150 degrees F so that the process goes as fast as possible. However, the microorganisms that capture ammonia gas die off around 140 to 145 degrees F. I suggest the maximum core temperature you ever want to see is about 135 degrees F. A medium-heat heap takes months longer, yes. But you'll end up with a larger volume of finished compost. And that compost will be more effective.

A quick, easy way to check the heap's core temperature is to push a pointed garden stake or sharpened tool handle about 4 feet long well into the heap and leave it there. When pulled out, you can gauge core temperature by holding the heated end in your hand; the temperature you want should feel uncomfortably warm but not so hot it's painful to hold tightly for a few seconds.

If a heap fails to get hot enough, next time add more green stuff, more manure, more COF. Use a thicker insulating straw blanket. If a heap gets too hot, tear it apart, add more soil, and remoisten; next time, include less seed meal or manure or more brown stuff.

Gardening without Composting

I struggled with lousy soil in Lorane, Oregon, for eight years and then homesteaded near Elkton on 16 acres of black Malabon silty clay loam, a highly productive Class I alluvial soil found along western Oregon rivers originating in the Cascades. The soil at Elkton withstood wheat farming that started around 1860. I knew it once produced flower bulbs. For at least 10 years before I bought it, the field still could be mined of enough grass hay to profitably cut and bale. It was as good as Cascadia offers. Elkton was far from any convenient source of organic matter in quantity. So I tilled in about ¼ acre of sod, spread COF, and started gardening. I never before experienced such a fine result. However, the garden was declining by the finish of the second summer. The soil organic matter level had dropped, and I was discovering symphylans, so it seemed a good idea to shift the garden to a new spot. And thus it was that I discovered the absolutely best way to manage soil organic matter when food gardening. Do not import compost or materials to make it with; till in some well-developed sod, and import nothing but balanced, concentrated nutrition—COF.

Either way, buying compost or importing materials to make compost with is risky business. There could be noxious weed seeds or diseased plant materials in that stuff. And these days it could contain long-lasting chemical residues that still act like herbicides. Instead, why not own enough space for several gardens but put most of the area into a pasture-like reserve that accumulates its own organic matter. Chapter 2 and the discussion of symphylans in Chapter 8 (page 176) fully describe the method.

Instead of having only one garden, I suggest having four. Even eight is not too many. One garden grows vegetable crops, another grows fruit and other perennial food crops, and the rest of the space grows deeply rooting pasture grasses, clover, and broadleaf herbs. Better to not remove any biomass produced by the grass plots and do everything possible to avoid soil compaction, which means if you have livestock larger than a *few* chickens that don't destroy the grass, have them graze different land. Instead of being used for grazing or hay making, the grassed areas are mowed like a hayfield, but everything lies where it falls.

When the time comes to move the veggie garden to a new area, simply choose one, mow the plot closely, spread COF, and then rototill in autumn. Till it again in spring, and start growing veggies there. No compost necessary.

If you're starting with infertile land (most likely the case, because that's usually the sort of land that gets offered to homesteaders), and you've deep pockets, then the best thing to do is remineralize the entire area and, if possible, replant the reserve to a complex mixture of grass, herbs, and legumes that maximizes biomass production. Mow these plots whenever the grass is forming seeds, and remove nothing. So you'll need a strong lawn mower, probably one purpose-built for this task, or a brushcutter—or you'll have to become skillful with a scythe. For more information, consult Robert Elliot's

The Clifton Park System of Farming (see Additional Reading, page 339).

Yes, gardens newly won from old sod are weedy, but if in recent years you've mowed the plot before any grass makes seed, the garden it makes won't be all that weedy. If you wield a sharp hoe and use wide-enough plant spacing, weeds will not be a problem. If you try this method but don't spread the plants out a bit and don't have a properly sharp hoe, you'll probably curse me.

One cubic yard of finely divided compost will cover 12 100-square-foot beds ¼ inch thick. Can those 12 beds produce enough vegetable crop waste to produce 1 cubic yard of finished compost? Answer: no way. Can they make that much compost by including the tops of green manures grown in every production gap on those 12 beds? Answer: closer, but still no way. Can this amount of land produce the equivalent of a cubic yard of compost each year by growing hay with no removals if the land is highly fertile? Answer: probably.

Chapter Four

PLANNING

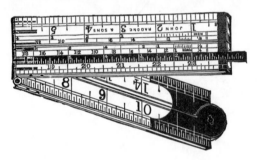

The strip system [a farming method widely used during the Middle Ages that steadily lowered soil fertility] has also been adopted for the allotments round our towns and cities without any provision whatsoever on the part of the authorities to maintain the land in good heart by such obvious and simple expedients as subsoiling, followed by a rest under grass grazed by sheep or cattle, ploughing up, and sheet composting the vegetable residue. Land under allotments should not be under vegetables for more than five years at a time: this should be followed by a similar period under grass and livestock.

—Sir Albert Howard, *Farming and Gardening for Health or Disease*, 1945

WHEN I WAS in the seed trade, I learned the average backyard garden is 1,000 square feet. I wish every backyard would have a food garden at least that large so that the family discovers how good vegetables can taste. Then that family might devote most of the rest of their yard to growing vegetables. And start demanding nutrient-dense food from the industrial food system. And be willing to pay a higher price for it.

Managing 1,000 square feet does not place big demands on a family's time. A veggie garden this size leaves room in the shadier parts of the backyard for the kids and pets. And that much garden land can, in high summer, produce what seems like a huge overabundance to people who deep down consider veggies an insubstantial garnish while real food consists of meat, wheat, and potatoes.

Your Engineered Garden

I thought it would be of great help to novices if together we begin planning your first 1,000-square-foot year-round Cascadian food garden. I'll provide minimal coaching; you provide the desire. And listen in, you experienced gardeners; you might learn something.

Start out by listing those vegetables you and your family prefer. Then rank your choices according to economic return from the space and time required. True, value is not only measured in dollars: What's the worth of tasting a raw ear of sweet corn seconds after tearing it off the stalk? That delightful moment might seem more valuable than a few pounds of potatoes or the three fresh heads of leaf lettuce that might have been produced in the same amount of space over the same amount of time.

In the right column is my ranking of garden vegetables by economic value. The ranking considers several factors—what the vegetable would cost at the supermarket in the season you could grow it, the per square foot yield, and how long

Economic value for the space required. Value lessens going from top to bottom. Vegetables in italics should be avoided by novices.

Fresh Herbs (Basil, Oregano, Thyme, Sage, Rosemary, Parsley, Etc.)
Carrots
Beets
Parsnips
Loose Leaf Lettuce
Most Other Leafy Salad Greens
Scallions
Garlic
Bulbing Onions
Spinach
Kale
Swiss Chard
Leeks
Kohlrabi
Potatoes
Broccoli
Rutabaga
Zucchini and Other Bush Summer Squash
Tomatoes *(Indeterminate, Staked)*
Cucumbers
Peppers
Snap Beans and Runner Beans
Cabbage
Cauliflower
Brussels Sprouts
Winter Squash
Sweet Corn
Eggplant
Cantaloupe and Muskmelons
Watermelon

the vegetable will occupy space before you can plant something else there. If this is your first-ever garden, I suggest avoiding everything from cauliflower to the bottom of the list.

The greatest economic return comes from salad greens and herbs. Lettuce, for example, produces one big head per square foot per two-month crop. Freshness makes a huge difference with salad greens, and the gardener can grow varieties that taste so good you'll want to eat salad by the huge bowlful. Fresh culinary herbs are expensive and remarkably tastier.

And the garden produces vine-ripe tomatoes the likes of which you can't buy.

FRESH VEGETABLES 12 MONTHS A YEAR

Please have a look at the planting calendar in the preliminaries of Chapter 9. Note that sowing can start with the first hint of spring and continues into autumn. And in Cascadia harvesting may happen every month of every year. Even when an extraordinarily harsh winter freeze kills the garden, there can still be root crops to dig. Yep, a broad assortment of fresh veggies year-round—but only with a plan.

Would you plan to work a few hours in October to harvest spring vegetables a month sooner? Earlier spring sowing is possible, even in clay soil, if you prepare the bed the previous autumn. Quick-maturing vegetables can be sown anytime from spring through midsummer. Not only can you, you *should* sow them again and again if you want a continuous supply of lettuce heads or radishes or cabbages or cauliflower or big central broccoli flowers.

Heat-loving vegetables must be transplanted out or sown during a short window of opportunity that opens when there is no more frost danger and closes a few weeks later. That single planting slot must establish the entire summer's supply of tomatoes, peppers, eggplant, melons, cucumbers, winter squash, and zucchini. These heat-loving species are what most people picture when they hear the word "garden." So most people fail to plan for autumn and winter. Consequently they harvest an abundance in July and experience an absolute glut during August and September, followed by scarcity. Or by nothing.

So make and follow a year-round garden plan. Why not make one right now! Get a large sheet of paper, a pencil, an eraser and a ruler, and draw a fairly accurate map of your existing or proposed garden space. Plan an imaginary garden even if you're landless right now. Besides, according to the Rules of Life, if you'll strongly visualize a hoped-for garden, imagine it with enough detail while allowing yourself to deeply desire it, the garden is far more likely to materialize.

IMAGINARY GARDEN PLAN

If this will be your first garden or if you're landless, I urge you to design an imaginary garden that is 33 by 33 feet. Divide that area into six beds, each 4 feet wide and 33 feet long, with (narrow) 18-inch-wide footpaths between them.

If you are new to food gardening, please do not plan for more than 1,000 square feet. You have so much to learn that if you take on more land, your mistakes will have such big consequences that you'll likely ruin the fun. Don't overwhelm yourself. Everything you attempt in the first

LOCATION AND INFRASTRUCTURE

To grow well, vegetables require the following:

- Free-draining soil at least 2 feet deep.
- Fruit-making crops need direct sunlight from 10:00 a.m. until 4:00 p.m. if they are to develop full flavor. Even longer hours are better. Root crops and brassicas will do okay with only four hours of direct sun during those six optimum hours. Leafy greens can produce acceptably in bright shade between April and the end of September, but most leaf crops do much better in full sun. Forget about winter gardening where the sun don't shine in that season.

COUNTRY GARDENS ALSO NEED

- wildlife (and wandering livestock) fencing,
- protection from strong winds, and
- a dependable and adequate water supply (see Chapter 5).

HILLSIDES

- Land sloping to the north at 3 percent (3 feet of fall in 100 feet of run) grows crops like it was located a few hundred miles closer to the North Pole. Land sloping to the south at 3 percent grows crops like it was located a few hundred miles closer to the equator. The sun provides more growing energy after the morning's humidity has dispersed, so the best-possible exposure is south-by-southwest facing.
- Land sloping more than 3 percent must be terraced or the soil will be soon lost to erosion. My interpretation of history is that after people terrace any land, they still eventually lose the soil. Civilization may endure for several thousand years, but eventually chaos reigns, the terraces are neglected, and soon the whole hillside washes away. See Carter and Dale's *Topsoil and Civilization* and J. Russell Smith's classic *Tree Crops: A Permanent Agriculture* (see Additional Reading, page 339).

year will be far more difficult than it ever will be again. Accept in advance that you will make many errors . . . but you can make them small errors.

Now, with a list in hand of what you're intending to grow, consult the planting calendar on page 186, and then begin reading up on the vegetable you ranked number one on your list. Use the sowing table at the beginning of each vegetable's section to estimate how much space it'll take to produce as much as you imagine that

you'll want, and also note when it'll be planted and when the harvest will happen (the number of days to maturity given in regional seed catalogs may also help with this). Then allocate bed space for this vegetable, and write in the sowing date and anticipated harvesting date or date when the crop will be finished.

Before you get halfway to the bottom of your wish list, the garden plan you've drawn out will probably be filled up solid. But there's actually much more space in your garden than you may see right now. Keep in mind that gardening is a four-dimensional process that you're mapping on a two-dimensional media and that one of those four dimensions is time.

Now please, you novices, don't think you can garden effectively without a plan on paper. I still make one. By late spring the much besmudged plan pretty much stays in my seed box, but that's because by then I've pretty much memorized it—and have already changed it too. I work out next year's garden plan early in winter while the mistakes of the previous year are still fresh, and then use my plan to help control myself when reading seed catalogs.

HOW MUCH?

I set out to produce at least half again more than I expect to need. Then I don't stress when insects or disease cause losses. If the weather doesn't cooperate, I can still be generous.

SUCCESSIONS

Suppose you're like me, addicted to green salads made mostly of tender lettuce hearts. Most lettuce varieties mature all at once, hold in prime condition for about one week, and then turn bitter. Rather than cycle from lettuce glut to famine to another glut, my patch grows several varieties that require different amounts of growing time. This way a single sowing date will yield prime lettuce for a month. For convenience I mix all my lettuce varieties into one packet. I sow this blend once a month from spring to the end

of summer. After mid-August, growth goes ever slower, so my late-summer lettuce sowings have only two weeks between them.

Draw that up on your own garden plan as though you were going to do the same thing! A mature average-size lettuce fits comfortably in 1 square foot of growing space. To harvest one head daily during as much of the year, it is possible you'll need to start a new patch of about 4 feet by 8 feet on a schedule like this: March 1, April 1, May 1, June 1, July 1, August 1, August 15, August 30. If you assigned each of those sowings to its own area and grew nothing else before or after the crop, then lettuce would occupy more than two of the six beds in our imaginary 1,000-square-foot garden, and most of the space assigned to lettuce would be empty for most of the growing season.

However, the area planted March 1 will be harvested in June. Ah! We'll have a vacant space come available. We could grow root crops for autumn harvest. Or cabbages. There are lots of options.

Now view the lettuce succession backward. We've already decided to sow lettuce during August. No sense having these beds do nothing from March through July. What could we squeeze in there that would be harvested by the end of July? Peas? Spinach? Broccoli?

The possibilities are so many that you'd best draw your plan with soft pencil and have an artist's eraser handy.

Here are a few successions I rely on: Bare beds in spring often get sown to shelling peas even if the peas would be far in excess of our table's requirement, in which case I consider excess peas to be green manure crops. In either case peas will be harvested by mid-June and may be immediately followed by large, slow-growing brassicas such as Savoy cabbage, broccoli, kale, rutabagas, or brussels sprouts. If I need a planting space in May, some green manure peas get yanked before they yield anything. Pea vines contribute to making strong compost. And better, pea roots leave the bed loose, fine textured, and open, ready to welcome the next crop.

Here's another: Start garlic in October on the bed where the spuds were just dug; the garlic is harvested the following June, and then brussels sprouts and other winter brassicas go in. Spuds, garlic, winter brassicas—three crops in two years. One reason I repeatedly use that pattern is our main crop of potatoes, the garlic crop, and the brussels sprout bed all require about the same amount of space.

Purple sprouting broccoli is done by May 1, and the last overwintered cauliflower will be cut by then too; both these beds will be perfect locations for summer heat lovers. Why not brassicas again? See Rotations, below.

ROTATIONS

The simplest crop rotation divides the garden in halves. One section grows frost-sensitive summer crops followed by a green manure over winter. The other half grows the spring garden followed by autumn/winter crops. And switch.

The spring garden is sown into beds that had been growing green manures over winter. The green manure crop dries the soil sooner; the dense, fast-rotting root system it leaves behind fractures the soil better than digging can. These green manures are not always turned under because doing that delays planting until the vegetation decomposes. Instead, they can be pulled from the bed, roots and all, or else mowed close to the soil, and the stubble can be chopped in. In either case, the vegetation is used to make compost. The Legumes and Green Manures sections in Chapter 9 explain this fully.

The summer garden grows on beds that previously produced autumn and winter vegetables. These beds usually come into spring in rather barren or weedy condition, showing the stumps of cabbage and remains of winter root crops. I mentioned already that in spring I often sow peas as green manures on these beds. The peas may be ripped out before summer crops go in. Summer crops are mainly planted in May in the Willamette. When the summer crops finish, immediately start green manures to grow over the winter, making the soil easier to prepare for spring sowing.

The autumn/winter harvest is mainly sown during July and into early August, with a few minor items started in June and September. These crops go on beds that produced the spring garden. Because there often is a month or even a six-week-long gap between the harvest of a spring crop and the sowing of the following autumn/winter crop, I may squeeze in a quick-growing buckwheat green manure, described in the Green Manures section (page 214).

This pattern prevents the same vegetable growing in the same place two years in a row plus facilitates an annual winter green-manure crop over a good part of the area. Thrifty!

Garden writers often assert that moving a crop to a different spot each year reduces insect problems. They do, *on the farm*, because the areas involved are greater than some insects travel. Farm rotations completely eliminate host plants from a large enough area that diseases fade away. Traditional farm rotations make sure that the following crop is one that can handle the root exudates left by the proceeding crop. Rotation is the key to raising grain without herbicides. Most of this wisdom does not apply to the food garden.

Garden writers east of the Rocky Mountains recommend multi-year rotations that allow vegetable gardening to go on indefinitely, but these do not succeed in Cascadia. I speculate eastern crop rotations work because there is a harsh winter. Soil freezing solid for months powerfully lowers insect and disease-organism populations. But Cascadian soils remain biologically active throughout winter. In Cascadia after growing vegetables for 3 or 4 years, mysterious troubles start.

The worst trouble comes from the symphylan, a small soil-dwelling root eater discussed at length in Chapter 8. The only effective way I know to eliminate symphylans is to abandon the garden until they die out and make a new garden where there aren't many, which means where unirrigated grasses and clovers grew for some years. For many suburban and urban gardeners, the closest optional garden is the front lawn. I can well appreciate how upset suburban gardeners get at the prospect of converting their backyard food garden into a rough pasture where grasses are allowed to grow chest high in spring before being mowed while the vegetable plots are moved to the front lawn. And then to trade off again a few years later. And to never water the lawn.

It is possible to extend the number of years you can grow sensitive vegetable species in the same garden plot before encountering troubles. Avoid planting most families in the same spot two years in a row: e.g., do not follow onions with leeks nor follow kale with cabbage or broccoli. Do not follow tomatoes with peppers or eggplants—or potatoes. Grow green-manure crops whenever possible because cover crops reset the soil's microecology to a balance that welcomes vegetables. By keeping compost imports to the minimum required to maintain a healthy soil microecology, you can slow symphylan population growth.

POSITIONING PERENNIALS

Fruit trees, small fruit like raspberries and currants, and perennial vegetables like asparagus don't fit into rotations. Locate perennials along the northern end of the garden, where their shade won't interfere with the vegetables. These plants also serve as a windbreak.

Strawberries and rhubarb are perennials but shouldn't be grown for more than a few years without being divided and moved or, as in the case of strawberries, replaced with new virus-free stock. So these crops do fit in the veggie garden, although they occupy their bed for more than a season.

THE SEED BOX

My own seed organizer functions like a sowing appointment calendar. Anytime I'm in doubt about what to plant, I look at what seed packets are waiting for me in this month's bundle.

Before learning better, I kept mine in a cardboard box in a back bedroom closet. Now, to better preserve vitality, I use large airtight plastic storage containers kept in a spare refrigerator. There is active silica gel desiccant inside the container because of the arithmetic of seed storage—drier plus cooler equals longer. The next chapter has much to say about seed storage.

In early winter I reorganize my old packets into rubber-banded bundles labeled for the month they'll first be planted. Thus, I also discover what new seeds I must buy. Some packets in a bundle get sown once and will not be needed again that year. Some packets will be required again; after the first use, these are transferred to the appropriate bundle.

Any packet that germinated weakly or slowly is tagged for discard as soon as its last planting of that season is done. (For more on this, see Chapter 6.)

Plant Spacing

The amount of uncontested root zone you allow for each plant has enormous consequences on how the crop grows. Interplant spacing controls how large your cauliflower and cabbages will be at harvest every bit as much as soil fertility and soil moisture do. Spacing determines how many side shoots broccoli will grow and how large they are, how long root crops can hold in the ground before losing quality, if lettuce will form hearts, if corn plants make more than one ear, and when and for how long the heaviest yield comes from crops like tomatoes and zucchini. Plant spacing strongly influences how often you must irrigate and how you will control weeds.

There are two usual approaches. The currently fashionable plant-spacing approach is called "intensive." With this method, plants are positioned very close together. I usually prefer the old-fashioned "extensive" method, where each plant is given much more growing space. Extensive was how people grew vegetables before John Jeavons. His book *How to Grow More Vegetables* has sold many copies since the 1970s and is still in print. By 1990 nearly every North American gardening book, magazine article, and extension bulletin was preaching his intensive approach or something very similar.

I think both methods have advantages. Intensive concentrates the harvest period of crops that yield over a long period, like tomatoes, zucchini, broccoli, and pole beans; if it is a cut-once-and-done crop, then intensive gives you more (smaller-size) units to pick for the amount of land involved, and usually you pick a week sooner. Spun this way, it can seem that intensive yields more. But with crops having the potential to provide an ongoing harvest over several months, the amount harvested from an intensive planting (and its quality) drops off greatly after a short initial burst. Extensive spacing of these same crops yields less at the beginning, but the amount harvested steadily increases because the plant has as yet unoccupied space to grow into. Extensive produces more for longer.

Suppose a cabbage variety can yield either 12 medium-size heads or six large ones from 36 square feet. The 6 large cabbages will slightly outweigh the 12 smaller ones; the smaller ones mature a few days sooner. Not much difference there. Cabbage is a cut-once-and-done crop. But if you compare what happens from putting either 4 or 12 broccoli plants into the same 36 square feet, the 12-plant bed will produce a dozen medium- to small-size heads followed by one set of smaller but still useful side shoots. After that, the side shoots get very small and woody. It soon seems sensible to pull these nonproductive crowded plants, making room for something else. The same area sustaining only 4 broccoli plants will yield 4 enormous heads that together outweigh the 12 smaller ones, followed by an abundance of large side shoots for another month or six weeks. Often the side shoots from uncrowded plants will be larger than the main flowers from crowded plants. Larger broccoli flowers taste better too. Choosing the best interplant spacing isn't a rote matter. For example, early-maturing broccoli varieties make considerably smaller plants.

The amount harvested from fruiting crops (tomatoes, peppers, eggplants, melons, cucumbers, zucchini) drops off greatly after their growing bed has been covered with leaves, which is also when root zone expansion starts being constricted. But when these crops experience little or no root zone competition, they continue growing fast, ultimately yielding far more.

On the other hand, if I were growing fruiting crops in a cool, short-season area, I'd use tighter spacing.

Jeavons asserts that intensive uses much less water for the amount of output. I'm not sure this is so, but I am certain intensive beds demand daily irrigation in hot weather while extensive plantings allow you to enjoy a week's summer vacation without requiring someone else to water the garden. Intensive demands bent-over, by-hand-with-fingers weeding while extensive allows most weeding to be done efficiently with a hoe while standing erect. Ultraintensive requires the timely raising of transplants so that there's always a seedling ready to immediately plug into any opening. Extensive allows you the ease of direct seeding most of your crops.

MARINA'S EXPERIENCE

New gardeners are often drawn to the intensive method because it is so commonly advocated. Some are attracted to the idea that precise plant placement maximizes yield. They see photos of perfectly grown beds at the point of harvest. But inexperience makes it very unlikely that they will achieve those results. Perhaps while they are enjoying a weekend away, the weather suddenly turns hot and their intensive beds become a wilted mess. Or crowded seedlings stop growing and never produce anything worthwhile. Sadly, this kind of discouragement can cause newbies to lose heart for the whole endeavor, while wider plant spacing would have proved more adaptable to inexperienced stewardship.

The intensive method breaks down when a bed is *overcrowded*. Put 6 broccoli plants into 10 square feet of bed, something I frequently see in other people's gardens, and you'll harvest woody, rather tasteless main heads only 2 inches in diameter, followed by a few small, rather woody side shoots. Crowd most varieties of cabbage that much, and half the plants do not form proper heads. Head lettuce cannot develop when overcrowded, nor will carrots make smooth roots of uniform size, while the majority of radish plants in an overcrowded row fail to make sweet, juicy roots. Crowded bush beans make slightly larger overall yields if measured by weight of beans taken from a given space, but you'll harvest small pods that take more time to pick and will be tedious to top and tail.

During 40 years of food gardening I've used seven quite different soils in two climates. I've tried everything from the closest intensive interplant spacing to dry gardening with extremely wide interplant spacing. So no matter what you have been told or what you may have done in previous years, please try my spacing (and fertilizing) recommendations at least once. See what happens.

Southern Oregon gardeners with deep, open soil can usefully provide heat-loving vegetables with half again more growing room than I suggest for the Willamette. If the growing instructions have peppers on 24-by-24-inch stations (576 square inches of root zone per plant), half again more growing room comes to about 30 by 30 inches (860 square inches). But if you grow peppers close to the Pacific or around Puget Sound, they probably need only 18 by 18 inches (324 square inches).

Lovers of giant beets can increase my recommended spacing by about one-third. Do the same if you want very large heads of cabbage, cauliflower, or broccoli. However, unnecessarily wide plant spacing makes useless gaps unless you are dry gardening. (See discussion on dry gardening in Chapter 5.)

These statements apply to most vegetables:

- If adjoining broccoli plants touch before you harvest their first set of side shoots, they were too close together.

- If you provide broccoli with all the growing room this book calls for and by the time you finish harvesting the first three sets of side shoots the plants haven't entirely filled their bed, you probably did not give the crop enough fertilizer.

I suggest starting out with the interplant spacing and fertilizing procedures recommended in Chapter 9, and then adjusting in the years to come. If your plants bumped this year, then next year increase spacing by 25 percent. Reassess this annually until the ever-larger plants you will grow either get too big to suit you or no longer touch at their maximum size, leaving wasteful gaps.

Layout: Rows, Raised Beds

I acknowledge that successful gardens are planted in ditches or on mounds of decaying vegetation and use rows running north to south or only running east to west. Or in circles. Or use complex interplanting schemes. All these approaches produce vegetables. This book describes techniques that I consider efficient and practical, and that produce nutrient-dense vegetables.

Most of my garden beds are 4 feet wide and 25 feet long. I arrange small plants like lettuce, kohlrabi, beets, and carrots in 4-foot-long rows across the bed with 16 to 18 inches between row centers. Sprawling plants like indeterminate tomatoes, zucchini, cucumbers, or melons may be positioned 4 or more feet apart straight down the bed's center, and for these crops a 4-foot bed is not quite wide enough. The big brassicas like broccoli, cauliflower, brussels sprouts, and autumn/winter cabbages are stationed 24 to 30 inches apart in a pair of rows 24 inches apart. A 4-foot-wide bed is perfect for two such rows. There are exceptions: to pollinate properly, corn patches should be at least three rows wide; corn is most productive when it's allowed 3 feet between rows. Winter squash spreads wildly, and so do most zucchini varieties if given half a chance, so for these vegetables I temporarily join two beds by digging up the pathway between them, making a growing area 25 feet long and 10 feet wide.

Paths waste potential growing room, so I make them only 2 feet wide, just enough to allow a wheelbarrow to pass. I once made them only 18 inches wide, but my wife complained that when those narrow paths are slippery, the neighbors must think she's drunk. I make beds 4 feet wide because any wider and I can't touch every spot without stepping on the bed. They're 25 feet long because few home-garden crops need more than 100 square feet and because I can, with a shovel, accurately toss compost halfway down the bed from a wheelbarrow located at one end. I find it simplest to calculate fertilizer applications in increments of 100 square feet because spreading 1 kilogram per hectare, or 1 pound per acre, or 1 gram per 100 square feet amounts to roughly the same dose. For example, spreading agricultural lime at 1 ton per acre (2,000 pounds per acre) is equal to spreading it at 2,000 grams per 100 square feet.

On flat ground the beds need not be raised any higher than it takes to distinguish them from the paths, unless you cannot squat or touch your toes. On gentle slopes beds should form low terraces more or less on the contour lines. The easiest way to make a raised bed is to move an inch of soil from what will be the adjoining path atop what will be the bed. That's enough raising. After adding compost and loosening up that bed, it'll stand a few inches above the path with its edges at a gentle-enough angle that rain or irrigation won't cause soil movement. However, you will inevitably move soil from bed to path when raking out seedbeds, when making furrows, and sometimes while hoeing weeds. So whenever the bed or a section of the bed is prepared for the next crop, an inch of soil from the surrounding paths should be shoveled back up. My current garden has a gentle slope. Because there is slight downhill soil movement every time I work the land, whenever I prepare beds for the next crop, I only take soil from the lower path and put that on top.

Difficulties arise from enclosing raised beds:

It can be very difficult to remove clumps of grass when their roots grab a plank.

Retaining walls restrict hoeing; they force the gardener into laborious hand weeding.

Raking easily combs lumps and clods out of the surface and onto the paths if there are no side walls.

Side walls make the bed too permanent. They make it awkward to temporarily combine adjoining beds.

Beds without retaining walls are easier to prepare for sowing seeds. First, clear the remains of the previous crop, and then spread all soil amendments except compost. Then soil is shoveled up from the surrounding paths and roughly spread over the bed. Next, the bed is dug, hoed, or otherwise loosened, which blends in the amendments. Then a thin topping of compost is spread, and finally, lumps in the surface inch are raked out and down onto the paths as the bed is leveled and the compost is mixed in—all at once. This practice concentrates organic matter where it decomposes most rapidly and also turns the surface inch into an excellent seed germination medium. Lumps of compost and clods that are raked off the bed get broken up and mixed together by foot traffic. Next time the bed is made up these have become soft, loose, humusy soil.

Garden Magic and Companion Planting

I am uncertain about vegetable friendships and antagonisms, or, as these phenomena are better termed, "companionate effects." The widely taught theory asserts some plant species grow better in close association with certain other species while other combinations are antagonistic. Therefore, we should arrange vegetables in compatible mixtures. Besides, the theory goes, interplanting deters or confuses harmful insects that hunt by smell.

I once read that onions would keep damaging insects away from all sorts of crops, so I tried alternating rows of bush beans and onions—the onions grew as usual; the bush beans were badly stunted. That same year everything else in my garden grew well no matter what it was next to, and it's been that way ever since. I suspect one reason is that my soil provides balanced and intense fertility that overrides most companionate effects.

I also have a rather biodynamical explanation for all of this. You've probably heard that marigolds deter unwanted insects. When I interplanted marigolds, I had little problem with insects. But when I didn't interplant marigolds, I also had little problem with insects. I don't deny that marigolds chase away bugs. Marigolds will deter most bugs most of the time *if you believe they will.* And I use another method more magical than marigolds; I'll explain shortly.

Now maybe you love flowers as much as vegetables, or even more. In that case, maybe you should interplant marigolds. Or maybe you use garlic in every dish. In that case you could deter insects by sticking a garlic clove into every nook and cranny in the garden, and then carefully work your spring garden around a vegetable that grows from October until harvest in June.

Please don't take me wrong: I ridicule nothing. I believe garden magic happens whether the gardener believes in it or not, is aware of it or not. The magician operating my garden is *me*; *you* are the powerful magician in your own garden. Now wouldn't it be a really terrific trick if I could become the magician who makes everyone's garden grow well. Maybe that's why I write these books and once sold those seeds.

What actually is magic? The word means bringing about change or transformation by intention. We decide that something will be so, and so it is. However, a successful magician must not have the slightest doubt whatsoever concerning the manifestation of her intention. None. Or it won't happen. So how do we overcome doubt? The usual confidence booster is to perform a magical ritual; prayer does it for some people. Biodynamic gardeners brew herbs and manure into "preparations," then meditatively stir these preps into water and spray the crops or soil, or insert the preps into compost heaps. Whatever the method, the cause of the result seems to be the *ritual* or the *magical object* or *God*, not us. I believe that the actual working force is the certainty the ritual creates. What you really believe is, *is*.

I believe insects and diseases are entitled to a tithe. After all, my garden shares their space, so 10 percent of what I grow would be cheap rent. Because I am generous, the bugs and diseases only take 5 percent. Really. I do not slap down the bugs except when they try to take more than their fair share. Which isn't often. So I don't bother with marigolds.

Ethical magicians require authority over or ownership of whatever they transform. So the first thing garden magicians do is grasp the space. We fluff up the soil, remove the existing vegetation, and put a fence around it. We sprinkle magical powders like lime and complete "orgasmic" fertilizer. These actions have to be done just so. The right kind and amount of lime(s). Measured quantities of sometimes hard-to-find ingredients in COF. We brew compost just so. And having done what we believe is needed to make the plants grow well, they do.

You may think I am going too far with this fantasy. Well, let me give you a couple of real-life examples from the years I ran Territorial Seed Company. An old-timer from southern Oregon wrote me a long letter demanding that I recommend his organic remedy for root maggots in radishes. This guy dissolved 1 tablespoonful of genuine sea salt in a gallon of distilled water (has to be *real* sea salt, has to be *distilled*—or rainwater—or it wouldn't work), and when his radishes got large enough to begin forming bulbs (which also alerts the mother cabbage fly to lay her eggs on the soil next to the just-about-to-appear food supply), this man sprinkled slightly sea-salty water on the soil immediately against his row of radishes. The result: no maggots—unless he failed to harvest soon enough. Eventually this deterrent stops working and larger unpicked radishes do get maggoty. His result was identical to what happened in my radish patch if I harvested soon enough too, but I didn't bother with the salt water.

I thanked him sincerely for sharing his method and told him I would try it out and tell others if it worked. And I am. Right now. Telling you. I am sure his method worked—for him—because he totally believed it would. If you believe slightly salty water will work for you, then it might. I mean, if you didn't find yourself in Heaven after your previous death, then your faith wasn't strong enough. Likewise, if you have any doubts about the sea-salt-in-water cure, then don't use it.

During the years I was running Territorial Seed Company, I paid close attention to what the head plant breeder at Oregon State University, Dr. James Baggett, was up to. Among his other projects, he trialed up to a dozen early hybrid eggplant varieties every summer—and would inevitably include one heat-loving heirloom, Black Beauty, that stood no chance of yielding anything. Why Black Beauty, I asked one day. Because, he told me, if one summer ever proved so warm that Black Beauty *did* yield, then Dr. Baggett intended to disregard all the eggplant results from this highly atypical year.

I was giving a garden talk in Seattle and a lady in the audience asked why my books had such unpleasant things to say about Black Beauty. She'd had fine results with it! She had just moved to Seattle from East Texas and had brought along treasured Black Beauty seeds that had been saved by her family going way back. The previous summer she transplanted Black Beauty seedlings next to a south-facing white wall, and in that position it grew fine and yielded well. And Black Beauty seed is cheap and you can save your own, while the hybrid eggplant seeds I was selling were pricey and then some.

I confess I allowed a mean-spirited impulse to run my mouth. At that time I possessed the generally recognized status of gardener laureate of the maritime Northwest, and with all the authority I could muster, I informed her of Dr. Baggett's trials with Black Beauty and about similar results doing my own eggplant trials at Lorane, Oregon. Then, immediately feeling ashamed for reacting so insensitively, I told her that since she had such good luck growing the family heirloom, she should continue to use it in her well-protected location. But I wouldn't be at all surprised if she no longer gets any fruit to set.

ROOT EXUDATES

Root exudates have many effects beyond influencing which microbes inhabit the area immediately around the plant's roots. They also serve to help the plant win its struggle for light, water, and nutrients by chemically suppressing competing species. The effectiveness of exudates as herbicides depends on the species involved. Some species can massively cripple certain other species. Some exudates can be positive for another species; this is often seen in forests. Both relationships, cooperative and antagonistic, happen in the garden.

Companionate effects carry on to succeeding crops. I already mentioned how onions interplanted with beans make the beans grow poorly. Soil that grew onions ends up saturated with onion root exudates. And the soil microecology now suits the onion. If an overwintered onion crop that gets lifted in May is followed by a bush bean crop sown in June, the beans won't grow well.

The suppressive effects of root exudates can go on a lot longer than most would think possible. If you harvest storage onions in August and plant bush beans on that spot the following May/June, the beans still grow less well. A farmer remembers that a whole field grew onions last year or even two years past, and as you would expect, traditional farm rotations allow for exudate effects. But it gets difficult to keep track of where things were even last year in a vegetable garden.

One way to reduce this sort of problem is to not grow vegetables for more than a few years on a certain plot, field, or garden. Sir Albert Howard, founder of the organic farming and gardening movement, knew that too. I suggest you reread the quotation that introduces this chapter. Incidentally, Americans frequently misunderstand the word "allotment." It refers to a large community garden plot whose minimum size of about 300 square yards was specified by law. To the British of that era, an allotment plot was an entitlement. The local council was required to organize one for any resident who requested it. An allotment was expected to produce a major economic result for the family. It was not a contemporary-style community garden whose average individual plot is under 20 square yards and whose main product is a sense of community.

Cloches and Cold Frames

An unheated greenhouse protects and improves a winter garden full of salad radishes, lettuce, spinach, and other cool-season greens. Daytime temperatures are higher, humidity is lower than outside, and there's no pounding rain so the vegetables remain tender and grow lushly. In summer the space grow okra, eggplant, and melons.

But back to what's practical and inexpensive. Cloches and cold frames grow crops nearly as well as structures you can walk into. And sometimes better. Although it's a great joy to step from a drizzly winter's day into a semitropical greenhouse, this proves an unnecessarily expensive pleasure because greenhouses don't retain heat as well as cloches. Warmer nighttime temperatures can be achieved passively by making the greenhouse knee high and managing it from the outside. The soil below a cloche or cold frame accumulates heat in the daytime that keeps a small air volume warmer at night than any unheated greenhouse could be.

For low-growing greens in winter I suggest making crude boxes of two-by-twelve planks— best to use slow-to-rot western red cedar if you can afford it. The frames should be no more than 10 feet long so that they can be moved by one strong person. They should be the same width as your raised beds or else as wide as the glass windows you find to recycle. The frames could last your lifetime if you get them out of direct contact with the earth when they're not needed. Doug fir frames need periodic treatment with a nonphytotoxic wood preservative.

The glass or clear plastic cover should slope enough that rainwater runs off. If the glass leans to the south, you'll get more light into the box. But I'm not a skilled carpenter, so instead of constructing tilted frames I rake the bed the frame sits on so that the sun-facing side is 2 inches lower than the pole-facing edge. Opened glasses are blocked from sliding off the frame by small pieces of one-by-two screwed onto the side. The windows are held open at various heights by a wooden block that started out as a four-by-four 6 inches long before a chunk was sawn out of it. There is no weather stripping, no crosspieces to fill gaps between window sashes, no attempt whatsoever to seal cracks. But these rough frames do allow plenty of light in while keeping out the rain. They raise night temperatures a few degrees. When the winter sun shines I prop the windows open to the full 6 inches. When frost threatens I close them. During mild rainy spells I keep a window partly open to prevent rot. I believe more advanced construction brings no benefit.

Where winter is harsh, Cascadians should use cold frames for growing salads. The Lorane valley floor at 900 feet elevation is always several degrees colder than nearby Cottage Grove, Oregon, at 640 feet of elevation. Living in Lorane I routinely used four such frames, two sown mid-September and two more sown mid-October. The September sowing was harvested midwinter; the October sowing was size up late winter to early spring. Immediately after being emptied during winter, the September frame was resown to another lot of mixed salad greens to eat in mid to late spring.

It's that simple—tender, sweet loose-leaf lettuce and spinach, mild young rocket, and escarole/endive salads all winter instead of an entire season exercising one's jaw muscles chewing tough cabbage and kale. Not to mention the occasional winter when everything freezes out . . . except what's protected in a frame.

The tunnel cloche is simpler to make than a low wooden box with a transparent lid but is less convenient. Basically it's a sheet of clear polyethylene stretched over supporting hoops to make a long half cylinder. The edges of the plastic may be held down with soil or by placing lengths of recycled two-by-fours on them. One or both of the cloche's ends may be opened for air circulation, or both of them closed against frost. I seal the ends by making the covering plastic long

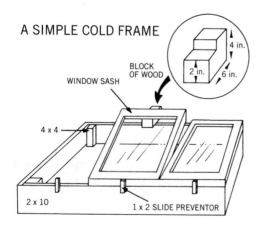

A SIMPLE COLD FRAME

4 in.

2 in.   6 in.

BLOCK
OF WOOD

WINDOW SASH

4 x 4

2 x 10

1 x 2 SLIDE PREVENTOR

enough to overhand the ends and reach the soil line, and then some. I anchor the ends to the soil with short lengths of four-by-four. The overlap can also be folded back, spread double over the tunnels' ends, and anchored in that position with the same wood tight against the sides, thus ventilating the tube on sunny days.

Tunnel cloches range in size from little tubes 1 foot high by 1 foot wide supported by stout wire hoops stuck in the ground to substantial 3- to 4-foot-wide hoops made of 10-foot-long lengths of thin-walled galvanized steel pipe also stuck in the ground. I prefer the larger hoops. I shaped mine with an electrician's pipe bender, the sort once used when steel pipe was used as industrial wiring conduit. When the ends are pushed 12 inches into the bed, the hoops are strongly self-supporting. The resulting arch is about 3 feet tall in the center. The bottom width matches my 4-foot-wide raised beds. Shorter-lived supports can be made of 1-inch-diameter black plastic irrigation pipe, sliding the ends over short metal or wooden stakes pounded into the ground. I prefer the greater initial expense of thin-walled galvanized steel pipe because it will last many years if the rusty ends are periodically repainted.

The best use for poly tunnels is to allow earlier planting of frost-sensitive crops and accelerate their growth. If frost threatens, even if it's forecast to go below 40 degrees F, close both ends in late afternoon. Otherwise, the end flaps are left open. With both ends wide open, daytime temperatures will still be 10 degrees higher than outside; night temperatures will still be a degree or two higher. This small improvement can make an enormous difference. After late May tunnel cloches gets too

Wide tunnel cloche on left side, X frame with tomatoes on right side. The X frame is braced better than the illustration suggests.

hot even with both ends wide open. I have kept the plastic on until late June by cutting 1-foot-diameter vents along the top, one hole between each hoop support. Doing this wrecks the plastic for reuse next year, so I used inexpensive poly film.

To be first in the neighborhood to harvest a ripe tomato, transplant already-blooming seedlings into a tunnel cloche three to four weeks earlier than would be possible without frost protection. Chapter 7 explains how to raise tomato seedlings to this standard. To keep the bed free of weeds, either crawl through the tunnel a couple of times before the plants get too big or else lift the plastic on one side, tidy up the bed, and then reanchor the plastic. To water a short tunnel, spray from the ends with hose and nozzle every few days or, far better, install a row of microsprinklers when the cloche is erected. By late June tomato plants should be touching plastic on all sides. With early varieties there may already be ripening fruit. At that point remove the plastic and let the vines grow over the path. Similarly, chitted (see Chapter 6) zucchini seeds will germinate in a tunnel cloche weeks before

Cloche and Cold Frame Calendar

Planting Date	Crops	Harvest Period
• September	Loose-leaf lettuce, mustard greens, spinach, endive	November to January
• October	Loose-leaf lettuce, mustard greens, spinach, endive	February to April
• February	Loose-leaf lettuce, mustard greens, spinach, bush peas	Mid-April to May
• March	Lettuce, mustard greens, kohlrabi, spinach, broccoli, cauliflower, cabbage, beets, chard, carrots	Mid-May to June
• Mid-April to Mid-May	Tomato transplants, bush beans, squash	June to the end of summer
• Mid to late May	Pepper and eggplant transplants, melons, cucumbers	July to the end of summer

Note: This rough schedule is for the Willamette Valley, Oregon, garden.

the last usual frost. These will start yielding a month or more ahead of normal.

Melons and cucumbers make faster early vine growth in low wood-box cold frames like the ones I use in winter. However, low cloches can reach solar-hot-water-heater temperatures in spring and must be opened wide whenever the sun shines. On warm sunny late May days the sashes may have to be removed entirely to avoid frying the plants and put back late in the afternoon. By the time the vines reach the edge of the box, it should be safe to remove the cover entirely, but to avoid disturbing growing plants, you may choose to leave the frame in place; the vines simply climb over and keep going.

The need to vent excess heat brings to mind one large plus from having a real greenhouse. In every passive solar-heated enclosure the temperature at the top will be far higher than it is at ground level. On a sunny late May afternoon an inadequately vented greenhouse can be

80 degrees F at the soil line and over 140 degrees F at the top. Few heat-loving vegetable species survive 120 degrees F. Many are severely stressed at 110 degrees F. No matter if you have a 3-foot-high tunnel cloche, a 1-foot-high box cloche, or an 8-foot-high greenhouse, top to bottom the temperature extremes will be about the same. In every sort of enclosure, at the midpoint between soil and the top, the temperature will also be in the middle.

A 1-foot-high frame forces all plants to grow into the hot zone. A 3-foot-high tunnel will have the middle temperature range at about 18 inches above the soil line; in this cloche low-growing determinate tomato plants spread out below the hot zone. So the lower your cloche is, the more attention must be paid to opening and closing the cover. And the higher the cloche (or greenhouse), the easier it is to keep destructively high temperatures above the level of the plants. The opposite prevails at night when the amount of heat rising from the earth keeps the small air space of a low cloche warmer than it can heat a room-height enclosure.

Winter Gardening

Winter stresses frost-hardy plants. They use energy to resist humidity-induced diseases. Pounding rain damages cells. Less light combined with chilly weather greatly slows sugar production. During periods of cloudy weather the plant survives by consuming food reserves. Frost adds to the burden because a plant must expend energy when adjusting to subfreezing temperatures.

Watching endive/escarole trying to survive winter demonstrates that mild, rainy weather can be harder on plants than clear, sunny days with frosty nights. Sunny winter days give them a chance to rebuild food reserves, maybe even grow a bit. Many endive varieties tolerate a 10 degrees F overnight low. So they often survive a dryish winter. However, when winter is rainy, overcast, and mild, endive starves; its disease resistance is reduced while disease-inducing moisture is constantly trapped in the dense rosette of thin leaves. The ever-weakening head slowly rots back. Endive/escarole make excellent cold frame candidates because merely by keeping off the pounding rain without significantly raising temperatures, they are able to reliably overwinter. Spinach is similar.

Winter cabbages survive rain and frost without any protection because they have thick, tough waxy leaves that easily shed water, and the heads are wrapped in many protective, insulating outer layers that keep moisture away from the vital core. Besides, it doesn't really matter to the gardener if the outer leaves you strip off anyway show a bit of damage.

Plants prevent their cells from bursting in subfreezing weather by converting reserve starch into sugar that acts like antifreeze in their sap and cellular fluid. That's why brassicas and chicories taste better after they've been well frosted a few times. Another chill-handling mechanism plants use is to pump water out of the cell as the temperature approaches freezing so that when the cellular fluid does freeze, it won't burst the walls. However, this effort depletes food reserves as the plant adjusts and readjusts.

Winter gardening is always uncertain. Getting a harvest depends on more than how low temperatures go. Sometimes the result depends more upon how the pattern of frosts develops. Plants handle severe frost far better after they've experienced a few light to moderate ones. But the plant may succumb if one of the first frosts of the year is severe. Here's an example from my own trial reports in Lorane. During the December 1983 freeze overnight temperature suddenly dropped to 7 degrees F and remained below freezing for several days. This occurred after a sunny autumn that only brought a few light frosts. Varieties that in previous years had survived an overnight low of 3 degrees F were destroyed at 7 degrees F. Why? During that mild fall the crops grew fast and were still tender when the freeze hit. Only one extremely tough winter cabbage variety called Wivoy survived. Tundra (TSC) and Wirosa (OSB) are similar varieties.

That same year the Vegetable Crops Research Station at Agassiz, British Columbia, experienced much frosty autumn weather and a few snowy days during November. Most of its winter trials survived that December freeze, withstanding slightly colder temperatures than we had at Lorane.

Breeding influences cold tolerance. Salad cabbages are tender because they have thin cell walls. Logically you'd expect freeze-hardy varieties to be chewy, and they are.

Winters are discouragingly severe at some locations. For example, folks in Whatcom County, Washington, can almost count on a savage blast of arctic air that wipes out their garden. My high-elevation Lorane garden was hit hard about every third winter. During the years I lived in Lorane I observed nearby Eugene, 420 feet elevation, where winter gardens survived four years out of five. Only undauntable people garden in the winter at elevations over 1,000 feet, and they must use especially hardy varieties.

I consider the Willamette Valley as "standard" or "average" for the entire bioregion. South of Yoncalla, Oregon, the hardiest crops survive most winters if the garden is under 1,200 feet elevation. On the south Oregon coast and in the redwoods, winters are sunnier and mild enough that crops grow slowly, so, for example, winter-heading broccoli can be grown and lettuce might be possible all winter. Winters are harsher as you move north of the Columbia and inland from Puget Sound. Washington State microclimate differences are pronounced. Only a few miles south of frigid Whatcom County, the Skagit Valley offers excellent and generally safe winter conditions. That mildness, combined with unusually dry summers caused by being in the rain shadow of the Olympics and Vancouver Island, has brought many international vegetable seed companies to the Skagit.

Most vegetables die if the root system remains waterlogged for days at a time. Large areas of the southern Willamette Valley have poor drainage. I've noticed a similar situation along the floodplains of various coastal rivers in both Oregon and Washington. The only farm crops that tolerate both waterlogged roots and Cascadian winter are flax and grass. If you're considering the purchase of rural property in the vicinity of Willamette Valley grass seed farms or even thinking of buying a city house in west Eugene, think again if you're a serious gardener, and for sure consult the Natural Resources Conservation Service. They have soil maps showing Class I agricultural soils in the same area.

If the ground has any slope, poor winter drainage can be improved by making raised beds and grading the surrounding paths to better carry away runoff. Some difficult situations can be fixed with a French drain, which is a 3-foot-deep narrow ditch with a perforated drainpipe laid along the bottom and then filled with coarse crushed rock. One such ditch can improve soil 50 feet (and more) from the ditch on both sides, assuming there is anywhere conveniently downhill from the garden site to receive that surplus water.

Areas exposed to frequent wind can be difficult spots for gardens. Fencing or living windbreaks (or both) raise the temperature considerably and may permit plants to make more growth.

WINTER YIELD

Because light fuels plants, a relatively small garden will overwhelm the kitchen from June through September; a 50-square-foot bed growing two zucchini plants fills a bucket every other day, and you get gallons each time you harvest 100 square feet of snap beans. Two indeterminate tomato vines on 50 square feet of bed will cover the kitchen counter with fruit from mid-July through the end of summer. In fact, unless a lot of summer food is to be preserved or the family is extremely fond of winter squash or sweet corn, only 1,000 fertile square feet provide a summertime overabundance.

The winter garden is another matter. Vegetables don't grow much from October through March; they endure. Essentially, the winter garden is in living cold storage awaiting harvest. Each winter my wife, Annie, and I go through about 100 square feet of carrots and about 50 square feet each of parsnips, rutabagas, leeks, kale, and endive. I grow a dozen brussels sprout plants for our own table and usually another six plants so that we can gift them to friends and family (100 square feet), a dozen big Savoy cabbages, and at least that same number of overwintered cauliflower (150 square feet). When I lived in Oregon, about 50 big heads of loose-leaf lettuce were required between October and the time unprotected lettuce *usually* freezes out (75 square feet). Add in miscellaneous items like rocket, sorrel, parsley, parsley roots, fennel, and so on, and add cold frames to extend the salad harvest, and the winter garden requires at least 1,500 square feet. That's in addition to the land growing the summer garden.

WINTER GARDENING TECHNIQUES

Constant humidity, combined with low light levels and cold, weakens plants and makes them susceptible to disease. Plants resist diseases better if they do not quite touch when fully grown. Then they get more light, and air can move freely between the plants to dry them off. When loose-leaf lettuce encounters an unusually warm autumn and *grows too much too soon*, its inner leaves tend to wrap themselves into semiheads that trap humidity. This is why I've lost my lettuce patch sooner in mild rainy winters than in mild dryish winters. Midsize lettuce seedlings can be considerably hardier than larger plants that are forming hearts, so gamble on an early spring lettuce crop (or a lettuce seed crop) by sowing some in mid-October. Many winters this sowing will not survive unless protected by a cloche or frame.

Practicing careful hygiene during autumn and winter improves air circulation and reduces gastropod population. Promptly transfer all trim, stumps, and decaying materials to the compost area. Thin and weed overwintering crops.

Plants that haven't been pushed to grow extremely fast tolerate lower temperatures. So don't side-dress winter crops after the end of August. Kelp meal contains hormones and phytamins that make a plant more cold tolerant. I think it wise to feed winter crops twice the usual amount of kelp meal when blending their complete organic fertilizer. Some gardeners spray liquid kelp every few weeks during autumn and even during sunny spells in winter. This is an effective, frugal practice.

Chapter Five

WATER

Drought is said to be the arch enemy of the dry-farmer, but few agree upon its meaning. For the purposes of this volume, drought may be defined as a condition under which crops fail to mature because of an insufficient supply of water. Providence has generally been charged with causing droughts, but under the above definition, man is usually the cause. Occasionally, relatively dry years occur, but they are seldom dry enough to cause crop failures if proper methods of farming have been practiced. There are four chief causes of drought: (1) Improper or careless preparation of the soil; (2) failure to store the natural precipitation in the soil; (3) failure to apply proper cultural methods for keeping the moisture in the soil until needed by plants, and (4) sowing too much seed for the available soil-moisture. *[Emphasis mine]*

—JOHN A. WIDTSOE, *Dry-Farming*, 1911

CASCADIAN GARDENS seem to require irrigation. Rain rarely falls between June and late September.

When it does rain in summer it usually doesn't amount to much. Most gardeners irrigate veggies with lawn sprinklers, but these put out water so fast they almost inevitably spread too much. Gardeners watering with hose and nozzle tend to spread too little. Either way, too much or too little, diminishes the result. And not just a little.

Most gardeners have seen plants get gnarly, or stunted in dryish soil and, when moisture stress is extreme, wilt and die. They have also seen plant growth speed up after irrigating. So gardeners water prolifically without realizing that overwatering leaches soil fertility, slows growth, and lowers productivity.

This chapter explains how the plant density you establish strongly influences how much water the garden will need, how often irrigation must be done, and how to construct an irrigation *system* that spreads water evenly and controllably. You may design a garden that needs watering once a week. Or one that may yield a bit more but requires watering almost every day in summer. Or if you're fortunate enough to have deep moisture-retentive soil, you may design a garden that during the heat of summer only needs irrigation every two to three weeks, allowing you to take worry-free summer vacations. On that kind of soil you also can dry garden, an extreme style that yields a good deal less per square foot but rarely needs watering, if ever. It's your choice.

A Gardener's Textbook of Sprinkler Irrigation

When it rains hard, the soil's pore spaces are temporarily filled with water. Soil air contains a high concentration of carbon dioxide produced by the microecology and plant roots. When the moisture inflow stops, surplus water drains and fresh oxygen-rich air gets pulled back into the soil pores.

The remaining moisture *adheres* to soil particles. To see adhesion at work, dip a small stone into a glass of water and then remove it. The stone is wet on the outside. A few drops may fall off, and then the rock, still moist, stops dripping. If this rock were a layer of soil being irrigated, when it stopped dripping we'd term the quantity of moisture still adhering to its surfaces its *capacity* to hold moisture.

As soil dries down, the films of water adhering to its particles get thinner; the thinner they get, the stronger they stick and the more effort it takes plants to extract that moisture. Plants cannot grow fast when they must expend a lot of energy getting moisture. Even a short period of moisture stress turns lettuce bitter. If a moisture-stressed cauliflower plant manages to form a head at all, it will probably be harsh tasting. Water-short zucchini become dry, fibrous, and sometimes bitter, while moisture-stressed winter squash vines don't set as many fruit and they'll be smaller fruit. Snap beans become thin and tough, radishes hot and woody.

When a plant can't extract soil moisture fast enough to keep up with the amount being lost in strong sunshine, it wilts—a self-protective action that reduces its rate of moisture loss. As the day cools down, or the sun goes behind clouds, or night falls, the plant straightens back up and looks okay the next morning. Actually, temporary wilting is a huge stress that slows growth for days after. Extreme moisture stress makes plants wilt and promptly die.

Root crops like parsley and carrots store water. By drawing upon this reserve they can transpire more moisture than the roots can take in, without wilting. However, enduring a moisture deficit makes the carrot or radish tough to chew and bitter tasting, while the parsley stops making new leaves. No wonder gardeners quickly learn to fear dry soil.

If the garden is important to your family's health and economy, then I think it is crucial to irrigate *systematically*. But investing in convenient equipment is not necessary; it is possible to get an excellent result with a cheap lawn sprinkler or even a hose and nozzle, as long as you know what you're trying to achieve, discover what your equipment actually does, and in the case of hose and nozzle, are willing to invest your time.

SYSTEMATIC WATERING

The least costly way to irrigate is with hose and nozzle. *You* wetting down the garden works quite well if you enjoy the task. But the garden gets watered too briefly if you don't relish the occasion. If the garden is hand-watered every single day but too briefly, moisture doesn't penetrate deeply enough before you move on. Under a damp surface layer the bed may have been sucked bone dry. The vegetables may never wilt, but they'll become severely stunted.

To avoid this possibility, John Jeavons recommends repeatedly wafting the spray back and forth across several square yards of bed (area A) until the entire surface sparkles and becomes shiny wet. During the few moments the surface is sparkling, the surface layer contains more water than it can hold against the force of gravity. Spreading even more water faster than the pore spaces drain would make water run off the bed and possibly wash topsoil down on the paths. Better to move on to the next few square yards

(area B), continue on B until that section gets sparkly, then return to A until the shine reappears, and then go back to B until the shine reappears, repeating this pattern until the sparkling shine lasts long enough. At first the shine only lasts a second or so, but as the soil gets saturated ever deeper, the shine lasts longer. How long you want the shine to persist depends on your soil type. In the edition of Jeavons's book I read, it says "long enough" can vary from a second or so on sand to 10 seconds on a clay soil.

That's quite a difference! How to choose? Jeavons suggests initially calibrating your soil's moisture-assimilating ability by trying different shiny times combined with digging some test holes to see how deeply the soil has become saturated. Without this check, gross overwatering or underwatering could result. The desired shiny time only has to be determined once.

Clayey soil holds a great deal of moisture but assimilates it slowly. So clay can show a sparkly surface for many seconds while being quite dry a few inches deeper. On the other hand, coarse sands usually take in water so rapidly that it can be difficult to get a shine to last more than an instant. However, sandy soil is the type most prone to leaching. Garden writers (including me) tend to generalize broadly from limited experience, so I'm not surprised Jeavons did his research on clay soil.

In my first few years of backyard gardening I painstakingly hand-watered exactly as Jeavons suggested and it worked, but I had a small business to manage. So I switched to a sprinkler system that achieved the same result without consuming my precious time.

A Wet to Dry Scale

Soil	Moisture Remaining
Permanent wilting point	20 to 33 percent
Temporary wilting point	50 percent
Minimum moisture for intensive vegetable beds	70 percent
Field capacity	100 percent

Available Moisture *(Inches of Water per Foot of Soil)**

Soil Type	Total Holding Capacity	Available Moisture
Sandy	1.25 inches per foot	1.0 inch per foot
Medium (loam)	2.5 inches per foot	2.0 inches per foot
Clayey	3.75 inches per foot	2.7 inches per foot

* When the soil has delivered all of its available moisture, it has dried to the permanent wilting point. Obviously, sandy soil has far less ability to supply moisture than clay soil.

Daily Moisture Loss in Summer, Willamette Valley *(Inches per day)**

Average Day	0.2
Hot Day	0.25
Very Hot, Breezy Day with Low Humidity	0.3

* This table assumes the sun is shining and the soil is growing a dense leaf canopy.

Amount of Water Needed to Bring 1 Foot of Soil from 70 Percent to Capacity

Soil Type	Irrigation in Inches
Sandy	¼ (0.25)
Medium (loam)	½ (0.50)
Clayey	¾ (0.75)

How much water?

Many vegetables grow very poorly when soil falls below 60 percent of its peak moisture-holding capacity. So be guided by this principle: *once the top foot of soil has dried to where it holds about 70 percent of its total capacity to hold moisture, it should be brought back to capacity again.*

Sandy soil covered by a dense leaf canopy can lose enough moisture in two sunny summer days to drop 2 feet of topsoil from capacity to 70 percent of capacity. This garden benefits from having yesterday's moisture loss replaced at the beginning of every hot sunny day. A clayey garden loses the same amount of moisture as a sandy garden does each day, but clay could be watered every three or four days and you'd spread three or four times as much water with each irrigation.

When plants are small, their root systems feed in the surface foot. In that case, spread the quantity of water recommended in the table "Amount of Water Needed to Bring 1 Foot of Soil from 70 Percent to Capacity." When the plants are two months old (after one month, if the vegetable makes a taproot), their root systems reach down 2 feet or more. And their tops probably have formed a canopy that transpires a lot of moisture.

Soil moisture should be measured 4 to 6 inches below the surface. Firmly squeeze a handful of soil from that depth into a ball—this is the classic "ready to till" test. If the ball feels wet or gooey, or sticks together solidly, the soil moisture is above 70 percent, unless you have sand that won't form a ball no matter how hard you squeeze. If the soil ball sticks together firmly but breaks apart easily, moisture is 65 to 70 percent. If the soil feels damp but won't form a ball when squeezed hard in the fist, then the soil is below 65 percent moisture.

Cascadian soils receive more moisture than crops transpire from midautumn through midspring. Some of this excess runs off the surface. Some passes through the soil and enters the water table. "Leaching" is another word for this circumstance. The soil dries down during March and April, although clay soils, especially bare clay soils, may not reach 70 percent of capacity until May.

Daily moisture loss varies with the season and with the amount of vegetation the soil supports. The scientific name for this loss is "evapotranspiration," meaning a combination of evaporation from the soil's surface and transpiration from leaves. If a bed is covered by a dense leaf canopy during June, about an inch of water is lost through evapotranspiration each week. During the intense light and heat of July and most of August, average water loss will be around 1½ inches per week. On days that bring a scorching east wind I call a "Umatilla," loss can exceed ⅓ inch each day. By September, losses average around 1 inch per week.

I determine how much to irrigate by assuming the soil is losing as much water every day as the chart says and spread 10 percent more than that amount.

DESIGNING SYSTEMS

Lawn sprinklers spread water thick and fast. This seems convenient. But how uniformly do they spread it? And how long does yours have to run in order to spread a half inch of water? Before you irrigate a veggie garden with a lawn sprinkler, please test its application rate and how uniformly it spreads water. Position a few irrigation-rate measuring gauges—cylinders like empty tin cans or straight-sided drinking glasses—in different parts of the sprinkler's pattern and operate the sprinkler for exactly 30 minutes when the wind is not blowing. Locate one gauge close to the sprinkler, put another a few feet inside the far limit of its throw, and put a couple more in between. After 30 minutes, measure the depth of water

---

THE BOTTOM LINE

Sandy gardens in Oregon should receive half an inch every two days in summer. In periods of extreme heat they should be irrigated every morning. Washington gardens should get about the same amount, but every three days. And Washington gardens almost never have to cope with periods of extremely hot dry winds.

Clayey soils growing large-size vegetables can easily accept 1 to 1½ inches of water. In Oregon this much every five or six days in summer is enough except in very hot weather.

Frequent light irrigation may be needed on all soils when sprouting seed, when nursing recently transplanted seedlings during hot weather, when nursing small seedlings until their roots penetrate far enough to find stable moisture, and for species with unusually high moisture requirements, such as radishes and celery. These extra needs are best supplied with hose and nozzle.

---

in each container, average those amounts, and then multiply the average by two to derive the sprinkler's *average application rate per hour*.

In my experience lawn sprinklers spread water at over 2 inches per hour. Perforated hoses and spot sprinklers designed to cover small areas usually put out an even higher rate. How much leaching do you suppose happens in a sandy garden from running this sort of sprinkler for 1 hour? The tin can test also reveals how uniformly the sprinkler spreads water. Usually, the ones closer to the sprinkler holding a lot more water than those on the fringes.

Agricultural (and institutional) sprinklers spread water more uniformly. They initially cost more, but durability makes them far less expensive in the long haul. I recommend them. Sometimes the local home-improvement store or big-box garden center department sells all-brass impact sprinklers resembling those used by farmers, but usually what's offered to consumers is designed for lawns, not vegetables. I suggest you buy commercial-grade crop sprinklers from a supplier that understands why there are optional nozzle sizes and a range of sprinkler head sizes.

But before buying any sprinkler, discover what your water pressure is because this factor may determine which, if any, sort of sprinkler is possible. Municipal water usually is well over 35 pounds per square inch (psi) at the street, so a pressure reducer can hold household pressure at a steady 35 psi. Homestead well pumps can be adjusted to produce between 30 and 50 psi. You can roughly test water pressure without a formal gauge with a hose nozzle that makes a strong smooth jet. A nozzle like that should throw water 40 to 50 feet if you have over 30 psi.

An ideal agricultural sprinkler for vegetable crops emits between 1 and 3 gallons per minute. My ¼-acre garden is covered by 40 1-gallon-per-minute sprinklers arranged in five lines holding 8 sprinklers each. I have enough water to operate 16 sprinklers at once. To get an idea of the number of gallons per minute your outlet can supply, measure how many seconds it takes to fill a 5-gallon bucket through a full length of garden hose with a nozzle at the end putting out its strongest jet. The nozzle mimics the back pressure from an array of smaller sprinkler nozzles. Before building a system that needs the entire amount, first see what happens if someone takes a shower while the bucket is filling.

Agricultural sprinklers come in a range of sizes. Large crop sprinklers use nozzles that can throw water over 50 feet; some *really* big sprinklers with nozzle openings the size of a 10-gauge shotgun barrel spray a mixture of water and dairy manure over a circle hundreds of feet in radius. Sprinklers most suitable for vegetable crops use nozzles between ⅛ inch and ¹⁄₁₆ inch. At its designed pressure a ¹⁄₁₆-inch nozzle can be expected to throw 25 feet; a ⅛-inch nozzle throws around 35 feet. Small-bore nozzles like this are better in the home garden because (1) they put out fine droplets that cause less soil compaction and (2) a shorter throw radius helps keep the water off adjoining buildings and neighbors' yards. The impact of large droplets breaks up soil crumbs and floats silt and clay particles to the surface, where they dry and form a smooth crust, much the same as screeding concrete lifts the fine sands to form a smooth skin. Crust formation is the last thing you want to cause; it blocks germinating seeds and stops air exchange.

Application rates between ¼ and ½ inch per hour are ideal for most food gardens. But low-application-rate sprinklers have limitations. A combination of sun plus wind plus high temperatures can evaporate much of a fine stream of water before it hits the ground. This means small-bore sprinklers should be run early in the morning on light soils before the sun gets strong and the wind comes up, or else all night on clay. A clay soil could be watered from bedtime to breakfast without leaching the root zone if the application rate is below ⅕ inch per hour. Watering at night is reputed to cause disease. Actually, watering *all night* prevents disease by continuously washing bacteria and fungus spores off the plants before they can germinate. This principle is well understood by nurseries that propagate healthy plants from cuttings by frequently misting them. What *can* harm plants is to turn off the water just before or soon after dark. This makes plants damp all night—ideal conditions for the multiplication of disease organisms.

Spreading water uniformly using only one sprinkler in one fixed position is nearly impossible because to achieve uniformity, the sprinkler must deposit nearly 10 times as much near the far edge of its pattern as in the center. Every point in between must get a different amount. Please *carefully read* the caption below the illustration on the next page.

The oscillating lawn sprinkler *seems* to overcome this problem by watering in rectangles. But this design spreads less uniformly than most circular sprinklers. I suspect the reason is that the

Achieving Uniform Water Application from a Single Sprinkler

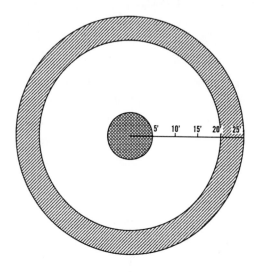

The formula for the area of a circle is: $A = \pi r^2$. Imagine water being spread by a sprinkler with a 25-foot-throw radius. The innermost 5 feet of the sprinkler pattern occupy 78.5 square feet (3.14 by 5 by 5). The area in the outer 5 feet of the pattern is 706.5 square feet, calculated this way: the area of the full circle (3.14 by 25 by 25) minus the area in the inner 20 feet of the pattern (3.14 by 20 by 20). Thus, the nozzle must deposit nearly 10 times as much water on the outermost 5 feet of the pattern to end up with the same thickness of coverage as it spreads on the innermost 5 feet.

cam that pivots the spray arm pauses at the turn-around points, putting too much water at the ends of its rectangular pattern and too little above the sprinkler itself.

The impact sprinkler can't spread water uniformly because when the rocker arm momentarily interrupts the nozzle jet (its bouncing rotates the sprinkler), it creates heavy, slow-moving droplets that fall close to the sprinkler. Most consumer-market impact sprinklers come with a

diffuser paddle or adjustable needle-tipped screw to shorten the water throw by diffusing the spray. But diffusing the stream makes it throw even less water to the fringes. The more diffusion, the worse this effect becomes. Agricultural-quality impulse sprinklers do not have diffusing devices; they come with precision nozzles that, if operated within the designed pressure range, achieve the best-possible compromise, putting only about twice as much water near the center of their coverage as on the outer half.

Farmers obtain fairly uniform distribution by positioning impact sprinklers in overlapping patterns. Any multiple sprinkler pattern still leaves a fringe area where fewer overlaps occur. On the farm, throwing some water beyond the margins of the field is of little consequence; in the backyard, it may be essential to keep all spray within your own yard or off your own buildings.

Fringe areas can be used for dry gardening. Or you can position a tall growing crop like climbing beans, asparagus, or sunflowers along the garden's edge to intercept the overspray.

Sometimes sprinklers are arranged in a square pattern, sometimes in a hexagonal pattern. The hex arrangement distributes water slightly more uniformly, but the square pattern works slightly better when the garden is close to buildings or where the sprinklers could throw water on the neighbor's property.

For the home garden the most useful, highly durable, and least costly ag-quality impulse sprinklers I know of (and personally use) are Israeli-made Naan 501s with ¹⁄₁₆ or ⁵⁄₆₄ nozzles (1.7 to 2.0 millimeters). Naans should be widely available through irrigation and farm suppliers

Comparison of High- versus Low-Application-Rate Sprinklers

Note: *There are intermediate nozzle sizes not listed in this table, such as ⅛ inch, etc.*

Nozzle Size (in Inches)	Operating Pressure (PSI)	Discharge GPM*	Radius (in Feet)	Spacing (in Feet)	Application (in Inches per Hour)
$\frac{1}{16}$	30	0.45	33	20 x 20	0.11
$\frac{1}{16}$	60	0.79	36	20 x 20	0.29
$\frac{7}{64}$	30	1.94	36	20 x 20	0.47
$\frac{7}{64}$	60	2.66	40	20 x 20	0.64
$\frac{13}{64}$	30	6.78	40	25 x 25	1.05
$\frac{13}{64}$	60	9.53	45	25 x 25	1.46
$\frac{5}{16}$	30	17.7	59	40 x 60	0.71
$\frac{5}{16}$	60	25.7	75	40 x 60	1.03

*GPM = *gallons per minute*

but are not at present. A good online source is www.growerssolution.com, offering both 501s and 502s (see below).

A sprinkler designed to throw water the maximum-possible distance has its nozzle angled about 12 degrees above horizontal. This "high-angle" design covers the largest-possible area with the fewest sprinkler heads while drawing the least number of gallons per minute. However, high-angle water streams are strongly affected by wind. High-angle sprinklers with ⅛-inch nozzles create application rates so low they allow watering a clay soil all night and half the next morning. Low-angle sprinklers throw a stream that is only a few degrees above horizontal. These are best for windier situations and for daytime use. However, their throw radius is shorter, so more low-angle sprinklers are required.

Naan 501 series sprinklers have low-angle nozzles. They are durable! My current set has been exposed to year-round sun and weather for 15 years now, and every one of them is still operating. Naan sprinklers are rotated by a brilliantly simple design that does not require close tolerances. There are only a few moving parts and no springs; Naans are quick to disassemble and clean if the nozzle becomes blocked. To disassemble a Naan, wiggle and lift the top cover to detach it from the two posts that hold it, remove the spinning wheel, pry up the nozzle using a flathead screwdriver or the back of a small peeling knife, remove the blockage, and then reassemble.

Sprinkler heads require a support stand and water supply that usually cost more than the sprinklers themselves. Conveniently, the Naan 501-U plus stand assembly includes a yard-long galvanized steel rod that supports the sprinkler head above most vegetable crops and a corresponding length of feeder pipe with a 7-millimeter quick-disconnect barbed fitting at

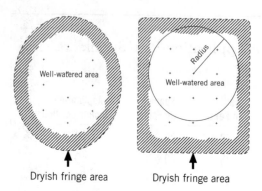

Well-watered area

Radius

Well-watered area

Dryish fringe area　　　Dryish fringe area

Using several correctly spaced sprinklers creates overlapping water patterns, permitting uniform coverage. The optimal spacing between sprinklers is about 60 to 70 percent of the sprinkler's throw radius. Left: sprinklers arranged in triangular patterns. Right: sprinklers arranged in square patterns.

the end—ready to plug and play. Naan also makes the 502 series, small-bore high-angle sprinklers that use the same stand/support assembly. If I were market gardening a half acre or more, I'd use the 502.

> Holes in supply lines for barbed connectors should be made with a proper punch so that the barb doesn't leak. Barbed connectors set with a nail almost inevitably leak.

Some gardeners avoid spreading water outside the garden by using part-circle impact sprinklers. Keep in mind that reducing an impact sprinkler's coverage to a half circle doubles its rate of application; cutting it to a quarter circle quadruples the rate of application. Impact sprinklers spread water even less uniformly when running in part-circle mode because while the head is reversing, the rocker arm's action deposits even more water close to the sprinkler. Part-circle sprinklers come with

other downsides. Actuating the reversing mechanism requires considerable force; this means they must use a large-bore nozzle that makes higher application rates and bigger droplets.

A simple way to restrict an ordinary full-circle impact sprinkler is to attach a shield made from a cutout tin can or a small plastic bucket to a garden stake pounded in directly behind it. This method does not increase the application rate (except immediately below the sprinkler), nor does it lessen uniformity of distribution.

Turbine-powered sprinklers are an enormous improvement over the impact design. The nozzle is rotated by a propeller spun by the water passing through. Multiple water streams emerge from a slowly rotating disk. One or two of these jets throw an undiffused stream that covers the outmost parts of the circle; others spread water close in. Some nozzle openings greatly diffuse the spray; others make a rather clean stream. The original was made by Toro. Now other manufacturers are in the business. I think the best design is the MP Rotator made by Nelson. It is not expensive, allows handy adjustment of the throw angle (distance), and can restrict the amount of arc covered without increasing the precipitation rate. (www.nelsonirrigation.com).

Agricultural sprinklers are designed to operate within a specific range of water pressures. Farmers understand that if pressure is too low to diffuse the spray properly, far too much water is thrown to the outer few feet of the pattern. The impulse arm's action still causes much water to be laid down near the sprinkler. Too little water goes into the midzone. The resulting distribution pattern is termed "doughnuting."

Consider the opposite. Operated at excessively high pressure, the water jet becomes too turbulent and breaks up too much—"sprays too much," as a farmer would say—actually reducing the throw distance while greatly increasing the amount laid down close to the sprinkler, making the fringes too dry.

Nozzles can be designed to diffuse properly at pressures ranging from 10 psi (for mini-sprinklers) to 100 psi most designs require from 30 to 60 psi. Homesteaders having their own well and pump can, within limits, adjust their water pressure. Naan 501s, for example, operate effectively from 20 to 50 psi. Under 20 psi they don't diffuse enough; over 50 psi they diffuse too much and operate so violently you might eventually wear them out.

High-angle sprinklers should be spaced no further apart than 65 percent of their throw radius. This creates enough overlap to equalize distribution and allows for (light) wind blowing the spray. Low-angle sprinklers are usually spaced at 75 percent of their throw radius.

The cost of supporting the sprinklers and of bringing water to them can much exceed the cost of the sprinklers themselves. Inexpensive sprinkler supports that can supply low gallonage heads can be made by gluing a plastic micro-sprinkler spike into the end of a piece of ¾-inch white plastic pipe that has its bottom end cut off at a sharp angle so that it can more easily be pushed into soft soil. The white plastic pipe carries no water.

If a permanent sprinkler system that covers the entire garden is beyond your interest or budget, uniform, precise irrigation can still be accomplished with a single impulse sprinkler

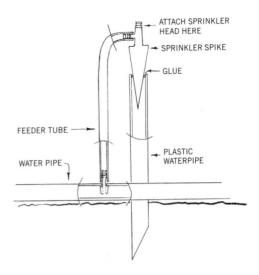

on a homemade stand tall enough to position the sprinkler above most crops, supplied by an ordinary hose. It is run for the same amount of time in each of the positions you'd have put a dozen sprinklers. I watered my trials ground this way for the first few years. I made the stand with

one sack of ready-mix concrete, a 5-gallon white plastic bucket, a few feet of ½-inch galvanized pipe, and some fittings.

DRIP

Drip systems are the last method I'd ever choose for vegetables. For six years I had to supply my household and irrigate a ¾-acre trials ground and a 5,000-square-foot kitchen garden from a 3-gallon-per-minute well. Three gallons per minute can't supply even one sprinkler nozzle large enough to be effective when the sun is strong or the wind is blowing. So as soon as I could afford to, I switched to drip tapes, lightweight plastic hoses with a pinhole every foot. I'll soon tell you more about that disappointing well and the lessons it taught me.

I came to know way too much about drip, and here are the downsides. Drip tapes are expensive even when purchased in 2,500-foot-long spools. They are short lived, but I did not care what a trials ground cost in terms of money, time, or effort—it was producing information that made everyone's garden grow better. Drip tubes are easily cut when hoeing. The emitter holes must face upward or else they rapidly become plugged with soil, but the tape moves with changes in temperature. To keep the water on narrow rows of young seedlings, the tubes have to be pinned firmly to the earth every few feet; and even so, it is not possible to germinate seeds or make sure every newly transplanted seedling gets watered when the drip line lengthens and shortens, twists and lifts as the temperature changes. Even though the water supply first went through a filter, every emitter hole on every line still had to be checked each and every time a line was turned on. Because the runs were over 100 feet long and went down a slope, I had to use "biwall" drip tubes. This design equalizes the pressure from end to end because there is

an inner, larger pipe with internal openings into 10-foot-long sections where the emitter holes are. With biwall pipe, when an entire 10-foot section stopped emitting, it could not be fixed.

Drip tapes, individual drip emitters, or soaker hoses do not suit sand because the water goes straight down without wicking out horizontally, leaving areas of totally dry soil. If the soil contains a fair amount of clay, water wicks out horizontally as much as 2 feet to either side of the drip line. Drip lines might be useful for permanent plantings such as raspberries, but given a choice, I'd choose sprinklers.

Microirrigation is a hybrid between drippers and crop sprinklers, using low-pressure black plastic pipes, quick-connect fittings, and cheap plastic spike stands holding miniature ultrashort-radius sprinkler heads with emission rates of a few gallons per hour, not per minute. Microirrigation provides an inexpensive alternative for establishing high-density orchards and vineyards, and for narrow ornamental beds around houses. I have used them in tunnel cloches. Microirrigation parts often are bubble packed in garden centers, but you'll find a broader range at urban irrigation suppliers. If you're considering microirrigation, don't assume the rate of application is low. Each sprinkler may not emit much water, but the nozzle doesn't throw far. And use a very effective particle filter! The nozzles are extremely fine.

Gardening without (as Much) Watering

Irrigation makes a huge difference. Some kinds of vegetables absolutely require irrigation. Irrigation hugely increases yield and usually increases quality. Irrigation always makes the outcome more certain.

But in case the need arises, I reckon you might like to know how to grow a garden without much or any irrigation. Understanding dry gardening also clarifies plant spacing. Even if you have abundant water, the information in this section can save you work and trouble.

HOW I GOT INTERESTED IN DRY GARDENING

In early May of 1978, when I was 36, I had just settled on a 5-acre Oregon Coast Range homestead. We'd come there by way of Los Angeles, where, like the biblical Jacob, I had spent the previous seven years earning the wherewithal. In early May the Lorane valley is covered with green grass punctuated by liquid sunshine and rainbows. New to Cascadia, I thought summer would be like that too.

Homesteading. I intended to grow as much of my own food as possible, raise a legal crop to pay the bills, live simply so as to need little cash. Because I had horticultural ambitions, my offer to purchase was subject to drilling a well delivering at least 15 gallons per minute (gpm). With that much water I could irrigate one acre. The fourth (and what I vowed would be the last since I was paying the bill) drilling attempt brought forth slightly more than 15 gpm, and I bought the place. The wells were drilled in April.

My 5 acres had been part of an exhausted pasture that no longer produced enough grass to profitably mow and bale, an east-facing hillside that before growing hay and fattening calves had lost all of its topsoil from a half century producing plowed crops. I rocked the driveway, put in a septic system and a power pole, and hauled in a new single-wide mobile home—not the dream house we'd wanted, but it was instant shelter that I could pay for without debt. I immediately built a tool/firewood shed with space for a workbench. We were free and clear with enough left in the bank to live frugally for 2 years if nothing went wrong.

To establish a food garden, I spread a few trailer loads of sawdusty horse manure and a few sacks of lime and cottonseed meal on the silty clay subsoil, and hired a neighbor who did custom tilling; then I erected a deer fence around the roughly 5,000-square-foot area and assembled an excessively permanent irrigation system using 10 small brass impulse sprinklers that emitted 1 gallon per minute each. All 10 sprinklers were turned on and off with one big gate valve. I used galvanized pipes for supply lines and risers, because I knew I was going to be there for the rest of my life. Wasn't I a clever young man! Unfortunately, every time I've *known* that something would be so for the rest of my life, I've been painfully wrong.

Summer arrived. Those lush green pastures browned off. The days got quite warm. My garden needed irrigating for the first time. So I opened up that big valve and stood outside the gate admiring 10 little impact sprinklers bouncing out crisscrossing streams, *psit, psit, psit*. But after a few minutes the pump shut down. Not yet knowing much about Oregon Coast Range wells, I spent hours repeatedly repriming and restarting the pump only to have it run for three minutes and then quit again. It wasn't a pump issue. The pump wisely turned itself off because taking 10 gallons per minute lowered the static level below the intake point. But I could run seven sprinklers.

Over the next month the well's output steadily decreased. I accordingly reduced the number of sprinkler heads I operated at one time. I was deeply worried. By mid-July the well could only sustain three sprinklers. Fortunately, a bit over 3 gallons per minute was the well's lowest production level. By running three sprinklers all night I could cover the entire garden in three nights.

Two years later that well was also called upon to supply Territorial Seed Company's ½-acre trials ground. Initially, I watered the trials with only one high-angle 2½ gpm impact sprinkler. I remember starting up that sprinkler at about 8:00 p.m., waking up by alarm clock at 2:00 a.m., stumbling down the cold dewy path barefoot, moving the sprinkler to its next regular position, going back to bed, and then shutting the system down at 8:00 a.m. so that the household could have morning showers. This went on four to five nights a week from June through August; on the remaining summer nights the water went to the kitchen garden.

For two years the trials ground depended upon my talent for getting back to sleep with cold feet. No wonder when the business could

afford drip tape, I started using it. With drip I could water the trials in the daytime.

Once I had to replace the pump during high summer. After only a few days without irrigation, my intensive kitchen garden began to complain. The more extensively spaced trials ground grew okay through seven days without water. I was forced to face how dependent my garden was on technology. The experience started me wondering how the original settlers managed. Asking that question led me to discover dry gardening.

Before the intensive system, garden books from east of the Rockies suggested arranging vegetables single file in rows 3 to 4 feet apart. Irrigation was desirable but not absolutely required east of the 98th meridian, a north–south line running through Dallas, Texas. It rained often enough in summer to keep things green, although some years there were rainless periods lasting weeks. Fortunately, drought does not necessarily start after two weeks without rain. John Widtsoe, the agricultural scientist whose wise words begin this chapter, defines drought as beginning when the crop is damaged. The onset of drought has little to do with how much time elapses between rains; it has everything to do with how the grower manages moisture already in the soil.

While investigating, I turned up an old guy growing unirrigated carrots on alluvial sandy loam on the Rogue Valley floor, the hottest, driest part of Cascadia. He sowed carrots in spring while the soil remained moist enough to germinate the seed. He soon thinned the row to 1 foot apart; the rows were 4 feet apart. Despite getting no rain and no irrigation all summer, his carrots grew to enormous sizes and the overall yield per area occupied by the crop was not as low as you might think.

I found hints in a book by Gary Nabhan called *The Desert Smells Like Rain* about Native Americans growing remarkable Arizona desert gardens using moisture left in the soil by a brief period of seasonal rainfall. I knew of native South Americans in the Andean highlands who grew food crops in their cool climate with only 12 inches of annual rainfall. And I discovered John Widtsoe's book, *Dry-Farming* (see Additional Reading, page 339).

My first dry-gardened vegetable happened by accident. I had sold Territorial Seeds; we resettled on 16 acres of Class I silty clay loam near Elkton, Oregon. I had a long list of plant breeding projects in mind, one of them being to develop an open-pollinated late Savoy cabbage out of a commercial hybrid because this kind of cabbage was a family staple food item, while the only remaining open-pollinated variety, Chieftain Savoy, had degenerated into a useless mess. (Incidentally, Chieftain has been restored by Tim Peters and is available again from Adaptive Seeds.)

I knew that irrigating seed crops while they are drying down lowers germination and vigor. So in late winter I dug up six fully headed out hybrid Savoy cabbages and transplanted them beyond the sprinkler system's throw. Big Savoys are usually arranged 24 by 24 to 24 by 30 inches, but for seed making I spaced them 48 by 48 inches because blooming brassicas make huge sprays of flower stalks. I did not intend to water these plants at all because cabbage seed forms during late spring while the soil is naturally moist. The seeds mature as the soil naturally dries down.

Seeds formed as expected. Except that one plant did something slightly unusual for a refined brassica—it started growing a new head among its seedstalks. Amazed, I watched this unwatered cabbage enlarge steadily through the hottest and driest summer I had yet experienced in Oregon. I realized I was being shown something, so I gave the plant absolutely no water, although I did hoe out a few weeds around it after I harvested the seedstalks. At maturity the head weighed seven pounds and was as sweet and tender as any other of its type when given all the water it could have asked for.

Because Nabhan pointed out the extreme plant spacing used by desert gardeners and I knew about dry farming carrots in southern Oregon, that huge unwatered cabbage *spoke!* Next spring I dry gardened a pair of 100-foot-long rows that were 5 feet apart center to center. I tried an assortment of vegetables I hoped could cope. I chose to dry-garden like a playful purist, to use absolutely no water at all, not even to germinate seeds. So I sowed everything before the soil dried out.

I tried kale, late-maturing Savoy cabbage, purple sprouting broccoli, carrots, beets, parsnips, parsley, endive, shelling beans, potatoes, French sorrel, and a couple of corn seeds. I also transplanted one compact bush (determinate) and one sprawling (indeterminate) tomato plant. (Each tomato seedling got a cup of water when I set them out.) Most of these vegetables grew surprisingly well. The plot produced extraordinarily good-tasting tomatoes until the end of summer. Kale, Savoy cabbages, and parsley fed us the following winter. The purple sprouting broccoli looked gnarly at summer's end, but it grew lushly as soon as the rains returned and produced abundantly the next spring.

Almost everything was pleasantly edible. The potatoes yielded less than I'd been used to and had a thicker than usual skin that stored better but also had a richer flavor. I found out later that potatoes grown dry often have more protein compared to those given all the irrigation they can seem to use. Unirrigated tomatoes were numerous, richer tasting, and smaller than usual with thicker skins. The enormous carrots were a bit chewy but tasted fine. The rutabagas grew huge but became inedible by summer's end. I could have eaten them in July.

The following year, I grew a pair of similar gardens. My insurance garden was, as always, thoroughly irrigated and the usual size so that no matter what came of my dry-gardening experiments, we would still have plenty. Another garden of equal size was grown entirely without watering.

By midsummer, some kinds of unirrigated vegetables looked fine, and others seemed severely moisture stressed. I recalled Widtsoe reporting on an 1882 dry-farming experiment where it took 1,100 pounds of water to grow 1 pound of dry plant matter on poor soil, but only 575 pounds of water to produce that same amount of plant matter on fertile land. Wondering if the real cause of what appeared to be severe moisture stress might actually be severe nutrient deficiencies, I tried foliar feeding full-spectrum liquid chemical fertilizer. Within days I could see it helped a lot.

I reasoned that I had fertilized the topsoil, but the topsoil had become too dry to feed the plants. The still-moist subsoil on this never-before-gardened area was infertile; it might take another few years of building topsoil fertility before many plant nutrients leached down that far. So I improvised a subsoil FertiGator. Next to some of the plants (and not others) I placed a 5-gallon white plastic pail with one ¼-inch-diameter hole drilled in its side just above the bottom. The bucket then was filled with liquid fertilizer that slowly emptied out, leaving a small wet spot on the surface. Most of the moisture had gone into the subsoil. I gave the lucky plants another such drink three weeks later.

Unfertigated winter squash vines looked moisture stressed all summer. Each unfertigated hill yielded about 15 pounds of very average-tasting food. When given just two 5-gallon fertigations, the vines extended twice as far and yielded about 60 pounds per hill. And the squash tasted good.

Some plants got fertigated with an equal mixture of liquid seaweed and liquid fish emulsion. Others were fed soluble chemicals.

Both approaches worked, but the chemicals worked better. At that time I thought the reason why was that chemical fertilizers offer far more phosphorus to the plants. Now I understand that fertilizers like Miracle-Gro and Peters are closer to being in balance regarding all 11 major plant nutrients than any honestly labeled combination of fish and kelp could possibly be.

Next year I grew only one garden with irrigated, intermediate, and dry areas. Water-loving species like lettuce, Chinese cabbage, and celery were assigned to an adjoining pair of fully irrigated raised beds 4 feet wide by 100 feet long. These two beds occupied about 15 percent of the garden. The rest was in long rows four feet apart. The two long rows closest to the sprinklers got enough overspray to mean something. The remaining area was either given no water at all, was fertigated, or in a few cases, was foliar fed. Everything worked! Many species grew surprisingly well. At the end of that summer I wrote a little labor of love about these experiments called *Water-Wise Vegetables.*

Dry gardening is possible because the plants draw upon last winter's rainfall stored in the subsoil. Leached Cascadian subsoils are not fertile enough to grow vegetables, but many of them hold a lot of moisture and some allow root penetration. Even if that subsoil is so compact or clayey that roots cannot survive in it, the moisture it contains still rises up slowly and replaces some of the water lost from the topsoil. Fertigation increases subsoil fertility and supplements that moisture. Fertigation enormously increases yield while using very little water.

If you doubt that vegetable crops can produce without watering, please go blackberry picking in August. Go where exhausted fields are fattening feeder calves on protein- and mineral-deficient grass. Notice that blackberries grow much better in some places than in others. Deep, open, moisture-retentive soil can be located immediately; that's where blackberries grow huge and lush. You'll find blackberry vines 7 feet tall covered with big, sweet berries; you'll find a lot more patches only 4 feet tall with smaller berries that may taste okay; you'll find places where stunted canes yield nothing worth picking. These differences are mostly an indication of how much soil moisture is in storage.

Now ask yourself how the forest survives rainless hot summers.

HOW SOIL LOSES MOISTURE

Imagine keeping a Cascadian garden entirely bare all summer by repeatedly hoeing it from March 1 through the end of August. On March 1 we scientifically measure the amount of water being held in a slab of subsoil starting 1 foot below the surface and going down to 2 feet. It'll be at capacity, holding all the moisture it can. Now suppose it proceeds to be a typically hot, entirely rainless summer. On September 1 again we measure the amount of water in that foot-thick subsoil layer. Most people would reason there would be little water found in the soil no matter how deeply we dug.

But that is not at all what happens! The hot sun does dry out the surface, but if we dug down 6 inches, we would encounter slightly damp soil. Go deeper and there will be a lot of moisture.

When topsoil loses moisture, it is slowly replaced by the uplift of subsoil moisture. However, the drier the soil gets, the slower subsoil moisture moves upward. If the top few inches get dry enough, moisture uplift stops almost completely. Frequent weed cultivation makes the surface inch get so dry and loose, it acts like mulch.

I suggest making a quick study of the root system drawings in Weaver's *Root Development of Vegetable Crops* (see Additional Reading, page 339). This free downloadable book makes it instantly apparent that the underground parts of most kinds of vegetables can be more extensive than the top. You'll realize from Weaver's drawings why spacing corn plants on a 4-by-4 foot grid provides each plant with sole access to all the soil its roots can reach. You'll discover which vegetable species make weak root systems. And perhaps you'll see why subsoil moisture can sustain widely separated vegetables through long, hot rainless months.

A field's moisture-supplying ability depends on depth of soil, on the subsoil's clay content, and on how much root penetration that subsoil permits. Theoretical calculations won't help you much; to find out if your site can support dry gardening, you'll have to run a performance test. I can assure you that there's a lot of water in storage if your soil is more than 3 feet deep and the subsoil contains at least 25 percent clay. If it is less than 3 feet to bedrock, or if it is sand, you can still use dry-gardening techniques to reduce the frequency of irrigation.

In the best of circumstances the upward movement of subsoil moisture will not fully support high-density crops. I suppose that's why intensive gardening and industrial vegetable production completely ignore the possibility. However, when given sufficient uncontested growing room, plants can forage enough moisture to support themselves through long rainless periods, even for months. If you can irrigate a dry garden, once every three or four weeks spread enough water to recharge the subsoil 3 or even 4 feet deep. Then the soil supplies the plants better for a long time.

> Modern vegetable varieties have been bred to make big yields from high-density irrigated plantings. Genuine heirlooms and some commercial varieties in use before 1970 direct more of their energy budget toward root formation. These varieties usually grow for more time before maturity and should be provided with more room to do that. Chapter 9 provides what little I know about specific varieties.

LOW PLANT DENSITY ALLOWS DRY GARDENING

The amount of water a crop transpires is determined by the nature and density of the leaf cover, amplified by wind and sun. In these respects, the crop functions like an automobile radiator. With radiators, the larger the metal surfaces, the colder the air, and the higher the wind speed passing over the cooling fins, the better the radiator works. In the garden, the more leaf surfaces; the faster, warmer, and drier the wind and the brighter the sunlight, the more water is transpired. Where there are no plants growing and a dust mulch has been created, little subsoil water will be lost. If a thick leaf canopy develops in summer, the rate of water loss will approximate what I recommend be added through normal summertime irrigation.

On sandy soil a crop with a full leaf canopy can experience moisture stress the day after being irrigated if it has been hot, sunny, and breezy and the humidity has been low. On a clay soil that same crop could comfortably grow through four or more days of such heat. But if those plants were given more growing space, they might grow entirely unstressed for an entire week without irrigation. And if that crop was separated enough that no leaf canopy developed, such that a considerable amount of bare, dry, dust-mulched earth were showing, this apparent waste of growing space would result in an even slower rate of soil-moisture depletion. This is dry gardening in a nutshell. And this is how to garden without having to irrigate so frequently in the same nutshell.

VEGETABLES THAT MUST BE IRRIGATED

Bulbing onions *(for August/September harvest)*

Cauliflower *(except overwintering varieties)*

Celeriac

Celery

Chinese cabbage

Lettuce *(for summer harvest)*

Winter radishes *(spring radishes grow on rainfall)*

Scallions *(for summer harvest)*

Spinach *(spring-sown varieties do okay without irrigation)*

CAN YOU DRY GARDEN?

Absolute dry gardening requires very deep, open, moisture-retentive soil, and most people don't have that. But anyone who stands atop more than 2 feet of soil can irrigate less frequently by lowering plant density.

Suppose you have a 100-square-foot bed. You could raise quite a bit of lettuce on that bed by irrigating frequently. Or bravely put only four indeterminate tomato seedlings in that space. I assure you, given adequate soil fertility and a bit of fertigation, four tomato seedlings *will* thickly cover that space by mid-August. A tomato plant given 33 square feet of competition-free growing room might survive the summer without fertigation while still making a useful yield. But if you could provide each vine with 5 gallons of fertigation every two to three weeks from mid-July through August, you would harvest five times as much.

I suggest digging a 3-foot-deep hole in your garden. Evaluate what you find against the table in the first part of this chapter, "Available Moisture (Inches of Water per Foot of Soil)." If you discover a plow pan, it should be broken up by deeply digging the entire garden. Otherwise, your plants will be forced to form roots in the topsoil only. If there is airless clay beneath a shovel's depth of topsoil, I can't advise you for sure. This might prove to be a great site for dry gardening. Then again, it might not. To find out for sure, conduct a trial.

Plant Spacing Possibilities in Relation to Irrigation (in Inches)

Some of the numbers in this table are the result of personal experience. And some of them are logical projections from that experience. Please use this chart as a rough guide for your imagination.

Potential rooting depth	1 foot	2 feet	3–4 feet	4–6 feet	6–10 feet
Frequency of irrigation	2–3 times/week	5–7 days	2 weeks	3–4 weeks	8–12 weeks
Broad beans, autumn sown	8 x 18	8 x 24	12 x 30	12 x 30	12 x 30
Beans, bush or snap	6 x 18	8 x 24	12 x 36	16 x 48	18 x 48
Beet	3 x 18	4 x 18	4 x 24	6 x 30	12 x 48
Cabbage, autumn/winter	24 x 24	24 x 30	30 x 36	36 x 48	36 x 48
Carrots	2 x 18	2 x 18	2–3 x 24	4 x 36	12 x 48
Cauliflower, autumn	24 x 24	24 x 30	30 x 36	36 x 42	don't know
Corn	8 x 36	8 x 36	10 x 42	24 x 48	48 x 48
Cucumbers	36 x 48	42 x 48	48 x 48	60 x 60	60 x 60
Endive (chicories)	12 x 18	12 x 18	18 x 24	24 x 36	24 x 48
Kale	18 x 24	24 x 24	30 x 30	36 x 48	60 x 60
Parsley	6 x 18	6 x 18	6 x 24	8 x 30	12 x 36
Parsnips	not possible	4 x 18	6 x 18	6 x 24	inedible
Peppers	18 x 24	24 x 24	30 x 36	36 x 48	36 x 48
Potatoes	12 x 42	12 x 42	15 x 48	18 x 48	20 x 60
Rutabagas	6 x 24	8 x 24	12 x 30	18 x 36	18 x 48
Squash, bush (zucchini)	30 x 36	36 x 42	42 x 48	48 x 72	60 x 72
Swiss chard	12 x 18	12 x 24	16 x 30	18 x 36	24 x 48
Tomatoes, indeterminate	24 x 36	36 x 48	48 x 48	60 x 60	72 x 72

Chapter Six

SEEDS

Caveat emptor.
[Let the buyer beware.]

You can sell the gardener the sweepings off the seed-room floor.

—An agribusiness suit telling me why I should repackage my company's cheap home-garden seed, 1979

I'D PREFER not to, but I could work garden soil with a digging stick and my fingers. I could grow a productive veggie garden without convenient irrigation. I know how to coax nutrient-dense food out of difficult soil. But I can't make up for lousy seed. To grow an abundance of great-tasting food, I require seed that comes up, grows strongly from the start, and then yields something delicious.

For some crops the planting period is only a few weeks long. If two weeks pass before I realize the seed I just planted is not going to come up, at worst there goes our chance for the year. At best, there's time to sow again, but likely because of the late start, the yield gets reduced. The very worst disappointment of all comes from a mislabeled seed packet that grows okay, resembles a familiar food crop when small, but ends up producing something that would only interest livestock.

The Garden Seed Trade

Garden seed merchants differ in responsibility and ethics. At the low end of the scale are vendors who buy their seeds from primary growers specializing in producing the cheapest-possible stuff. At the other end of the spectrum are people with a deeply felt commitment to providing effective seeds; their main concern is the customer's success. Regardless of their position on a scale of ethical behavior, almost all seed merchants repackage seeds bought from large producers known in the trade as primary growers.

Primary vegetable seed growers do international business mostly through a network of distributors, rarely direct to the farmer. Their names are unknown to gardeners and they prefer it that way. The largest primary growers are headquartered in Holland, Japan, and the United States, with others domiciled in the United Kingdom, France, and Taiwan. Most serve the garden trade only incidentally. A few primary growers specialize in supplying cheap garden seed to catalog and seed rack merchants.

Farmers are knowledgeable, demanding, repeat customers. If a seed purchase didn't germinate well or failed to grow properly, the farmer loses and their neighbors hear about it. Farmers and market gardeners who remain in business buy what the trade calls "commercial-quality" seed, which means it comes up strong and will produce as described if nothing wrecks the crop. In contrast, home gardeners are uncertain customers who blame disappointments on weather, the phase of the moon, or their own lack of ability.

Most gardeners will accept degenerated varieties, leftovers, low-germination seeds, and suspect lots (that started out with good intentions but ended up producing numerous off-types)—stuff that a frank seed-biz senior manager once described to me as "the sweepings off the seed-room floor." If gardeners do blame the seed, we merely grizzle to ourselves. We haven't lost enough to sue. We almost never demand a refund. Such pushovers!

The garden seed supplier offering only open-pollinated varieties may honestly provide homestead grown. Their customers know in advance this seed was raised by a network of well-intentioned amateurs who often see their own opinions about "heirloom" or "open pollinated" rather than what's actually growing in front of their eyes. But when a slick catalog self-righteously praises open-pollinated varieties with old, familiar names, and especially if the company wraps itself in the patriotic flag if antihybrid, anti-GM propaganda, you might be offered stuff actually produced by a primary grower specializing in cheap garden seed.

Sometimes low-end seed can be useful. Assuming germination is adequate and the variety is generally suited to Cascadian conditions, then seeing variations in the leaf shape or height of kale plants, or the stalk width or color of chard, or scallions with slightly bulbous bottoms may not matter all that much to a gardener. On the other hand, how about having an entire patch of iceberg lettuce go to seed before heading up? Or seeing the sweet, mild tender scallions you thought you were growing turn out to be fibrous and pungent. With refined vegetables like salad radishes, munching carrots, bulbing onions, heading lettuce, brussels sprouts, cabbage, broccoli, or cauliflower, plants that vary too much from the ideal usually produce little or no desirable food. I never start refined vegetables with cheap seed.

I've trialed shoddy salad radish varieties that yielded at best, two or three true-to-type roots per 10 plants. One seed packet produces skin colors varying from pale pink to mottled crimson. Many of the radishes have thick, roughened skins, coarse or multiple taproots, and huge crowns. Many plants fail to make a bulb. Sometimes the first radish in the row tastes okay, and the next one fries the taste buds. Gardeners using seed like this soon opine radishes won't grow for them. In contrast, commercial-quality open-pollinated radish seed yields seven decent radishes and a couple of rougher but usually acceptable ones (to the home gardener) for every 10 plants. These days the commercial trade uses extra-fancy hybrids sold by the thousand seeds, not by weight. Varieties like this are worth the asking price, because if they are given good growing conditions, almost every seed sprouts and makes a perfect radish.

Please do not choose cheap seed if you are short of money. It will prove far less costly to invest a few more dollars. As of the date of this book's publication, R. H. Shumway's sells an ounce (about 3,500 seeds) of home-garden-quality, open-pollinated radish they call "Early Scarlet Globe" for a very low price. Stokes Seeds sells an ounce of commercial-quality, open-pollinated (OP) radish seeds for half again more, while a packet holding 5,000 of their most expensive hybrid radish seeds sells for slightly

more than double Shumway's price. But most Stokes OP seeds can make a decent radish, and almost every hybrid seed can make a perfect or near-perfect one. And with decent storage that packet can be counted on to germinate well for more than 5 years. With excellent storage maybe 10 years.

An ethical home-garden seed merchant does not uncritically accept what the primary grower's salesperson or catalog says about a variety, nor choose to sell varieties according to trade gossip or the reports of research institutions trialing varieties for use in industrial agriculture. They choose what to sell after evaluating their own variety trials. Doing trials means the varieties offered suit the climate where the merchant's trials ground is. The trials may be done organically to better match home-garden conditions. A garden seed merchant with enough commitment to do trials also maintains effective germination standards. From that kind of company you can expect excellent seeds from more than 9 packets out of 10.

PICTURE-PACKET SEED RACKS

Picture-packet seed racks are found at supermarkets, garden centers, hardware stores, and national discount store chains. The larger displays offer a wide choice. The photos are gorgeous. They're widely available, so gardeners assume picture-packet seeds must be okay.

But they often aren't. Picture-packet companies distribute as broadly as possible, so every variety offered in Cascadia may not suit Cascadia's climate. Rack jobbers must feel that high overheads force them into cutting every possible corner. After giving half of the gross proceeds to the store, they still must cover the cost of large numbers of unsold dated packets that must be discarded before next spring. Rack jobbers also suffer credit losses.

Covering all those costs requires a very high gross profit margin. Consequently, most picture packets are filled with the most inexpensive seed obtainable. Selling cheap seed remains profitable because uncritical home gardeners rarely realize why 25 percent of their cabbages have volcanic holes running down the center of the head, or why a third (or all) of their Green or Purple Vienna kohlrabi aren't round as illustrated on the packet but taper to a point like a Cambodian temple. Inexperienced gardeners think kohlrabi is supposed to get woody rapidly when the main thrust of breeding work on commercial-quality kohlrabi varieties has been to delay that from happening. They rarely wonder why the coarsely budded foul-flavored side shoots on their De Cicco, Waltham 29, or Italian Green Sprouting (Calabrese) broccoli are often larger than the pathetic main head when the photograph on the picture packet shows the glorious head that variety used to produce before it was replaced by hybrids. When chard goes to seed a few months after sowing . . . it's cheap seed; it is not your fault. But gardeners usually blame their own fertilizing, or their watering, or the weather that season.

CATALOG SALES

Buying garden seed through the Internet or a printed catalog doesn't guarantee getting productive, strongly germinating varieties. A formal garden-seed trade survey I made in the early 1990s for *Harrowsmith* magazine showed the majority of catalog sellers did not conduct significant variety trials. Or perform grow-outs. Or even routinely germ (germination) test the older seed in their warehouse. I have no reason to believe it's any different 25 years later. Here is my short list of ethical seed suppliers whose offerings are especially relevant to a Cascadian garden.

Adaptive Seeds: Collecting rare and endangered vegetable, grain, and bean varieties from around the world and producing high-quality seeds, Andrew Still and Sarah Kleeger responsibly steward this Willamette Valley homestead business and deserve a Very Well Done! Their priorities are new Cascadian-bred open-pollinated varieties and regional heirlooms, winter garden varieties, early maturing varieties adapted to Cascadian latitudes, and quality open-pollinated varieties for commercial growers. Beans of all types are a special focus, and they have a good selection of grain seed as well as uncommon varieties of familiar vegetables. In recent years I included Adaptive's varieties in trials I continue to do; all germinated well and were useful. *Contact Adaptive Seeds, 25079 Brush Creek Road, Sweet Home, OR 97386 or via www.adaptiveseeds.com.*

Johnny's Selected Seeds: In the early 1970s founder Robert Johnston Jr. set out to supply high-quality seeds to gardeners and homesteaders in the northernmost tier of states and southern Canada. Rob's vision has not been diluted, even though Johnny's business has increased enormously. The company is now employee owned. Their catalog offers the same great seed in tiny trial packets or farmer-size amounts. The company breeds some varieties and produces its own seed for these. Johnny's runs acres of trials, and last I heard Rob is still actively involved. Keep in mind Maine summers are warmer than Oregon's, so Johnny's heat-loving varieties take longer to ripen in Cascadia than the catalog says. Winter in Maine means frozen soil, so Johnny's autumn varieties often mature quickly; some can't grow through Cascadia's winter, although some do. Johnny's maintains commercial germination standards. *Contact Johnny's Selected Seeds, 13 Main Street, Fairfield, ME 04901 or via www.johnnyseeds.com.*

Osborne Seed: Operating at Mount Vernon, Washington, for 30 years, they offer an impressive range to Northwest vegetable farmers and market gardeners and will accept home gardeners' orders. Osborne conducts variety trials in several locations on both sides of the Cascades and publishes trial results in an informative online blog. Their smallest packet suits a serious gardener who understands how to store seeds. Osborne's offering of winter and overwintering varieties is broad and useful. *Contact Osborne Seed, 2428 Old Highway 99 South Road, Mount Vernon, WA 98273 or via www.osborneseed.com.*

Stokes Seeds: Before I started Territorial, I bought most of my seed from Stokes. Located near Saint Catharines, Ontario, Stokes runs a very large trial ground. The company supplies the same high-quality seed to gardeners and large vegetable growers in southern Canada and the northern United States. Most of Stokes's varieties are of commercial quality; the catalog makes it obvious, at least to me, the few that are not. I've never been disappointed by Stokes. Americans: Stokes maintains a US warehouse to avoid customs hassles. *Contact Stokes Seeds Inc., PO Box 548, Buffalo, NY 14240. Canadians: Box 10, Thorold, Ontario L2V 5E9 or via www.stokeseeds.com.*

Territorial Seed Company: I started Territorial. I intended my business to serve Cascadia like Johnny's serves the short-season north. In 1985 I sold Territorial to Tom and Julie Johns. Just as it was when I owned the business, Territorial's bulk seed is stored in a climate-controlled room and is germ tested twice a year. Territorial runs large variety trials evaluated primarily on the potential for success in the home garden. These days, Territorial sells a great deal of seed to people living east of the Cascades; from my founder's perspective, pursuing this possibility has diluted the business's original focus but has not lowered its quality standards. Territorial is the primary grower of some locally renowned or especially well-adapted noncommercial varieties. Tom Johns has evolved to embrace biodynamic agriculture, and their trials ground and seed productions are moving toward formal certification. Territorial has (non-picture-packet) seed racks at locations throughout the maritime Northwest and a few in Alaska. *Contact Territorial Seed Company, PO Box 158, Cottage Grove, OR 97424 or via www.territorial-seed.com.*

Thompson & Morgan: A major English garden-seed seller, their US arm is primarily focused on ornamentals, but they still offer a decent veggie selection, including British specialties like sea kale. *Contact Thompson & Morgan Seedsmen Inc., PO Box 397, Aurora, IN 47001 or via www.tmseeds.com. Canadians are still able to import seeds from England and may find T&M's much broader UK online catalog of more interest. Canadians would do better to check out Tuckers Seeds in the UK; I buy from them.*

Uprising Seeds: Brian Campbell and Chrystine Goldberg started about a decade ago near Bellingham, Washington. I don't know much about them yet, but their catalog looks very promising. Their trials ground focuses on open-pollinated varieties. They reference the producer of each seed they offer if they have not grown it themselves. This is not the other Uprising Seed Company, which sells cannabis seed. *Contact via www.uprisingorganics.com.*

West Coast Seeds: A year after I started Territorial Seeds, a Vancouverite, Mary Ballon, came up my driveway to demand a seed rack for her garden store. Mary brushed aside my initial objections and every cross-border obstacle that Agriculture and Agri-Food Canada imposed. Then she started placing other Territorial Seed racks in southwestern British Columbia. This subsidiary arrangement went on for some years after Tom and Julie Johns took over Territorial; then Mary struck out on her own as West Coast Seeds and modeled it after Territorial, big trials ground and all. A few years ago Mary sold West Coast and retired. The new owners continue to run a serious variety trials grounds and offer excellent winter varieties. West Coast Seeds ships seeds to the United States but cannot send anything that has been in contact with soil, like garlic or seed potatoes. *Contact West Coast Seeds, 3925 64th Street, Delta, BC V4K 3N2 Canada or via www.westcoastseeds.com.*

OTHER CATALOG SEED COMPANIES

The Cook's Garden: Unusual varieties of gourmet interest, especially salads. *Contact The Cook's Garden, PO Box C5030, Warminster, PA 18974 or via www.cooksgarden.com.*

Fedco Seeds: Started in 1978, it soon became a co-op/membership amalgam that evolved into providing seeds, fruit trees, and more than 40 types of potatoes, garlic, and more, as well as a wide range of gardening and farm supplies. Their catalog descriptions are down-home and informative. They sell modern open-pollinated varieties, reselected heirlooms, original heirlooms, and approximately 150 hybrid varieties out of 1,050 offerings. Fedco sources about one-third of their seed from their network of small seed farmers. *Contact Fedco Seeds, PO Box 520, Waterville, ME 04903 or via www.fedcoseeds.com.*

Nichols Garden Nursery: Known regionally for their plant starts, Nichols also has a full range of thoughtfully chosen vegetable seeds featuring varieties from university breeding programs as well as garden classics and uncommon species. Nichols sells Oregon Homestead, Carol Deppe's version of Sweet Meat squash, and the similar but smaller variety, Katy's Sweet, as well as varieties from the Kapuler family breeding projects (next, below). *Contact Nichols Garden Nursery, 1190 Old Salem Road NE, Albany, OR 97321 or via www.nicholsgardennursery.com.*

Peace Seeds: Peace seeds arose from the fertile mind of Alan Kapuler, PhD (Harvard, 1960s, molecular biology). The catalog offers about 150 remarkable varieties, one-third of them bred and produced by Dr. Kapuler. There are food plant species from South America and beyond, all with potential for Cascadia. All seeds are certified organic. *Contact Peace Seeds, 2385 SE Thompson Street, Corvallis, OR 97333 or via peaceseedslive.blogspot.com.*

Richters Herbs: No one compares to Richters when it comes to herb seeds. No one. *Contact Richters Herbs, 357 Highway 47, Goodwood, Ontario L0C 1A0, Canada or via www.richters.com.*

Vesey's Seeds, Ltd.: Vesey's mainly sells the highest-quality European varieties and has conducted trials on its 5-acre trials ground for 60-odd years. Prince Edward Island can count on cool summers, so Vesey's summertime varieties perform well in Cascadia. Vesey's happily supplies customers in the United States. *Contact Vesey's Seeds Ltd., 411 York Road, York, Prince Edward Island, PE C0A 1P0, Canada or via www.veseys.com.*

Log House Plants: Log House deserves recognition for its 30-plus years of supplying well-grown transplants of regionally appropriate varieties. Log House was the first grower to introduce grafted tomatoes, eggplants, and peppers in the United States. *Log House Plants is a wholesale nursery in Cottage Grove, Oregon, but you can check their website for the nearest retailer: www.loghouseplants.com.*

Getting the Most Out of Seed

I learned a lot from Territorial's germination lab about making seeds come up in the garden. Laboratory germination tests are done under ideal conditions for each particular species. A certified lab uses a climate-controlled cabinet that provides the ideal temperature (or daily range of temperatures that imitate the daily day/night cycle) and light (or not) as needed. Whatever medium the seeds are germinated in (or on) is sterile and kept at ideal moisture at all times.

MOISTURE, BUT NOT TOO MUCH

Does it surprise you that most kinds of seeds germinate less well in wet soil? That's because irrigation or rain drops soil temperature . . . and the seed needs warmth to sprout rapidly. Cold, wet soil conditions also are ideal for the development of a fungal disease called "damping-off" that attacks seedlings before they emerge and continues to kill seedlings until their stems have formed a toughened skin, a thin bark. You can recognize damping-off when a newly emerged seedling suddenly falls over because a scaly collar that pinches off circulation develops at ground level. Damping-off doesn't thrive in warm soil at only 70 percent of total moisture capacity, but seeds germinate excellently.

Seed testing labs coax the highest-possible percentage of germination from most species by placing seed between or atop sheets of sterile, damp (not soaking wet) blotting paper. The way the lab brings blotting paper to the correct moisture is to immerse it in water and then squeeze out most of the water by wadding the paper up in a tight fist. Try that yourself with a dishrag and see how a damp dishrag feels. That's the ideal moisture content for sprouting most kinds of seeds.

For a few species, like corn, germination lab protocols specify sterile soil as the sprouting media instead of blotter paper. In that case powdered, oven-sterilized, dry loamy soil is slowly moistened until a handful squeezed into a ball will barely stick together and will easily break apart into fine particles. (Note that this technique is also used to determine optimum tilling moisture—70 percent of capacity.) To maintain ideal moisture, germination tests in soil are done in airtight containers.

When I ran Territorial Seed Company's perversely practical germination lab, we used ordinary *unsterilized* garden soil at about 70 percent moisture in seedling trays covered by clear plastic lids. The uncounted seeds (I avoid unnecessary work) were rather thickly sown in furrows across the tray and covered to the usual depth they would be covered in the garden. I was not interested in determining a specific percentage of germination; what I hoped to see was a dozen lines of vigorous seedlings emerge from that tray within a short few days. If a row didn't show good vigor then I might count out 100 seeds and do a sterile test on blotter paper before deciding what to do with that seed lot.

When I first started doing germination tests, the seedling tray was not covered. It had to be remoistened frequently; in this case, the germination percentage results were never half as high. Yes, you have to water sprouting seeds,

sometimes, but there are ways to slow drying out so that you water less often. And there is a best time of day to do this watering. I'll soon explain.

THE SPROUTING MEDIUM

You can't expect the shoot emerging from a tiny celery or cabbage seed to push aside a pebble or a lump of hard earth above it. Maybe a husky bean seedling could overcome those obstacles. Commercial seedling growers use container growing media designed so that small seeds germinate successfully. They are light, friable, and hold a lot of moisture without becoming soggy or airless. Similarly, we gardeners can make seedbeds that are slower to dry out and remain loose long enough to allow emergence.

Tiny seeds must be positioned close to the surface where the soil dries out fast. The appearance of the shoot says the seedling has put down roots where the soil remains moist after one hot day. Before emergence, the gardener must keep the germinating seed moist. But watering the seedbed lowers temperature and can create crusts that block emergence. By remembering that sprouting seeds prefer damp rather than wet soil, we can avoid unnecessary watering on cloudy days. We can irrigate in the morning so that within hours the seedbed warms back up. The worst thing would be to water sprouting seeds so late in the day that the bed can't heat back up until midmorning the next day. If your soil forms crusts or the surface dries out rapidly, try filling the seed furrow with a light, loose, moisture-retentive material. Doing this is not much trouble. Finely sifted compost, or a container medium as recommended in Chapter 7 are suitable.

Most people use rotary tilling or spading to conveniently blend in compost or manure. But I assert that in most soils and circumstances, it is better to rake compost into the surface after digging or tilling in fertilizers. That way the surface inch is converted into a friable germination medium that is much like the potting mix delicate seedlings do best in.

The generally accepted rule for sowing depth is three times the length of the seed's largest dimension. In early to midspring the soil's surface stays constantly damp, so I start very tiny seeds (French sorrel, some herbs) by scratching a shallow furrow (¼ inch deep) and sprinkling them into that furrow *without covering them*. Enough seeds bury themselves between soil crumbs. Light watering with a fine spray will put some of these seeds a bit further under and perhaps wash a bit of soil off the sides of the furrow down over them. I get very good emergence this way as long as I sow early to midspring. I do almost the same with slightly larger celery seeds, but celery must be sown late in spring, so I cover the seeds with sifted compost.

For the usual small seeds like cabbage family, carrot, or lettuce, place them in a furrow or small depression about ½ inch deep and cover; huskier seeds (spinach, radish, beetroot, Chinese cabbage) go in about ¾ inch deep; large seeds (squash, cucumber, melon, beans, corn, peas) I inch deep. Bush beans sown in the heat of midsummer go in 1½ inches deep.

Before sowing, restore capillarity! Gardeners usually dig or rototill before sowing or transplanting. But cultivation temporarily shatters the network of capillary connections that bring up subsurface moisture. (Moisture uplift resumes as the bed resettles.) But have you ever seen this happen? The entire garden is rototilled into a fluffy damp carpet on a sunny late-spring morning the day before it is "put in," but the perfect smoothness is blemished by a few footprints. By late afternoon the loose surface has dried in the sun. Early the next morning the footprints are again moist while the rest of the field remains dry on top. Foot pressure restored capillary uplift. However, the sun again shines on that moist footprint; it soon dries out.

Now imagine what would happen had someone dropped seeds atop that footprint immediately after tilling, and then covered these seeds to the appropriate depth with a mulch of loose fine soil, or with a compost/soil mix that wouldn't crust over. The seeds lie on damp earth, exactly as they rest on damp blotter paper in a germination testing lab. The moisture would be protected by the loose soil mulch. Unless conditions got hot and windy, it would not be necessary to irrigate these seeds for several days, perhaps not irrigate them at all until they emerged. There's no need to pound soil down to restore capillarity; make a fist and gently push it into tilled earth an inch or two. Stop pressing when you feel resistance start to increase. Another way is to irrigate after digging the bed and wait one week before sowing. This gives time for the soil to resettle by itself.

Gardeners have more success with big seeds—beans and peas and corn—because they're planted deeply enough that the soil doesn't dry out so fast. But even for these, it is wise to restore capillarity first. Then you won't have to sow them quite so far down, and they'll emerge faster and at a higher rate. Most gardeners, including me, make furrows in recently dug soil with the corner of a common garden hoe. When sowing in hot weather, a better way to make a furrow is to first rake the bed almost perfectly level and then press the narrow edge of a piece of one-by-two into the soil about a half inch deep or to lay the handle of your hoe across the bed and press it in.

When sowing inexpensive small seed in rows, I often sprinkle it into furrows from which I will ultimately thin out most of the seedlings that do come up. When I start expensive hybrid seeds for larger-size vegetables, I first fertilize and dig/rake the bed. Then I gently compress the planting spots. The purpose is not to make a fist-size hole with rammed earth on the bottom; the goal is to make *firm* soil under a *shallow* depression. Then four or five seeds are carefully counted out and placed on that depression (best in knuckle dimples) and covered to the right depth with fine, humusy earth. Even if several hot, sunny days follow, I usually get good germination without watering more than once.

PROGRESSIVE THINNING

If only one seed is sown for each plant ultimately desired, there will be many large gaps in the row while pests and soil diseases kill a portion of those seedlings that do appear. Better to sow three to five seeds for every plant desired at each position and gradually thin out the extras. When starting small seeds in a regular grid pattern like 18 by 24 inches, sow four to six seeds in a group the size of a 25-cent piece at every position.

When sowing large-size seeds like beans or one of the cucurbits, three seeds per position is usually enough to ensure that two seedlings emerge. Then gradually remove the less desirable seedlings until there remains only one strong plant at each position.

Suppose the growing instructions call for a final spacing of 4 inches between plants in the row. To achieve that, sow one seed per inch and then thin gradually, what I term "progressively." To end up with one plant per inch (salad radishes, for example), sow three seeds per inch. After the row emerges, thin this way: shortly after germination, remove enough seedlings that no one touches another. After growing for a week, they'll probably be touching again, so thin again. Repeat this a few times, and the row will be properly spaced.

TEMPERATURE

A germination cabinet is set to maintain the ideal temperature for the kind of seed being tested. Experienced gardeners sow when soil temperature is in the right range. But they do not need a soil thermometer to find out. They pay attention to nature's soil thermometer—the emergence of bulbs each spring and the procession of blooming fruit trees. When the earliest spring bulbs come up, overwintering alliums also start growing, so it is time to side-dress them; when Asian plums bloom, it is time to sow radish, spinach, and alliums. Apples bloom over several weeks, depending on variety. I have read that when the middle range of apple trees are flowering, it's usually safe to plant out tomatoes. When I lived in frosty Lorane, I learned that most years when the cow parsnips growing by the ditch across the road started blooming, it was safe to plant out tomatoes.

Sowing according to soil temperature works better than doing it by the calendar. Spring's main milestone occurs when the soil temperature measured an inch or so below the surface has reached 50 degrees F, the critical minimum for germinating some cold-tolerant species. When the first daffodils emerge, Cascadian soil will be 40 to 45 degrees F, too chilly for seed to sprout. From that point dark-colored loams warm up a lot faster than moisture-retentive clays do. Southern exposures warm up the most rapidly. Western slopes are warmer than east-facing ones. North-facing slopes make for late gardens.

Soil temperature changes rapidly near the surface. In mid to late February to mid-March the air may be nippy, but when the sun shines strongly, the surface inch of dark-colored soils can exceed 70 degrees F. At night, these same soils drop below 50 degrees F, but will warm back up quickly if the sun comes out. However, if the weather becomes cloudy or worse, rainy, you get a germination failure.

Spring's unstable weather causes germination failures. But not planting early can result in a late harvest, or none at all. That's the eternal dilemma when growing food. If we miss our window of opportunity, there will not be another until next year. And that's one reason knowingly selling weak seeds to gardeners seems a crime. A thinly germinating, weakly growing lot can produce the worst outcome, because we'll keep on hoping those slow-growing seedlings will finally come right. Sometimes they do.

CHITTING

Early sowings made in chilly soil germinate better when you presprout the seeds. British garden books call this practice "chitting." To chit corn, peas, beans, and other large-seeded legumes, first thing in the morning place the seeds in a jar, cover the top with a square of plastic window screen held on with a strong rubber band, and then cover the seeds with tepid water for six to eight hours. Keep the seeds in a warm place in the house. Do not submerge them any longer than eight hours or the awakening embryos may run short of oxygen. Then gently rinse with more tepid water, immediately drain all free water, and position the jar on its side so that the damp seeds get the best-possible air supply. Rinse and drain like this two or three times daily for the next few days. As soon as root tips begin to extend from the seeds, immediately sow them because the fast-emerging roots easily break (that kills the seedling), and worse, will soon tangle inseparably. Gently position sprouting seeds in the furrow without breaking off emerging roots, which kills the seed. You can count on nearly 100 percent germination from large seeds that already were sprouting when put into the soil. Chitting also alerts the gardener should they be about to sow an ineffective seed packet.

Chitting makes germinating small seeds in summer's heat (lettuce, carrot) far more certain. When their roots are just beginning to emerge, the seeds are gently stirred into fine, or sifted, damp compost so that they can be uniformly and gently distributed along the bottom of a furrow and then covered. Presprouted small seeds emerge quickly. You'll also need quite a bit less seed per length of row than you previously thought, you'll get a far higher percentage of emergence far quicker, and you'll save heaps of time thinning.

In the Cucurbits section, page 281, I suggest a slightly different way to chit squash, cucumber, and melon.

QUICKER THINNING

Gardeners, usually unsure about how well a packet is going to perform, sow thickly, and when they end up with too many seedlings, if they have any sense, thin the row promptly however much time that takes. Some try to avoid all this uncertainty, and the thinning, by using transplants. Farmers use costly and complicated seeding machines to avoid wastage and reduce thinning to a minimum. Here's a simple technique that works as well or better than anything farmers have and costs nothing. When growing small-size vegetables in rows, put ¼ or ½ teaspoonful of raw (not chitted) seed into a quart or two of sifted compost or sifted moist soil (at 65 to 70 percent of capacity) and thoroughly blend the seed in. Then distribute this mixture along the furrow and cover to the appropriate depth. You'll do much less thinning.

A heaped ¼ teaspoon kitchen measure of strong carrot seed carefully mixed into a gallon of compost can start about two carrots per inch along about 50 lineal row feet. The same amount of strong lettuce seed might establish twice that length of row. One gallon of compost will not fill the furrow. Top it up with more compost or soil. Thinning a few tight clusters out of a row started like that takes only moments. There

will be few gaps exceeding 1 inch. There's no way to be exact about how much seed to use because seed size varies and the percentage of seedlings that will emerge vary greatly from lot to lot and also by soil conditions. But even if you put in too much seed, the thinning you must do to correct it will prove far less work than had you sprinkled seed into that furrow by hand. If you'll buy seed in fairly large quantities and store it so it doesn't rapidly lose vigor, then you'll be able to predict from past performance how much seed it takes.

SAVING ON PURCHASES

Most gardeners worry that this year's seed packets will not germinate next year. Some throw away what remains in their old packets every year and start with all new (to them) seeds. I disagree. If the packet sprouted vigorously and grew well this year and if the variety pleased you enough to want to grow it again next year, and if there's unused seed to carry over, you should use this seed next season. Even if you've already had that packet for several years, if it sprouts strongly this year, it'll very likely carry over to the next. But if the seed packet sprouted weakly this year, then by all means, discard any remaining stock before the next season comes around.

If there's a good chance you'll grow a variety more than once, buy a money-saving larger-size packet. The only time you won't save much is with very expensive hybrids. Gram for gram some hybrid seeds cost as much as precious metal while the cost of packeting, mailing, promotion, etc., is the minor part. Vegetable seed usually retains good vigor for three to seven years from the date that seed lot was harvested, if it is stored in a cool part of the house where humidity is not high. I wish I could give you a chart of anticipated seed life by species, but there is no simple way for a home gardener to determine how intrinsically vigorous any seed lot is at the time of purchase, nor can we know how many years have passed between the time of its harvest and our purchase of it. So we can have no firm idea of how much longer any particular lot of seed might last. But despite the uncertainty, it still pays to buy enough to plant for several years.

You can easily make seed last several times longer than it does when stored in a cardboard box in the spare bedroom closet. More precisely, let's distinguish "normal household storage conditions" as a stable 68 degrees F and 70 percent relative humidity (RH). The rule of thumb used in the seed trade is that every 18 degrees F drop in stable temperature, combined with lowering of the seed's moisture content by 1 percent, doubles storage life. At 70 percent RH, seeds stabilize at around 13 percent moisture content. Storing seed in an airtight container with a large sachet of silica gel (at least as much weight of active silica gel as there is seed in the container) lowers seed moisture by several percent. If you also lower the temperature to a stable 40 degrees F, the storage life might be trebled. A packet of strong, recently harvested brassica seed might retain good vigor for five years kept at household room conditions, but stored with a sachet of silica gel in an airtight container in the fridge, it might last 15 years. Silica gel can be purchased from hobby/craft suppliers because it is used to make dried flower arrangements. It can also be obtained from chemical suppliers. Sometimes small bags of it come free when you buy new electronic equipment, and tiny sachets of it are found in some vitamin jars; I save and reuse every tiny bit that comes my way.

Silica gel lowers humidity until it has saturated itself with moisture. Most silica gels are color indicated; when they are dark blue, it is fully activated; light blue, losing potency but still working. When the gel turns pinkish, it has adsorbed all the moisture it can and it is time to bake it blue again. I recharge silica gel when it gets to the light blue stage by putting it in an oven at 212 degrees F for a few hours while the gel crystals are spread out an inch thick in a roasting pan. Make the oven much hotter than 212 degrees F, and you'll destroy the gel; you'll know you did that because it'll come out of the oven black instead of dark blue. If silica gel seems unfindable, a few inches of fresh dry powdered milk on the bottom of the jar will do almost as well.

To achieve the cooler part of the cooler/dryer equation, store the seed in the crawl space under the house or in an old refrigerator that also stores apples and overflow produce. Even an airtight desiccated container on an unheated bedroom's closet shelf is far better than holding your seeds in a cardboard box on that shelf and is enormously superior to keeping seeds in a cardboard box outdoors in a shed. Humid conditions and frequent temperature change speeds up seed death.

Temperatures above 68 degrees F and relative humidity above 70 percent age seed faster than normal. Seed held at 86 degrees F and 80 percent RH lasts half as long. Keeping seed in a damp place where it can get hot (such as a greenhouse) leads to dead seed. They can be killed even faster by putting the box of seeds you just picked up at the post office into a car with closed windows and parking that in the sun while you go shopping.

Grow Your Own Seed

Homegrown seed can be as vigorous as commercial stuff or more so. Even though your part of Cascadia might not provide the ideal microclimate for a species to form seed, gardeners can afford to have their soils provide minor nutrients in abundance and contain much more organic matter. Cascadia's low-humidity summer and moderate temperatures greatly boost dry seed vigor.

Chapter 9 details how to produce seed vegetable by vegetable. This section provides information that applies to all of them.

Vegetable seed divides into two broad groups: dry and wet. Wet seed forms and matures inside a moist fruit. After separation from the pulp, the seed has to be dried. Here we're describing tomato, pepper, eggplant, squash, asparagus, cucumber, melon, etc. To produce highly vigorous wet seed, you must allow each fruit to become totally ripe while still attached to the plant. The other sort, dry seed, usually forms along branches or in pods and (hopefully) dries down in the field. To produce vigorous dry seed, you must allow the majority of the seed on each plant to pretty much dry down before harvesting,

which means avoid overhead watering while the seed finishes. Biennials that survive winter can be left where they are to make seed, or if the soil supports dry gardening, transplanted to an unirrigated seed-growing area at the first sign of spring, where lower humidity while the seed is maturing makes it stronger. In order to end up with highly vigorous seed from annuals like beans or peas in an irrigated garden, you may have to handpick seedpods. Take pods one at a time when it first starts drying down; that's when the stem end of the pod wilts becomes floppy, signifying there no longer is a connection to the plant's vascular system. Handpicking enough pods to sow next year's crop isn't much trouble.

Wet or dry, only fully ripe seed can be vigorous. With dry seed, the home seed grower should delay harvesting until some seed has gone past ripe and fallen off the plant—around 10 percent of the total. Species that mature dry seed at summer's end don't fit Cascadia's climate. Late September brings repeated morning dew and humid days. This slows drying and lowers vigor. Rain is worse. If the late-season weather doesn't cooperate, yank and then dry the nearly mature plants under cover before threshing; the seed won't be quite as vigorous as it might have gotten, but it still may sprout better than most of what you'd buy from commercial sources. How vigorous it'll be depends on how close to finished the seed was when the plants were harvested.

When raising wet seed, allow the fruit to go on past dead ripe before you pick it. If you'll then hold the overripe fruit in a warm place for a few days to a week, the seed within may continue to ripen. Extract the seed before the fruit begins to decay. Wet seeds that mature before mid-February receive the benefit of more solar energy. Wet seeds that mature in the last half of September will not be very vigorous.

Raising your own seed inevitably means being a plant breeder. There is no avoiding this responsibility. You must choose which plants to propagate. Even if you make seed from all the plants you started with, that too is a choice. If you're serious about producing your own, I recommend reading Suzanne Ashworth's *Seed to Seed*, John Navazio's *The Organic Seed Grower*, and Carol Deppe's *Breed Your Own Vegetable Varieties*.

POLLINATION

Some species like beans and tomatoes need no intermediary to pollinate. In fact, their flower's structure usually prevents insects from entering until it has fertilized itself. Some usually self-pollinating species like peppers, runner beans, and fava beans make flowers that are not entirely immune to insects; these species occasionally cross-pollinate but mostly self-pollinate. Some species transfer pollen from plant to plant. Seeds that are fertilized this way are "cross-pollinated." The plants of some outcrossing species have a gender; they make either pollen or ovaries, and only the females develop seeds. Asparagus, spinach, and hemp do this.

Some species both self- and cross-pollinate at the same time—cucurbits, alliums, corn, the brassicas, and all the biennial root crops except beets (which are so entirely self-incompatible they only cross). Vigor in these kinds of vegetables is maintained by the ongoing exchange of genes in each generation; selfed (self-pollinated)

seeds are, by definition, inbred, and won't be nearly as vigorous. So from these species, if the variety is open pollinated, you should expect to get a percentage of inbred seeds producing weak plants that usually get thinned out. I find it useful to think of open-pollinated varieties of cucurbits, alliums, corn, brassicas, and biennial root crops as collections of similar hybrids mixed with self-pollinated inbreds.

Strictly self-pollinating species rarely cross even if grown in close proximity. Occasionally one flower produces a few outcrossed (hybrid) seeds because an unusually aggressive bee or small insect manages to transfer pollen between plants. Then a whole bunch of potential new varieties are created. To create new varieties, plant breeders force a cross in a normally self-pollinating species.

You can produce seed for several varieties of the same self-pollinating species in the same garden at the same time. If an unwanted cross shows up, it will be a rare event. The greatest likelihood is that the cross will be recognizable in the first generation, so you may yank it like a weed; there's no more problem. A few normally self-pollinating species are prone to outcrossing and need some isolation. These include peas, peppers, and runner beans. But an unanticipated outcross might prove interesting; perhaps you'll wish to make it into a new variety. Getting a first-year cross to become a uniform and true-to-type variety can take several generations of clever selection.

Self-pollinating species can be carried forward through many generations using seed taken from only one plant without any loss of vigor.

Backyard gardeners easily can and should save their own seed from self-pollinating species.

Bee- or wind-pollinated varieties reproduced from only a few plants become ever more inbred with each generation, making the variety soon lose vigor and become nonproductive. To maintain an outcrossing variety, you must involve a great many plants in each and every generation. This is an extreme example of inbreeding: if a seed crop consists of one plant, then all the seed must be self-fertilized (unless a bit of pollen comes from a distant garden somehow). After two or three generations of selfing, the seed won't sprout well; if it comes up, it won't grow so well. The technical term describing this is "inbreeding depression of vigor." Plant breeders intentionally inbreed to obtain genetic uniformity and then outcross in a controlled manner to restore vigor.

If you reproduce an outcrossing variety from only half a dozen plants, it'll suffer from inbreeding depression of vigor within a few generations. I would not attempt to make seed of an outcrossing species unless I had at least 10 or, better, 25 plants involved. For some species it takes at least 100 plants. Or 300 plants. In all cases you'll have to make a large amount of seed when you do make it, and you must be able to allocate enough land to do that. Naturally, seed-saver clubs soon come to see the sense of specializing and trading, or else they entirely give up on most outcrossing varieties. These clubs usually concentrate on self-pollinated annuals like beans and tomatoes.

With outcrossing species, the more uniform the gene pool is, the less vigorous the variety becomes. So a vigorous open-pollinated variety must actually be a mixture of quite similar hybrids that cross in every generation. When choosing parent plants, allow as much difference as possible to remain *in unimportant aspects*. For example, slight color variations or slight variations in leaf shape are not important traits, but tightly beaded broccoli florets are required for the best flavor.

To turn wild plants into garden vegetables, select the most likely plant(s), inbreed, then repeat. The more refined the line becomes, the more inbred it must be. Growing seeds for an outcrossing vegetable like kale is relatively easy because it is still close to being a wild plant. You might succeed at maintaining a kale variety for quite a few generations by growing only four plants in each generation. But with the highly inbred cauliflower, if you reduce the gene pool below 50, you'll likely see a complete breakdown of the variety within a few generations. Practically speaking, seeds for large-size refined brassicas and sprawling cucurbits must be produced by seed companies or by market gardeners with enough space to grow a great many plants from which to select many near-perfect plants to form seed. Someone with a large backyard might be able to involve 50 small-size vegetables such as onions or kohlrabi in a seed production. But 50 full-grown cabbage plants making seed occupy a minimum of 800 square feet and better, 1,200.

To produce seed from an outcrossing variety, start by sowing many extra seeds, thinning progressively. You can make valuable selections in early stages. Once the row is a few weeks old and solidly established, remove the weakest plants; these are either inbreds or possess poorly adapted traits. A few weeks more and it's time to remove all supervigorous seedlings, the ones standing head and shoulders above the rest. They are extra vigorous because they are endowed with the most genetic diversity; if these seedlings were to be used for parent plants, they would produce wildly variable progeny. What you're aiming at is making seed from the middle range of vigor, using plants that are as diverse as you can afford to allow. Until the desired plant density has been achieved, continue to remove plants that are very different from what you desire as best you can tell when they are small.

HYBRID VERSUS OPEN-POLLINATED

The following opinions have been used like propaganda for the virtues of heirloom and open-pollinated seed. I do not agree with any of them. I sense selfish motives pushing these assertions:

- Gardeners using hybrid seeds are supporting an international conspiracy to control global food production.
- Hybrid varieties belong in the same immoral category as chemical fertilizers, synthetic herbicides, and pesticides.
- It is not possible to grow your own seeds from hybrids. Once hybrids replace open-pollinated varieties, we will no longer be able to grow our own seeds. Then we all will be Monsanto's slaves.
- Hybrid varieties are not nutritious, nor do they taste as good as the old-fashioned sorts.

Territorial Seed Company's first catalog (1980) offered only open-pollinated seeds because at that time I ignorantly opined that hybrids were less nutritious and couldn't be used to produce seed. In the first year I started a half-acre trials ground. To fill it, I asked my suppliers for samples of their open-pollinated varieties; I completely ignored their hybrids. But those sly Dutch primary growers knew I didn't yet appreciate what hybrids were all about and slipped in a few unasked-for hybrid packets. And finding a bit of extra room here and there in my rows, I grew them.

The hybrid seeds germinated faster and grew more vigorously. In contrast, some of the open-pollinated varieties barely came up. So I asked myself: If a vendor would send me a weak trial sample, wouldn't I be a fool to put that variety in my catalog? Inquiring about this I was told that many of those open-pollinated varieties were no longer in commercial use; seeds for them were rarely produced, which is why I was sent old, weak seed. (The word "rarely" was proved to be a fib because these OP varieties soon vanished from their catalog.) Hybrid varieties are big-volume commercial items that get produced frequently, so hybrid seed is fresh, strong seed. I was promised that I would always be sent vigorous, high-germination seed when I ordered hybrids.

The few hybrids in my 1980 trials proved highly productive and were good eating. The open-pollinated varieties grew a significant percentage of off-type nonproductive plants while the true-to-type majority did not grow as well as the hybrids. Ah, I realized, that's why the commercial trade now prefers hybrids.

Taste

I had been instructed that traditional open-pollinated varieties tasted better and were more nutritious, but what was revealed on my trials grounds was the opposite. Many of the hybrids had superior flavor, so my next year's catalog offered a few hybrid varieties and I removed its antihybrid rhetoric.

Some hybrid varieties do make awful eating, but all hybrids should not be judged by them. There is a cabbage called Stonehead—perfectly round, fast growing, hard and dense as a rock, pretty appearance, so uniform the farmer can cut the whole field on the same day and make lots of money. Flavor? Like dry paper, and tough. Then why is there a Stonehead? Because it is ideal for making the thinly sliced, canned sauerkraut preferred by Americans; the taste need not be in the cabbage: it develops from fermentation, salt, and flavoring agents, but the cabbage must not turn to mush when it is sliced thin and canned.

Once a plant breeder and I were cruising his small fruit trials at the North Willamette Valley Research and Extension Center. It was June; I was stuffing my face. We reached a strawberry variety that made very red fruits the size of Asian plums; they were so hard that you about broke a tooth. And they were extremely sour. Why this variety? I asked. Oh, said the breeder, we're very proud of that one! WTF? I thought so loudly that he went on about it. This variety is for freezing. These berries are still firm when you thaw out the package, and as for sweet . . . it already has lots of tart flavor. The cannery simply adds sugar.

Hybrids can be used to make seed

Antihybrid propaganda says using hybrids enforces dependency on the seed company and is a form of enslavement. Actually, seeds can be grown from hybrids. Sometimes it takes a few generations before you have usable seed. And sometimes you get productive seed right away. I bred an open-pollinated carrot out of an unusual F_1 hybrid called Merida and an open-pollinated kohlrabi from a widely used F_1 hybrid called Kolibri. The open-pollinated Merida came out nearly the equal of the hybrid. My open-pollinated kohlrabi grows and tastes the same and is nearly as uniform as the Kolibri F_1—at least my first seed production grows great.

The kohlrabi project was easy. Every plant in a hybrid variety has virtually identical genes, so there is no need to use more than a few plants the first time seed is produced. My seed from 12 Kolibri F_1 plants grew a crop so uniform you might think Kolibri actually is an open-pollinated variety, not an F_1 hybrid. I've been using seed from that production for the last five years and hope it'll last another five before I am tempted to see what happens when I grow the next open-pollinated generation.

However, to get seeds from Merida, I needed some secondhand experience. The parent lines used to make this variety had been so highly inbred that Merida F_1 is totally self-sterile. The first time I attempted to make seed from about 20 plants, not a single seed formed—exactly like the antihybrid propaganda claimed would happen. So at Carol Deppe's suggestion, I grew Merida F_1 again, and this time next to it I grew a row of Armstrong, an open-pollinated variety that was not too different in shape and color. This time I got lots of seed from Merida. Carol said I could just as well have crossed Merida with a similar-looking hybrid variety and harvested lots of seed from Merida.

In the next generation I backcrossed (Merida x Armstrong) to Merida F_1 by planting a short row of the cross next to a short row of the original. The backcross produced seeds on the Merida F_1 row containing three-quarter Merida genes. The result is now so genetically similar to Merida F_1 that I can't tell the difference, but it freely makes seed. I've carried open-pollinated Merida through several succeeding generations and the variety seems stable.

Umpqua broccoli was developed by a self-educated Oregon breeder named Tim Peters. Tim told me he started with Green Valiant, an excellent F_1 hybrid. Green Valiant had a lot of self-sterility bred into it. It set only a few seeds in the F_2, but the next generation after that it set seed like a normal open-pollinated variety. I do not know how many more generations it took for Tim to work out the kinks. Umpqua is uniform, productive, and far better eating than the raggedy open-pollinated broccoli varieties remaining in the cheap end of the seed trade.

In the event gardeners were forced by circumstance to begin growing their own seeds and had mainly hybrid varieties to start with, within a few years we could have a full range of open-pollinated varieties.

Hybrids lack nutrient density

Most modern vegetable varieties, including most open-pollinated varieties, provide less nutrition than they once did. In private conversation Alan Kapuler suggested this explanation: For thousands of years each agricultural family grew their own unique varieties. Genetically, some varieties produce more nutrient density. The children born to families whose varieties lacked nutrient density tended to die from childhood diseases. Thus less-nutritious varieties tended to disappear along with the family that grew them. Thus, for thousands of years our food crops have been selected for greater nutrient density.

About 1870 vegetable and fruit varieties began to be bred for industrial agriculture. Consequently, some varieties of fruit now look ripe when they really aren't; vegetables have been redesigned to sit longer on the supermarket shelf or hold up better when trucked across continents.

And now genetic engineering is being applied to achieve greater profit. Catering to public opinion, many garden seed merchants have promised to never knowingly sell seed or plants that are genetically engineered. I see nothing *inherently* wrong with genetic engineering. GE is but a tool to bend plants to the shape we wish them to be. If our goal was to increase nutrient density, genetic engineering could be useful. But since our goal is to shape plants toward higher profits, GE lets us move our food crops away from being nutrient dense even faster than we already have. And I have read reports of livestock not thriving on GE feed and of Indian farming villages getting sick (and some people dying) when pollen released by nearby GE crops was blowing through their village.

The best reason I know to preserve and use *genuine* heirlooms is their promise of higher nutrient density. However, just because a variety is open-pollinated and was used in commercial production before the Second World War does not make it an heirloom and does not mean it is more nutrient dense. In truth, there aren't many useful heirlooms left; those profiting by cultivating gardeners' prejudices often sell degenerated open-pollinated varieties like Waltham 29 broccoli that were bred after World War II and widely used in industrial agriculture. And what of the actual heirlooms? It may be possible to rescue some outcrossing varieties that have been through generations of inbreeding and poor selection by backyard seed savers, and some garden seed sellers are working on that—including Territorial.

Instead of deciding the issue of hybrid versus open-pollinated by ideology, I think we are best guided by our tongues. I use what tastes and grows the best.

TRANSPLANTS

My well-beloved had a vineyard
In a very fruitful hill;
And he digged it, and cleared it of stones,
And planted it with the choicest vine. . . .
And he looked that it should bring forth grapes,
And it brought forth wild grapes.

—Isaiah 5, The Holy Scriptures
(Masoretic text)

JUST LIKE PICTURE packets, eager-looking seedlings are available from supermarkets, health-food co-ops, drugstores, garden centers—I remember the independent bookstore in Cottage Grove selling Log House starts. Some of these are nearly to equal my best homegrown; others are weak, likely to die soon after transplanting. The problem is how to distinguish which from what.

Buying Transplants

A healthy transplant looks sturdy—thick stemmed and stocky, not tall, spindly, and thin stemmed. The seedlings should have formed at least three pairs of completely developed leaves, and these leaves and the stems supporting them should be springy and strong, not weak and flimsy such that wind will tear them apart. The seedlings should have made enough roots that the soil ball won't fall apart during transplanting but won't have become pot-bound.

POT-BOUND SEEDLINGS

To inspect the root system, first support the soil by sliding the gap between your second and third fingers around the stem, fingertips facing the soil; then invert the pot into your hand and firmly tap the bottom until the root ball loosens. Then ease the pot up. If few or no root tips are visible, the soil ball will break apart during transplanting. If you intend to transplant immediately, don't buy this one. So many roots will be damaged that this seedling is likely to wilt and will probably go into shock when set out. It was produced in a constantly warm greenhouse and heavily fed to speed up top growth even more. If you're determined to have this plant, then it's better to grow it for a week in that pot while it hardens off and its roots fill the container. Then plant it out.

If roots have wrapped themselves around the outside of the soil ball, the plant has become pot-bound. Fertigated daily, the top growth can look good for several weeks after becoming pot-bound. But until it starts putting roots into the surrounding soil, that seedling may wilt unless you water it daily. With fancy brassicas like cabbage, cauliflower, and broccoli, becoming pot-bound in the seedling stage can make them head up before they develop into full-size plants. After paying the price of those transplants and assigning valuable garden space to them, you won't enjoy harvesting broccoli or cauliflower heads the size of a teacup.

Pruning off the largest pair of leaves when transplanting pot-bound seedlings reduces the amount of water the roots have to supply and allows you to bury the root ball deeper, where the soil doesn't dry out rapidly. Even though you have removed some of its sugar-manufacturing ability, without moisture stress this seedling will resume growth much sooner and ultimately grow bigger than if you had not pruned it. Still, this pruning is a setback.

If numerous root tips are visible at the outer edge of the root ball and only a few roots have just begun to wrap around the outside, the seedling is perfect for transplanting. The soil ball will hold together; the root system immediately expands. This seedling needs no special watering beyond an initial drink when transplanting.

A transplant can go from being insufficiently rooted to being slightly pot-bound in one week. Wholesale nurseries often sell insufficiently rooted seedlings when terrific spring weather creates greater demand than had been anticipated. And at the end of the main transplanting window you find pot-bound seedlings on the sale bench.

SOFT SEEDLINGS

You can inspect a seedling's root system. Robustness is not as easy to spot.

When soil fertility is high, moisture always abundant, the temperature pleasantly warm at all times, and wind nonexistent, plants form larger thin-walled cells holding more water. They get bigger faster. Luxuriant plants are so fragile that a strong breeze may tear the leaves right off their too-flexible stems. Delicate tissue like this transpires a lot of moisture. This kind of seedling inevitably wilts or gets sunburned when first experiencing outdoor conditions. After experiencing its first chilly night, a soft seedling goes into shock that stops it from growing for a week or more. If it is transplanted on a windy day, it may get shredded.

When the environment is normally stressful, plants form smaller-size, tougher leaves on shorter, stockier stems; they make a stronger root system. Seedlings like this are much less likely to be damaged by handling, winds, or insects. In this respect, I think seedling plants and children are very similar.

Transplanting can so shock a soft seedling that it falls prey to disease and insect attacks, or at the very least, stops growing until it adjusts. For example, a pepper seedling that has not yet experienced a night below 60 degrees F and is suddenly put outdoors will be shocked when exposed to a nighttime low of 45 degrees F.

When growth resumes a week later, the new leaves will be smaller, the stems tougher and wiry. A soft seedling that is chilled that strongly on several consecutive nights may become diseased and die. A pepper transplant that already had experienced a few low-50s nights would not be badly shocked until an outdoor night falls below 40 degrees F.

Cold, hard rain can shock a hothouse plant. A light frost stuns an otherwise-frost-tolerant brassica seedling that never before experienced temperatures below 50 degrees F. Loss of root hairs, almost inevitable when transplanting, is also a shock. Put yourself in the place of a warm, comfortable soft seedling that, without any preparation, gets exposed to wind, rain, root damage, strong direct sunlight, never-before-experienced low overnight temperatures, soil diseases, and predatory insects—all at once. It is easy to see why transplanting is so often fatal and why transplanting does not necessarily lead to harvesting much sooner than direct seeding.

I had a close look at the difference between hard and soft seedlings while I was growing a tomato trial at Lorane. Frost after the last usual frost date is the usual thing at 900 feet above sea level. So I'd always grow extra tomato transplants and hold these in my cold frame for another 10 days or so after transplanting the rest, just in case.

One year I planted out the tomato trial on May 30, as usual. There was a frost on June 13, not that unusual. I lacked enough reserve tomato transplants to fully restore the trial, so I filled the gaps with seedlings from the local garden center. Where mine looked stocky, thick stemmed, and

How to Transplant

If you follow these directions, you'll almost never have a seedling wilt.

- Prepare the bed for a low-demand crop. Then make a hole about 4 inches deep and 8 inches across. Pour a generous half cup of COF into that hole and mix it into the soil going down another 4 inches. Then refill the hole and smooth the surface.

- Now make another hole in the center of the diggings. Make it slightly wider than the root ball and deep enough that the seedling's bottom leaves will be just above the soil line when the hole is refilled. Without damaging its roots, invert the seedling, tap it out of the pot into your other hand, and place it into that hole. Do not immediately refill the hole with soil.

- From a bucket of tepid water containing liquid fertilizer or compost tea, scoop out a pint and carefully but quickly pour it into the hole. Take care not to wash soil away from the transplant's roots. Immediately, before the water soaks in, push enough loose growing medium back into the hole to form a muddy slurry that coats the root ball while filling in the cavity; now the seedling is perfectly mudded in. It will not wilt and won't need any special watering.

tough, the garden center seedlings were spindly, light colored, and delicate. My reserve seedlings started growing as soon as they were set out; the commercial ones went into shock. Mine were untroubled by insects; the others were badly chewed by flea beetles, and I had to spray them twice. Although the garden center seedlings did eventually get to growing, my homegrown plants ended up much larger, bore more heavily, and generally ripened earlier.

Assume that any seedlings you buy are soft. The easiest way to harden them off is to transplant them into a pot that holds about twice the soil volume of the one they're in and then grow them in a cold frame until the larger pot has filled with roots. This delays transplanting about one week, but the seedlings grow much faster in the frame than they could outdoors. If you don't have a cold frame, on the day you bring them home, put the transplants outside in bright shade to become accustomed to wind and to light that is unfiltered by glass or plastic, and bring them back indoors before sunset. The next day, introduce them to direct morning or late-afternoon sun, and bring them in at night. Give them full sun (if there is any) throughout the third day, and at night put them in an unheated building or an enclosed back porch. Let them experience the following night outside in a protected spot, such as hard up against the sun-facing wall of your house, unless the low temperature is forecast to be below 40 degrees F for frost-tolerant species, 45 degrees F for tomatoes or squash, or below 50 degrees F for tender species like peppers and eggplant. After a week on this routine they'll transplant with a much higher likelihood of thriving right away. If you've potted them up a size, it may take two weeks before the seedling grows enough roots to transplant.

Raising Your Own

These days I do not purchase transplants; I do not grow many for myself either. That's because raising transplants requires far more time and attention than direct seeding does, and if there is much difference in result, I'd say the direct-seeded crop does slightly better. I got quite skillful at raising brassica and celery transplants when I did trials for Territorial Seed Company. These days I know better; I only raise seedlings for tomatoes, peppers, eggplants, and basil. The rest of my garden crops are directly seeded. I urge you to do the same.

To grow great transplants, you must control light and temperature as well as moisture, growing medium, ventilation, and fertility. Success will come only to the degree that each of these factors is properly provided for. Direct seeding lets nature handle more of the job.

TEMPERATURE

Temperature determines how many days it takes seeds to sprout or if they will sprout at all. To quickly summarize, semitropical varieties such as melons, peppers, and eggplants sprout poorly or not at all below 70 degrees F. Most other vegetable species will sprout below that temperature

Raising Transplants Outdoors

Here's how to direct-seed many sorts of vegetables that are usually started as purchased transplants.

- Mix up some seedling mix/potting soil (described shortly). Take a bucket of it out to the garden. In recently worked soil wherever you'd want to set a transplant, dig out one shovelful of soil (making a little hole about 4 inches deep and 6 inches around). Pour in ½ cup of complete organic fertilizer. Mix the fertilizer into about a quart of soil at the bottom of the hole with your fingers. Then fill the hole back in with the loose earth you just dug out. Take an empty half-pint mason jar and press it into that spot, making a half-pint-jar-size hole. Doing this also restores capillarity below the spot. Then pour a heaping half-pint of seedling mix into the hole and press it down gently. With your fingertip, make a depression ½ inch deep (or deeper for larger seeds like squash or cucumber) in the middle of that core of seedling mix, and into that little hole count out four seeds, and cover them.

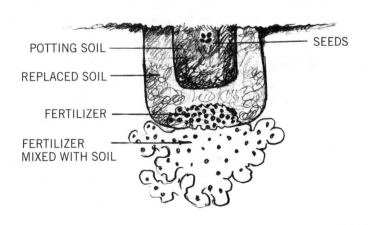

POTTING SOIL

REPLACED SOIL

FERTILIZER

FERTILIZER MIXED WITH SOIL

SEEDS

but do best when stably held between 75 degrees and 82 degrees F. I suggest that when germinating seed indoors, you aim for 75 degrees F, except with lettuce, spinach, celery, and celeriac, which won't sprout well at all above 70 degrees F and do best in the low to mid 60s.

In their first weeks after germination, tomato seedlings do best at 60 to 65 degrees F during daytime and not below 50 degrees F at night. Heat lovers, like peppers, eggplants, melons, squash, and cucumber, grow fast enough between 65 and 72 degrees F in the daytime. Temperatures over 75 degrees F make tropicals grow faster, but they get soft. Below 65 degrees F, tropicals grow too slowly. Dark period temperatures for tropicals should not drop below 60 degrees F until they've developed two pairs of true leaves; then teach them to be comfortable at 50 degrees F during their dark period. Cool-weather seedlings—the coles, alliums, celery, parsley, and lettuce—get spindly and weak when grown at temperatures that tropicals would find ideal. All these (except celery) do best at 60 to 65 degrees F in the daytime and 45 to 55 degrees F at night. Celery must not experience dark period temperature below 50 degrees F, and maybe it is better kept above 55 degrees F.

A compromise temperature range is needed if you wish to grow many species at once. Seedlings grow well at normal household temperatures. They thrive between 68 and 70 degrees F in the daytime and 52 and 60 degrees F at night. They need slightly higher temperatures while seeds are germinating.

GROWING MEDIA

Seedlings have delicate root systems. To promote rapid growth, their growing medium must remain light, airy, and loose. Even if you have excellent garden soil, you should not use it as a container growing medium. The problem is that small containers growing substantial plants must be watered daily. When soil containing more than the slightest amount of clay is moistened, it swells. When it dries again, it shrinks. Daily swelling and shrinking compacts soil. You can actually see the medium settle lower in the pot as the seedling grows. This compaction reduces soil air; there is less space for roots to develop. Growth slows. A container-grown seedling that takes four weeks to reach the four-leaf stage in a proper seedling growing medium might need six or seven weeks to achieve the same size in pure garden soil.

Commercial seedling raisers use blends of lightweight materials like coir, peat moss, vermiculite, pearlite, and compost. The bagged growing media found in garden centers are often mostly bark- and sawdust-based compost prefertilized with chemicals and (if you're lucky) lime, but even when prefertilized, they contain only enough N-P-K to grow a second-rate plant for a few weeks. After that, keeping the plants fed becomes your problem.

Here are two typical recipes for commercial growing media. I'm not suggesting you use them. I am suggesting you consider the intention behind their formulation and then do something better. Both of them contain aglime because it is extremely expensive to make a soluble fertilizer that provides calcium; without calcium plants simply shrivel, and if it is merely in short supply, they grow poorly.

University of California mix

This growing mix, being sand-based, is inexpensive but weighs a lot and has no buffering capacity.

75 percent coarse sand
25 percent sphagnum moss
Add to each cubic yard of mix:
7½ pounds agricultural lime
2½ pounds dolomite lime
3 pounds 10-20-10 chemical fertilizer

Cornell University "peat-lite" mix

Using a mix like this in a bedding plant operation reduces the amount of strength needed to move plants around. The vermiculite in it retains more moisture and adds what is termed "buffering capacity," to be explained shortly.

11 bushels sphagnum moss
11 bushels horticultural-grade vermiculite or pearlite
5 pounds dolomite lime
1 pound superphosphate
12 pounds 5-10-5 chemical fertilizer

Steve's seedling mix

My own seedling mix is not sterile. I garden on a silty clay loam that has a high buffering capacity, and I include proper humified compost so that my growing medium has an even higher capacity to hold on to plant nutrients. If my garden soil was sandy and lacked clay, I'd substitute vermiculite for coir or sphagnum moss. If my garden soil were clay, I'd decrease the amount of soil in the medium to 25 percent and also add pearlite.

Thoroughly blend:
1 part by volume best garden soil
1 part by volume sifted humified compost
1 part by volume sphagnum moss or, slightly better, coir
Blend into each cubic foot (5 gallons) of this blend:
1 cup complete organic fertilizer (COF)
¼ cup finely ground agricultural lime

Sphagnum moss comes in compressed bales, is sterile, and has the capacity to soak up 10 to 20 times its own weight in water. Moss provides almost no nutrients and has a very acid pH, about 3.5. It also contains natural fungicidal substances that inhibit damping-off diseases. Sphagnum moss is usually sold finely ground and dehydrated. Old bales often break apart into large hard lumps. Slow to take up water when completely dry, peat moss should be thoroughly remoistened before use. Drop any hard chunks into a 5-gallon bucket, cover with water, and they will expand and loosen in an hour or so. Then squeeze out the excess moisture.

Vermiculite is made from mica, a naturally occurring volcanic mineral. Mica bursts open like popcorn when heated. Once popped, it weighs only 6 to 10 pounds per cubic foot, has a pH of about 7.0, and holds a lot of water. Like clay, vermiculite has a strong ability to hold plant nutrients. This trait reduces the amount of fertilizer lost when water passes through the pot, stabilizing nutrient availability. Unlike clay, vermiculite remains loose after going through many wet-dry cycles. Vermiculite comes in four horticultural sizes: #1 is too coarse for bedding plants, #2 is the regular horticultural grade, and the very fine #3 and #4 are used in commercial greenhouses as germinating media for extremely small seeds. Vermiculite is sterile.

Pearlite is made from a naturally lightweight form of lava called pumice. The rock is crushed and heated until it pops like vermiculite does, expanding the particles to small, spongy bits that are very light, weighing 5 to 8 pounds per cubic foot. Pearlite will hold three to four times its own weight in water. It has almost no ability to hold nutrients the way clay and vermiculite do, has a pH of about 7.0, and is used to lighten and aerate soil mixes.

Composts are highly variable; some batches make seedlings grow noticeably better, some do little, and some contain so much incompletely decomposed woody material that they interfere with growth. Compost holds a lot of water and loosens soil. Composts are not sterile and that's a good thing. Seedlings are far healthier when growing in a medium that contains decomposing organic matter and a complex microecology. Compost also provides buffering capacity, some more so than others.

Some bagged composts contain a large fraction of forest industry waste; this stuff is okay for growing shade-tolerant houseplants or for mulching ornamentals but interferes with rapid growth when used to raise vegetable seedlings. My advice is not to expect much growth stimulation from bagged compost.

Coir is coconut husk fiber. It is slow to decompose, lightweight, and naturally stays loose. Coir holds an enormous quantity of moisture yet still holds a lot of air when completely wet. Growing media with plenty of coir in them do not need watering as often,

nor do they shrink as much as ones based on sphagnum moss when they dry out. Coir is a renewable resource while sphagnum moss took thousands of years to form, which, for practical purposes, constitutes nonrenewability. Coir is usually sold in compressed dry bricks that must soak up water before use. While being rehydrated, the material naturally crumbles as it expands to many times its compressed volume. Dry, compressed coir contains no nutrients. So a coir brick could be rehydrated with liquid fertilizer.

Coir is separated from coconut husks after soaking them in water for an extended period. It often originates as a third-world homestead product. Sometimes the soak water is seawater, and the resultant coir contains so much sodium that it can damage plants. Make sure the coir brick you purchase is "low sodium" or is in bricks labeled "horticultural grade."

Soil from a fertile garden brings with it a healthy microecology, something no commercial-grown seedling can enjoy.

WATERING

Large seedlings in small containers have to be watered daily. On sunny days when they're close to transplanting size, they may need watering both late morning and midafternoon. This requirement makes it essential to use a soil mix that can rapidly reabsorb water after pretty much drying out and that won't shrink too much as it dries. If the growing medium shrinks away from the sides of the pot, water you add to the top may run down the sides and out the bottom without really wetting the contents. If the

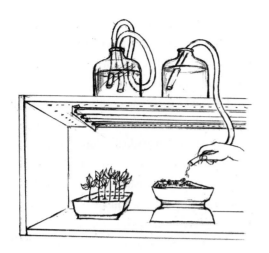

stress off my arm and hand, I stand the bucket atop an inverted bucket next to the frame.

A bucket siphon system also serves to fertigate small plants in the garden. Carry the bucket in one hand and the broomstick in the other. Place the outlet near the soil, and siphon fertigation solution straight into the root zone of a growing plant.

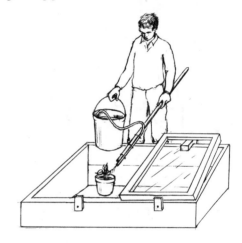

CONTAINERS

Commercial seedling raisers aim to produce the largest-possible number of seedlings from each precious square foot of growing bench, so they use a small pot or cell. They can do this because they are always present to water when necessary. The home gardener should use containers providing at least twice as much soil volume per plant as the ones you'll see on a sales bench. Doing this results in stronger seedlings and takes pressure off you.

Many factors can influence the growth rate and ratio of top to root, including light levels, temperatures, species, varieties, and soil mixes. Generally, a 3- to 4-inch-diameter (or square)

surface crusts over, water uptake may slow down so much that the soil looks saturated when an inch down it actually is dry. Unlike coir, once sphagnum moss has fully dried, it is difficult to remoisten. For that reason, I find that about one-third moss by total volume is the maximum safe level, and also for that reason, I prefer coir.

Growing media can be disturbed unless you water gently. For the home gardener, the best method I know of is to use a ¼-inch (internal diameter) plastic or rubber siphon tube to drain a gallon jar, plastic milk container, or bucket located 1 to 2 feet above the seedlings. If you want more water pressure, increase the reservoir's height above the seedlings. This method provides water at room temperature, not cold and shocking, straight from the tap.

I water seedlings in a cold frame from a 5-gallon bucket using a siphon. I tie one end of ¼-inch internal diameter tube to an old broom handle that allows me to conveniently move the gentle stream around in my cold frame. To provide enough water pressure while taking the

Fertigating small plants.

the growing medium about ⅜ inch deep with the blunt end of a pencil, sow the seeds in that hole, and flick a few bits of growing medium over them. Then seal each pot or tray in its own small airtight plastic bag until seedlings emerge. If your soil mix is not sterile, sow four seeds per pot or cell and then gradually thin the extra seedlings with a small pair of scissors. Extra seedlings allow for losses from damping-off and the later removal of any weak seedlings. If the growing medium is sterile, start three seeds.

I do not recommend using peat pots or expandable peat pellets. It is hard enough to keep a small container moist without having a lot of water evaporate through its sides. The sales pitch for these is that you reduce shock by planting the pot, and the roots grow right through it. I've seen very few roots actually go through a peat pot's walls; I've seen these pots strangle seedlings. If you use peat pots, be sure to tear off the bottom at planting time. The trouble with expanding peat pellets is that it is not possible to mix aglime or COF into them. Plants lacking calcium nutrition do not grow well, while the only liquid fertilizer I know of that does contain calcium is one of the most expensive brands found at shops selling gear for indoor cannabis growing.

LIGHT

During the usually cloudy Cascadian spring windowsill-grown seedlings grow slowly, and become spindly and weak. There are two effective solutions: indoor grow lights and protected outdoor spaces such as cold frames. I prefer to use both.

pot will provide adequate room for small-seeded species to grow three or four pairs of leaves. Peppers, eggplants, and tomatoes benefit from plenty of hardening-off time, so I finish them in 7-inch pots. Melons, cucumbers, squash, and beans get big fast and should be sown in 5-inch pots unless you intend to transplant the seedlings within a few days of germination, in which case 2-inch pots will do.

The best way I know to get strong seed germination in a container or cell tray is to first bring the growing medium to an ideal moisture level (70 percent of capacity) and then fill the containers. Do not pack medium into the container; keep it loose, but not so loose that it settles a lot the first time you water. Poke a hole into

Configuring and Using Fluorescent Lights

Number of Tubes	Maximum Height above Top of Seedlings	Width of Strongly Illuminated Area	Period of Growth with Sufficient Light
2	2 inches	6 inches	4 weeks
4	3 inches	9 inches	6 weeks
6	4 inches	12 inches	8 weeks

Light quality and light intensity have profound and immediate effects on growth. When given low-light levels many plants develop elongated, thin stems. The name for this stretching out is "etiolation." You can easily etiolate a container plant to an extreme degree by putting it in a dark closet for a few weeks. The stems soon become vine-like; new leaves are almost white and barely develop. Cool-white fluorescent tubes provide enough light in the right spectrum to grow seedlings to about their four-leaf stage, just the right size to transplant. Fluorescent bulbs are available in 2- and 4-foot lengths. An array holding from two to six parallel cool-white tubes suspended over the growing area can produce enough stocky seedlings for a home garden. The minimum light intensity vegetable seedlings require is the maximum light intensity fluorescents can create when the tubes are positioned close together and suspended *only 1 to 2 inches above the top leaves.* As the seedlings grow, the lamps must be raised, or else the height of the shelf holding the seedlings must be lowered, or else individual plant containers must be on props that are gradually lowered as the seedlings grow. When I used fluorescent lights, I preferred the last option, because at any one time I was growing a mix of species started at different times. Fluorescents generate heat. If you'll locate the lights where the day and night ambient temperature is 55 to 60 degrees F, you probably create the right temperatures for the seedlings.

Recently I've been using a 250-watt high intensity lamp (HID). It has several advantages over fluorescents:

- More light means my seedlings grow more than twice as fast as they do under fluorescents.
- The seedlings are stockier and a lot stronger.
- Compared to fluorescents, the HID lamp consumes much less power to produce much more plant growth.

HID lights come in two general types, high-pressure sodium (HPS) and metal halide (MH). For vegetative growth, you get more bang from each watt with MH bulbs. I use a 250-watt metal halide over a 2-by-3-foot growing bench. I think this lamp could do about as well illuminating 3 by 3 feet. The bulb, its required ballast, and a reflector to equalize light distribution cost more than a fixture holding four 40-watt fluorescents that are capable of illuminating an area 1 foot wide by 4 feet long. What takes four weeks to develop under a 250-watt MH bulb takes eight weeks to accomplish under fluorescents. The bottom line: a 250-watt MH bulb supports 50 percent more growing area and produces double the growth rate in exchange for using half again more electricity for half the duration. It'll get even cheaper. Pretty soon you'll find *inexpensive* LED assemblies putting out a perfect spectrum for vegetative growth.

HID bulbs generate heat. A 250-watt bulb must be about one foot from the top leaves. The light intensity is so high that leaves 30 inches from the lamp still can get enough light.

Plants need a dark period. Four hours of darkness in each 24 can be enough. But after being pushed that hard, the seedlings of some species experience an even larger transplanting shock when you put them into a shorter day length. I suggest a stable 16-hour illumination period and a timer to keep it regular.

FERTILIZERS

Whenever I've put enough COF into a soil mix to grow a seedling to transplanting size, I've inadvertently reduced or sometimes wrecked seed germination. The solution is moderate but balanced fertility in the growing medium (especially calcium) supplemented by liquid fertilizer. But supplying balanced nutrition from concentrates is not always straightforward. Fish emulsion is usually 7-2-2 or thereabouts: too much nitrogen. Ideally you'd want 5-10-5. With organics I think the best compromise is liquid seaweed concentrate diluted to one-quarter the recommended strength combined with fish emulsion at one-quarter recommended strength, in all water. If you're going to use liquid organic concentrates, in addition to aglime I suggest also mixing bonemeal or guano into your potting mix at ½ cup per 5 gallons. Compared to fish emulsion

I've gotten better results with Miracle-Gro or Peters 20-20-20 diluted to one-quarter the recommended strength and included in all water.

I think ongoing fertigation is synergistic in that the more the sun shines or the more light intensity, the faster the seedlings grow and the more water they transpire, so the faster they intake nutrition. I dilute fertilizer this much because providing all the nitrogen a plant can tolerate results in lush leaves and spindly stems. If you use concentrates at or close to full strength, including organic concentrates, the seedlings soon get overdosed. You'll soon see a faint yellow/brown fringe developing on the leaf margins. Immediately flush out the pots with pure water and from then on reduce the fertilizer concentration to what I recommend.

A few years ago my local garden center opened a hydroponics aisle featuring a huge display of liquid fertilizer concentrates. Most of them are two-part hydroponic fertilizers that must be diluted and mixed immediately before use. I tried using an A-B fertilizer to supplement my own transplant-raising mix (against advice), and sure enough, because my growing medium has buffering capacity, before too long the plants began to suffer from toxic imbalances. My local shop also sells liquid organic concentrates compounded for growing cannabis in soil or soil-like media. Some of these work better than fish, kelp, Miracle-Gro, or Peters. Almost every grow shop in the world provides a mind-boggling assortment of liquid fertilizers. I couldn't test them all. However, Canna is the largest-selling brand worldwide, so I tried that one. Canna's Terra Vega is designed for soil-based media. It rapidly grows stronger seedlings than any other fertilizer concentrate I've ever used. Terra Vega's written instructions are targeted at skilled growers who measure the concentration of their nutrient solutions with an electrical conductivity meter. Instead of becoming confused, mix Terra Vega at two kitchen measuring teaspoons per gallon (2.5 milliliters per liter). Although the label suggests using up to 4.5 milliliter per liter on an indoor cannabis crop growing under extreme luxury conditions, do not use more than what I recommend on vegetable seedlings.

COLD FRAMES

After the seedling has germinated and produced two pairs of true leaves indoors, it can grow on to transplanting size outdoors in an inexpensive cold frame cobbled together from recycled materials. On a frosty night a tight frame with fitted windows, all joints caulked, all gaps sealed, can increase nighttime temperatures quite a few degrees. Even a hastily constructed, drafty frame keeps nighttime temperatures warmer enough to make a big difference. When frost is predicted, old wool blankets or tarps can be spread over the frame. The family garden needs a cold frame no larger than 3 feet wide by 5 feet long, 18 inches tall at the back and 10 inches high at the front, built very much like the one described in Chapter 4.

Having both a cold frame and an indoor grow light is advantageous. By mid-March the light level in the frame exceeds what fluorescents produce, so in a frame you get faster growth from frost-tolerant species while you simultaneously harden them off. March/April daytime temperatures can be kept cooler than indoors (advantageous for cool-season transplants). This makes the cold frame a fine place to put half-grown brassica transplants. After a few weeks in the frame, they'll be stocky and strong and ready for transplanting.

By mid-April the cold frame will be comfortable for tomato seedlings. If four- or five-week-old tomatoes are transplanted into 10-inch pots and put out in the frame in mid-April, they'll be hardened off and have flowers (and maybe fruit) on them when you transplant them a month to six weeks later. About the time no more frosts are expected and the frame has been emptied of tomato seedlings, it becomes a suitable environment for hardening off peppers, eggplants, melons, and cucumbers, where they can grow fast for a few weeks while waiting for summery weather.

A hot frame is a cold frame with a source of heat below it. In the old days frames were placed above pits filled with fresh, strong manure that heated naturally. Now most people use thermostatically controlled electric cables buried in the soil. I used one like that when I did trials. Hot frames enable a gardener to germinate seeds and grow seedlings entirely outside. Hot frames are not necessary if you can live with seedlings in the house for a month or two every spring; however, most serious gardeners will eventually want a cold frame.

ASSORTED SUGGESTIONS AND RESTATEMENTS

In commercial greenhouse operations, fungicide-treated seeds are sown in sterile media. The germination media is brought to the ideal moisture content, seeds are sown in it, and then the sprouting trays are covered with clear, airtight lids, placed on electrically heated benches, and kept at optimum temperatures until the seeds sprout. There is no damping-off. The germination rate achieved will be very close to that of a germination laboratory. If (costly) very high germination hybrid seed is used, the grower can have automatic seeding equipment place one seed in each cell and end up with nearly every cell occupied, with every plant in the tray looking great.

If something like my growing medium and untreated seed are used, germination percentage will drop. If the variety outcrosses and is open-pollinated, some seedlings will not be vigorous or desirable. Consequently, the gardener should sprout three to five seeds in every container or cell, and then gradually cull weaker seedlings until only one remains. With this approach, damping-off diseases let nature assist thinning.

For most species, trays and pots that are germinating seeds can be put above the fluorescent light bank, where the heat generated by the lamps and ballasts creates quite warm conditions. In fact, this place can be too warm. In that case, use spacers to create some airflow below the germinating containers.

The mantle over a fireplace insert or a shelf near the woodstove may be a good spot if it doesn't get too warm there. Inside the kitchen oven with the oven lamp turned on can also be quite workable as long as no one accidentally bakes your seeds. Atop the hot water tank isn't always a good spot because they're too well insulated these days. Garden centers and mail-order seed companies sell electric heat pads to put under germinating seedlings. Keeping a 250-watt HID lamp running 24 hours a day above a tray of germinating seeds (until they sprout) will do it too.

Maintain the moisture level by sealing the germinating tray or pot in a clear plastic bag until the seedlings emerge. After germination, thin progressively. Don't let plants force one another's stems very far off vertical as they compete for light. Thinning is best done with small, sharp scissors. By the time the seedlings have started their second pair of true leaves, thinning should have been completed. Then they're about ready to be moved to a cold frame if you've got one.

Growing Guide, A to Z

Planting dates in this section are for the Willamette Valley, Oregon. Gardeners to the south of this area might start seedlings a few weeks earlier; gardeners much north of the Columbia River should start seedlings a week or two later.

Beans Grow transplants only if your aim is to achieve the earliest-possible harvest. About three weeks before the last frost date, sow two seeds per individual 3-inch pot. Sprout at 70 to 75 degrees F. Thin promptly to one plant per pot. Grow under lights for about one week and then move to a cold frame until the first pair of true leaves are fully developed and the next pair is forming. Transplant outdoors when there no longer is frost danger. An early start like this is

A Typical Transplanting Calendar

Sow under Lights	Species	Move to Cold Frame	Transplant in Garden
February 1	Autumn leeks	April 1	May 1–31
February 1	Bulb onions	March 5–15	April 1–15
February 15	Early cabbage, broccoli	March 5	April 1
February 15	Celery, celeriac	April 15	May 15
March 1	Cauliflower	March 20	April 10
March 1	Earliest possible lettuce	March 20	April 10
March 15	Tomatoes	April 15	May 1–15
April 1	Peppers, eggplant	May 5	June 1–15
April 15	Squash	April 25	May 1
May 20	Cucumbers, melon	June 1	June 5–10

Note: Dates in this table are for Willamette Valley, Oregon, gardeners. South of Drain, Oregon, these dates may be a week or two too late, even more so in the redwoods. North of Longview, Washington, and at higher elevations in western Oregon, these dates may be a week or two too early.

almost essential to obtain any yield from lima beans. Sowing chitted bean seeds works nearly as well.

Beets Grow transplants to achieve the earliest-possible harvest. A beet seed usually produces a cluster of seedlings. In March, sow two seeds per individual 3-inch pot or cell. Sprout at 65 to 70 degrees F. Grow for two to four weeks at 60 to 70 degrees F under lights and then transfer to a cold frame, if available. Do not thin unless you end up with more than four plants per pot. Hold in a cold frame until the seedling clusters are 4 to 5 inches tall. Do not allow beet seedlings to become pot-bound. Transplant clusters 12 inches apart in rows 18 inches apart. Although growing beets in clusters of four may seem crowded, by using sufficient spacing when transplanting clusters, almost every plant will form a good

(although not perfectly round) beet. It's best for this purpose to use a less-refined open-pollinated variety, one with variable maturation, like Early Wonder.

Broccoli To me it only makes sense to raise seedlings in order to harvest the first broccoli of the year a few weeks earlier than is possible from a directly seeded crop. And don't be too eager—early broccoli is a risky bet because transplants checked by cold conditions may not head out well and early seedlings face the most root maggots.

Sow in February, three to five seeds per individual cell or in a 2- or 3-inch pot. Broccoli sprouts fast at 70 to 75 degrees F. Thin progressively. Grow two to three weeks under lights with temperatures under 70 degrees F daytime, above 40 degrees F at night. Lower dark period temperatures make stockier seedlings. Transfer at the two-leaf stage to a cold frame, if available. When seedlings have three fully developed true leaves (usually this happens five to six weeks after sowing if you use a cold frame), they should be well rooted and ready to set out. Try to schedule transplanting during the earliest week you could direct-seed broccoli. Reckon transplants give you a few weeks' head start. When transplanting outdoors, consider using hot caps or else transplant into a cloche.

Brussels Sprouts If an early harvest is desired, grow transplants like broccoli, use an early maturing variety, and expect to fight aphids from the moment sprouts start forming. Better the crop is direct seeded in June and scheduled to begin harvesting mid to late autumn when the aphid season has passed.

Cabbage For earliest heads, use an early variety and grow like broccoli.

Cauliflower Cauliflower is more sensitive to chill and maggots than cabbage or broccoli. Schedule the crop so that it will be transplanted around the end of March. After April I cauliflower is better direct seeded. For early crops I recommend using a variety developed especially for this season such as Snow Crown.

Celery and Celeriac Between February 15 and March 15, sow clumps of four or five seeds in 2- or 3-inch pots or cells. Seeds sprout best between 60 and 70 degrees F. Thin gradually to reduce light competition. Grow at 65 to 75 degrees F during the day, 50 to 60 degrees F at night. Celery requires nearly three months of bright light in light, loose, fertile growing medium to attain transplanting size. Move to a cold frame for the last weeks but not before nighttime temperatures in the frame are reliably above 50 degrees F. Too many hours' exposure to temperatures below 45 degrees F makes celery seedlings bolt prematurely. I prefer to direct-seed celery between May 15 and June 1, before the arrival of hot weather makes achieving germination nearly impossible, but late enough that cold nights won't induce premature flowering.

Sweet Corn You can harvest a week sooner by starting transplants about two weeks ahead of the last usual frost date. Sow three seeds per 3-inch pot, and thin promptly to two plants per pot. Corn seedlings become pot-bound very quickly. Transplant pairs of corn seedlings every 20 to 24 inches in the row; make the rows 30 inches apart. Corn will do ever so slightly better spaced one plant every 10 to 12 inches in rows 30 inches apart, which is about how I direct-seed it.

Cucumbers Cucurbits fill a seedling container in short order. Cucumber transplants should be sown when tomato seedlings are transplanted out. Raising cucumber transplants makes more sense north of the Columbia.

Put two or three seeds, 1 inch deep, in a 2- or 3-inch pot sealed in a poly bag. The ideal germination temperature range is 75 to 80 degrees F. Cucumber seed will sprout at 70 degrees F, but takes longer. Remove the poly bag as soon as the shoot appears; this lowers humidity and prevents disease. Grow at 70 to 80 degrees F in the daytime, over 55 degrees F at night. Thin to the best plant per pot before the second true leaf fully develops. Transfer to a cold frame for a final week of slight hardening off; it is impossible to make cucumbers (or melons) very hard. Transplant very carefully; the roots are easily damaged.

Eggplant Eggplant grows like peppers, but note that young seedlings are even more sensitive to temperatures below 50 degrees F than peppers are.

Kale Kale grows like superbroccoli, so vigorous that direct seeding is preferable. Kale is much better tasting in fall than during the heat of summer. Raising transplants seems pointless to me.

Kohlrabi Don't raise transplants. I always direct-seed about April 1 and fully enjoy them before hot weather hits. For fall harvest, direct-seed about August 1.

Leeks If summertime harvest is desired, raise transplants like onions and be sure to use faster-growing less-frost-hardy leek varieties of the sort intended for late summer/autumn harvest. If autumn/winter harvest is desired, direct-seed leeks in a nursery bed outdoors. (See Onions, below, for more details.)

Lettuce Raise transplants only for the earliest-possible spring harvest, and otherwise grow like broccoli. I direct-seed lettuce, never transplant it.

Melons Grow like cucumbers, but note that melons are even more sensitive to low temperatures and damp conditions in the seedling stage.

Onions If your goal is to raise prizewinning lunkers or have the earliest-possible scallion harvest, raise transplants. Start them in February and push them hard. The best way is to sow eight seeds per inch, in rows 3 inches apart on a deep seedling tray; if using cell trays, sow four to six seeds per 2-inch cell. Sprout seed between 60 and 70 degrees F. Grow at 50 to 70 degrees F in the day and 40 to 50 degrees F at night. Do not thin. After seedlings have grown about 4 inches tall, use sharp scissors to take the top inch off the leaves—give the leaves about a 25 percent haircut. This promotes thicker stems and better-developed root systems. After the leaves grow another 2 inches, cut off ½ inch, and so forth. Use a 16- to 18-hour light period.

Transplant when stems are about ³⁄₁₆ inch in diameter, or by May 1 at the latest no matter their size (as long as they're large enough to survive transplanting). Onions transplant bare root, so separate the individual seedlings by gently shaking them apart.

Parsley Slow to germinate, parsley is often transplanted, although it establishes readily if directly seeded in midspring after the soils have warmed but before hot days make the soil dry out quickly. Direct-seeded parsley forms a proper taproot, so it handles dry soil better. Otherwise, grow parsley transplants like broccoli, but note that germination can take 14 to 17 days and is best at 60 degrees F.

Peppers Many gardeners set peppers out at the same time as tomatoes. This subjects pepper seedlings to overnight temperatures they can't handle easily. It is far better to go through a few weeks of hardening off, and then transplant larger but hardier pepper seedlings a few weeks after the tomatoes go out.

Start pepper seedlings six to eight weeks before the last expected frost. In 3-inch individual pots or 2-inch cells, sow a clump of four seeds. Sprout this heat-demanding seed at over 70 degrees F (best at 75 degrees F). Grow at 65 to 75 degrees F in the day, above 55 degrees F at night. Thin gradually to one plant per pot or cell.

After tomato seedlings have been planted out, pepper seedlings should be potted up a size and hardened off until summer is really on—around mid-June. Then transplant.

Squash Squash may be hardier than cucumbers, but they are equally difficult to transplant and need bigger pots than cucumbers do, since the seedlings start out larger and grow faster. I suggest germinating squash seeds at 70 to 75 degrees F. Start them two weeks before the last anticipated frost, and sow three seeds in a 4-inch pot. Once germinated, thin to two plants and move them immediately to a cold frame, if available. Grow the pair of seedlings only four

to seven days, until their roots hold the soil ball together enough to transplant without causing too much damage. Open-pollinated summer squash varieties these days don't get much plant breeder attention, so they sometimes produce plants that are not true to type. Best to delay thinning open-pollinated summer squash to a single plant per position until the pair of plants have formed their first fruit.

Tomatoes For the earliest-possible harvest, transplant large, hardened-off seedlings with fruit already on them. Sow about March 1. Move the seedlings to a cold frame around April 1, and transplant a few weeks later into a tunnel cloche. Another strategy: hold the tomatoes in 1-gallon pots in the cold frame until late May, setting out 18-inch-tall seedlings already bearing fruit. Tomato seedlings can be started indoors as late as April 30. Sow a cluster of four seeds in each 2- or 3-inch pot or cell, ½ inch deep. Sprout at 70 to 75 degrees F. Grow under lights. Hold temperatures at 65 to 75 degrees F in the day, 50 to 60 degrees F at night. Thin gradually to one plant per pot. Harden off. In a cold frame try to keep nighttime lows above 40 degrees F.

Chapter Eight

PESTS

Soil microorganisms interact with higher plants. Given identical soil conditions the composition of the microflora changes sharply with the type of plants growing on that soil. Plants are a very strong ecological factor, favoring certain species of bacteria, fungi, actinomycetes and other inhabitants of the soil while discouraging others. As a result of wrong agricultural practice the soil becomes infested with harmful microbial forms. By use of suitable plants in the crop rotation, one may change the microflora of soil in the desired direction, and eliminate harmful organisms, in other words—restore the health of soil.

—N. A. Krasil'nikov, Soil Microorganisms and Higher Plants, 1958

MANY ORGANIC GARDENERS believe that before a plant suffers from insect or disease trouble, it already was malnourished. Another way of saying this is that once the soil has been built up enough, disease and insects will not cause problems. Thinking this way leads to spreading too much compost because insects and diseases will occasionally cause problems no matter what the gardener does. I would say *most of the time* a strong, healthy plant will either be uninteresting to pests or will handily outgrow insect damage.

A well-nourished plant succumbs to disease *only* when environmental conditions are very stressful.

Natural Immunity

Before going into the seed business, I used garden center transplants. One spring I had three excess cabbage seedlings. Rather than waste them, I experimented: I dug up a never-before-used never-fertilized spot on the garden's edge and planted them, blending in only a little "complete" *chemical* fertilizer, but no compost and no lime. The other cabbage seedlings grew big and healthy on properly prepared ground. No problems. The seedlings on the fringe were severely attacked by flea beetles, which I sprayed. Then they were attacked by root maggots, and one died. In the end cabbages from fertile garden soil were around 5 pounds each and fine tasting; the two survivors on the fringe weighed in at less than 2 pounds each, had a harsh taste, and chewed tough.

I once grew a brussels sprout trial involving 96 plants, 8 plants each of a dozen different varieties. Aphids find just-forming brussels sprouts an irresistible treat. All early maturing varieties get heavily infested and must be sprayed again and again. Before any variety in this trial even started forming sprouts, all eight plants of one poorly adapted variety had aphids all over the large leaves, something I had never seen before nor ever since, while all the plants of the other varieties were untouched. In another case, disease

picked off a single tomato plant while other plants of the same variety touching the diseased plant remained healthy. Probably something damaged that plant when it was a seedling. Or maybe it was a genetic mutation. Or maybe that spot got too little COF. Or maybe . . . maybe speculation about what I did wrong is of little use. Maybe it's best to just grow half again more than I think I'll need and accept minor losses with minor concern.

Sometimes insect populations reach plague levels that no plant can outgrow no matter how healthy it is. Overwhelming insect attacks most often happen in gardens located near insecticide-protected farm crops because agricultural poisons kill off the beneficials. And sometimes unusual weather favors an insect that is rarely seen in normal years.

Diseases usually strike when plants become stressed. Sometimes there's nothing to be done. During an extremely poor summer in the 1980s, all the tomato plants growing outdoors in all of Cascadia had already become badly stressed by cold, damp conditions and lack of sunlight. The straw that broke the donkey's back was the stress of seed formation. When tomatoes first started ripening, a disease called "late blight" raced through the entire territory, scything down every tomato plant except for a few strong ones that had grown in greenhouses or under the protective eaves above a sun-facing white-painted wall.

PESTICIDE VERSUS FERTILIZER

I must spray cabbage worms or forego growing many kinds of brassicas. Fortunately, what I use is entirely nontoxic to other species. Otherwise, nothing else always requires fighting.

Before you rush to spray pesticides, first look closely: Is the plant significantly outgrowing the problem? Are we talking about a few odd pinholes in the leaves, or is it severe? Loss of less than 10 percent of a plant's photosynthetic area reduces the outcome by the same minor percentage. Usually, leaf-chewing insects and slugs are only a small annoyance to a fast-growing plant. When transplants are being chewed down as fast or faster than they are growing, the real problem may be that they were put out too early. Spraying pesticide can help fend off the problem until weather conditions improve. Sometimes the problem was caused by sowing too few seeds. If you start many more seedlings than the final number of plants ultimately wanted, you can benevolently allow pests to help you thin out the weaker individuals. Slug baits and pesticides may be a valuable short-term springtime solution while waiting for growth to accelerate.

At summer's end chill and decreasing light levels can trigger diseases and bring insects like spider mites and whiteflies on fruiting crops; these plants are hardly worth fighting for since their season is virtually over.

Certain vegetables are fussy about soil type; these species may be attacked by insects or disease, and there is little or nothing that can be done short of importing a bed of special soil. I have experienced globe artichoke, celery, celeriac, melons, radishes, and caulis growing poorly in heavy soil. And brussels sprouts prefer heavy loam.

GARDENING AIKIDO

I try to coexist with nature. I prefer to think of pests helping me in the same way gardeners who return nonperforming seed packets for credit give their supplier a heads-up. An important step along this gentle path is to grow a large-enough garden. Then you remain sanguine, even when a crop fails. Some years the sun just doesn't shine often enough, the tomatoes get diseased, melons and cucumbers succumb to powdery mildew, eggplants won't set, peppers don't mature, corn is very late and not very sweet, French beans become covered with aphids. But at least you can eat a lot of greens and root crops.

Another way to avoid doing battle is to reject what I call the American Sanitary System, something I judge by its acronym. The industrial food system requires that food should be entirely free of any evidence that a bug ever touched it. Why, imagine the utter horror of finding a blanched cabbage worm in a frozen broccoli packet! Why not change your attitude; accept insects. There's a big difference between a plant showing the effect of an occasional insect and one that has been severely damaged. As long as the plant is still growing fast, a few (even a few hundred) pinholes in the leaves don't matter. And what's the worry about an occasional scar on a cucumber's skin? As long as the cook can peel off the damage without wasting too much time, why fight it?

Pest Control

Sometimes circumstances demand taking action or you won't get a harvest. Still, it's always best to choose the least harmful option. The Organic Materials Review Institute (OMRI) evaluates fertilizers and pesticides along these lines. An "OMRI Listed" designation does not necessarily mean the product is completely natural; it means *permitted for use in organic agriculture*. OMRI charges substantial fees to check out a product before listing it, so not being on the OMRI List could mean that a small manufacturer chose not to apply for listing. Getting a product on the List sometimes requires balancing safety with almost religious doctrines about the concept "organic."

For the certification bureaucracy the word "organic" means a naturally occurring material created by a living thing. Pyrethrins are a naturally occurring mixture of similar chemicals extracted from chrysanthemum flowers with hexane. Hexane is also used to extract vegetable oil from oilseeds. The word "organic" also carries religious connotations that sometimes require mental gymnastics. An organic certification rabbi could argue that hexane is a natural material distilled from crude oil and that the extraction process does not alter pyrethrins chemically, so it can be certified "organic."

"Inorganic" means not of biological origin. Currently approved inorganic substances include ground-up sulfur, diatomaceous earth, and other natural mined materials like rock phosphate and guano. These can be OMRI Listed because they have not been chemically altered and are not poisonous. Sodium nitrate and potassium chloride are soluble fertilizers, once considered acceptable for certified organics because they also are natural mined substances. These two are no longer approved for use—and for good reason.

"Synthetic" means made by human beings. But here is where distinguishing acceptable from unacceptable confuses ideologically minded people because some natural insecticides are far more dangerous than many chemical pesticides. For example, nicotine extracted from the tobacco plant was used since colonial times as an extremely potent insecticide, and it certainly is an organic, naturally occurring substance, but nicotine is so toxic to mammals that its use was discontinued in industrial agriculture when far less dangerous synthetic insecticides came on the scene. Rotenone is a naturally occurring chemical extracted from a tropical root. It was long used as an insecticide by organic growers but is now rejected by certification bureaucrats because of possible links to neurological damage with prolonged exposure. I dusted bush beans with rotenone one afternoon only to find thousands of dead worms on the bed's surface the next morning after an unexpected rain washed the dust into the soil.

The newest pest controls are *biological*, including bacterial cultures, viruses, fungi, living parasitic nematodes, and beneficial insects as well as chemicals manufactured by these organisms. *Bacillus thuringiensis*, or Bt, is probably the most familiar example; it is a strain of bacteria that targets leaf- and fruit-eating caterpillars.

Spinosad is another very useful option, described in the short list following.

A lot of people think that certified organic produce is unsprayed, but nothing could be further from the truth. Industrial organically grown crops must still conform to the American Sanitary System, so they get sprayed more often than conventional crops because OMRI-approved sprays are less effective and break down faster than the pesticides used in industrial agriculture. This is part of why certified organically grown produce costs more.

For most OMRI-approved pesticides to be effective, the insect must directly contact the spray and, though tedious, you must spray the undersides and inner recesses where most of the eggs and juveniles are hiding. This is essential. An insect wandering through a few hours after spraying won't be killed.

Insects develop resistance to naturally occurring poisons the same as they do with synthetic poisons, which is why it is wise to alternate products with each spraying. OMRI-approved pesticides kill bees, so early mornings or shortly before dark are the best times to spray.

Seven Springs Farm in Virginia provides an unusually broad selection of OMRI-certified products. Their catalog online links to full product information and usage tips.

PESTICIDES

Pyrethrins quickly kill aphids, flea beetles, asparagus beetles, cucumber beetles, leafhoppers, cabbage loopers, and cabbage worms. I would use pyrethrin products containing piperonyl butoxide, a natural synergist that makes pyrethrins more effective. Certified organic producers are not allowed to. A high concentration pyrethrin product like PyGanic, 5 percent, is more effective on adult hard-shelled insects. The typical garden center pyrethrins strength is about 1 percent. Some pesticides combine pyrethrins with a botanical oil—pyrethrins get the adults; the oil smothers the larval stages. Pyrethrins may require respraying every few days.

Bt (*Bacillus thuringiensis*) is not a contact insecticide. What you mix in water is a culture of living bacteria, often resembling dry baker's yeast, that effectively poisons a family of moth larvae when they eat some sprayed plant material. Susceptible species include three kinds of cabbage worms, corn earworms, tomato hornworms, and tomato fruitworms. Be sure to add a few drops of liquid soap, mild dishwashing liquid, or an organic sticker/spreader, or else the spray rolls off brassica leaves. Use as little water softener as possible because these substances may damage leaves in high concentrations. I find about a scant measuring ¼ teaspoonful of low-suds dishwashing detergent is enough for a gallon of spray. Bt has a limited shelf life. My Bt remains effective for more years, stored under refrigeration with my seeds.

Spinosad is a naturally occurring poison the OMRI likes. It is extracted from cultured *Saccharopolyspora spinosa*, a bacteria. Spinosad kills numerous pests, but its effectiveness varies according to which life stages are present. Spinosad controls cabbage worms, leaf miners on spinach, beets, and chard, and many kinds of thrips. Use of a surfactant/penetrant is recommended for maximum absorption into leaf tissue if used for leaf miners. It is a good choice to alternate with Bt for caterpillars. Spinosad's effectiveness against mites, aphids, flea beetles, and whiteflies is erratic.

Spinosad is toxic to honeybees and other foraging insects, so spray when they are not present. While still wet, Spinosad is an effective contact poison. After it dries, a sprayed leaf must be eaten for Spinosad to be effective. A Spinosad bait, Seduce, is used for earwigs and cutworms. Spinosad is the ingredient added to iron phosphate in Sluggo Plus, which kills slugs as well as earwigs, sow bugs, and others.

Neem oil pressed from the seeds of the neem tree (*Azadirachta indica*) and its potent extract *azadirachtin* are worth mentioning. Neem oil is widely regarded as entirely safe for mammals. It acts as a repellent for mealybugs, beet armyworms, aphids, cabbage worms, thrips, whiteflies, mites, fungus gnats, beetles, moth larvae, mushroom flies, leaf miners, caterpillars, nematodes, and Japanese beetles. Neem oil is not considered a threat to birds, earthworms, or beneficial insects if it is not applied directly to their primary habitat or food source. Neem oil also controls black spot, powdery mildew, anthracnose, and rust (fungus), so it is sometimes packaged as Rose Defense or with different names for other specialized uses. The oil is viscous and works best if you premix the needed amount in warm/hot water and use warm water in the sprayer, or else it will clog the nozzle. You may have to clean the sprayer with hot soapy water afterward too.

The *azadirachtin* content of neem oil varies widely depending on the concentration in the seed itself as well as processing methods. Most neem oil has very little. Azadirachtin concentrate is much more potent. As well as disrupting feeding, azadirachtin acts like a hormone that prevents juveniles from developing into adults. Azadirachtin alone is usually not sufficient by itself if there are already large numbers of adults, so it is often combined with a fast-acting insecticide for best effect. It is very popular with indoor growers and gardeners with greenhouses for use against spider mites. An application lasts 10 to 14 days but is pricey, so it may be impractical for large areas. Studies report that so far no insects have shown resistance to repeated uses.

One caution: neem oil can leave a bitter taste behind that just won't go away. It can work well on seedlings or half-grown vegetable plants, but its long-lingering aftertaste might not please you when it is sprayed on the edible parts of vegetables or on medicinal herbs.

Insecticidal soaps such as the Safer brand have been in use for a few decades now and have a record of effectiveness. Old garden books recommend pouring dirty dishwater over vegetable plants to kill bugs. The insecticidal power of soaps varies greatly according to the kind of fat used to make them. The spray of insecticidal soap products must contact the insect directly; make sure it heavily covers the entire plant, especially underleaf. Soaps have proved most useful for small insects such as aphids, thrips, mites, and leafhoppers, and less so with larger insects. The soap can make plant foliage susceptible to sunburn. Young transplants, stressed plants, and certain species may be adversely affected, especially seedling-size cole crops and spinach, so test before dosing the whole crop. Do not spray insecticidal soap during intensely sunny afternoons.

Insecticidal oils, also known as *horticultural oils*, kill insect eggs, larvae, and adults of soft-bodied species. The product may be a single type of oil or combination formula involving paraffin, canola, fish, or sesame oil, possibly in combination with rosemary, eucalyptus, garlic, clove, etc. Oils have repellent properties; they disrupt feeding or smother pests (or both). To be effective, the oil must thoroughly coat the foliage, but leaves must breathe in order to function normally, and the oil inhibits this to some degree, and can be destructively more to some species. Be careful. Do not use horticultural oil when temperatures are below 40 degrees or over 90 degrees F. Be sure to water plants well before spraying. Young plants, plants with thin leaves, and plants under any kind of environmental stress are likely to be more susceptible to injury, so test first. *Hot pepper wax* is in much the same category as far as mode of action and cautions are concerned.

Diatomaceous earth is the fossilized remains of diatom, an algae that protects itself in a shell made of silicon—like glass. The form used by gardeners is an abrasive powder so fine and so sharp that it is able to penetrate the exoskeletons of insects, causing their dehydration and death. The form used to filter water doesn't kill insects. It must be thoroughly dusted above and below in order to directly contact insects. Accomplishing this requires a pump duster. People dusting diatomaceous earth must wear masks. Some gardeners swear by it. Researchers have concluded that diatomaceous earth is rendered ineffective when coated by clay, making it short acting

against symphylans. Still, a handful worked into each planting spot in spring may allow seedlings to outgrow symphylan pressure.

Floating row covers are an organically approved control for cabbage root maggots. They are very lightweight spun fabrics that pass light, wind, and water but screen out insects. Spun fabrics raise temperature like a cloche does. The thicker fabrics provide several degrees of frost protection but allow less light through and resist wind more. Usually the fabric is laid loosely over the row, and plants lift it as they get taller. Thicker fabrics may be supported by lightweight hoops. For insect control, either method requires that the edges are held down with soil so that bugs can't fly in or crawl in. Row covers fail if they are placed over an area already infested with eggs or larvae. Slugs have a way of showing up too, so don't just cover and forget about it.

Row covers prevent insect pollination, so when used to accelerate early vine growth on cucurbits, they must be removed for fruits to form. Leaf and root crops can remain covered from seed to harvest, though you must temporarily lift the cover to remove weeds and thin. Covers also protect cabbage, broccoli, and cauliflower from cabbage butterflies and their subsequent caterpillars. Flea beetles will be stopped, as will thrips on onions, leaf miners on beets, and spinach and early season cucumber beetles.

APHIDS TO WILDLIFE

Aphids

Aphids, sometimes called plant lice, are small, soft-bodied insects that cluster on leaves and stems, sucking plant sap and causing leaves to curl and cup. Sometimes there are only a few that cause no apparent problem. Aphids multiply with amazing rapidity, exploding from none to a serious threat in hours. Aphids can overwhelm stressed plants. When something has more than a few aphids on it, the most likely causes are crowding, moisture stress, or imbalanced soil. Your initial questions should be: Do the plants have room to keep growing without competition? Is there sufficient soil moisture? Are surrounding crops growing fast (soil fertility, in general)? If the crop has been bearing for a while, has it become exhausted?

I have read that some ants raise aphids to milk a sweet secretion from them. I've never seen this happening. However, I have had occasion to eliminate ant nests whose members were invading my kitchen. The ant baits you can buy these days are based upon borax, which is an essential plant nutrient that happens to be poisonous to ants. Make your own bait by dissolving a scant ¼ teaspoon of ordinary laundry borax into a generous tablespoon of slightly heated (liquefied) honey. If these ants take sugar, a feeding frenzy develops and persists a few days, and then the ants fade away.

Aphids can be sprayed off with a hose and nozzle, but more soon appear unless you've remedied the underlying stress. Pyrethrins are effective, as are insecticidal soaps and pepper wax repellents. To eliminate aphid clusters developing on newly forming brussels sprouts in September, grow varieties that don't start fattening their sprouts until October or later. (See Chapter 9 for more information on growing brussels sprouts.)

Aphids sometimes cover plants when they approach the end of their life cycle. If aphids appear on hot weather crops late in summer, I'd ignore them and start eating something else. Besides, the fruit coming from those exhausted plants won't taste nearly as interesting as it did three weeks before.

Beneficial insects

Your vegetable garden and ornamental beds already sustain beneficial insects. Rural and suburban sites that are close to extensive areas of mixed, unsprayed vegetation usually have plenty of helpful bugs. Native bees work the vegetable garden. Parasitoid wasps lay eggs into other insect species' eggs and larvae, thus destroying the viability of the host. Ladybugs eat aphids, mites, and other undesirables. Spiders have voracious appetites. It is possible to buy starter populations of some beneficials, but this is more relevant to greenhouse operations than gardeners. Predators travel in search of prey. If your garden and its immediate surroundings will naturally feed them, they will come.

To help beneficials prosper, grow ornamentals that feed harmless insects that predators like to eat. Sweet alyssum is a quick-growing annual that will self-sow, though not invasively, and has the type of flat, shallow flowers that small insects seek out for nectar and pollen. Love-lies-bleeding, asters, cosmos, and calendula helps. Growing thyme, dill, and borage also help. (For more information, see Chapter 10.) Many seed companies sell assortments of insect-attracting ornamentals.

The best spot to release beneficials is near the veggie garden in a permanent patch where both perennials and annuals grow, ideally anchored by a shrub or tree such as an elderberry, which also has flowers attractive to beneficials. This area also provides a winter refuge for insects and spiders.

Fava beans and clover are favored by certain beneficial insects, so cover cropping helps too.

Cabbage root maggots

Cabbage root maggots are larvae of a small insect resembling the common housefly. The sly fly usually doesn't lay its eggs next to a cabbage family plant until the root system has become big enough to support her brood (when the stem approaches ¼ inch in diameter). The larvae feed on roots.

The gardener discovers maggots when the weaker-rooting members of the family—cabbage, broccoli, cauliflower, and sometimes brussels sprouts—wilt and die on a sunny spring day. Lesser infestations stunt plants so much that they barely grow. The maggots also tunnel through turnips, radishes, and the lower portions of Chinese cabbage leaves. They tend to leave rutabagas alone, or at most scar up the thick skin, which is peeled away before cooking. Direct-seeded brassicas outgrow maggot damage better.

The only way brassicas can survive maggots in spring is to grow roots a lot faster than the maggots eat them. That means you must somehow provide excellent seedbed conditions in a season when the soil is usually too wet to work up properly, and supply plenty of plant nutrients at a time when the cool soil isn't releasing

them rapidly. COF helps greatly. The variety you choose also has a lot to do with how vigorous the root system will be. When I owned Territorial, I did brassica trials without any maggot protection. In the case of radish and turnip crops, variety makes no difference; only timely harvest can get them out of the ground before the maggots have invaded.

Gardeners can avoid much trouble by direct seeding brassicas after the maggot's April/May population peak. By early June the cabbage fly population has decreased greatly while the spring maggot hatch has finished feeding and now is pupating in the soil. So mid-May through July is less stressful. Maggot levels increase again in late summer when the pupae hatch out, but by then brassicas have grown large enough to withstand considerable predation, while light intensity has dropped so much that even if plants do lose some roots, they are not likely to wilt.

The late E. Blair Adams, research horticulturist at the Washington State University Puyallup Research and Extension Center, did extensive trials on traditional remedies. He found that dustings of wood ashes—once widely recommended—actually attracted the cabbage fly; he speculated that ashes helped anyway because in unlimed, acidic, calcium-deficient soils, wood ashes provide some calcium that boosts brassica growth enough to compensate for the increased predation the ash caused. Diatomaceous earth did not kill the soft-skinned maggots. Blair found that burying the root system deeper by persistently hilling up soil around the stems increased the survival rate.

Cone bug shields protect plants in their earlier stages (see illustration). Plastic screen is easier to work with than metal, and cones made with plastic will lie flat for storage, but the metal screen forms a stiffer cone. For a transplant-size cone, cut screen in a wide triangle from a piece about 30 inches wide by 20 inches high. Then make it curve as illustrated and join the side edges. Window screen is easily machine sewn. If you use nylon thread, it should last several seasons. If you want to skip the sewing, just form the cone by bringing the edges together. Staple the overlap to a slender piece of wood. There should be 4 to 6 inches of wood at the bottom edge to insert into the soil, anchoring the cone. To keep out the bugs, if you haven't sewn the cut sides before stapling them to the wood, you'll need to use more staples or run a bead of caulk to glue the gaps together or make the join between two wood strips, one inside and one out. When you set the cone, make sure the bottom edge is buried in the soil. Protective cones can have plastic bags slipped over them for extra warmth if very cold weather threatens, but if you forget to remove the plastic, the plants cook.

BUG CONES from WINDOW SCREEN

Cut a 36" circle of screen and divide in half. A lightweight 24" wood support such as a lattice strip is needed for each one.

folded edge

For each half circle: Fold in half, bringing cut edges together. Machine or hand sew or staple with closed staples ½" in from cut edge.

Place wood piece between layers underneath joined edges, leaving about 6" of wood stake to anchor into soil. If stapled and not sewn, press a bead of caulk along seam for tighter seam. Let dry if needed.

Position over transplant, pressing wooden support into soil, spread cone, and anchor edges of screen with soil.

The best control Blair could come up with was the collar. Gardeners had long used tar-paper collars slit halfway across so as to lie flat on the ground and fit tightly around the stem. Blair said a sawdust collar works better. Fine sawdust about 1½ inches thick extending 4 inches from the stem, carefully maintained, will prevent the fly from laying its eggs on the soil's surface.

Experiencing her own sawdust collars being disrupted by hand-watering, and wishing to avoid sawdust because it decreases soil nitrogen, Marina discovered that a collar of pumice also discourages the fly and isn't dislodged by the hose stream.

Radish and turnip crops can be protected by sowing seeds on the soil's surface instead of in a

Maggot protection using sawdust.

furrow and then covering that seed with a 6-inch-wide band of sawdust one inch deep. Timely harvest is still absolutely essential because the swelling roots push the sawdust aside.

Since Blair did his work, a biological remedy has come available. Beneficial nematodes effectively attack root maggots in the ground. If large numbers are suspended in water and then poured into the soil close to brassica seedlings, they actively knock off maggots as fast as they hatch out, even breeding and maintaining fairly effective population levels for a while. Best results are obtained when the nematodes are applied at soil temperatures above 60 degrees F (and below 90 degrees F). In early spring their effectiveness can be erratic because in the Willamette Valley, measured 4 inches below the surface, some years it takes until mid to late May before the day/night average on most soils warms to over 60 degrees F.

Parasitic nematodes are cheap to culture but have a short shelf life at room temperature. It's preferable to buy nematodes from a refrigerated case in a feed and seed or a specialty garden center, or on the Internet.

Spun-fiber row covers effectively prevent cabbage flies from reaching plants if their edges are meticulously anchored with soil. This technique is especially useful for Chinese cabbage and turnips. Row covers are discussed at greater length as a technique for controlling carrot rust flies.

Cabbage worms

There are three common sorts. The caterpillars we most notice are greenish and quickly eat their way to being over 1 inch long. They start as clusters of small yellowish eggs laid by white-winged day-flying moths on the undersides of the leaves of cabbage family plants. A similar but half-size larvae makes smaller holes but is more destructive; it comes from a night-flying brown moth. The worst damage of all in my garden comes from jillions of tiny diamondback moth larvae. Huge numbers of their tiny parents flit about each plant. The larvae are so small they're hard to spot, but the damage they do is quite apparent. All these annoyances lessen as summer fades. After a few sharp frosts only an occasional slow-moving larva will be seen.

In a very small garden painstakingly handpicking cabbage worms and tossing them away from any cabbage family plant can be sufficient control except for diamondback larvae. These are so small that it is nearly impossible to remove them by hand. I rely upon Bt. It remains highly active for no more than a week after spraying, although there's a noticeable residual effect from spores released by decomposing victims. There are reports of cabbage worms developing resistance to Bt, so entomologists recommend alternating it with Spinosad. I don't bother. From whenever moths appear until mid-September, I suggest spraying Bt on all cole crops except perhaps kale and rutabaga, on this schedule: one or two days after each irrigation or rain, or every two weeks no matter what. If you must water sandy soil every two days, then spray once a week on a day you don't irrigate. Exposure to sunlight degrades Bt, so concentrate on spraying the undersides of leaves. Spray heavily into the growing point and especially the leaves forming and then protecting heads of cabbages.

Carrot rust flies

Carrot rust flies can be thick in Washington State and British Columbia. I saw a few larvae in Lorane, none in Elkton. In late summer the fly begins laying eggs. Its maggots tunnel through carrots, mature and pupate quickly, and are soon laying eggs themselves. The autumn population increases several hundredfold each month. There'll be a few flies active early in spring, but it becomes safe to plant carrots after mid-May. Carrots remain relatively unharmed so long as they're lifted by late summer. Carrots become increasingly infested in autumn.

For decades gardeners have prevented the fly from laying eggs by covering their carrot crop with window-screened frames. Spun-fiber row covers also give a gardener a maggot-free crop. If carefully anchored with a sprinkling of soil all around the edge, the fabric makes an effective insect barrier. Put the row cover over the bed as soon as the seeds have been sown. Remove it to weed and thin carrot seedlings; do this when they

are 3 or 4 inches tall. Thin to about 150 percent of their normal spacing (to allow for the loss of light through the fabric). Then carefully recover the bed.

Storing carrots during winter by carefully laying sheets of plastic over the carrot tops and putting a few inches of straw over that for insulation might prevent the fly from gaining access, although it may also make a haven for field mice, who enjoy carrots as much as humans do.

Flea beetles

Flea beetles are tiny black fast-moving insects that make pinholes in leaves. They primarily eat members of the cabbage family, beet seedlings, and tomato transplants. They particularly like thick, juicy brassica cotyledons (the first leaves that emerge after germination). In large numbers flea beetles kill seedlings. Fast-growing, healthy plants usually are not seriously damaged.

Overwintering adults migrate from surrounding fields in spring, feed, and then lay eggs in the soil. During the summer larvae feed on various roots including potato tubers, usually without causing significant skin damage. After maturing into adults, the beetles then feed unnoticed until they hibernate in fall. Composting garden debris in autumn instead of allowing them to remain in place over winter is supposed to eliminate flea beetle shelters, but if the garden is close to acres of pasture or there's a messy backyard or untended vacant block on the other side of the fence, your own garden hygiene brings no benefit.

In spring you can limit flea beetle damage to tolerable levels by raising husky, well-hardened transplants that don't go into shock when set out, by not sowing too early, and by sowing thicker. If seedlings are being heavily damaged, they're probably not growing fast enough. In that case, the best strategies may be a dose of liquid fertilizer or immediately sowing again if the slow growth was due to unsuitable weather. A temporary green manure using cheap radish, broccoli rabe, or turnip seed may attract flea beetles and take the pressure off nearby crops. Severe infestations can be sprayed with pyrethrins or Spinosad.

Leaf miners

Leaf miners are the maggots of a small fly similar to the cabbage fly or carrot rust fly. They tunnel through beet, chard, and spinach leaves, although they'll also mine bean, blackberry, lettuce, and other leaves. Only a few insecticides work on leaf miners because they're protected from direct contact by being inside the leaf. But Spinosad, especially with a penetrant added, can rescue spinach, beets, and chard crops.

I've never seen a leaf miner in my garden, so I can't say anything from personal experience. However, I once sent a section of spun-fiber row cover to a Washington State gardener who complained of leaf miners ruining every beet crop he planted. The gardener carefully covered most of a beet bed after the seedlings were large enough to thin and weed, and kept the cover in place undisturbed until harvest. His unprotected beets were thoroughly ruined. Under the cover there was a fine harvest, though the fabric did reduce light levels somewhat so the beets made smaller bottoms than he would have liked. As with carrots similarly being protected against carrot fly larvae, light reduction can be compensated for by establishing a lower plant density.

Slugs and snails

Slugs and snails are fewer in a clean garden. They hide under debris during the days so promptly move garden waste to the composting area, and eliminate daytime hiding places such as tall weeds around the garden's fringes, boards, empty feed bags, or buckets on the soil. If slugs are eating too many seedlings in spring, next time try sowing a few weeks later when seedlings grow faster. Sowing more seeds and then thinning progressively provides some for the slugs and enough for you. Banding a little COF along seedling rows or below transplants might increase growth rates sufficiently that slugs are no longer a serious threat.

Gastropods can be trapped or poisoned. The best trapping method I know uses wooden planks laid on garden paths. Slugs hide under them during daylight hours. The gardener can turn the boards over, handpick the slugs, and drop them into a jar of detergent solution, salt water, or gasoline, or sprinkle a bit of salt on them. Or feed them to the chickens. This works on medium- and larger-size slugs; getting the tiny ones seems too painstaking. That's why I no longer use this method. A slightly wacky friend of mine enjoyed going out at night with a bright camping lantern and a pair of sharp scissors, snipping hundreds of slugs in half. He did this twice a month and got sufficient control.

If you find the banana (or tiger) slug, several inches long and yellowish to orange-brown, relax—they only eat decaying material and not fresh leaves, so toss that one somewhere it can be happy; no need to kill it.

Slug and snail baits made with metaldehyde are acceptable to me. Metaldehyde is a simple poisonous chemical similar to wood alcohol. It quickly breaks down into harmless substances. Slugs love to intoxicate themselves to death with metaldehyde in the same way they'll happily drown themselves in a dish of stale beer. Bait need not be placed among your vegetables to reduce slugs; it may be sprinkled in a narrow band outside of the garden and on paths around a bed. Slugs travel at random; snails seem to return to the same hideout every morning. A bait barrier will kill slugs entering the area, while those already in the garden will die when crossing a path. Reactivated every few weeks, a bait barrier can steadily reduce in-the-garden populations.

I make slug (and rodent-feeding) traps out of foot-long sections of plastic gutter drainpipe. The bait is placed in the middle with a long spoon. Don't use traps if dogs may get at them—metaldehyde baits attract some dogs and are fatal to canines even in smallish amounts. Better in that case to use the tried-and-true method of old-time organic gardeners and fill an old pie tin

with stale beer. Newer formulations of minipelleted metaldehyde baits with added bittering agents are less appealing to pets but still very toxic if consumed.

To get slugs out of your food, submerge vegetables in cold water for 10 minutes and then rinse well; slugs suffocate and sink to the bottom.

Symphylans

Most Oregonians and many north of the Columbia don't realize their soil hosts this garden wrecker. Symphylans may not live in the glacial sands spread over much of Western Washington north of Chehalis. About this I am still uncertain. Otherwise, assume they are present. Symphylans hide in the soil and are too small to notice unless you intentionally set out to find them. Symphylans are not mentioned in nationwide garden guides. Typically, the Cascadian gardener starts out in a previously ungardened spot and enjoys a few hugely successful years while, unnoticed, the symphylan population steadily increases. Then the gardener comes to think certain (symphylan-susceptible) species are hard to grow. Some give up gardening altogether. Few know what really happened.

Luckily, I was warned about symphylans the year I settled in Lorane. Discovering I was a serious homestead food grower, the garden center owner at Cottage Grove said I would soon be plagued by symphylans but wouldn't be able to control them with anything organic gardeners knew about. "The only thing that will kill symphylans is Dyfonate."

He pointed out a large chemical sack on a high shelf above the window. "All the farmers around

Slug traps.

here use it before growing vegetables or straw-berries. They couldn't harvest anything without it. Now, *you* can't legally buy Dyfonate—it takes a restricted-use pesticide applicator's license, and you've got to go to school for it. But I'll be happy to supply you with a few pounds and explain how to use it." (Dyfonate has since been withdrawn from sale because it is too dangerous.)

"No thanks!" I said with the overconfidence of the inexperienced true believer. "I can handle any pest that comes along without chemicals!" I eventually did discover how to control sym-phylans without poison, but I can't say I'm happy about what I've learned.

Imagine a centipede ³⁄₁₆ inch long. A flat-tened, flexible, wire-thin tube of white or pale brownish-pink, multiply jointed like a cray-fish's tail, and fringed with 12 opposing pairs of stubby legs. A pair of long whiskers probes forward. That's the symphylan. This tiny, shy soil dweller moves fast through cracks and soil pores. It instantly flees light. Its speed, color, and small size make it hard to spot. It lives for several years, breeds relatively slowly, and can live 5 feet down or lurk near the surface. Like most soil ani-mals, the symphylan can only survive in a moist environment. A single individual will generally remain within a radius of 15 or 20 feet. That's an important fact; keep it in mind. Several dozen symphylans can hide in a shovelful of soil and yet only someone intently looking for them may ever realize their presence. To find out if you've got symphylan problems, put a shovelful of soil on a large sheet of cardboard and carefully inspect every crumb as you move the soil from one side of the cardboard to the other. An Oregon State University entomologist I pestered about this pest said 10 or more symphylans per shovelful is about the level at which they become a problem.

Forget about control with beneficials. A few soil dwellers do prey on symphylans but not effectively. Having a very high organic matter content does assist predator beetles to get more symphylans, but increasing organic matter helps the symphylans just as much or more.

Symphylans mainly feed on decomposing organic matter and tender root tips in the top foot of soil. Above all things they seem to pre-fer juvenile roots just emerging from sprouting seeds, which kills the seed. Unirrigated pastures only have a few symphylans because to survive the summer, symphylans must move to moist soil deep in the earth where there is little to feed them. I speculate symphylans do best in deep soils that hold the most moisture. The only Cascadian soils I *think* don't host symphylans are glacial sands that dry out thoroughly and deeply. Because my locational survey is based on gar-dener reports, I'm still not sure.

Symphylans much prefer eating the roots of some vegetables over others. The species they concentrate on are considered "hard to grow" in local lore. In a garden without many symphylans, these same species seem easy to grow. I suspect one reason behind Territorial Seed Company's success was that my variety trials were conducted on symphylan-infested ground, so I chose the most aggressively rooting varieties.

Symphylan problems arise after a new garden plot has been used for a few years: Strawberries don't grow well anymore. Cauliflower is stunted, spinach and beets germinate but fail to grow, and then much of the stand that did sprout disappears before the seedlings get well established. What's happening is that the root-grazing symphylans are pruning rootlets. With heavier infestations, spinach and beets don't even seem to germinate. Heavy infestations stunt broccoli and cabbage, and may affect peppers, beans, celery, and a wide range of other species. Tomatoes, carrots, corn, parsnips, parsley, lettuce, fava beans, and members of the squash family seem relatively immune.

After symphylans started wrecking my trials, I learned everything I could about their habits. I imagined that before the Americans arrived, symphylans mostly lived in the moist, rotting forest duff, munching decomposing wood and occasional root tips. The woody stuff wasn't very palatable, and the root tips were few and not too tasty. There weren't many symphs. Or maybe they mostly lived in camas meadows. When homesteaders cleared the forest, plowed the meadows, and started farming, the amount of soil organic matter dropped markedly, further reducing the symphylan population and maybe selecting their population for individuals that preferred root tips. However, most pasture species aren't appealing to symphylans, and neither are the roots of most grains (which are also grasses). Nor are fava beans, as I found by experiment. (I describe a useful symphylan-suppressing rotation using fava beans in the Green Manures section, page 214.)

Local lore about the symphylan goes, "They weren't in the garden until I brought in a bad load of manure. Now they're a plague." That's half-correct: The symphylans weren't brought to the field with the manure; the manure fed them. Upping the level of decaying crude organic matter lets their population increase. But when the farmer or gardener also begins to irrigate and ups the organic matter content as well, the symphylan feeds and breeds much more effectively. Which brings me to the first symphylan-handling technique I worked out.

One morning I was leaning on my hoe, contemplating a long row holding 48 three-leaf-stage cauliflower seedlings that had been transplanted about three weeks previously and had not yet grown at all. All six plants of all eight varieties had been static. I carefully dug up a seedling with a handful of soil around it, inspected its roots, and found a dozen symphs feeding. In a flash of insight I saw it from a symphylan's viewpoint. The nasty gardener (that was me) had tried to starve them all by tilling everything in. No more root tips. He then set out a row of transplants surrounded by much bare soil. Naturally, every symphylan from many feet away flocked to the few little growing plants and nibbled away, wreaking havoc. Maybe, I mused, if I fed the symphylans something tastier than cauliflower roots, they'd eat my vegetables less. How about buckwheat roots? That's a sweet-tasting, tender plant, the seed is cheap, comes up quick, and grows fast, and, most important, buckwheat is easily hoed out. So I grabbed a 5-pound bag from the seed room, thickly scattered buckwheat seed several feet to either side of the cauliflower seedlings, rototilled it in shallowly, and sprinkler irrigated. Three days later the area was carpeted with buckwheat seedlings. One day after that all of the little stunted cauliflower plants started growing normally. As the cauliflowers grew, I hoed back the buckwheat. With a little more research I probably could have worked out frost-hardy trap crops for use early in spring, like spinach maybe, or some fast-growing brassica. But there was no point. This method did work, but using it made too much work for me.

Gardeners have long and often been taught that the best way to eliminate problems arising in their Garden of Eatin' is to add more compost. But in symphylan country, when it comes to manure or compost, least is best. If you add just enough compost to keep the soil's microecology thriving, you might use a plot for more years without building a symphylan population that is too high to tolerate.

The only effective strategy I know that massively reduces an existing symphylan plague is several years' rest from growing vegetables while growing unirrigated plants that do not sustain symphylans. The most practical way is the multiyear grass-clover rotation I've mentioned previously. Long rotations into unirrigated pasture grasses may be possible in suburbia by shifting the vegetable garden to a different part of a large backyard or by gardening the front yard for a couple of years and then the backyard. Remember, this is pasture grass that will be growing in garden soil, so it'll be 5-foot-tall hay you mow down in May.

The ability of symphylans to travel through soil means that to virtually eliminate them from an area, there must be a barrier at least 20 feet wide between that space and any soil that favors them. That barrier can be a never-watered strip of closely mown lawn grasses.

There is hope. Territorial offers a mustard variety that's decomposition products discourage symphylans. A spring green manure with this mustard may provide summer crops with a window to get going in. Presently there is ongoing investigation into using Certis's PFR-97, an insecticidal fungus, as a soil drench, but trials have been inconclusive. Perhaps more promising is the use of crab or shrimp meal extracts. Jim Brackens of Pacific Gro makes liquid fertilizers out of fishery waste, and Gary Kline of Black Lake Organic has been experimenting with their use for symph control—shells of shrimp and crab are composed of chitin, and the naturally occurring fungi that degrade their shells are thought to weaken the exoskeletons of symphs when soil is drenched with the diluted extracts. Recently Gary said to me in private correspondence:

About the use of shrimp meal and crab meal (or their liquefied versions being produced by Pacific Gro) . . . I am very confident that we have gotten 99 percent control of [symphylan] larvae and adults in our worm castings by mixing shrimp and crab meal in liberally and waiting a few days and visually monitoring that it takes effect, which it always has done for us.

Wildlife

If you share your environment with deer, don't think for a moment that you can grow a garden without an effective fence. I've seen neighbors trying that, and they inevitably experience midnight visits, ending up minus the top two-thirds of their broccoli plants and all of their carrot tops. At minimum.

Other neighbors tried jerry-rigged fencing, and they too experienced midnight visits. Certain acquaintances reckoned that anything in their garden was "good groceries." They were expert shots with a .22 who cared not a whit about hunting regulations; their freezer was usually filled with venison, but their gardens functioned more as a deer attractant than a source of vegetables. Those neighbors who got a dog to keep the deer out of the garden learned that dogs sleep soundly.

The Department of Fish and Wildlife has long recommended this design. Hung on tall, thin treated poles are two courses of ordinary 3-foot farm field fence, the second course atop the first. And above 6 feet of field fence are three courses of barbed wire, each wire 6 inches above the next, so the top wire is 7 feet 6 inches high.

There is no need to stretch the field fence. Deer are turned aside by almost any obstacle. These days there is a far-less-expensive option. Sturdy black plastic deer mesh can be strung on 10-foot T-posts driven in 2 feet and spaced about 10 feet apart. It goes up fairly quickly, can be moved or added on to, and lasts at least 10 years if you get the heavy-duty kind—the mesh costs about a dollar a running foot.

Moles eat worms and insects; they do not eat roots but they do destroy plants as they tunnel. Moles are not easy to trap but they can be poisoned. However, garden center mole poisons often fail to work because they are too old. The bait must smell right; the scent attractants fade away. I suggest asking at farm supply shops. A local pest control business may manufacture fresh poison baits of the sort used by farmers.

Chapter Nine

HOW TO GROW IT

The gardener is the servant of the plant.

—Louise Howard, *The Earth's Green Carpet*, 1947

THE GARDEN WRITER'S challenge is to explain how-to in a way that is easily understood across a wide range of intelligence, ability, and experience. The instructions should be almost impossible to misinterpret and, if wrongly applied, should still not do any lasting damage. Like I said, a challenge.

How to Use It

This chapter recommends Cascadian methods that make the best use of time and energy and produce veggies that look as good as anything on display in the supermarket, taste great, and are nutrient dense. I'm not saying that other approaches fail to produce vegetables. But I am confident that if you actually do what I suggest, you'll see a great result.

FAMILY GROUPS

This chapter is organized either by botanical classification, such as "alliums" and "brassicas," or by similarities in how the group is cultivated, such as "root crops." Grouping vegetables this way leads to an almost effortless crop rotation. After harvesting something belonging to one group, you grow something on that spot belonging to a different group.

All the vegetables in each group are cultivated similarly. If you're new to all this, after you succeed at producing one vegetable, the others in that group should seem easy to grow.

Following are the family groups:

Solanums: eggplants, peppers, tomatoes

Legumes: beans, peas, lentils, chickpeas, green manures

Greens: celery (and celeriac), corn salad (mâche), endive and escarole, lettuce, mustard, leaf parsley, spinach, chard, rocket (arugula), cilantro (coriander)

Brassicas: broccoli, brussels sprouts, cabbage, Chinese cabbage, cauliflower, collards, kale, kohlrabi, rutabagas, turnips

Roots: beets, carrots, chicory, Hamburg parsley, parsnips, potatoes, radishes

Cucurbits: cucumbers, melons, pumpkins, winter squash, zucchini

Alliums: garlic, shallots, leeks, onions

Miscellaneous: asparagus, sweet corn, horseradish. I consider each of these vegetables unique and its own rotational group.

PLANTING DATES

Cascadia's climate has similar characteristics from south to north. The bioregion begins where redwoods grow in northern coastal California, and from the Oregon border continues northward between the coast and the Cascades. Cascadia also includes the Lower Mainland and islands of British Columbia. Folks in coastal southern Alaska say they find this book useful, although it is too cold to winter garden that far north. Ranging from north to south there are differences in the length of the frost-free growing season, in how warm it gets in summer, and in how frosty it gets in winter. It would be impractical to provide a specific planting calendar for each subregion. Instead, I provide cautious suggestions for the Willamette Valley, safe dates that are in the middle of the range of Cascadian possibilities. Cascadians outside the Willamette must adjust these dates according to local knowledge and previous experience.

The 30-year usual frost dates for Portland are May 2 and October 6. North of the Columbia's influence and in the hills surrounding the Willamette Valley there are fewer frost-free growing weeks and the average temperature is lower. Accordingly, hot weather crops grow less rapidly. Close to the Sound, on an island in it, or right on the coast, it'll be even cooler in summer but not as cold in winter. Those gardening where it is cooler than the Willamette should plant

Local Planting Dates

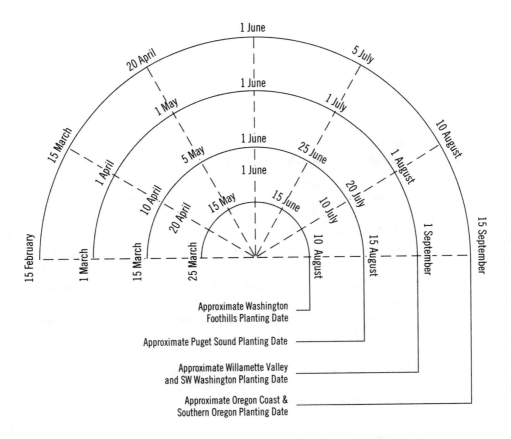

1 June

20 April

5 July

1 June

1 May

1 July

1 June

10 August

15 March

5 May

25 June

1 August

1 June

1 April

10 April

15 May

15 June

20 July

10 July

20 June

10 July

15 February

1 March

15 March

25 March

20 April

10 August

15 August

1 September

15 September

Approximate Washington
Foothills Planting Date

Approximate Puget Sound Planting Date

Approximate Willamette Valley
and SW Washington Planting Date

Approximate Oregon Coast &
Southern Oregon Planting Date

spring crops a week or three later than the dates given in this chapter. Autumn arrives earlier and there's less winter growth in cooler districts. Fall and winter crops should be sown a week or two sooner in those areas.

Spring arrives sooner close to and along the Oregon coast, but summer, if you can even call coastal summers "summer," comes a few weeks later than it does in the Willamette. However, go inland past the first big hill and the day can be nearly as warm as it is in the Willamette.

Central Oregon coastal gardeners can start spring crops a few weeks ahead of Willamette Valley gardeners, but their summer, autumn, and winter crops should go in about the same date as the Willamette requires.

South of Drain, Oregon, spring arrives a few weeks earlier. Gardeners along the southern Oregon coast or in the Umpqua and Rogue Valleys should start their spring/summer crops a week or two earlier than Willamette gardeners. Those at higher elevations have a shorter frost-free

Year-Round Planting Calendar

- **February**

  Entire month Transplant asparagus roots

  15th Sow peas, favas, spinach

- **March**

  Entire month Sow peas, favas, spinach, mustard and related Asian greens, radishes, parsley, bulb onions, leek nursery scallions

  15th Transplant earliest broccoli and cabbage seedlings

  17th Saint Patrick's Day ritual—sow at least one potato

- **April**

  Entire month Sow peas, scallions, spinach (summer varieties), beets, turnips, radishes, kohlrabi, chard, carrots, lettuce, broccoli, cabbage, parsley, sorrel, cauliflower

  1st Transplant earliest cauliflower

  after 15th Transplant onion seedlings, sow leek nursery

- **May**

  Entire month Sow cauliflower, cabbage, beets, radishes, chard, carrots, lettuce, broccoli, winter leek nursery bed, scallions, potatoes, lettuce

  15th Sow snap beans, squash (summer and winter), basil, dill, dry beans, sweet corn. Transplant tomato, celery, and celeriac

- **June**

  Entire month Sow cucumbers, summer squash, melons, snap beans, beets, carrots, lettuce, broccoli, fall and winter cabbage, brussels sprouts, cauliflower, scallions

  15th Transplant peppers and eggplant

- **July**

  Entire month Sow lettuce, transplant leeks

  before 15th Sow parsnips, carrots, beets, fall cauliflower, bush snap beans, scallions

  after 15th Sow rutabaga, kale, winter beets, spinach, overwintering broccoli

- **August**

  Entire month Sow endive, spinach

  before 15th Sow overwintering cauliflower, loose-leaf lettuce

  after 15th Sow overwintering bulb onions

- **September**

  before 15th Sow endive, corn salad, garlic and shallots, field turnips (as green manure)

- **October**

  Entire month Sow green manures: favas, crimson clover, field peas

Note: This rough schedule is more or less right for the Willamette Valley garden. North of Longview, along the coast, and at higher elevations, spring dates might be too early while sowing dates after midsummer might be a bit too late. South of Drain, Oregon, spring dates might be a bit too late while dates after midsummer might be a bit early. Starting dates for transplants are found in a similar schedule in Chapter 7.

season and must adjust accordingly. Gardeners around the California redwoods can sow spring and summer crops as much as four weeks ahead of the Willamette Valley.

Fall comes later south of the Willamette, and the sun shines more often in winter. Gardeners south of Drain may sow autumn and winter crops a week or two later than the Willamette Valley requires. Gardeners around the redwoods might hold off planting the winter garden by as much as four weeks.

GARDEN PLANNING AND QUANTITIES

Yield depends upon soil conditions, plant spacing, the weather, the variety—and skill. I can't know how much of any particular vegetable your family will want, how many sit at your table, or what you choose to serve guests. So in the growing information to come, I share what I do. To briefly summarize, Annie and I almost never eat out. We enjoy at least once-a-week dinner visits involving grandchildren who *love* my veggies. I am probably one of the most skillful vegetable growers you could ever hope to meet. I like to show off (and inspire) by giving away surplus by the boxful. We are vegetableatarians because eating mostly vegetables most of the time is the most healthful way for us. I make every effort to supply the table with an abundance of fresh veggies 12 months a year.

SUGGESTED VARIETIES

Heat-loving varieties that are productive east of the Cascades often fail when they experience Cascadia's cool nights. East of the Cascades frost-tolerant vegetables must be harvested before the soil freezes; varieties that work there may not withstand heavy winter rains and lack of light in the maritime Northwest. Overwintering varieties that make such a difference in the spring food supply are simply not available from seed companies east of the Rocky Mountains.

Fortunately, Cascadian gardeners are supported by several reputable regional seed companies selling well-adapted, honestly described varieties. I hope you will act in your best interest and buy from Cascadian seed suppliers if at all possible.

In this chapter when I specify a variety, the company selling it may be referred to by these abbreviations (contact details are in Chapter 5):

ADA = Adaptive Seeds
JSS = Johnny's Selected Seeds
NIC = Nichols Garden Nursery
OSB = Osborne Seed Company
STK = Stokes Seeds
TSC = Territorial Seed Company
WCO = West Coast Seeds
UPR = Uprising Seeds

DRY GARDENING

This chapter suggests ways to make the garden require less water. I have much more to say about this in Chapter 5.

PLANT SPACING AND GENERAL CULTIVATION METHODS

Most of the suggested layouts in this chapter refer to slightly raised semipermanent beds that are 4 feet wide and as long as you like. This method is discussed in Chapter 4. The suggested spacings will entirely fill up the bed in well-fertil-ized balanced soil receiving abundant irrigation.

This chapter recommends the use of complete organic fertilizer on all crops. COF is not the only way to grow a successful garden, but it is certain to give you a great result. The amount of soil fertility a crop needs is distinguished as low, medium, or high demand. All this is discussed at length in Chapter 2.

- *Low-demand crops* grow great on the basic amount of COF—one full batch of the recipe on page 29 (about 2 gallons) per 100 square feet.
- *Medium-demand crops* usually need more. Start them like a low demand crop and be prepared to side-dress.
- *High-demand crops* need even more side-dressing but rarely in excess of 2 additional gallons of COF per 100 square feet.

Vegetables
A to Z

Solanums

Garden solanums are botanically related heat-loving frost-intolerant fruiting perennials that originated in the semitropics or tropics. In Cascadia these vegetables are grown as summer-season annuals. All require full sun at least most of the day if the harvest is to be flavorsome and abundant.

Cascadia's chilly late-spring nights stop most solanum varieties from setting fruit. Cool summer nights slow ripening, reduce fruit size, and sometimes prevent the development of full flavor. Beefsteak tomato varieties ripen very late in Cascadia and do not develop the depth that makes them so treasured east of the Cascades. Chili varieties often fail to get as hot as hoped for. In trials in Lorane, Oregon, a tropical chili variety, Serrano, made hardly any vegetative growth outdoors, much less formed fruit. Out of a great many hybrid eggplant varieties, only a few yield dependably in the Willamette.

In the 1970s Cascadian gardeners expected to harvest more green tomatoes at summer's end than had ripened. It was considered normal for peppers to set and ripen only a few fruit, rather late, and for eggplants to remain fruitless most summers. That's because in Cascadia it is a rare evening that doesn't prompt wearing a long-sleeve shirt, even in July and August. An entire summer seems to pass without a single night that holds above 60 degrees F. These days well-adapted solanum varieties are available to Cascadian gardeners.

Most of your neighbors will put tomato seedlings out on the area's last usual frost date. I suggest a smarter strategy: Put yours out two weeks later than that, and as often as not you'll end up harvesting ripe fruit before they do. You also won't be replacing frosted-out seedlings. Also delay setting pepper and eggplant seedlings out. Nights approaching but not reaching frost shock solanum seedlings severely. Shocked seedlings attract leaf-eating insects. If your seedlings often die soon after being set out, or are immediately and severely attacked by flea beetles, or what looks like a yellow ladybird beetle with black spots—locally termed "cucumber beetles" (a.k.a. *Diabrotica*)—you're probably setting out soft seedlings and doing it too early.

Some folks prod slow-growing spring solanums with extra fertilizer; doing this often works against you. Stunned seedlings *must* take in whatever nutrients are dissolved in the soil moisture, but a nongrowing plant cannot build new tissue with these resources. Fertilizer elements (salts) build up to toxic concentrations in the plant's sap, stunting it. The shock of cold nights stunts it even further. The overfed seedling becomes diseased, is attacked by insects, or dies outright. In a slow-to-come summer, it is far better practice to erect a temporary cloche over the seedlings, and then *after* they are growing fast, side-dress or fertigate them.

Most garden books say tomatoes prefer acidic soil. Actually, all solanums tolerate a wide pH range, although they grow best at pH 6.4. What they cannot tolerate is a lack of calcium. If you'll depend upon COF, your soil will gradually move into the ideal range of pH and nutritional calcium always will be abundant.

Solanums can use a lot of nutrients *when environmental conditions allow rapid growth*. Initially prepare their entire bed for a low-demand crop. Then work ½ cup of COF into about a gallon of soil immediately below where the seedling will be placed. As soon as they start growing fast, side-dress. About mid-July, side-dress them again. That should carry the crop until its growth inevitably slows toward the end of August.

There is time to start a green manure crop after these heat lovers finish.

Solanum flowers are self-fertile. Small insects (not bees) cause occasional crossing in peppers, rarely in eggplants, almost never in tomatoes.

Crosses are almost always less desirable than either parent. Organic gardens contain many more small insects than insecticide-sprayed commercial fields, so crosses occur more readily in gardens than professional plant breeders expect. Given more growing space than most people think they need, solanums require much less irrigation than people usually give them. This is especially the case if they are given occasional fertigation.

EGGPLANTS *(Solanum melongena)*

Eggplants are the most heat-demanding garden solanum. To reliably bear fruit in the Willamette Valley, even the earliest hybrids require a black plastic mulch that heats their soil a few degrees and slightly warms the night air. Close to the coast, in the Coast Ranges and north of Longview, Washington, only the use of large cloches or a greenhouse allows eggplant to yield.

SOW	HARVEST	TRANSPLANT
Early April	Late July to early October	Early June
POSITIONS	**SEEDS**	**THIN**
24 x 24 inches	N/A	N/A

Culture

Set eggplants out in the first half of June. Don't rush. Wait for warm soil and milder nighttime temperatures. You should prewarm their bed. A week before transplanting spread both compost and COF for a low-demand crop, dig the bed or row, and level it with a rake. Then spread a sheet of black plastic over the entire bed surface, anchoring the edges with soil or better, by wrapping the edges of the plastic once around a two-by-four. Make the black plastic wide enough to be anchored just at or a bit beyond the edges of the bed; leave as much plastic as possible exposed to the sun (also keep it clean, free of loose soil on top). Cut out small holes that you can just put a hand through on stations 24 by 24 inches, and then with your hand work about ½ cup additional COF into the soil below each hole. Black plastic soaks up more solar energy than lighter-colored soil can and also helps hold that heat in at night, creating a slightly warmer microclimate—a little difference that, in this case, makes all the difference. Slugs find life under black plastic the next thing to paradise. They are capable of denuding a transplant almost overnight. So it is wise to spread a tablespoonful of slug bait close to each hole under the plastic. Do this the day before you transplant. Fertigate through a small hole in the plastic if growth slows before September, because with black plastic mulch you can't side-dress. After it rains, or after you irrigate for the first time, there will be small puddles where the plastic has low spots. At every one of these spots make a small hole or slit to allow water to flow into the soil.

Garden planning

A well-adapted hybrid may produce 6 to 8 large fruits; small-fruited types 15 to 20. In a cool summer you'll be lucky to get even a few, and they'll be smaller than usual. Eggplants neatly follow early peas or an overwintered green manure.

Insects and diseases

Unstressed, well-nourished eggplants are rarely bothered. Problems with aphids, whiteflies, or spider mites after mid-September are caused by decreasing light intensity and cooler nights; don't resist.

Harvest

Pick the fruit young while the skin is shiny and thin, before any seed develops. In early September unburden the plant by harvesting all full- and half-size fruit. This action helps small fruit enlarge if sunny, warm temperatures prevail.

Saving seed

Eggplant varieties cross occasionally. For commercial purity, varieties must be isolated by over 1 mile. I suggest growing only one variety if you're producing seeds. Seeds mature about two weeks after the fruit reaches full size and the skin has toughened. Black-skinned fruit often turn brownish when the seed is ripe; white-skinned varieties turn yellowish. Crush over-mature fruit into a large mixing bowl half-filled with water, loosen the seeds attached to the pulp by rubbing it with your fingers: the seeds settle on the bottom; the pulp floats to the top and can be skimmed off. Finally, put the seed into a sieve or strainer, and rinse well. Spread the seeds on a sheet of newspaper to dry thoroughly at room temperature.

Varieties

Early open-pollinated varieties may be productive in the Rogue Valley or in the redwoods; even the earliest produce scantly in the Willamette Valley. Black Beauty, the open-pollinated heirloom that is still popular in most of the United States, rarely yields anything in Cascadia. Uprising Seeds says their Diamond produces lots of fruit in their field, even during a cold summer. I'll soon find out if Diamond works because up to now my trials demonstrate it requires hybrid vigor to produce more than a few late fruit where nights are cool. Some early hybrids yield acceptably in an average Willamette summer; most "early" hybrids are early only where nights are warm, not in Cascadia. Territorial Seed Company, Nichols Garden Nursery, and West Coast Seeds offer the most reliable varieties. Small-fruited Asian eggplant hybrids are usually the earliest of all. Be careful if you buy from Osborne Seeds: many of their varieties seem intended for market gardeners east of the Cascades.

Dry gardening

Use a black plastic mulch. Set seedlings on stations 36 by 36 inches; give each plant 2 gallons of fertigation solution on July 1, 4 gallons July 20, 4 gallons August 10, and 3 gallons August 30.

PEPPERS *(Capsicum annuum)*

South of Drain, Oregon, open-pollinated varieties used in California agriculture do okay. In the Willamette Valley, only early varieties, open-pollinated or hybrid, do well. North of Longview, Washington, and along the coast, only the earliest hybrids might be productive; they will usually need cloches or greenhouses or at minimum, a sheet of black plastic over their bed—like eggplant.

SOW	HARVEST	TRANSPLANT
Early April	Late July to early October	Early June
POSITIONS	SEEDS	THIN
24 x 24 inches	N/A	N/A

Culture

Pepper transplants do best when set outdoors after warm conditions settle in. Black plastic mulch is not necessary. In poor Willamette summers I've seen improved results from growing peppers under plastic tunnel cloches or under spun-fiber fabric until their first fruits are ready to pick. North of the Columbia, and along the coast, peppers are a low-demand crop. In warmer areas they can be a high-demand crop. Transplant on stations ranging from 18 by 24 inches in cool districts to 24 by 30 inches in warm areas. Prepare the bed and planting stations as though for eggplants. Peppers make rapid vegetative growth from the time the nights warm up (usually mid-June) into the first week of September. If growth slows during summer I suggest fertigating one time as a quick test. If more nutrients make faster growth, immediately side-dress COF or fertigate again every time growth slows.

Some varieties make brittle branches that break when they're heavy with fruit. Sometimes the entire plant will lean because of the weight of its fruit load. Be prepared to set a few stakes around the plant to attach heavily laden branches to.

Garden planning

Expect well-grown hybrid bell varieties to yield six to eight supermarket-sized fruits per plant in an average Willamette Valley summer. Small-fruited sweet varieties make dozens. Open-pollinated varieties will be less productive. In a warm district four big chilli plants should make enough hot sauce to supply one fanatic for one year.

Insects and diseases

Rarely an issue. Heavy symphylan infestations stunt peppers more than other garden solanums.

Harvest

All peppers, sweet or hot, change color from green or yellowish green to red (or yellow, orange, chocolate, or sometimes purple) as they ripen, developing more flavor in the process. Thick-walled hots such as jalapeño and Hungarian Hot Wax also develop both flavor and increased potency as they ripen. Thin-walled hots like cayenne should turn red and then dry out while still on the bush, but September's weather usually does not cooperate. Before frost or excessive rains ruin the peppers, yank the entire plant, roots and all, shake the soil off the roots, and hang the plant upside down in a cool, dim place. Most chilies will then ripen and dry out.

Here's a recipe for raw (unfired) chili sauce that keeps for one year in our fridge. The potency and flavor depends entirely upon the sort of peppers being used.

Using a meat grinder, finely mince a few pounds of ripe destemmed chilies, seeds and all. Optionally, mince a few cloves of garlic as well. Into the bowl containing minced chili (and garlic), pour (and stir a bit) enough household vinegar to generously coat every piece, and let the vinegar soak into the chili for *no more than one minute* because you do not want your hot sauce tasting of vinegar. However, that brief soak lets an open jar keep for months without going moldy instead of weeks. Promptly drain the vinegar by pouring the chilies into a big strainer above a large mixing bowl. Press out as much vinegar as possible. I suggest

you consider bottling the vinegar! This brief soak has transformed it into a Louisiana-style cayenne sauce that keeps indefinitely. Then put the minced chili back into a bowl, and stir in enough light olive oil to more than generously coat every piece. Fill small glass jars with oiled chilies (do not pack them too tight), leaving about an inch of air space, and then top off the jar with more oil, making sure there are no air bubbles in the chilies, ¼ inch of oil covers the solids, and ¼ inch of air space remains at the top. Seal the jars tightly. Unopened jars last at least 12 months in the fridge; opened jars last a month or two, so use small jars that'll be consumed quickly. I find pint jars are about right.

Saving seed

Isolate varieties by at least 20 feet. Isolate sweet from hot varieties by at least 50 feet. To end up with high germination seeds from sweet peppers and thick-walled hots, allow a fruit to fully ripen and then some on the bush—allow the skin to wrinkle a bit before harvest. Then let the fruit ripen for another week indoors—but immediately extract the seeds if you spot any sign of rotting. Separate the seeds from the pithy core and spread them on a sheet of newspaper to fully dry at room temperature before storage. Seeds inside thin-walled hots are ripe when the fruit has dried down on the plant.

Varieties

Yield depends on how well the variety handles chilly nights. Small-fruited varieties usually are the earliest and yield more overall. Widely available open-pollinated bell pepper varieties that are used in industrial agriculture such as

Cal Wonder, Keystone Resistant Giant, and Yolo Wonder will be late to set and mature fruit in the Willamette, although these types do reasonably well in southern Oregon and are entirely okay in Northern California.

Hybrid varieties appear with much fanfare, then quietly vanish a few years later. Peppers come in many colors and flavors. Pepper lovers should experiment freely with early ripening varieties. Stokes and Johnny's catalogs offer varieties whose days-to-maturity range from 60 to 85 days. It is a reasonable guess that any variety in their catalogs needing more than 70 days from transplanting to first harvest is too late for Cascadia. Territorial and West Coast are safe sources—nothing in their catalogs should be too late. Adaptive provides quite a few interesting open-pollinated varieties.

Dry gardening

Grow on stations 30 to 36 inches apart in rows 4 to 5 feet apart; fertigate each plant with 2 gallons July 1, 4 gallons July 20, 4 gallons August 10, and 3 gallons August 30.

TOMATOES *(Lycopersicon esculentum)*

Tomatoes are the easiest to grow garden solanum and will be productive if you choose well-adapted varieties.

SOW	HARVEST	TRANSPLANT
Early April	Late May to early June	July to early October
POSITIONS	SEEDS	THIN
Determinates: 36 x 48 inches Indeterminates: 48 x 60 inches	N/A	N/A

Culture

Tomato varieties use one of two possible branching patterns—determinate or indeterminate.

Indeterminates grow an endless vine that forms side branches at every leaf notch, in a repeating pattern of two weak side branches and then one strong side branch. All the side branches form side branches on that pattern. If all branches are allowed to grow unhindered, the result is an almost-impenetrable tangle with much rotting fruit under it. So it's best if all the weak side branches are pinched off as soon as they appear and the strong ones are held up off the ground to prevent fruit rotting. Given a long hot summer, good soil, and root room, indeterminates grow enormous plants.

Determinate varieties usually form compact, ground-hugging bushes that set and ripen fruit a few weeks sooner. They do not require training or pruning and do not benefit much from being put inside wire cages to hold the fruit above the soil. Yes, without support a percentage of the fruit will inevitably be lost to slugs; some fruit will be damaged by contact with moist soil, and some will be overlooked, but these losses are more than offset by ease of growing. Depending on the variety's vigor, determinates should be spaced from 24 by 24 to 48 by 48 inches; highly dwarfed determinate varieties can produce fruit while growing in a few gallons of container medium.

In frosty, short-season Lorane, taking advantage of every possible growing day mattered. So I transplanted early determinates like Oregon Spring or Siletz into a tunnel cloche about three weeks before the last usual frost date. I'd grow them under plastic until the entire bed was covered by vines pushing against the side walls. The cloche cover would be removed early in July (see the illustration on page 91), and I'd start harvesting almost immediately.

If indeterminate vines are allowed to sprawl without staking and pruning, they set far too many fruit for them to develop full size or top flavor. Picking untrained indeterminates is difficult—even finding much of the ripe fruit can be difficult—and for sure one-third or more of the fruit will rot or be damaged by slugs and sow bugs. Indeterminates are often propped up in wire-mesh cages, but grown this way they are not easy to prune. Better, tie them to stakes or against trellises. I have trained vines up strong strings stretched from top to bottom of an X frame, much like an oversized clothes-drying rack. The strings are 1 foot apart; the plants are 2 feet apart in the row. Under the X, transplant two rows of seedlings, plants 24 inches apart in the row. When the plants have developed about eight pairs of leaves, prune off all side branches except a single strong one, leaving only the main leader and one vigorous side branch. As these two leaders grow, guide each one around and around its own string. For the remainder of the season *pinch off all side branches as soon as they appear*. Your goal is to have only two nonbranching vines from each plant. Pruning takes only a few minutes each week. In a hot summer the vines may climb beyond the top; in that event allow them to drape over the top beam and hang there. Trellising and training produce slightly earlier-ripening, tastier, and much larger, blemish-free fruit.

An alternate indeterminate training method ties the vines to wooden stakes pounded in where and when they're needed as the plant grows. I use full dimension (rough-sawn) one-by-ones 4 feet long with a sharpened tip. Remove all the weak side branches as soon as they start to develop but retain almost all the strong side branches. The strong branches are tied to the stakes 18 to 24 inches above the ground. Any strong leader that would overcrowd the space is removed. In a warm summer each plant will eventually be supported by 12 or more wooden stakes about 18 inches apart, reaching out as much as 4 feet from the center and many stakes will support two leaders. If you use this method, position your seedlings at least 5 feet apart in all directions. In southern Oregon, or on extraordinarily good soil in the Willamette, that could be increased to 6 feet apart in all directions. If the summer is a good one, tomatoes prefer to be a high-demand crop.

It is possible to direct-seed early determinate varieties if you don't care that the first ripe fruit appears a few weeks later than usual. Direct seeding is the easier way to grow enough tomatoes for making sauce by the gallon. Simply put a pinch of seed in the ground about ¼ inch deep; do this about the same day you usually set tomato seedlings out. Keep the spot moist until the seeds emerge—usually one week. Progressively thin the seedling clusters to a single plant. Directly seeded tomato plants don't get as large as transplanted seedlings, so use positions 3 by 3 feet the first time you attempt this.

Garden planning

I think it's best to grow tomatoes following an overwintered green manure; the best one is cereal rye. A 100-square-foot bed can be completely filled by one aggressive early determinate plant and three indeterminates. Four plants on this much space keep our kitchen counter covered with fresh tomatoes for more than two months. Most sauce varieties are determinate and can go on positions 3 by 4 feet apart.

Insects and diseases

Tomato hornworms, common in California and fortunately rare in Cascadia, are killed by spraying Bt. Fruitworms, also rarely seen, can be reduced by spraying Bt weekly from the time tomatoes first start ripening. Whiteflies bother stressed plants. If this happens in September, the cure happens next year when you provide your tomatoes with more growing room and maybe better soil.

Most of the diseases that tomatoes have been bred to resist attack industrial crops raised on depleted soils and are of little or no concern to Cascadian gardeners. I have already discussed the rare occurrence of tomato late blight. Early blight makes dead spots with yellow halos on leaves. It attacks when the weather is cool and humid. Delaying transplanting until a few weeks after the last usual frost date helps. Remove any infected leaves and, if possible, improve air circulation. One local (excellent) variety, Legend, is resistant to both early and late blights. Two tomato problems seem to be diseases but actually aren't. If large amounts of water are added to dry soil, tomatoes may respond by temporarily curling their leaves. The other, blossom-end rot, most affects the first fruits to ripen. These blacken at the blossom end and then rot. Tomato leaf curl can be prevented and blossom-end rot can be reduced by the same action—providing a steadier moisture supply. End-rot occurs because dry topsoil interferes with calcium uptake while there is not enough calcium in the subsoil. The lime in COF will reduce the frequency of blossom-end rot. The gypsum in COF provides a quick calcium hit and helps move this element into the subsoil. You might remedy end-rot by sprinkling a cup of gypsum over the actively feeding fringes of the plant's root zone and shallowly hoeing it in.

Harvest

Determinates enormously overbear; removing two-thirds of all new flower clusters beginning mid-July will increase fruit size and flavor. You can encourage more tomatoes to ripen before frost. Beginning September 1, remove *all* flower clusters as they appear and also remove most of the smaller tomatoes that never will attain full size. Withholding or greatly reducing irrigation starting late August is another way—if it doesn't rain in September. The plants respond to moisture stress by ripening everything in a great hurry.

Allowing tomatoes to get fully ripe on the vine often means sharing them with slugs, birds, and whatever. If you lose too many, try harvesting when the fruit turns orange. Within days they'll be red-ripe in the house and will taste 98 percent as good. Unblemished full-size green tomatoes ripen indoors during October and November, and sometimes into December. They never have quite the vine-ripe flavor, but they're enormously better than anything you can buy. To slow ripening as much as possible, keep cool (50 to 55 degrees F), give plenty of air circulation, handle gently, and check them every few days for coloring up. When a tomato starts turning yellow-orange, bring it into the warm kitchen to finish ripening. There is a unique late-ripening indeterminate variety called Longkeeper (TSC). Longkeeper should be covered with full-size green tomatoes at summer's end, some showing the beginnings of a yellowish blush. Unblemished Longkeepers ripen indoors over a longer period than most varieties. Their tough skins develop a natural wax, like some winter apples do. Longkeeper is a good candidate for direct seeding because the last thing you want from it is ripe tomatoes during the usual growing season.

Saving seed

A few old varieties (Golden Jubilee) occasionally get cross-pollinated by insects and need the same isolation as peppers. Modern varieties only self-pollinate. To get very strong seed simply half fill a small glass jar with the seedy gel from the cavities of a few early ripening tomatoes that had been allowed to go past table-ripe while still on the vine. Put the jar in a warm place so that the gel ferments quickly. Stir the ferment once daily. Depending on the amount of natural acidity in the fruit, after three or four days the solids rise to the top and the seeds settle to the bottom. At that point *gently* run water into the jar with the intention of floating the pulp to the top. Wait until the seeds resettle on the bottom and then gently pour off most of the pulp and refill the jar. Repeat this sequence a few times. With the pulp mostly eliminated, pour the seeds into a strainer, wash in cold water until they're completely free of pulp, and then dry on a sheet of newspaper. The trick to ending up with high germination is to start with fully vine-ripe fruit and conduct the fermentation speedily by keeping it warm, around 70 degrees F. Cold ferments lasting more than a week often result in dead seed.

Varieties

Midseason varieties east of the Rockies yield much unripe fruit in Cascadia and usually fail to taste as good as they do where summer nights are balmy. Any variety described in Johnny's or Stokes's catalogs as needing more than 72 days to mature probably shouldn't be attempted north of Yoncalla, Oregon, and count on their early varieties taking more days to first ripen in Cascadia than the catalog says. Beware: it seems a garden seed trade requirement to introduce a few new, incredibly wondrous, better, greater, faster, quicker tomato varieties every year. Only Cascadian seed company offerings may be depended upon.

The sooner fruit sets, the sooner it gets ripe, but most early tomato varieties fail to pollinate successfully if the flower opens on a night when the temperature falls below 50 degrees F, a usual occurrence during May and the first half of June. Unpollinated ovaries abort (fall off); no fruit gets set until some of the nights are warmer. Dr. James (Jim) Baggett, the vegetable crops breeder at Oregon State University (OSU), released a group of open-pollinated determinate varieties that do set fruit on cold nights. Starting with an unusual (but relatively tasteless) Russian variety that instead of aborting, set and then ripened seedless fruit when its early flowers failed to pollinate, Baggett bred a series of early setting, good-tasting determinates including Legend, Santiam, Siletz, Gold Nugget, and Oregon Spring. You can depend on these.

In the late 1970s OSU's Willamette was widely considered the best slicing variety available, but Willamette was infamous for having as many green tomatoes remaining at season's end as it had ripened. Dr. Baggett crossed Willamette with that parthenocarpic Russian stock and produced Legend. I grow Legend every summer and urge you to try it. It is better than Willamette in every way possible. Legend is a supervigorous determinate that needs no staking or training. I give each of mine a 5-foot circle to occupy. A locally based world-renowned chef whose kitchen we sometimes supply with our surplus opines that Legend's flavor is equal to that of Brandywine. I still consider Fantastic Hybrid (TSC) to be about equal to Legend, but Legend, a determinate, is easier to grow. Indeterminate varieties like Celebrity, Big Boy, Better Boy, Big Beef, Moreton, and Rutgers—popular back east and sometimes offered in Cascadia—produce far better back east. Early Girl hybrid does work pretty well in Cascadia. One year in Lorane I trialed Moreton and Rutgers, both open-pollinated and generally reputed to be among the best-tasting eastern varieties of all. I harvested a few average-tasting fruit in the last half of September.

Large-fruited indeterminates that routinely win Territorial's taste-off contests include Cosmonaut Volkov, Black Krim, and Brandywine. I treasure Brandywine. The major seed catalogs east of the Rockies present a bewildering assortment. Be cautious.

Gardeners who make more than a few quarts of tomato sauce or paste should make it from varieties bred for that purpose. Salad or slicing varieties simmer down to very little. Processing varieties almost always make tidy determinate bushes. The fruit has a higher percentage of solids and fewer seeds. Sauce varieties cook down rapidly; some varieties are firm enough for whole-pack canning.

In the same way that small-fruited peppers are more productive in cool conditions than the fancy large-fruited varieties, most cherry tomatoes are early and prolific. James Baggett's Gold Nugget has a mild-but-rich flavor, makes a small tidy bush, and has been the first to ripen in my garden year after year. Its first clusters of ripe fruit are supremely delicious; then overbearing dilutes the taste. But by the time this happens, there are better-tasting and much larger tomatoes. I suggest avoiding Red Cherry, Yellow Pear, and Yellow Plum. These are wildly vigorous indeterminate heirlooms with great flavor but are late to ripen and too rambling for comfort, except perhaps for dry gardening south of Drain.

No matter what disappointment happened with it last year, I always put in one Golden Jubilee (indeterminate) in my warmest, best-protected spot. Jubilee was released by W. A. Burpee in 1942, and there's a good reason it is still grown by so many gardeners east of the Rockies. Jubilee produces the most delicious, rich-flavored, large, firm ripe-mango-yellow slicing tomatoes you've ever tasted, but many summers it fails to ripen much fruit and will be the first variety to become diseased when conditions turn cool and damp. The regional seed companies offer far-better-adapted yellow determinate varieties, although in terms of flavor, every one I've trialed proved a pale imitation. You can find Golden Jubilee seed online.

Dry gardening

Use indeterminate varieties (or a supervigorous determinate like Legend) because an indeterminate's root system is every bit as aggressive as its vines. Grow on stations 5 by 5 feet or even 6 by 6 feet; stake and train; fertigate with 2 gallons July 1, 4 gallons July 15, and then 5 gallons twice in August. I've had good results from the Fantastic hybrid and the aggressively sprawling Red Cherry. Any indeterminate cherry variety should do. Try dry gardening with Gold Nugget (determinate) too, spaced 3 by 3 feet. In a hotter than usual summer unharvested moisture-stressed Gold Nuggets dry on the vine into sugary, slightly tart raisins.

Legumes

L egumes manufacture some, or all, of their own nitrogen requirement in collaboration with a family of soil-dwelling bacteria called rhizobia, which form pinkish nodules on their roots. Without rhizobial nodulation, legumes would have to obtain all their nitrates from the soil as other plants do. Legume green manures (clovers, favas) create a great deal of nitrogen. Garden legumes (beans and peas) cannot make all the nitrogen they could use and do much better when fertilized like other low-demand crops.

I know you've been told differently, but please believe me. In the world of gardening, falsehoods and half-truths have been repeated so often they seem to be the truth.

Rhizobial nodulation is a plus for garden beans and peas, but is not necessary if you use COF; in fact, the amount of nitrogen released by COF may hinder rhizobia for about two months after it is spread. Some farm soils are so devoid of life that for legume crops like soybeans to develop rhizobial associations, their seed must be inoculated before sowing. This step is very rarely needed in garden soil.

Garden books and magazine articles often parrot a fantasy about how actively growing legumes supply nitrogen to nonlegumes sharing their root zone, and beans and peas put useful amounts of nitrogen into the soil that benefits following on crops. The truth is, useful quantities of rhizobially produced nitrates do not leak into the soil, and very little nitrogen remains in the nodules or in legume roots after harvest. Virtually all rhizobially manufactured nitrogen becomes chlorophyll, the dark green protein in the leaves. This nitrogen later becomes the protein component of legume seeds.

You could be viewing vibrant green patches of small-seeded favas, clovers, or field peas mixed into cereal grains growing over the winter. Turning under a still-growing legume green manure does effectively increase soil organic matter and soil nitrogen. Overwintering green manures, legume or not, preserve soil fertility by capturing soil nutrients that might otherwise be leached. On slow-to-dry-out soils a green crop allows spring tillage weeks earlier because it transpires a lot of moisture. All this in exchange for sowing a few dollars' worth of seed and a bit of work in October.

I said before that snap beans and garden peas do not produce enough rhizobial nitrates to fully supply their own requirement. Clovers are far better nitrogen fixers than legume vegetables; a strong stand of crimson clover, turned under when its flowers appear but before any seed formation begins, can supply enough N for a low-demand following-on crop, such as carrots or beets. Turning in a thick stand of small-seeded fava beans may put enough nitrogen in the soil to grow a medium-demand crop.

Pea and fava bean seed may fail to germinate if spring weather is too cold. Similarly, garden beans are often started before the soil has warmed up enough to really suit them. Germination is more certain if the seeds are first chitted (see Chapter 6).

Legume seeds contain a lot of protein, but I don't think it's the best dietary practice to satisfy most of your body's protein requirement with them. If you believe you need more protein, the best thing to do is regularly fill your belly with raw chlorophyll from dark green leafy salads and cooked spinach, mustard greens, or Swiss chard. Chlorophyll is a complete protein whose amino acid balance is perfect for humans.

The problem with eating legume seeds is that, although high in protein, they are even richer in carbohydrates. The human digestive system does not readily process cooked proteins and carbs at the same time. That's why pea soup, baked beans, chickpea hummus, lentil soup, and so forth cause intestinal gas in almost everyone.

Wind is the minor concern. When the body attempts to digest an impossible combination of starch and protein, it makes both wind *and* toxic waste products that degrade health and cause disease. Vegans concerned about getting enough protein eat too many legume seeds. These folks develop the same deadly diseases that people eating too much overcooked red meat get. If you want a high protein meal, I suggest a large green salad and a belly-filling serving of steamed snap beans.

The key to getting strong planting seed from all legumes is to allow the seedpods to dry down completely on the plant without remoistening them when you irrigate. If it is about to rain or if you must irrigate the area where *Phaseolus vulgaris* bean seeds are drying down, handpick pods that are mostly dry and bring them inside to finish where they get good air circulation. However, do not pick any pod before its vascular connection to the plant has ended. This is revealed when the stem end of the pod gets floppy (wilts). From that point the pod is not receiving any more food from the plant and may as well dry down indoors as hang on the bush. Do not remove the seeds from the pod before they are dry and hard, because the embryo within is extremely delicate.

BUSH BEANS *(Phaseolus vulgaris)*

Pole beans came first. These untidy creatures were bred into half-tall climbers that fit a waist-high garden fence. And then half-tall varieties were bred down to have very short interstems that eliminate costly trellising and provide a shorter, concentrated, and more profitable harvest period. Some bush varieties mature so uniformly and bear so heavily that they can be harvested mechanically—once over, all done.

The flavor (and probably the nutritional content) of bush beans, even of old bush varieties, never equals the pole bean. I reckon that's so because the crowded leaves on bush varieties shade one another while their root systems have been compressed like their tops. Compare that with how the well-separated leaves of pole beans gather more direct, unfiltered light and how their aggressive roots reach far.

SOW	HARVEST	TRANSPLANT
Mid-May to mid-July	July to October	N/A
BETWEEN ROWS	SEEDS	THIN
18 to 24 inches	4 inches apart	8 inches

Culture

Bush beans fail to germinate if soil temperature falls below 60 degrees F for long. The first sowing can be difficult. Young seedlings get stunted by bad weather. So don't rush. In the Willamette, make the first sowing mid-May. Chitting helps.

Bush beans are a low-demand crop. Sow seeds 1½ inches deep, one seed every 4 inches in rows 18 inches apart. When the seedlings are well established, thin to an average of 8 inches apart in the row. There are a few old, almost-heirloom home-garden bush varieties that grow with extreme vigor; arrange these in rows 24 inches apart, the plants 1 foot apart in the row. Unsettled weather between sowing and emergence may wreck germination; if a small fraction of this sowing eventually struggles to the surface, the seedlings may be exhausted and won't grow fast for a few weeks, if ever. That's why I try to sow beans just before a dry, sunny period. If poor weather hits between sowing and emergence, the best strategy is to immediately resow. This later sowing may end up maturing beans ahead of the first sowing—while markedly outyielding the earlier attempt. When I must resow, I put the new rows in between the existing ones. Whichever sowing ends up dominating the area is allowed to grow on.

Garden planning

Bush beans usually produce intensely for a few weeks and then pretty much quit. To eat bush beans all summer, sow a new patch every few weeks. The final sowing should be around mid-July. For earliest harvest, sow chitted bush bean seeds under a cloche about two weeks before the last usual frost; remove the cloche several weeks after the last usual frost date.

Insects and diseases

In a poor spring leaf-eating insects may chew faster than the leaves can grow. Control them with pyrethrins or Spinosad until it is warmer. In decent weather and on good soil, bugs should be no problem. Many older bean varieties are sensitive to diseases that you could spread by harvesting damp plants. Just in case, wait until the morning dew has evaporated before harvesting.

Harvest

Snap bean bushes are brittle—their leaves are easily damaged by rough handling—so be deliberate and gentle when detaching the pods. The plants don't thrive in windy locations for the same reason, although being close to the ground, bush varieties handle wind a lot better than pole beans. The young pods go from mostly developed and still tender to overgrown and tough in a few days. Frequent harvesting will extend their production period because once a plant is forming even a few seeds, it stops setting as many new pods.

Saving seed

The official story is that natural crosses are extremely rare, and so isolation is unnecessary and seed can be saved from only one plant. Carol Deppe says that this is true where pesticides are frequently used, but in an unsprayed garden beans do cross fairly frequently. The Organic Seed Alliance suggests separating varieties by 10 feet in the garden; by 20 feet if in commercial productions.

Varieties

Green, blue, yellow, filet, flageolet, haricot, Dutch, English, Romano, Guatemalan, purple-mottled, longpod—feel free to explore without much risk of failure. The main difference I find is that the pods of some varieties develop strings and seeds (and get fibrous) more quickly than others. Recently I trialed a dozen industrial bush varieties in current use plus a handful of the traditional home-garden ones. In every case the old varieties had better flavor; the modern varieties yielded more over a shorter period, made smaller-size seeds, and sometimes had more visually appealing pods.

I find interesting taste differences among bush bean varieties when the pods have not been cooked. For raw eating I prefer Blue Lake types, of which there are many. When cooked, all bush beans taste about the same to me, although there are marked differences in mouth feel. I suspect the tough ones were bred for canning or freezing.

Filet varieties feature very slender, perfectly round pods that should be harvested at half size. They're pretty when artfully arrayed on oversized restaurant plates but not very different when they get past the eyeballs.

Purple-podded types turn green when cooked. They're slightly more vigorous sprouters in cool soil and make better growth under cool conditions. Purple beans should be considered for early sowing under a cloche. I don't think Royalty Purple Pod is as good as a new variety called Royal Burgundy.

Bush wax beans do not have a soft, warm, waxy texture the way some old pole wax types did; they're only a different color—same flavor as green pods.

Dry gardening

Grow plants 1 foot apart in rows 3 or even 4 feet apart. They'll go weeks between irrigations. It's better to use pole varieties for absolute dry gardening; the habits of their root systems match those of the aggressively spreading vines.

POLE BEANS *(Phaseolus vulgaris)*

Pole beans must grow a week or two longer than bush varieties before producing pods, but many climbing varieties yield all summer, ultimately providing quite a bit more for the space and time involved. In this respect, pole beans and indeterminate tomatoes are similar. I no longer grow bush beans except when doing trials.

SOW	HARVEST	TRANSPLANT
Mid-May to early June	Mid-July to October	N/A
BETWEEN ROWS	SEEDS	THIN
5 feet	4 inches apart	12 inches

Culture

Climbing varieties naturally twine around rough poles or up a trellis, fence, or strings. Willamette Valley canneries used to zigzag a string between two stout parallel wires for vines to climb: one wire stretched tight a few inches above the ground, the top wire about 7 feet up. The pioneers used tall tripods made of skinny, rough poles with the bark left on and grew one plant up each pole. I've let pole beans climb the deer fence in a neighborhood where deer were rarely seen. When growing trials, I used plastic "fishnet" hung from a stout steel wire stretched over the tops of a 100-foot-long line of pointed two-by-two posts driven into the soil about 1 foot deep and 6 feet apart.

Pole beans are a low-demand crop. Sow as soon as there is no more frost danger. Place the seeds 1½ inches deep, one seed every 4 inches, and thin so that the plants average 12 inches apart. You'll enjoy a longer harvest period if the vines can keep growing because their row has plenty of uncontested soil on either side.

Garden planning

One sowing is all that's required unless you're in redwood country, where a second sowing made soon after the summer solstice yields into October. Ten row feet produce all the beans my family can eat fresh. Snap bean fanciers might consider growing a bush variety to fill the gap until the pole beans start bearing.

Insects and diseases

Like bush beans. Reaching above the wind-slowing ground effect that shelters bush varieties, pole beans struggle in breezy sites.

Harvest

Take pods at 90 percent of full size, or else they start forming seed and string. It is essential to keep pole varieties picked clean. Allowing even two pods to form seeds on a vine greatly reduces further pod set. If gently and completely picked and not crowded, most pole varieties will produce until the end of September. Production drops off as the older leaves blister, look obviously aged, become inefficient photosynthesizers, and worse, block the light that triggers growing points to form new bearing side branches. I remove old blistered leaves as they appear. To keep production high after mid to late August, foliar feed.

Saving seed

Like bush beans. You're just wasting money if you don't let at least one good plant make seeds for next year.

Varieties

Blue Lake pole provides slow seed and string development and slender, attractive round pods—this is, after all, the variety that made the Willamette Valley canning industry. Kentucky Wonder—either strain, brown or white seeded—has a richer, beanier flavor than Blue Lake. The harder to find brown-seeded Kentucky Wonder has rather rapid seed and string development, but is the best all-purpose variety for dry gardening.

Kentucky Wonder Wax (WCO) is available again! I hope this is the original heirloom, but can't find that out for myself because I can't legally import bean seed. The original Wax provides a unique and genuinely waxy mouthfeel and a distinct bland but pleasant taste.

Oregon Giant is an old-fashioned early maturing variety with huge, watery, tender, mild-flavored, mottled purplish-green pods and large, fast-developing seeds good for shell beans. Cascade Giant is Dr. Jim Baggett's superior version.

I discovered Musica, and Territorial still sells it. Musica has long been my favorite. I cover a 10-foot-long by 7-foot-tall net with it every year. Musica provides everything—very long, very wide, very thin pods that remain very tender to full size and, in my opinion, have the best flavor of all *P. vulgaris* varieties. Musica grows okay outdoors, but it was bred for the Dutch greenhouse trade. It has thin leaves that are easily wind damaged, and it doesn't yield much when nights are too cold for it. When flowers open on the day before or after (I don't know which, or maybe it's both) a night this edge of "too cold," they may curl into a J-hook. And after a windy

day there may be a period of low productivity while it regrows new leaves. But so what!

Climbing purple varieties are an excellent choice for coastal Oregon and north of the Columbia.

Dry gardening

The best variety I know is Kentucky Wonder (brown seeded), sometimes called "Old Homestead" for good reason. Adaptive has several climbing varieties likely to be as productive, or better. Sow a few seeds every 18 inches down the row and make sure there's an entirely uncontested space at least 3 feet wide on either side of their supports. Thin to one plant in each position. Fertigation will more than double production. Give each plant 3 to 5 gallons once a month, early July, early August, and early September too, if they're still going strong.

RUNNER BEANS *(Phaseolus multifloris*, also called *P. coccineus)*

Runner beans are popular in England, where people think the *P. vulgaris* snap beans do not have nearly as much flavor. The Brits are correct!

SOW	HARVEST	TRANSPLANT
Mid-May to early June	Mid-July to October	N/A
POSITIONS	**SEEDS**	**THIN**
3 x 5 feet	3 per position	1 per position

Culture

Grow like pole beans on tall trellises or other supports. Runner beans start yielding a week or so later than *P. vulgaris* pole beans. They cope with cool, humid conditions. The vigorous vines run much longer distances than *P. vulgaris* and promiscuously throw side-branching vines. Give runner beans plenty of space. I suggest 3 feet apart in the row. I locate my row down the center of a 4-foot-wide raised bed. In the redwoods and on the southern Oregon coast, where there are only a few light winter frosts, *P. multifloris* may regrow in spring from its dahlia-tuber-like roots. For this reason, runners have been called "seven-year beans." However, allowing second-year plants to grow on is not a useful practice. So many vines come up that overcompetition results in many small, misshapen pods. It's better to dig up the tubers in autumn and get rid of them. The University of Florida Institute of Food and Agricultural Sciences Extension says the tubers are eaten by South Americans; others say they're poisonous. My guess is that the native South Americans know how to prepare them, probably much like people leach cyanide from cassava leaves.

Runner beans often fail to pollinate in hot, dry weather. If yours are flowering, but pods don't form, try heavily misting the vines an hour before dark.

Harvest

They're best for eating as snap beans when the pod is half to three-quarters grown. The immature seeds are eaten as shelling beans. I've used dry runner bean seeds like ordinary dry beans. The original Native American type had dark seeds. It was grown primarily to produce edible dry seeds. I've been told that dark-colored seeds from some varieties are toxic like the tubers are. I suppose it would be wise to soak the seed overnight, pour off that soak water, add more water, and boil them for 1 hour and pour off that water too. Then finish cooking. Like other beans, having unoccupied soil to grow into and keeping the vine picked clean so that no seed starts developing helps maintain production of new pods. As soon as the vines get crowded or run out of root room, the harvest diminishes greatly.

Saving seed

Bumblebees often cross-pollinate runner beans, so seed savers should grow only one variety. Otherwise, collect seed like *P. vulgaris*. Seed formation does reduce pod set. Because the vines are so vigorous, allowing one plant to only form dry seed is impractical in the home garden. However, I inevitably collect dozens of seeds from overlooked pods. The Organic Seed Alliance suggests isolation of 800 feet for home-garden purity and half a mile for commercial productions.

Varieties

The Native American heirloom Scarlet Runner develops seeds rapidly; this type is useful for producing shelling beans or dry seed but makes a poor choice for snap beans. Most modern varieties offer slow seed, string, and fiber development and long, attractive pods. Some have white flowers and white seeds most have red flowers and mottled purplish seeds. Sunset (TSC) has peach-colored flowers and black seeds and is Marina's favorite. My favorite, Scarlet Emperor (WCO, NIC), has slow seed development; tender, handsome pods; a sweet, full-bodied flavor; and showy flowers. Thompson & Morgan offers several.

Dry gardening

Thin to one plant, on positions 5 feet apart. In Elkton, Oregon, runner beans stayed alive and grew slowly without any watering, but they could not forage enough soil moisture to produce much without fertigation. During July and August, and into September if they're still setting pods, fertigate each plant with about 5 gallons every three weeks.

FAVA BEANS *(Vicia faba)*

Large-seeded varieties have long been called "horse beans" by the few Americans aware of them. That's because for many decades Windsor has been the only readily available variety in the United States. Windsor makes barely acceptable eating as a shelling bean during its short season, but it tastes awful after drying down and then being rehydrated and cooked. Windsor is not winter hardy in most of Cascadia. There are better varieties.

Small-seeded varieties are locally termed "bell beans"; the English call them "tic beans" if spring sown and "winter beans" if the variety is cold hardy enough to withstand fall sowing. The English often eat large-seeded favas, but unfortunately their small-seeded varieties have been selected for use as green manure or animal feed. In my Lorane trials, four small-seeded English varieties survived a typical winter, but when cooked their flavor was foul. The beans I once ate at a Palestinian restaurant in the Old City of Jerusalem were delicious, and I know they're a human staple throughout the Middle East. I believe small-seeded favas perfectly match Cascadia's climate and should be selected for increased cold tolerance and pleasant-eating qualities when used as dry beans.

SOW	HARVEST	TRANSPLANT
Overwintered: October Spring: March to early April	Late April to mid-June	N/A

BETWEEN ROWS	SEEDS	THIN
2 feet	4 inches apart	12 inches

Culture

Favas are a cool-season crop. If your garden generally grows vegetables well, then no COF is needed before sowing favas. Otherwise, consider them a low-demand crop. Sow March through early April. Sow later and heat will degrade the crop before you harvest much. You'll get better germination in early March by presprouting the seed (see Chapter 6). Place one seed 1½ inches deep every 4 inches in rows 24 inches apart. Thin to 1 foot apart in the row. Expect large-seeded varieties to grow at least 3 feet tall.

Where winter is not too severe, sow in October. Large-seeded favas freeze out between 18 to 20 degrees F. One winter trial in Lorane some plants in a row of Aquadulce Claudia survived 12 degrees F and went on to make seed. Favas that do survive winter grow taller and start setting seed a few weeks earlier than spring sowings.

Garden planning

A dozen plants produce enough shelling beans for a few ample servings each week during the harvest period. Favas finish when June warms up; grow brassicas, cucumbers, or melons after them.

Insects and diseases

Disease makes black spots on the leaves. British organic farming books assert that occurs only in infertile soils. In 40 years of growing fava beans in garden soil, I have experienced no leaf disease except the time I tried overwintering a small-seeded green-manure variety where the clay soil was soggy most of the winter. After I put in a French drain, favas overwintered there without difficulty. Pea weevils chew chunks out of fava leaves in spring, but this minor damage causes little loss of yield and should be overlooked.

Harvest

All the early flowers fail to set pods. This is normal. Seedpods will set as soon as conditions are warm enough. Harvest pods before the seeds are full-size because they quickly get starchy and develop tough skins.

Large-seeded varieties tend to fall over (lodge) from the weight of seed forming high on the stalk; some gardeners support the top-heavy stalks. I find providing generous interplant space grows a stockier plant capable of holding up the weight of forming seed. Large-seeded favas overwinter reliably in southern Cascadia and grow taller than spring sowings. To prevent overwintering favas from lodging, pinch off the growing points at the beginning of spring regrowth. This encourages formation of several shorter stalks.

Seeds mature and dry down when summer turns warm. Most large-seeded varieties hold their seeds tightly in protective pods that don't shatter. Take your time about harvesting. The seeds of small-seeded varieties are held less securely. Once the seed has dried, some (or many) pods split and some seed falls on the ground. These sorts may be harvested as soon as most of the pods are mostly dry and allowed to finish drying down while spread out on a tarp.

I process and clean the seeds right in the fava patch after the stalks have finished drying on a tarp. If rain threatens before they're fully crisp, I cover them with another large tarp. One sunny afternoon after the night's moisture has been baked out and the pods are really crisp, I scuffle-walk on the stalks, breaking the seed free. Others beat the stalks with a flail or pair of thin sticks about the length of a policeman's baton. Winnow in a light breeze or in front of a window fan until the seed is clean. Without assistance I have threshed and winnowed 100 pounds of seed in about 2 hours.

Saving seed

(See the previous section, Harvest.) Favas do cross-pollinate. Varieties must be separated by 800 feet or more to stay pure.

Varieties

Large seeded: Almost all US seed companies, including Territorial and West Coast, only offer Windsor, a large-seeded, bitter-tasting, mealy-centered shelling bean with a tough skin that dries into a cookable seed with an even tougher brown skin that leaves a bitter aftertaste and tends to form a rough cud in your mouth. Windsor is not winter hardy (except perhaps in Northern California or along the southern Oregon coast). Ianto Evans, one of the founders of Aprovecho, a nonprofit rural-life-improvement organization near Cottage Grove, Oregon, collected fava varieties from indigenous Latin Americans. These have been selected for winter hardiness and are now sold as a mixture called Ianto's Return by Adaptive Seeds.

Small seeded: I discovered a pleasantly edible winter-hardy variety I named Sweet Lorane. It was hiding within a diverse collection of small-seeded favas obtained from the USDA Plant Introduction Station in Pullman, Washington. Each of the packets I was originally given contained several hundred seeds, one or two seeds from each variety, all mixed; the packets were labeled Nepal, Afghanistan, Yugoslavia, and Pakistan. I planted every seed I had been sent and overwintered this collection through several generations, allowing winter to eliminate many plants. The only selection I made during those years was to only harvest seed from plants that stood erect with a full load of dry seed. The majority of these varieties did not taste very good. Most of them had such tough skins that even after hours of cooking, your mouth ended up working a fibrous cud with a bitter taste. That's why I've seen hulled, small-seeded favas sold in Canada. A few of these plants made such bitter seeds, I thought they must be poisonous. Eventually I discovered a strong plant that made delicious seeds—Sweet Lorane. All its seed grew true to type so that no purification was required, a fortunate thing since at that time I didn't know much about plant breeding. Territorial is again offering Sweet Lorane after allowing it to disappear for quite a few years. I hope it didn't get crossed with something.

Small-seeded varieties make taller, more vigorous plants than large-seeded types. Sow small seed in rows 36 inches apart and thin the rows so that the plants stand 1 foot apart. If you'll keep the patch well weeded during winter and spring, you'll harvest more.

Dry gardening

Not a problem. Spring or fall sown, favas totally suit Cascadia's rainfall pattern and need no irrigation. Broad beans should be one of Cascadia's essential survival crops along with Turkish opium poppy varieties that overwinter to produce deliciously sweet light-brown oily seeds. These are a basic staple food in parts of Turkey where the climate is too dry and the soil too infertile to grow wheat.

FIELD BEANS AND HORTICULTURAL BEANS *(Phaseolus vulgaris)*

P. vulgaris seed production can be difficult in Cascadia. Most varieties are harvested in the second half of September, but typically unsettled weather at that season rarely helps the seed to dry down. Even if it doesn't rain, there are heavy dews. Consequently, achieving earlier harvest makes success a lot more certain. Hotter summers south of Yoncalla allow a much broader choice of variety.

SOW	HARVEST	TRANSPLANT
Late May	Late August or September	N/A
BETWEEN ROWS	**SEEDS**	**THIN**
18 inches	4 inches apart	8 inches

Culture

Grow like bush beans. With irrigation, sow seeds 4 inches apart in rows 18 to 24 inches apart. Thin most varieties to 8 inches in the row. Stop all watering when the first pods start drying out, and absolutely stop irrigating by September 1. Without irrigation, sow seeds 6 inches apart in rows 36 to 48 inches apart. Thin when established to 12 inches in the row. Keep the area entirely free of weeds. Grown without irrigation, beans quickly come under moisture stress, which reduces seed set and prompts earlier drying but also lowers yield.

Garden planning

Yield depends greatly upon variety, weather, and soil conditions. Irrigated yields average 50 to 100 pounds per 1,000 square feet.

Insects and diseases

Same as bush beans. If you've seen weevils crawling out of a bag of bean seeds in the spring, they can be eliminated by freezing the seeds for a few weeks shortly after you finish cleaning them. But freezing may damage the embryo unless the seed has been first dried to a very low moisture content, so it's probably best not to freeze the seeds you're planning to sow for the next crop. The pinholes that weevils leave behind after emerging from your planting seeds will not reduce their germination, nor does anything pupating bean weevils left behind seem to ruin the beans for consumption; I assert that because I've cooked and eaten beans after the weevils infesting a bag exited their seeds and proceeded to crawl all over Territorial's seed room. Fortunately they were not looking for dry seeds to lay eggs on.

Harvest

If the rains didn't normally return until mid-October, you'd harvest when 90 percent of the leaves had yellowed and the pods had dried to a crisp but very few seeds had yet shattered from the pod. You would pull the plants from the dusty, dry earth, pile them on a large tarp, and dry them to a crisp in a few more Indian summer days before threshing. However, in most of the maritime Northwest, most varieties need to be harvested before most of the leaves have yellowed, and then bunched and hung or loosely stacked on a porch and carefully turned every few days until they are dry.

Threshing can be done with flails or by banging the plants (held by the stems at the root end) against the inner wall of an oil drum. I prefer to spread the dry material on a tarp and then scuffle-dance on it. Then winnow the seeds by slowly pouring the mixture of plant fragments and seed back and forth between large plastic buckets in a moderate breeze or in front of a window fan.

Saving seed

Isolation of 20 feet between varieties is enough for home-garden purposes. Still, variation naturally develops in most bean varieties. You can maintain uniformity by flagging a few perfect plants each year, harvesting them separately, and planting this selected seed next year. For the highest uniformity, choose what seems to be a perfect plant, choose a dozen pods from that plant, and then grow out the seeds in each pod in its own line and then continue to increase planting seed only from lines where every plant is perfectly true to type.

Varieties

Many well-adapted varieties are offered by regional seed businesses. Taylor Dwarf Horticultural (Speckled Bays) (WCO) is widely grown west of the Cascades because it is one of the earliest. Black Coco is the best-eating dry bean I know of. When I owned Territorial, every July I'd take the contents of every unsold packet of Black Coco to the kitchen pantry. Seeds from most kinds of *P. vulgaris* beans make decent eating, including snap bean varieties. When evaluating a dry bean, I soak a tablespoon of seed overnight, drain soak water, add more water, bring it to a boil, and then simmer for exactly two hours without salt or any other seasoning. Drain, cool, taste. A few varieties like Black Coco taste great all by themselves. Most need seasoning. Some varieties will have objectionably tough skins after two hours of cooking, and some of these will still have tough skins after eight more hours. This may not be the variety's fault. Bean seeds develop harder skins as they age. Latinos know dry beans should be eaten within a year of harvest. Asians have the same concern about old rice.

Dry gardening

Most varieties work okay, but the unirrigated yield will be much lower. Kentucky Wonder (brown seeded) makes very edible dry seed. See the information on dry gardening in Bush Beans, page 202.

LIMA BEANS *(Phaseolus limensis)*

Limas are heat lovers. I never managed to harvest more than a few seeds. Territorial's catalog asserts Jackson Wonder is early enough. Good luck! You'll have a better result if you transplant large-as-possible lima seedlings about the time you'd put out eggplants. The so-called Oregon Lima is not a lima at all but an heirloom white-flowered, white-seeded runner bean with rapid seed development, useful as a shelling bean.

SOYBEANS *(Glycine max)*

Soybeans are a heat-loving seed crop. In warmer climates they can be a broad-acre crop driven by rhizobial nitrogen, but to yield much in Cascadia's cool soils they must be fed more nitrogen than the soil ecology can provide in early summer. Start soybeans with enough COF in their bed for a low-demand crop. Sow about the same time you put out pepper and eggplant seedlings because soybean seeds germinate poorly in cool soil. Soybeans grow only vegetation until, triggered by day length, they entirely cease making new leaves and stems and form flowers at nearly every leaf notch. Because Cascadians have to sow rather late to get soybeans to germinate (chit them), and because early vegetative growth is slow under cool conditions, the bushes tend to be small when flowering starts, so yields are low. For this reason (and because irrigation is required), soybeans are not a regional basic staple. Territorial sells varieties primarily for eating in the green seed stage, what the Japanese call "edamame beans"; the TSC website provides full cultural information. Steamed edamame beans make wonderful summertime snacking, but in my opinion, those seeking food self-sufficiency through legume seed crops should learn to love favas, garbanzos, lentils, and pea soup.

PEAS *(Pisum sativum)*

Shelling peas are a frost-tolerant spring crop. Almost any variety can be productive in Cascadia *if you can get it to come up and start growing early enough*. Unfortunately, if harvest extends into hot weather, an unavoidable regional disease called "enation" wipes out nonresistant varieties. The right variety of snow peas can produce in Cascadia's summer.

SOW	HARVEST	TRANSPLANT
Mid-February to mid-April	May to mid-June	N/A

BETWEEN ROWS	SEEDS	THIN
24 inches	1 inch apart	Do not thin

Culture

Peas are a low-demand crop. Sow bush varieties one seed per inch, about 1 inch deep. Make the rows 18 inches apart for very dwarfed varieties; 24 inches apart for regular varieties. Do not thin. Keep the bed thoroughly weeded until the vines make a semi-self-supporting tangle that prevents hoeing. You may have read in old garden books about giving peas fences to climb up, but few modern shelling varieties can attach themselves to a trellis, even if one is offered.

The few remaining tall shelling varieties are heirlooms that require a 6-foot-tall support. Climbers are not enation resistant; they must be sown very early and encouraged to grow very fast

in order to mature before disease takes them. Sow chitted seeds 2 inches apart in single rows, with several feet of empty ground on either side. I have succeeded at harvesting tall climbing peas, but I can't say their slightly better flavor is worth the trouble.

Garden planning

A 25-square-foot patch of bush peas should cover half of two adult plates with peas every few days over a 10- to 14-day harvest period. I'd sow a new pea patch every two weeks from late February through mid-April. By the time the mid-April sowing has been harvested, the bush beans are coming on and numerous heat-related pea diseases (including enation) are getting fierce.

Any bed that had grown autumn/winter crops is a good candidate for a spring-sown bush pea green-manure crop. Even if the peas aren't needed in the kitchen, the vegetation becomes compost while decomposing roots create a friable planting bed for the next crop.

Insects and diseases

Pea diseases are numerous—wilts, yellows, mildews, streaks, and enation, which is the main Cascadian problem. Pea enation is spread by the green peach aphid, which appears when the weather turns warm (and the vines are beginning to form seed). Enation makes the pods look mottled and warty, ends flowering and pod set, and then kills the vine. In my experience peas are able to resist disease while they are making vegetative growth but succumb when they fall under the stress of seed formation, especially in warm conditions. There's not much an organic gardener can do about pea diseases except to grow peas in raised beds to enhance soil drainage, boost overall vigor by making the soil properly fertile, and choosing resistant varieties. The most effective home-garden measure is scheduling—finish harvesting peas before summer's heat appears. The farther north you go, the longer shelling peas can grow into summer. The cool Skagit Valley produces industrial crops of shelling peas.

Harvest

Shelling peas fatten rapidly and are best eaten when the seeds are not quite full-size. We harvest a patch every other day. Snow peas should be picked before strings and seeds form, which is also when their pods get fibrous. A few snow pea varieties don't toughen rapidly. If allowed to fatten for another day or two, they become much sweeter and the half-size pea seeds within are delicious, but strings must be stripped out. Snap peas become much tastier if picked after they've fattened and formed strings and half-size seeds.

Saving seed

Pods inevitably get missed; a few days later when you harvest the patch again, it's sure you'll spot these past-it pods because when overdone, their color lightens and the skin wrinkles. If all you want are enough seeds to plant next year, allow these overdone pods to remain on the vine until the pod's stem end wilts. Then *gently* detach the pod (the seeds inside are still soft; if you crush them even slightly, you may damage or kill the embryo). Allow them to finish drying indoors. Small insects, often crawling ones, not just bees, transfer pollen. Most authorities say peas

are self-pollinating and need no more than 10 feet of isolation. However, I have seen a good deal of crossing. Probably these experts are working on conventional breeding/seed production sites, where pesticides have reduced insect populations. I suggest organic gardeners provide 50 feet of isolation from any other flowering pea variety if you're saving seed.

Varieties

Old standards like Little Marvel, Lincoln (small, extra delicious peas), Dark Skin Perfection, Early Frosty, and Freezonian may produce a harvest if it comes in before enation appears. Early sowings produce reliably north of Chehalis. Alderman, also called Tall Telephone, is the only tall shelling variety still readily available. I suggest only attempting Alderman on well-drained dark-colored loam or sand that heats up quicker and encourages spring growth.

Enation-resistant varieties were developed by Oregon State University. Regional seed companies offer Maestro (TSC) and Cascadia (WCO). Dr. Baggett's highly enation-resistant Oregon Sugar Pod became the basis of a snow pea farming industry in the Willamette Valley. An improved variety, Oregon Giant, has larger pods than OSP. Both varieties yield in midsummer *if you keep them picked clean*. But if you allow seeds to develop in more than a few pods, disease will probably take over.

A belly full of peas sits heavy. Digesting juicy snap pea pods doesn't sap my energy. The original Sugar Snap is a 6- and sometimes 7-foot-tall climber with far better flavor than any of the dwarf snap varieties that came out after it was released. The original Sugar Snap is often a bit too late to produce a full yield before enation takes it out. Seeds plump up quickly in the original Sugar Snap, and as they do, the pod gets ever sweeter. Even though allowing that to happen means strings must be stripped out, we prefer to harvest pods with half-developed seeds.

Super Sugar Snap is a new so-called improved highly disease-resistant variety that climbs only 5 feet high and starts yielding sooner. It does cling to its supports better than the original. However, seed development has been retarded because flat pods without any seed inside is what the supermarket and restaurant trades want. But if you wait for pods on this variety to plump up, they toughen, seeds still do not form, and sweetness does not increase much

Alaska is the traditional American variety for making pea soup. Capucijners, a traditional Dutch field pea with a unique flattened seed, cooks quickly into a delicious, rich brown gravy. Desirée (ADA) is a Capucijener type. If a homesteader wanted to grow legume seed as a major dietary staple, peas and their relatives, garbanzos and lentils, would be far more likely than vulgaris beans.

GARBANZO BEANS (*Cicer arietinum*) and LENTILS (*Lens culinaris*)

Garbanzo beans (chickpeas) and lentils form short bushes that resemble peas. They're frost hardy but not quite as cold tolerant as peas. They must be spring sown, their seed dries down in July, and they are best assigned an area where irrigation can be withheld around harvest time.

Culture

You'll get the best results by treating chickpeas and lentils as low-demand crops whose rhizobia do not manufacture their full nitrogen requirement. Sow as soon as the soil is warm enough to germinate the seeds. That will be mid to late March in the Willamette—risking earlier sowing increases the chance of there still being plenty of soil moisture while seeds are forming. Chitting the seeds helps them get up and grow earlier. Place seeds about ¾ inch deep, three to four seeds per foot, rows 24 inches apart. The first time you grow them without irrigation, try rows 36 inches apart. Thin garbanzos to about 8 inches apart in the row, lentils to about 4 inches apart.

Harvest

Like dry beans, but less stressful because harvesting occurs in stably dry conditions. If you get a lot of empty pods, the most probable cause was a shortage of phosphorus. Next time prepare their row with a full dose of COF. Next most likely cause, the variety is adapted to the northern Indian winter, not Cascadian spring.

Saving seed

When you grow them to eat, you've also saved seed to replant.

Varieties

I find the small black garbanzos supposedly from Afghanistan particularly tasty and tender—300 percent better than the big, tough yellow ones. Any bag of lentils or garbanzos sold for food should sprout and do okay. Iranian, Pakistani, and Indian specialty grocery stores usually have several varieties in a range of colors. Carol Deppe has long been interested in garbanzos and sells a popping variety. Find her business, Fertile Valley Seeds, at www.caroldeppe.com.

Green Manures

Any green-manure variety sold by local feed and grain dealers will be well adapted to the climate and probably will cost a lot less than seed sold by catalog. Most green manures are sown in October. They overwinter and must be disposed of in spring before or, at the latest, when they start blooming.

CRIMSON CLOVER *(Trifolium incarnatum)*
Crimson clover is an excellent green manure, although it fails on poorly drained sites and will disappoint on acidic, infertile soils. It is reliably winter hardy and easily eliminated in spring. Sow late September through October; earlier is better. One pound of broadcast seed thickly covers 500 to 1,000 square feet. (Farmers use 15 to 25 pounds per acre when precision planting.) If possible, rake the seeds in about a half inch deep. Early in November, try scattering clover seeds into beds of brussels sprouts and olrecea kale after the base leaves have been removed. This lets enough light in for clover to survive. If the temperatures aren't too cold, the seed sprouts, gradually gets more light as the winter progresses, and takes over the bed by spring.

Crimson clover blooms in April. A rear-end garden rototiller can turn this vegetation under if this is done before flower buds develop. I've done the same with a combination shovel. But if the soil has been too wet to work and now the flowers are opening, do not even try to turn the vegetation under because it's become woody. If it doesn't hopelessly tangle the tiller, it's decomposition will interfere with your next crop. Instead, pull the vegetation out of the ground (or mow it close to the soil with a scythe or brushcutter), rake it up, and make it part of your next compost heap. Then chop complete organic fertilizer (COF) into the bed with a common garden hoe. Clover stubble decomposes rapidly. After one more week you'll be able to rake out a seedbed.

You can prepare a quick rough seedbed late February through March by chopping in crimson clover with an ordinary hoe. At that tender stage, everything will completely rot in a few days. Beware of other types of clover. Crimson clover is an annual that dies after making seed. Better, it is easily killed with a hoe or tiller. It can be recognized by its intense crimson flowers. Perennial clovers such as red (pink flowers) and Dutch White form strong root clumps that spread through underground runners that resist death. I know this from sad experience, because a garden store owner once sold me Red clover seed when I asked for Crimson. I was hoeing out clumps of it for the next three years.

FIELD PEAS *(Pisum arvense)*
The Austrian winter pea is usually winter hardy in Cascadia. In October broadcast enough seeds to establish plants on 4-by-4-inch average spacing. Put seeds 1 inch under with a rototiller or by hoeing. Peas can be grown alone or in combination

with tall-growing cereal rye. The peas don't much interfere with the grain's growth, while the strong rye stalks physically support the pea vines. But plowing in the lush tangle demands a powerful tractor. Be prepared to scythe down the vegetation before any seeds start forming, rake it off the bed, and use it for making compost. Field peas (more so when combined with cereal rye) leave the soil in a beautifully crumbly condition.

FAVAS *(Vicia faba)*

Use small-seeded favas for green manuring because compared to large-seeded varieties, this type grows taller, produces more biomass, and certainly requires less weight of seed to cover a given area. Turning under a dense stand of favas provides at least enough nitrogen to grow a low-demand crop. Maybe more. In October (and even into early November in southern Oregon or Northern California) sow 1 inch deep, 3 inches apart in the row (probably half will germinate). You want to end up with plants 6 inches apart. Make the rows 12 inches apart. Or broadcast 5 to 10 pounds per 1,000 square feet and hoe in or rototill in shallowly. Favas make an excellent spring-sown green manure but won't grow as tall nor produce as much nitrogen. Before blooming starts, fava stalks are brittle, so they can be turned under by a front-end rototiller. Once seeds start forming, the stalks become fibrous and tangle all garden tillers. Like crimson clover, fava stalks can be scythed or taken down with a brushcutter, raked up, and composted, and then the stubble can be hoed in. Favas become woody weeks later than crimson clover, making favas better for green manuring heavy soils.

Varieties appropriate to spring sowing east of the Cascades, often called "bell beans," are sometimes sold in Cascadia. These do not reliably overwinter north of the Yoncalla Valley. Sweet Lorane is hardy enough to use as an overwintering green manure throughout Cascadia.

In Lorane I effectively cleaned up a symphylan-infested trials plot by growing a three-year-long fava bean dry fallow/green manure. In autumn of the first year, I established a fava seed crop by sowing 6 inches apart in rows 4 feet apart and thinning to 1 foot apart in the row. The wide between-row space allowed me to conveniently keep the plot free of weeds during spring and early summer, ensuring that the soil wouldn't be weedy several years later when it again grew vegetables.

The plants made seed that I did not harvest. Some stalks collapsed under the weight of ripe seed. No matter. When the fall rains began, I rototilled the plot shallowly, setting most of the bean seeds an inch under. This action also eliminated germinating weeds. An excessively dense stand of favas appeared because 50-plus pounds of dry seed sprouted on every 1,000 square feet.

The favas overwintered and set what seed they could (being so crowded). Weed growth was strongly suppressed. The entire leggy stand lodged (fell over) in one huge tangle while the seeds formed. No matter; enough seed still matured in that snarl to permit yet another very dense stand of favas to be established when I rototilled shallowly in fall (starting year three of the rotation). The next spring I turned the favas under as early as possible in April, waited a few weeks for the stalks to decompose, and then put the area back into vegetables.

Symphylans were very few in number after three years of only fava roots to eat and no irrigation, while organic matter content had been maintained. (See Chapter 8 for information about symphylans.)

CORN SALAD (*Valerianella locusta* var. *olitoria*)

This very hardy salad vegetable is fully covered in the Greens section, page 218. As a green manure it'll be flowering by April. Even in bloom, the vegetation is very tender (although no longer edible) and can be easily chopped into the bed with a hoe, creating a very fine seedbed.

Broadcast and shallowly rake in about 1 ounce of seed per 100 square feet of bed mid to late September after the heat of summer is over. Seed is widely available.

GRAINS (*Poaceae* or *Gramineae*, true grasses)

To grow winter cereals as green manure, scatter a quarter pound of seed over 100 square feet in the month of October, then till, rake, or hoe it in about a half-inch to an inch deep. Let it grow. In spring, turn it under. Seems simple, eh? Well, usually it works out best to mow and then rake up and remove the vegetation.

Any winter-hardy cereal works—wheat, barley, oats, rye—but problems can arise. Sow too much seed, and the stand gets so leggy, it falls over (lodges). Then it can't easily be mowed. Heavy, late-tilling soils pose another difficulty. As seed formation progresses, the stems (and leaves) rapidly become woody. Tender young

cereals rot in two weeks if turned under before there's any sign of seedstalks appearing. When wet soil conditions delay turning the crop under until seed stalks develop, if you do dig it in, the advanced vegetation rots so slowly that another crop can't be started there for a month or even six weeks, resulting in a very late garden—or a very poor showing if the gardener ignores all that decomposing straw and plants anyway. The thing to do in that case is mow the vegetation close to the soil line and then rake it up for making compost. Then work the soil.

The grain that farmers say yields to the disk most easily is winter wheat; I suggest using local varieties. Sometimes these can be purchased from farm suppliers as animal food and occasionally in health-food stores. Barley, oats, and spelt create more leaf and longer stalks than modern wheat varieties. If you have use for very strong and extraordinarily long straw for insulating compost heaps, or for summertime mulching, *and* you want an easy way to prepare ground for cucurbits and solanums, the best grass grain of all is cereal rye. I do not mean ryegrass of the sort found in pastures, but *cereal* rye. Seeds to plant can be purchased from a bulk-food or whole-food shop. Cereal rye makes an extremely long, strong straw. Depending on variety, the seed heads top out between 5 and 7 feet.

Please, never consider turning cereal rye under unless you have sandy soil (that allows early tillage) and a powerful tractor, and are sure you can do this job before there's the first sign of seed heads. I wait until after the seed heads have pollinated (so the stubble doesn't resprout) and then mow rye close to the soil line with a brushcutter (or scythe). The tough straw dries in the sun for a few days and then I rake it up. Then I dig fertile hills, spread COF over the rest, and plant. Spaces between hills can be dug up at my convenience, or not dug at all because the fast-decomposing rye root systems thoroughly fracture the bed a foot deep.

Be sure to cut the rye before any half-formed seeds could ripen while the straw is drying down. Tilling or digging after mowing is not essential because rye roots are so fine, dense, and quick to rot that the bed almost tills itself. However, tilling or digging does make absolutely certain all the rye is dead. Hoeing COF into the stubble will eliminate any rye that has not been killed. Cereal rye straw will be the longest, strongest straw you ever had, and there'll be a great deal of it.

BUCKWHEAT *(Fagopyrum esculentum)*

Buckwheat grows in early summer. It is not frost hardy. It quickly matures seed on natural soil moisture if you want a fast but low-yielding summertime grain crop.

I suggest growing buckwheat on bare areas occurring in late May that you intend to plant vegetables on in July. Buckwheat grows so rapidly in June that it quickly shades out competing weeds and grasses. Sow it after mid-June, and shortening days force it into bloom while still too small to suppress weeds or produce much biomass. Before blooming starts, buckwheat stalks are so brittle they do not tangle rototillers and rot quickly in garden soil, forming a fine, loose seedbed within a week of turning them under. Beware, though: after the seeds start forming, the stalks will take weeks longer to decompose and *will* tangle garden rototillers.

One pound of seed covers 300 to 500 square feet and should be broadcast and tilled or hoed in about 1 inch deep.

THE GRASS LEY

If it is at all possible in your situation, I recommend periodically rejuvenating vegetable ground by converting it to unirrigated grasses and other typical pasture species for at least three years. The procedure will give you a lot more benefit if you'll establish a well-considered diversity rather than letting the weeds take over. You should mow the plot once or twice a year but take no biomass away from that land, no bagged up grass clippings, no hay making, no grazing.

The British know much about converting fields to temporary pasture, which they call a "grass ley." The best books about this are Newman Turner's *Fertility Pastures and Cover Crops* (currently in print by Acres, USA) and Robert Elliot's classic *The Clifton Park System of Farming*, circa 1900 (see Additional Reading, page 339).

I use this inexpensive, readily available seed mixture. The amounts given are enough to plant from 1,000 to 2,000 square feet: ½ pound of whatever variety of quick-growing perennial ryegrass is being offered by my local farm supply and 2 pounds of cocksfoot (*dactylis glomerata*), also called orchard grass, a deeply rooted species that gradually overwhelms the ryegrass. I also include 4 ounces of red clover, and if I can find seed for it, 4 ounces of wild chicory. Do not include any vetch seeds, or you'll have their hard-to-weed-out descendants troubling your garden for years. Blend uniformly. In October, ideally the first half of the month, broadcast the seed over just loosened ground (so it falls into cracks and crannies), or else work the soil shallowly after broadcasting the seed.

Mow the minipasture in spring after the grasses pollinate but before any seed could mature. Orchard grass grows tall and strong, so I use a brush cutter. Allow the hay to rot where it falls. Be prepared to mow a second time, and even a third time if there's been summer rain, before the grass completely abandons its attempts to form seed.

To convert the grass ley back into garden, see the information about eliminating sod in Chapter 2. When back in vegetables again, the area will produce excellently for three or four years. Better, the ley creates so much organic matter that you'll probably not need to import any compost or manure (or both) for a few years.

Greens

I assert without exception and with only one qualifier: when it comes to greens, the faster they grow, the better they taste. I feed most kinds of greens like medium-demand crops. But when greens are pushed by providing lots of nitrogen without balancing the other essential nutrients, they only appear to thrive. They grow big and fast, but are tasteless and appeal more to insects than to children. Supermarket stuff. It's best to push them with COF or something like it.

Most leafy green vegetables have been bred to make fast-growing tops at the expense of strong root development, so during summer maintain plenty of moisture in their beds. Only Swiss chard and New Zealand spinach can go through moisture stress without losing much eating quality, although they won't grow as much new leaf. Crowded greens grow slowly; slow growth lowers eating quality. Once plants have touched, thin the row so that they can continue growing fast. If the soil is moist and they aren't growing fast, side-dress them.

I do not grow cut-and-come-again greens mixtures. I much prefer lettuce hearts and mild (young) rocket. So once a month from March through July I start 100 square feet of mixed leafy salad vegetables. In August and September I sow lettuce and spinach by the 100 square feet each, and corn salad and endive in patches of 50 square feet because these beds must carry our kitchen through autumn and, hopefully, through winter. If you want to become an expert at growing winter salads, sow a short row of mixed lettuce varieties on August 15 and make another sowing as soon as that one germinates. Continue doing this until the last sowing fails to germinate. Thin progressively and keep well weeded over the winter; you'll observe how the seedlings of various sizes and varieties handle winter, and maybe you'll see what they do in spring, if they survive.

You waste money buying greens transplants. Yes, true, greens seedlings generally are transplantable. But you'll find that it takes less effort, it is less costly, and you'll be able to grow a wider range of varieties if you direct-seed greens. That's especially true of growing celery.

CELERY (*Apium dulce*)
and CELERIAC (*A. rapaceum*)

Growing celery (or celeriac) by direct seeding in the correct month demands much less work than raising your own transplants, but anyone who has examined celery seeds wonders about getting these minuscule things to come up and grow. Actually, direct seeding can be the easiest way.

The wild species that humans coaxed into becoming garden celery is a swamp plant that makes a long taproot and weak, shallow, and generally inefficient surface feeding roots that do not spread far. Transplanting wrecks celery's taproot—another reason to direct-seed the crop.

Celery is poorly adapted to heavy soil. If that is your situation, the celery bed should be especially well amended with organic matter. Attempting celery on clay is one occasion when thoroughly double digging a great deal of compost into the subsoil may be required, not optional.

SOW	HARVEST	TRANSPLANT
Mid- to late May	August until freeze out	N/A
POSITIONS	**SEEDS**	**THIN**
2 x 2 feet	Clusters of 10	The best plant per station, progressively

Culture

Raising celery transplants takes 10 to 12 weeks of attentive care, and for all that you end up with a second-rate root system. Direct seeding gives much better results, but only if the crop is not started too early. Yes, celery seed sprouts easily in chilly soil. Yes, it grows outdoors in April; the seedlings survive frost. But to avoid seeing the plants go to seed prematurely, it's essential to have the seedlings emerge just after the usual last frost date. The same is true of celery transplants. Do not set them outdoors before you transplant tomato seedlings or they'll almost certainly go to seed in July. Even if you wait long enough, transplants you buy may still go to seed prematurely if the nursery allowed them to experience many chilly nights. I suggest that if you buy transplants, get small, younger ones and make the purchase 10 days after tomatoes usually get transplanted in your area.

When preparing the celery bed, give it twice the usual amount of compost and make sure that compost gets blended into the surface two inches. *Locate this moisture-demanding crop where it will be convenient to water it frequently.* Arrange your plants on positions 24 to 30 inches apart in rows 24 inches apart. Your seedbed should rake out to a condition resembling commercial potting mix. If it doesn't, then at every position you want a celery plant, make a half-pint mason-jar-size hole. Fill that hole to heaping full with something like the home-brewed potting mix described in Chapter 7. Then slightly compress that sowing position to restore capillarity, but not so much as to form a brick. Then using a fingertip, make a shallow depression about the size of a 25-cent piece and in it, scatter a dozen celery seeds. Cover them ¼ inch deep.

Celery seeds must be kept moist until they germinate more than two agonizing weeks later. In warm weather that can seem impossible because the tiny seed must be close to the surface. That's half of why I urged you to start them in moisture-retentive potting soil. I water the seed almost every morning. Should the day be warm and sunny, I gently spray my celery bed again in the afternoon. Close observation and almost daily watering for two weeks may seem like a lot of trouble, but if there is any way you can manage to direct-seed celery, let me assure you making this effort comes to much less work than raising your own transplants.

Progressively thin each growing position after germination. Don't rush it. For their first six weeks, the seedlings will be very small. All during summer it is essential that celery grows rapidly or else the stalks will be pithy, stringy, and tough. Slow-growing celeriac roots, especially if under moisture stress, get tough, fibrous, and knobby. So I water my celery bed almost every time I have occasion to visit the garden. If growth slows during summer, fertigate abundantly every two weeks or side-dress, keeping in mind that the surface feeding roots do not extend more than a foot from a full-size plant. Make the last side-dressing about mid-August so that the plants harden off as fall approaches.

Grow celeriac exactly like celery; however, celeriac makes a smaller plant, so arrange it on 18-by-24-inch to 24-by-24-inch centers. Do not crowd celeriac or you'll mostly harvest leaves. Celeriac roots are peeled, then steamed, fried, or pureed into a thick celery soup. It tastes like starchy celery. I love celeriac slowly fried, atop a wood stove, in butter to a golden-brown crisp.

Garden planning

Six healthy plants should be enough to enliven your salads and soups from late summer into autumn, rarely through winter and the following spring. Mature plants can be protected under a tunnel cloche over the winter, where they'll make more winter growth and have a better chance of surviving.

My household can use a dozen celeriac roots over a winter. In frostier areas, hilling up an inch of soil over the edible bottom when fall weather checks their growth will protect them from freezing and then rotting.

If growth was only average to poor, then in early October quite a bit of light will still be hitting the soil around the plants; in that situation, sprinkling crimson clover seed in the celery or celeriac bed may establish a noncompetitive green manure that will take over in spring or when the celery freezes out. If the bed grew well, the leaf canopy will be so dense that clover won't be able to get established.

Insects and diseases

Celery diseases are rarely found outside commercial growing areas. I've had no problems. Marina lost her celery patch to a virus of some kind one year, but never before or after. Besides, if a home garden does catch a celery disease, the cure was in the soil preparation or variety choice before sowing, not in any treatment.

Premature bolting (going to seed before going over the winter) is caused when seedlings experience too much chilling (below 45 degrees F).

Harvest

Do not take the entire plant. During late summer cut or break off some of the larger stalks and leave others to sustain the plant. After the plant is developing side shoots around the base, take the entire center and at the same time remove all but two or three side shoots. These will develop during autumn—being more open, they'll resist humidity-induced diseases better.

If the plant survives winter, its unopened flowers and tender stalks below them make useful salad greens.

Take the first celeriac when they've reached the size of grapefruit, and hope they get a lot larger than that.

Saving seed

Celery is biennial. Experiencing cold spring weather makes celery seedlings react as though they had overwintered, so they bolt in summer. Any propensity to make seed the first year suggests undesirable genes, so first-year bolters should be destroyed. Celery is pollinated by insects. It crosses freely with celeriac. A celery-celery cross might make highly vigorous and useful plants, so isolate celery varieties by at least 200 feet (or more), and consider allowing the occasional superhybrid to grow on, should one appear when planting seeds you produced yourself. The Organic Seed Alliance suggests 800 feet of isolation for home-garden purposes. A celery-celeriac cross will not prove useful. Fortunately, there's no need to grow celery and celeriac seed in the same year, since the species makes very long-lived seed. Even if the crop freezes out most winters, Cascadian gardeners should still be able to keep a variety going. At least southern Cascadian gardeners can.

The Alliance also asserts that 80 celery plants are needed in every generation to maintain a variety's genetics. I take this to mean that I'd best not count on making more than one or two productions from only a few plants before my variety develops inbreeding depression of vigor.

Because of the species' weak root systems I suggest mulching plants intended for seed making. Celery flowers are similar to those of its relative, the carrot, but are smaller. Individual flowers ripen irregularly over many weeks and should be taken individually just before the seed starts to detach by itself. Spread drying flowers under cover on a tarp.

Varieties

I suggest using a commercial quality celery variety. "Utah" strains work well. If the catalog says the variety is used in California commercial production, it'll do okay in Cascadia. Avoid "Florida" selections.

Currently there's much interest in heirlooms. Pascal types are supposed to be more resistant to early bolting, but my experience does not confirm this. From trials I know Golden or Golden Self-Blanching types have shorter stalks and less vigorous growth.

Quality celeriac selections are free of big lateral roots and are smoother, reducing waste. I urge you to not use cheap or amateur-produced celeriac seed.

There's an easier-to-grow variant called "cutting celery," or Chinese celery. It grows like parsley and will tolerate moisture stress far better than stalk celery. We use it for cooking or minced finely in salads. Like other celeries, to avoid premature bolting it should not be started too early in spring. Cutting celery is far more likely to survive winter, especially under a cloche.

Johnny's offers two varieties, an ordinary sort and Par-Cel, a refined yet vigorous plant that makes much larger stalks than most. I grow my own Par-Cel seed. Adaptive sells a Belgian heirloom called Hollow Pipe of Malines.

Dry gardening

No way, José, unless you've got a naturally sandy swamp to grow them in. Maybe cutting celery could get through a long dry summer without dying if given minimal fertigation and resume vigorous growth when the rains return.

CILANTRO A.K.A. CORIANDER

(Coriandrum sativum)

SOW	HARVEST	TRANSPLANT
Once a month, late April through mid-September	Late summer sowings do not go to seed quickly	N/A
BETWEEN ROWS	SEEDS	THIN
12 inches	One per inch	Do not thin

This is a quick-growing low-demand crop. Sow cilantro seeds from midspring through the end of summer. The seeds go 1 inch apart in a furrow 1 inch deep. Cilantro grows like a small white carrot with a big top; its row should be in the middle of an empty bed space at least 1 foot wide.

When seed making begins, cilantro's flavor becomes too strong for me to tolerate, especially so in warm weather. When experiencing long (and lengthening) days, cilantro goes to seed as soon as it has grown tall enough to use. If not sooner. When experiencing short (and shortening) days, it grows quite large before going to seed. I suggest sowing a short row about once a month starting in April and continuing through mid-September. Cilantro is frost hardy and survives a mild winter.

If you want to produce seed for planting or for culinary use, simply allow a spring sowing to go to seed. Yank the plants with roots still attached after most of the seeds have become brown or at least tan and about 10 percent of them have detached. Spread the plants out on a tarp under a roof (that also keeps the sun off), where they have excellent air circulation while they slowly finish ripening their seed. Then strip dry seeds from the branches.

I've trialed named varieties that are supposed to stand longer before going to seed. Maybe they do by a few days. I suggest buying an ounce of coriander seed from the bulk bins at the health-food store and planting that.

CORN SALAD *(Valerianella locusta var. olitoria)*

In England, small grains like wheat, barley, and oats are collectively named "corn." What North Americans call "corn," the English call "maize." Corn salad was once a biennial weed that came up in the stubble of harvested grain fields. The domesticated version still is rather uncivilized, and if allowed to go to seed in the garden, it may naturalize. Fortunately, corn salad is an easy-to-eliminate weed.

SOW	HARVEST	TRANSPLANT
Early September	Mid-October to March	N/A
BETWEEN ROWS	SEEDS	THIN
12 inches	Three per inch	When harvesting

Culture

Corn salad grows great on fertility remaining after the harvest of summer vegetables. The seeds will not sprout until soil temperatures have dropped well below their summer peak. Sowing early in September will result in more autumn harvest, but it may be too hot then for the seeds to sprout. Corn salad seed does not germinate at high rates. Sow three seeds per inch, ½ inch deep in rows at least 12 inches apart. Do not thin much until harvesting begins. (See the Green Manures section, page 214, for another slant on growing corn salad.)

Garden planning

Sow corn salad after any crop that finishes in the month of September. A few row feet provide enough tender thin leaves to balance tougher greens like finely cut Savoy cabbage or escarole/endive. Fifty square feet repeatedly fills a big salad bowl and also serves as a green manure crop. Corn salad goes to seed in April and becomes too strong tasting to eat a few weeks before that happens.

Insects and diseases

None that I know of.

Harvest

Gradually thin the row and use the thinnings. Once the plants stand more than 2 inches apart, you may continue to eat thinnings or else harvest by cutting off some side branches so that the plants continue producing.

Saving seed

In late April lightweight, irregularly shaped seeds develop quickly, promptly detach, and travel when the wind blows. As soon as flowering begins, pull every other row to increase between-row spacing to at least 24 inches. Slip a sheet of cardboard under the plants to catch falling seeds. Collect seeds daily; spread them out to finish drying indoors. Corn salad seed lives two years, maybe three.

Varieties

The differences concern leaf size, not flavor or hardiness. All varieties survive Cascadian winter. Medallion (JSS) is unusual, bred for spring sowing and summer production.

Dry gardening

It is best to start the crop mid-September with some irrigation, but corn salad may be sown early October if there has been rain.

ENDIVE/ESCAROLE *(Cichorium endivia)* and OTHER CHICORIES

Supermarket endive usually tastes too bitter; after a few hard frosts homegrown tastes sweet with only a slight hint of bitterness. Growing endive (escarole) can increase your midwinter salad security. Freeze-out for most lettuce varieties is about 21 degrees F; some exceptional strains survive brief exposures to 19 degrees F. Consequently, unprotected lettuce rarely

survives winter. But I have witnessed endive/
escarole survive 7 degrees F (under plastic as well
as outside the plastic) with no sign of damage.

SOW	HARVEST	TRANSPLANT
Late July	Mid-September to March	N/A
BETWEEN ROWS	ROWS	THIN
18 to 24 inches	Two per inch	Progressively

Culture

Endive is a biennial. Most varieties go to seed
prematurely when spring sown. If sown early in
summer, it grows okay but is too bitter in hot
weather. Consequently, I target endive for fall
and winter harvest. I sow in July; later in the
month is better. To fill a winter cold frame, sow
as late as October 1.

If you treat endive as a medium-demand
crop (side-dress), you'll grow huge rosettes.
Sow seeds ½ inch deep, two seeds per inch, in
rows at least 18 inches apart. Thin promptly
and progressively so that the seedlings don't
touch in the row. Full-size plants should not
touch each other in the row nor touch the
adjoining rows because leaves more readily
develop rotting black spots when plants lack
air circulation. Gardeners in southern Cascadia
where wintertime sunshine is more frequent
may sow unprotected crops in early September. In well-ventilated cloches, endive can be
crowded without becoming diseased.

Garden planning

Salad greens get scarce in winter. Finely chopped
endive can seem mighty desirable in January/
February, but unprotected plants start rotting
back to stumps by Christmas. A cloche, a cold
frame, even a sheet of glass or plastic propped up
on cement blocks, anything that keeps off damaging rains and increases daytime temperatures just a
bit encourages more growth and prevents disease.
Cold frames filled with endive (and spinach) can
be started on beds that grew melons, cucumbers,
corn, tomatoes, or other hot-weather crops.

Insects and diseases

Leaf disease is not a problem under glass
or plastic.

Harvest

Harvest every other plant in the row to make sure
there is excellent air circulation.

Saving seed

Chicories are self-pollinated biennials. Plants that
survive winter may be allowed to form seed right
where they are. The gnarled tiny-blue-flower-
covered seedstalks grow waist high.

When chicory seedstalks have partly dried,
cut and let them dry under cover until they are
brittle. Getting the seeds out of some varieties
can make you sweat. The best at-home system
I ever devised is to spread the stalks out on a
concrete walkway or slab and dance on them
with a scuffling, sole-scraping motion. (I had
one resistant variety I had to batter with the butt
end of a 3-inch-diameter, 5-foot-long wooden
staff until the seeds separated.) Then pass the

seeds through a sieve to eliminate chaff. Winnow out the dust and any fine chaff by pouring the mixture from bucket to bucket in a mild breeze. Endive seed is long lived. One plant will produce about an ounce of seed.

Varieties

There are two better-known types: *Endive* has deeply cut and frilled leaves. *Escarole* forms broad, plain leaves that wrap into semiblanched hearts. *Frisée* is an endive with especially narrow, deeply cut, frilled leaves resembling mizuna; frisée isn't too bitter to eat in summer. American-bred endive or escarole varieties are intended for California or Florida agribusiness and are not likely to be as cold hardy or rain resistant as the species can be. Look for catalog language like "handles bad weather" or "tolerates low temperatures" and Dutch- or French-sounding names. Adaptive Seeds has several varieties of endive/escarole selected for winter hardiness.

Radicchio makes a round, dense head like a small purple cabbage. It is best sown during July. To form decent heads, you must thin carefully; no crowding allowed. Winter regrowth will provide bright purple-red leaves for early spring salads if you don't cut off the growing point when harvesting the main head. Like endive, radicchio is prone to disease when damp all the time.

Sugar Loaf or Sugar Hat or most properly *Zuccerhut* forms a conical green head somewhat like romaine lettuce. It is also prone to rotting in winter, but it can produce more leaves after the head is cut; the regrowth is disease resistant and also good for eating. Virtus (JSS) is this type. *Grumolo* sorts are way too bitter to eat

during autumn, but their tops naturally die back in winter. Very early in spring their regrowth is rapid and much milder. They'll balance a cabbage salad. *Catalogna* is like a wild dandelion, an annual whose flower stalks are picked before they open. It's easy to grow but too bitter for me to eat. As the Asians do with bitter melon, the Italians must know what to do with Catalogna.

Dry gardening

Chicories make deep, moisture retentive taproots, similar to carrots. Start endive and other chicories two weeks before the heat of summer arrives. Sow this crop where the subsoil moisture has been preserved by keeping the surface bare from early spring. If possible, immediately after sowing apply just enough irrigation to deeply saturate a foot-wide band of soil immediately beneath the seeds. Thin the row steadily and promptly to 24 inches apart. Make the between-row space 3 to 4 feet. That way you probably won't have to water them all summer. If they get too overgrown by the time the rains return, cut off the tough, bitter tops without damaging the growing point and use the regrowth during winter.

LETTUCE *(Lactuca sativa)*

It is a common misconception that lettuce provides little nutrition, although little nutrition correctly describes iceberg types. Icebergs also are the most difficult type to grow; these days I don't bother. Nonheading or semiheading varieties are easy to grow; nutritionally the leafy green varieties are the equal of any other leafy green vegetable, rich in high-protein chlorophyll.

Semiheading types (butterhead, Batavian, cos/romaine) given too much nitrogen tend to blow up (loose, poorly shaped) or suffer internal tip burn (thin blackened edges on interior leaves). COF supplies nitrogen in balance, so side-dressing COF discourages tip burn while making your lettuce grow as fast as it can.

Lettuce forms a dense network of fine roots that decompose rapidly after harvest, leaving the ex–lettuce bed in a beautiful condition for the next crop.

Lettuce must be both tender and naturally sweet or I don't eat much of it. Most varieties turn bitter in hot weather, and all varieties do when they're under moisture stress, or if they have much competition or grow slowly for any other reason. Lettuce handily survives moisture stress by using water stored up in its core and taproot. To the eye it may not seem to suffer other than to grow slowly. To the eye, not the mouth.

SOW	HARVEST	TRANSPLANT
Sow once a month from early April to mid-August	60 to 90 days after sowing	N/A

BETWEEN ROWS	SEEDS	THIN
18 inches	Two per inch	Progressively

Culture

Sow from April through mid-August. The use of cold frames can extend sowing dates both earlier and later. In new gardens lettuce is best considered a medium-demand crop. After the soil has been improved for a few years, lettuce may grow like a low-demand crop. Sow two seeds per inch ½ inch deep in furrows that are 18 inches apart. Ideally, one seedling per inch will emerge. Thin the row progressively without permitting any crowding. Eat the thinnings if you wish. When mature, the heads should barely touch.

Garden planning

I eat large (belly-filling-all-by-itself) green salads. So throughout spring and much of summer I start a 25-square-foot patch of mixed lettuce varieties roughly once a month. By the time I cut the last heads from one patch, I am harvesting the quickest-yielding varieties from the next sowing. I do not use cut-and-cut-again salad mixes; I prefer eating the choicest bits—the semiblanched inner hearts of full-size plants.

About mid-August I suggest sowing a much larger area using only the hardiest varieties. This will be the last unprotected crop. Sometimes, small lettuce plants that haven't yet begun to form hearts will survive frosts that destroy larger plants. For that reason, a "take-a-chance" sowing might be attempted the first week of September. You might see those small seedlings survive a mild winter, make big heads in spring, and then, if you don't harvest them, make seed.

Protected by crude cloches, lettuce can be started as late as October 1. I suggest this approach for making seed.

Insects and diseases

I've never had any problems, except for having to wash slugs (and occasionally a few aphids) out. If you do get more than a few aphids in your lettuce, it means the plants are crowded, thirsty, or malnourished, so they are stressed and slow growing or nongrowing.

Tip burn or internal browning on leaf margins is usually caused by calcium deficiency induced by hot weather. Repeated use of COF reduces and eventually eliminates it.

Harvest

I feed the coarse outer leaves to our chickens while we gourmandize on the tender inner bits. Many varieties turn bitter soon after reaching harvestable size and then go to seed very quickly. Others retain good eating qualities for a few weeks after maturity. Lettuce varieties mature over a range of about three weeks. Each variety remains in peak eating condition for a week at best. So I mix all my favorite varieties into a single seed packet. Sowing a mix lengthens the harvest period to about a month. I thin so as to leave some of every type. This is easy to achieve because lettuce varieties are recognizable at a very small size.

Saving seed

Lettuce varieties very rarely cross-pollinate. No isolation is needed. Commercial seed is grown in Southern California close to the ocean because in that coastal strip's mild, frostless conditions, the seed crop can be sown in spring and ripens during long days and intense light. In Cascadia a spring sowing may not start flowering in time to mature its seed. Lettuce seed absolutely must be harvested by the end of August when the lengthening dark period instructs the plant to cease ripening seed and resume vegetative growth. If the seed has not matured by then, it never will.

A more certain approach is to raise big transplants—sowing the seeds indoors, say, mid-January—and set well-hardened-off transplants out mid-March. If your spring-sown attempts fail to finish in time, next time try this gamble: sow shortly before the first anticipated frost; attempt to overwinter small seedlings, under a cloche. During severe winters lettuce seedlings freeze out in a frame. But lettuce seed lives many years, so it is possible for this region's gardeners to keep their own seed going by trying every year.

Ripe lettuce seeds detach and scatter on a light breeze. Individual branches ripen at their own pace. Take plants or branches one at a time after 10 percent of the seed has been lost. Spread them on a tarp protected by a roof where the seeds finish ripening. On a sunny dry morning in late August or early September drag the tarp into full sun and hope the stalks dry to a crisp by midafternoon. Otherwise, return it to shelter and try again the next sunny day. Then thresh out the seed by rubbing the brittle, thoroughly dry plants between the palms of your gloved hands or else hold a rain dance on them.

Lettuce seed is not easy to thinly sow by hand. I see little reason to bother winnowing the seed to perfection because when seeds are mixed into some chaff and dust, it is easier to distribute them evenly in the furrow. If you want perfectly clean seed, then sprinkle the mixture out of a bucket held a few feet above a similar receiving bucket. Do this in a *mild* breeze or better, use a window fan or else you'll see more seed blow away in wind gusts than you'll collect. If your soil has been fully remineralized, the seed will be fat and heavy; most of it will fall straight into the receiving bucket without blowing away. And it'll germinate strongly for many years.

Varieties

Just about any loose-leaf variety will grow in Cascadia, although a few varieties bred for lower latitudes become confused by Cascadian day lengths and bolt almost before hearting up. My personal favorites among the common varieties are Slobolt (a hardy Grand Rapids strain that, like the name suggests, is slow to go to seed), Buttercrunch, and Valmaine (a romaine). Slobolt is not easy to locate these days, but Two Star is similar. So is Simpson Elite (TSC). I also treasure Winter Density and Little Gem, which are small-size romaines that handle cold well.

Boston, Bibb, or butterhead types usually do best in late summer/early autumn. New types constantly appear faster than I care to trial them, but I know that Nancy (JSS) and the heirloom Continuity (also known as Merveille des Quatre Saisons) are excellent. I've recently trialed Red Cross (JSS), a new and improved version of Continuity, and it truly is improved.

Batavians are semihearting varieties originating from romaine-butterhead crosses. They're highly popular in Europe; the ones I've trialed are exceptionally winter hardy, great tasting, and hold at maturity for a long time without getting bitter. Compared to other varieties they're also slow to go to seed. Territorial once sold two similar Batavians, Sierra (reddish tints) and Nevada (green). Sierra was the superior variety, but now only Nevada remains. Magenta (JSS) is similar to Sierra.

Dry gardening

Early spring sowings may reach full size before the soil dries down too much. Nursing an outdoor August sowing until the rains begin or starting a cloche in September would make excellent use of a limited water supply.

MUSTARD (Brassica alba, B. nigra, B. chinensis, B. juncea, B. rapa)

Mustards are not well known to Casacadians but should be because they're the first spring-sown crop that can be harvested. They are rarely damaged by the cabbage root maggot. Mustard seeds germinate in cold weather. It is extremely frost hardy. Cooked mustard greens are delicious. Young leaves of the milder sorts are good in salads.

SOW	HARVEST	TRANSPLANT
Spring: early to mid-March	Spring: mid-April to mid-May	
Summer Pac Choi: May/June	Summer Pac Choi: July/August	N/A
Autumn: mid-June to mid-August	Autumn: Late September to March	

BETWEEN ROWS	SEEDS	THIN
18 to 24 inches	Two per inch	Progressively

Culture

In order to yield much, spring mustards must be sown as early as the seeds can be made to germinate and then helped to grow extremely fast so that the plants produce something useful before going to seed. Mustards sown after mid-July go to seed the following spring. Success with the fall harvest is certain and a winter harvest is likely. But achieving success with spring-sown mustards is not so easy.

In early spring all Cascadian soils are saturated with moisture. The amount of water a soil holds determines how fast it warms up in spring. Sands or sandy soils have one-third the water-holding capacity clay soils have, so sands warm up sooner. This difference in root zone temperature makes an *enormous* difference in the growth rate.

If spring-sown mustard is to attain decent size before inevitably bolting, it must be sown *very* early and grow fast from the beginning. Mustard seeds sprout in chilly soil, but in order to grow *fast*, the seedlings must find plenty of nitrogen (and other nutrients in balance). Cold soils don't release much nitrogen.

You can help. Grow mustards in raised beds where the surface inches dry out sooner and, thus, warm up faster. Soil dries faster when the clay in it does not hold too much exchangeable magnesium; COF is designed to gradually correct the magnesium excesses so commonly found in Cascadian soils. On clays it may be worth the trouble to start spring mustard under cloches.

Sow early to mid-March in furrows about ½ inch deep, four seeds per inch, the rows about 18 inches apart. In spring, in addition to the usual COF worked into the bed before sowing, immediately after germination blend 1 tablespoon of blood meal into each cup of COF and side-dress that cup close to each four or five row feet of seedlings. Do not let the fertilizer touch the seedlings because blood meal may damage leaves. Thin progressively.

Autumn mustard may be considered a low-demand crop that usually does not need side-dressing. Sow mid-July through mid-August. Separate the rows by 24 inches because the plants will grow much larger. Thin late sowings to 12 inches in the row.

Garden planning

Spring or fall, eight row feet usually provides plenty. Spring-sown mustards bolt late April to early May, making space for heat lovers. Fall crops that survive winter will go to seed by April. It's best to follow them with root crops or heat lovers.

This paragraph is speculative, something I'm currently testing. Beds that grew the autumn/winter harvest are barren early in spring. If they're not needed for spring crops, why not plant mustards as a quick green manure that gets turned under when it starts going to seed? I've been hearing about using mustard-family green manures because their breakdown products act like soil pesticides/fungicides against some undesirable species—like symphylans, maybe? Territorial sells a cover crop called "Mighty Mustard Kodiak." When decomposing in the soil, it releases high levels of glucosinolates that prevent nematodes and other soil-dwelling pests from reproducing. Another vegetable that might work for this purpose is rocket/arugula.

Insects and diseases

In spring flea beetles feed on slow-growing seedlings. The best solutions are lots of extra seedlings that get thinned progressively, fertile soil, and cloches or cold frames to enhance growth. If all else fails, spray pyrethrins or Spinosad.

Harvest

After progressively thinning spring mustards to about 3 inches apart in the row, start harvesting for the table by taking every other plant until the in-the-row spacing is 12 inches. With the fall/winter crop, thin to about 12 inches apart in the row and then harvest about half the large leaves from standing plants; take them when mostly developed but not old and tough. Unopened mustard flowers make passable broccoli.

Saving seed

Mustard flowers are bee pollinated. Even though several distinct species are considered mustard greens, it is safest to assume that every variety freely cross-pollinates. Crosses rarely produce superior progeny, so do not permit more than one variety to form flowers. Mustard seeds last 7 to 10 years, so a seed saver could keep several pure varieties going. The small yellow flowers become typical brassica seedpods containing five to eight seeds. When half of the pods have turned yellow brown and the seeds within them have turned brown black, cut the stalks close to the earth, and finish drying under cover on a tarp until crisp; then thresh out the seed by walking on the straw and winnow. Allowing unharvested flower stalks to mulch the ground results in a self-perpetuating mustard thicket that only needs weeding and a once-a-year addition of compost and COF, best done early in spring.

Varieties

Some Asian imports have been grown by Europeans for so long they've acquired American names: Green Wave and Southern Giant Curled (both *B. juncea*) are both hot and mustardy and feature gorgeous frilly leaves. Green Wave is slightly later to bolt to seed in spring. A much better, sharp-tasting variety is Miike (Red) Giant (*B. juncea*). It's sweet, complexly flavorful, and beautiful as well, with reddish-purple tints and broad, thick stalks. Tendergreen (*B. rapa*), is mild and bland; American selections have deteriorated into much variability and earlier bolting. Komatsuna (WCO) is the original slower-bolting Japanese variety that, while still mild, has good flavor.

Many sorts of Hon Tsai Tai and Pac Choi have become available; all of them have celery-like stalks, broad and spoon-shaped green leaves, and a pleasant, mild flavor. Some varieties make large plants that grow through autumn; some make miniature heads in short order and then bolt. Most Pac Choi strains work in spring and again for fall/winter harvest. Black Summer (JSS) is a remarkably bolt-resistant good-tasting hybrid that makes smallish heads. I plant a short row of Black Summer once a month from early spring through the end of summer. Open-pollinated varieties like Nichols's Shanghai or Territorial's Chinese Pac Choi work in summer too, but to get the high production and uniformity required for market gardening, Black Summer is best by far.

Green in Snow (ADA) is from China and is, as its name implies, the hardiest-known mustard, suitable only for fall and winter. Mizuna (*B.*

juncea var. *japonica*) is another sort suitable only for autumn/winter because it bolts too soon when sown in spring. Mizuna makes a dense rosette resembling endive and has a mild flavor. If you're growing salad mixes for profit or admire extraordinary plant breeding, I urge you to try a hybrid mizuna variety.

Dry gardening

Start a row mid-August; provide enough water in a narrow band to germinate the seeds and then just enough more to keep the seedlings alive until the rains return. Then side-dress.

PARSLEY

Parsley is like a carrot grown for its tops, with this difference: if leaf production falters, side-dress and remove any unharvested old leaves that are turning yellow. (See Parsley Root in the Roots section, page 267.)

SPINACH (*Spinacia oleracea*)

The cool maritime Northwest so perfectly matches spinach's requirements that much of the global spinach seed supply is grown in the Skagit Valley. Most varieties go to seed when days are lengthening, so when growing the spring crop, apply all the cautions in the mustard section concerning cold soil, strong balanced fertilizer, and early sowing. Spinach is extremely cold hardy but gets diseased in winter when there is too much moisture. It almost always survives winter under plastic.

SOW	HARVEST	TRANSPLANT
Spring: mid-March	Spring: May	
Summer: mid-April to June	Summer: June to mid-September	N/A
Autumn: mid-July to mid-August	Autumn: mid-September into winter	

BETWEEN ROWS	SEEDS	THIN
18 inches	Two per inch	Progressively

Culture

For spring harvest, sow ordinary varieties in the first half of March *and not after that*. For late spring and summer harvest, only use varieties bred to be bolt resistant during long days, and sow these from mid-April through June. Use any disease-resistant sort for late summer, fall, and winter harvest; sow from mid-July through mid-August. Spinach seed germinates best under cool conditions; a spell of hotter-than-usual weather ruins germination, so when starting fall crops, be prepared to resow. Once up and growing, spinach seedlings handle heat.

Spring and summer spinach are medium-demand crops. Sow seed ½ inch deep, two or three seeds per inch, in rows 18 inches apart, and thin progressively so that plants don't quite touch. In spring, side-dress blood meal–fortified COF or other high-nitrogen (but balanced) fertilizer immediately after germination. For summer crops, side-dress with regular COF. Spinach is more winter hardy when grown as a low-demand crop.

Delay the initial thinning until the seedlings have formed their first true leaf and are growing fast because there may be mysterious disappearances, especially if your soil has many symphylans or does not provide balanced and abundant nutrition. Supermarket spinach has small leaves on much elongated stems because it's grown crowded so that it can be harvested and bunched efficiently. If you'll thin the row progressively, you'll end up with giant leaves on strong, stocky stems that are quicker to wash, and you can conveniently discard the stems if you wish to.

Garden planning

Fifty square feet sown in March provides many salads and all the cooked spinach a couple can use. If we did not eat the entire crop, what remains becomes a fast-decomposing green manure when chopped in with a stout hoe. Spring spinach germinates and grows well when sown into the rough seedbed formed after young crimson clover has just been chopped in. For fall harvest, commit a larger area than you'd use for the spring or summer crop because unprotected spinach doesn't grow much after October. Undiseased plants that survive winter may provide a spring harvest if side-dressed when the earliest bulbs emerge.

Insects and diseases

Symphylans prefer spinach; they can make whole rows of seedlings disappear; fewer symphylans merely stunt spinach. If you are having difficulties, consider them a strong suggestion from serendipity that now may be the time to rotate your current vegetable garden out of vegetables for a few years. Find out for sure. Do a symphylan count. (See Chapter 8.)

Ongoing stresses from rain, frost, weak light, and high humidity make winter spinach prone to leaf diseases. In my trials some disease-resistant varieties produce new growth during winter while old standards gradually succumb to mold and rot. I thin my fall/winter crop to wider in-the-row spacing—8 to 10 inches—so air can move freely around leaves and molds don't form so readily. A cloche or even a drafty cold frame will let spinach overwinter reliably and be modestly productive. Periodic foliar feeding with kelp extract may help too.

Saving seed

Hybrids have replaced most open-pollinated varieties. Don't hesitate to make seeds from a hybrid and, henceforth, consider it your own open-pollinated variety. It will be somewhat less productive and less uniform than the hybrid you started with, but these down points don't matter much in the garden. The climate around Puget Sound is near perfect for making spinach seed because seeds forming when temperature much exceeds 75 degrees F have less vigor.

Ordinary varieties sown before April bolt before June and ripen their seed in midsummer. So do any plants that overwinter. Making seed for summer varieties can be difficult because even when sown early in spring they start making seed so late that it fails to ripen. I grow my own seed for an extremely bolt-resistant, no-longer-available open-pollinated summer variety called Steadfast. For Steadfast to start forming seed in time, I must overwinter the plants. Ideally, seed-making plants should be located where general garden irrigation won't reach them during the critical few weeks the seed is drying. Spinach is wind pollinated and readily outcrosses; varieties must have at least a mile of isolation to remain pure.

The species makes exclusively male or exclusively female plants; both sexes put up a stocky central seedstalk. Males open small sacks that release pollen, and then there's nothing left of the plant; only the females form seed. Because males bolt before the females, breeders have developed all-female hybrids that amateurs probably shouldn't try to involve in making seed.

When the seedstalks begin browning off, start checking daily for plants that are ready to harvest by tugging gently on them. Only take stalks that easily lift from the soil. However, some varieties may not yield this way. You can also gauge when to harvest by looking at the seeds. When they've turned brown/tan and about 10 percent of them have detached by themselves, it is safe to harvest. I spread the plants on a tarp on the garage floor to fully dry. When the stalks are crisp, remove the seed by rubbing stalks between gloved palms or by holding a rain dance on a heap of them. Then sift/winnow. Many seeds will still be in hard-to-break-up clusters. Seed clumps and a fair amount of dust in your seed bag won't matter for home use.

Varieties

Bloomsdale strains have been the usual thing for a long time. Their thick, savoyed (crinkly) leaves make great eating. All Bloomsdales go to seed quickly when spring sown. Tyee, a hybrid, is slower bolting than the Bloomsdales and just about as tasty. It's disease resistant enough to overwinter and make some regrowth where the winter sun shines more often.

For harvesting in summer, use slow-bolting varieties. All the seed companies I recommend except Adaptive offer at least one of this sort. These days they're all hybrids.

Giant Winter is a traditional open-pollinated spinach variety with extraordinary disease resistance. After overwintering, its flavor can be disgustingly sweet.

Dry gardening

Spring spinach varieties arranged on normal spacings grow fine on natural rainfall.

Around mid-May start a summer variety. Thin gradually and carefully to 1 foot apart in rows 3 feet apart. Given enough growing room and open subsoil, spinach may not need watering.

For starting the fall/winter harvest, you'll probably have to irrigate (just a small quantity of moisture concentrated into the row) in order to get the seeds to sprout and to keep the row barely growing until the rains return; for those reasons, it is best to delay sowing until mid-August.

SWISS CHARD (*Beta vulgaris* subsp. *cicla*)

Chard is a beet that makes large, succulent leaves and rough, unusable bottoms. Primary growers produce seed in the Skagit Valley because chard survives a lot of frost and makes the strongest seed when it develops in cool, dry conditions. It will survive relatively infertile, unwatered soil but will thrive, produce much more, and taste better if well fertilized and irrigated like other greens.

SOW	HARVEST	TRANSPLANT
April to mid-July	Mid-May to mid-March	N/A

BETWEEN ROWS	SEEDS	THIN
18 to 24 inches	Six per foot	Progressively

Culture

Chard is a low-demand vegetable that forms a subsoil-feeding moisture-storing taproot. Sow only once between April and June, six seeds per foot, seeds ¾ inch deep, in rows at least 18 inches apart, better 24 inches apart. Thin progressively until the plants stand 12 to 18 inches apart, and eat the thinnings. If growth slows or production seems inadequate, side-dress with COF or fertigate.

Alternatively, grow chard as though it were ordinary spinach. Sow in rows 12 to 14 inches apart, and harvest entire sections of row as soon as the plants are large enough to use. That way you only eat small, tender leaves. The downside is that you have to sow a new patch every month from April through August. The Europeans use thin-stemmed varieties bred especially for this style of cultivation.

Garden planning

Eight row feet sown in April and ultimately thinned to about six plants yields a gracious plenty from June into winter and sometimes through next March. Chickens (and English sparrows) love chard, but we don't give them too much of it because too much oxalic acid (in chard leaves) prevents our chickens from forming such strong eggshells. We find the same thing happens from feeding them too many spinach and beet tops.

Insects and diseases

I've had no problems. Leaf miners could cause difficulties and Spinosad handles them, but I doubt I'd want to eat the leaves after spraying. (See Beets in the Roots section, page 262, for information on how to handle leaf miners and also Chapter 8.)

Harvest

One method is to take about half of the largest leaves and all the small clusters naturally emerging around the base. What you take will soon be replaced. Alternatively, in late September cut out the entire central area, permitting a few of the side shoots forming around the base to take over. My wife, who does most of the harvesting, thinks this approach results in more and better-tasting leaves during winter.

Saving seed

Chard crosses with other beets. (See Beets in the Roots section, page 262.)

Varieties

Fordhook was originated by the W. A. Burpee Company nearly a century ago. It seems plenty hardy and is well adapted to the entire region. Ruby or Rhubarb chard tends to bolt prematurely; delay sowing red-stalked varieties until late May.

There are slight flavor differences and variations in color. I prefer the taste of a variety with chrome yellow stalks and grow my own seed for it.

European varieties bred to be grown like spinach are not available from North American suppliers. Canadians: Tuckers in the United Kingdom sells this variant as "Leaf Beet/Perpetual Spinach."

Dry gardening

Swiss chard fits dry gardens. Sow in April while there remains enough soil moisture to sprout the seeds. Don't use a red variety. Depending on how often you want to water it (maybe never) and how deep your soil is, thin the row progressively to as much as 3 feet apart; make the rows 4 feet apart. Harvest some leaves in summer but allow at least half to remain; there'll be more new leaves after the rains return.

Assorted Cooking Greens

SANTOH *(Brassica rapa Pekinensis)*

Santoh is a type of nonheading Chinese cabbage grown just like the heading sort. Santoh may be slower than heading varieties to go to seed from early sowings and handles rain and frosts better in autumn. Adaptive Seeds currently offers this hard-to-find item. Tokyo Bekana (JSS) is a refined, market-garden variant.

BROCCOLI RABE *(a.k.a. rapa, raab, or rapini)*

Broccoli rabe is a turnip green grown like mustard. The most rapid spring grower of all leafy greens, rabe fills the pot before any other new crop can be harvested, but it bolts fast. The leaves and unopened flowers are edible but not particularly choice.

EDIBLE CHRYSANTHEMUM *(Shungiku)*

This leaf vegetable actually is a small-flowered member of the chrysanthemum family used as a stir-fry green in Japanese cookery. If you've never eaten proper *sukiyaki*, let me tell you that Shungiku's flavor is distinctive and interesting *when the plants are young.* Shungiku is easy to grow. It can be sown from April through August. Harvest it before the flowers develop; then it becomes too strong tasting to enjoy. For a continuous supply, make successive sowings about three weeks apart. Don't plant more than a few row feet.

NEW ZEALAND SPINACH *(Tetragonia)*

New Zealand spinach grows wild on windblown infertile sand next to ocean beaches, but it also loves heat and produces abundantly in rich soil. The plants spread rapidly, thickly covering the bed and then some. It tolerates light frost. New Zealand spinach should be harvested every few weeks by removing about half the length of each branching stalk. Do this, and the plant regrows even thicker than before. Don't, and the plant makes an impenetrable tangle you can only pinch a few tips from.

About the time you would normally sow cucumber seeds or put out pepper plants, sow pairs of seeds about 1 inch deep on stations about 18 by 18 inches apart. Four positions should provide enough. Thin each position to a single plant, and have no worries if a spot comes up blank because the entire area will still be lushly covered before the end of July. Lightly steam the leaves and stem tips. The flavor seems naturally salty; I believe this is due to an extraordinarily high concentration of minerals.

MALABAR SPINACH (*Basella alba*)

Malabar spinach is a tropical vine that thrives when eggplant and peppers do. In Cascadia it only twines about 3 feet up a stick or garden stake. Tasted raw, the thick leaves resemble fresh, raw okra. There are two quite similar types, green and red leaf.

VEGETABLE AMARANTH

(*Amaranthus tricolor*)

Seed catalogs suggest this plant is useful in summer salads, and true, the colorful leaves are pretty, but I do not like their flavor when raw. In my universe amaranth is a summer cooking green. It grows like a weed in rich garden soil, soon reaching 3 feet tall and more, shading adjoining crops. Sow the small seeds shallowly as soon as there is no more frost danger.

Minor Salad Greens

These greens are basically refined weeds that thrive on residual fertility. The types that add variety to winter salads are especially helpful.

GARDEN PURSLANE (*Portulaca oleracea*)

Garden Purslane is a domesticated version of the low-growing weed found in almost every garden. The succulent leaves and upright thick stalks resemble the jade or money plant people often grow indoors. Purslane is not frost tolerant. Raw, it has a crunchy, bland taste, pleasant in summer salads in small amounts. Garden purslane only needs thinning and weeding. Start a few plants after the last frost. Harvest by cutting a few stalks an inch or so aboveground; the plant will regrow from the base. When seed heads appear, immediately cut that stalk off at the base; these are tough and inedible, and allowing seed development will reduce future leaf growth.

FRENCH SORREL (*Rumex scutatus*)

French sorrel is a derivative of sheep's sorrel, a common, fast-growing, and hard to eliminate edible weed in acidic soil that becomes scarce as aglime raises soil pH. The garden variant is an excessively productive perennial that needs nothing beyond a bit of compost once a year. Sorrel leaves have a pleasant lemony taste during cool weather; in small quantities it improves winter and early spring salads. Sorrel's flavor becomes too intense for me to enjoy in warm weather. Sometimes a winter freeze burns off all of the leaves, but this will not kill the crown. Leaves shoot up again in early spring.

Sow early in April. Spread the entire packet of tiny seeds in 4 feet of very shallow, freshly scratched furrow. Do not cover them. The seeds fall into cracks and crannies and germinate in a few weeks without you attending to them so long as the weather remains mellow and moist. Thin progressively to about 4 inches apart.

The entire row will make unwanted seedstalks in summer, but some plants make many more seedstalks and do it sooner, so you might select a shy-to-make-stalks plant from which to propagate a new permanent row. When seedstalks appear, cut them all off about an inch aboveground. Leafy regrowth will start immediately. If you're lucky, you'll find a plant that does not put up seedstalks. If that happens, mark it. In the row's second spring, dig the best plant. Divide the crown, and plant a short row. Root pieces transplant easily almost anytime, much like horseradish.

ARUGULA (*Eruca vesicaria* subsp. *sativa*)

Often called rocket, arugula is a very fast-growing, low-demand brassica with a delicious peppery flavor that spices up salads. Like French sorrel, rocket's flavor gets awfully strong in summer but stays mild tasting in cool weather. During long days rocket goes to seed before it is barely large enough to harvest. It also gets too peppery too fast for me to bother with it in hot weather. I grow rocket mainly for late summer to winter harvest.

Sow about eight row feet in March and again in April. Sow every few weeks between mid-July and the end of September. *Thinly* sprinkle the fine seed into a ½-inch-deep furrow across a raised bed, cover, and keep moist until it sprouts, usually in about three days. You may progressively thin the row or not thin at all (either way, soon after germination you should reduce any thickly overseeded clusters). Cut leaves as needed. There is no way to keep arugula from going to seed quickly when the days are long. In hot weather you could cut the plants off an inch aboveground and later use the regrowth, but after being cut back it'll mainly produce more seedstalks and some strong-tasting leaves. I think it is best to start a new row every few weeks.

One or more of your later sowings may survive winter and then make seed like other brassicas do. However, arugula will not cross with other brassicas. Because I grow my own rocket seed, I can afford to use it as a green-manure crop.

ANISE HYSSOP (*Agastache foeniculum*)

Judging by its flowers and seeds, this is a member of the mint family. Anise hyssop is not invasive like common garden mints. Sow late in April, a time when still-frequent rainfall combines with sufficient warmth to ensure germination. Barely cover the tiny seeds. Thin progressively. You only need a few plants, maybe only one. An occasional leaf in a mixed green salad provides a strong anise hit. The purple flowers attract bees. The plants will drop fine seeds that may naturalize into an easy-to-eliminate weed.

MINUTINA (*Erba stella*)

Minutina is useful as a *small part* of autumn/winter salads. To get the fine seeds to germinate, sow them early to mid-September in a shallow furrow. Barely cover the seeds with fine compost, and water gently every morning unless the previous day had not seen any direct sunshine. Thin progressively until seedlings stand 3 to 4 inches apart in the row. The chewy leaves should be finely cut. Minutina will go to seed if it survives winter and may naturalize.

ORACH (*Atriplex hortensis*)

Orach comes in two varieties, green and purple. I prefer the purple strain. Leaves from young purple orach plants have a mild flavor that in small quantities, used as an accent, brighten up salads. Sow seeds (resembling parsnip seeds) April through June. I grow orach like ordinary spinach but need only a few row feet. Orach grows fast; it makes a 6-foot-tall plant that soon goes to seed and loses culinary quality before that happens. Let an odd plant make and mature seed and it'll naturalize, but makes a very easy-to-eliminate weed.

Speaking of weeds: I had a few purple orach plants self-sow on the fringe of a large area soon to be covered with winter squash vines. I did not eliminate them and saw an extraordinary example of plant antagonism. In the rich soil the orach grew enormous, spreading plants 6 feet tall and 5 feet around. Their roots probably extended 4 feet from the center. The squash vines did not expand anywhere near them. I pulled out the orach; one month later the vines still did not cover that ground.

Brassicas

Cascadians can count on coles during a constantly cloudy, cool summer, the sort I call a "cabbage year." Brassicas are nutritious: F. H. King said in his classic survey of sustainable agricultural systems *Farmers of Forty Centuries* (see Additional Reading, page 339) that the labor that built the Great Wall of China was fueled more by cabbage than by rice. The fodder crop yielding the most protein per acre is not, as you might think, alfalfa or beans, but chlorophyll-rich kale. Chlorophyll is a complete high-quality vegetable protein as valuable as any animal protein, maybe better, in that raw kale is more acceptable to most people than raw flesh. The human body extracts much more nutrition from raw protein with far less digestive effort

while producing much less toxic residue. In other words, it thrives on raw proteins.

Brassicas include kale, rutabagas, cabbage, cauliflower, broccoli, brussels sprouts, collards, Chinese cabbage, some relatively unknown Asian vegetables, as well as related species I discuss elsewhere, such as radishes and turnips under "Roots," plus mustards and arugula under "Greens." The English wild ancestor resembles ordinary kale. Coax the tiny terminal bud into becoming a giant while compressing the main stalk and you get a cabbage. Axial buds (at the side branches) morphed into brussels sprouts and the stem was thickened into kohlrabi, while the naturally larger flower clusters on wild Italian cabbage became broccoli and cauliflower. Unfortunately, the more breeders accentuate one aspect, the less vigor the variety has.

Coarse brassicas are easy-to-grow low-demand crops that still resemble their wild ancestor. These include kale, collards, and purple sprouting broccoli. Cabbage and brussels sprouts are medium-demand crops. If you feed them like high-demand crops and give them enough growing room to benefit from all that nutrition, they become *huge*. Cauliflower, fancy kohlrabi, and Italian broccoli are high-demand vegetables requiring loose, airy soils holding lots of fertility and moisture.

"Low," "medium," or "high" demand mostly refers to the amount of nitrogen the vegetable requires, but all brassicas require high levels of available calcium. Not only will a calcium deficiency stunt them, but with cabbage and brussels sprouts even a brief calcium shortage can cause internal browning of leaf margins. The small quantities of both lime and gypsum in COF markedly improve the growth of brassicas.

Cabbage root maggot damage varies by type of brassica and by the season. Mid to late spring is the peak in maggot population. Maggots are rare during summer, only to reappear in modest numbers at summer's end when the sun is not strong. In autumn they did not visibly damage my aboveground brassica crops; I doubt it's that easy around the hugely out-of-balance Skagit. Expect unprotected Chinese cabbage, turnips, and winter radishes to be totally wrecked by the autumn flush of root maggots. Rutabagas go relatively undamaged. Otherwise, the intrinsic strength or vigor of the root system determines how much protection the gardener must provide. My suggested sowing dates consider the maggot population's peaks and valleys. The growing instructions also specify direct seeding of all brassicas because root systems of direct-seeded crops overcome maggot damage much better.

Cabbage worms can completely ruin many kinds of brassica from late spring through midsummer. Unchecked, they turn leaves into lace. Fortunately they are easily and effectively controlled with Bt or Spinosad. Flea beetles make pinholes in brassica transplant leaves in spring, especially in transplants that were not hardened off. Direct-seeded crops usually require no protecting if you plant plenty of seed and thin progressively. (For more on all these brassica pests, see Chapter 8.)

The family is also troubled by a soil-borne disease called clubroot. I have never seen clubroot-infected plants or even heard of anyone whose garden has the disease, but I feel honor bound to alert you. Infected roots swell into twisted irregular knobs that can't assimilate nutrition. Mysteriously stunted (sometimes wilting) brassicas with swollen, knobby roots are proof. Soil can become infected by importing bedding plants, from compost made from infected plants, and even from the gardener's shoes after visiting an infected garden.

If clubroot is present in your garden, protect visitors with gardens of their own; do not let them walk in yours. Do not compost your brassica wastes; instead, burn them or send them to the landfill. Clubroot is not easy to eliminate; to achieve that, the garden must be kept entirely free of all brassicas as well as certain host weeds for seven years. However, even three or four years without brassicas will greatly reduce the fungus's effect. See the *Pacific Northwest Plant Disease Management Handbook* online, and read the section on "Cabbage and Cauliflower—Clubroot." A few varieties carry genetic resistance to one or more strains, but resistance to one strain does not necessarily mean resistance to the variant infecting your plot.

Broccoli, ordinary cauliflower, and cabbage first make a genetically predetermined number of leaf pairs along a main stem, and then they must flower or head up. Leaf pairs develop at roughly the same rate whether or not the plants are growing lushly in good soil or are stunted in poor soil. However, the yield depends on how large the plants got before they headed or flowered. Uncrowded, later-maturing varieties inevitably yield more than earlies because they have time to grow larger before flowering or heading. Your task is to cultivate their potential for rapid growth, by side-dressing once or twice before they start forming heads or flowers. All brassicas for fall and winter harvest should be side-dressed for the last time around the end of August so available nitrogen declines during October. That way they'll develop maximum frost resistance.

Overwintering broccoli and cauliflower flower only after experiencing increasing day length following months of winter chilling. The larger the plant has grown when flowering commences, the larger the flower will be. These crops are most winter hardy at about one-third full size. Your task is to get them to that size when winter sets in, hope they survive, and then push them hard in spring as soon as they can grow fast. Parenthetically, on highly leachable sands, winter brassicas will be healthier if they're lightly side-dressed in early October and again in early winter, using the version of COF for glacial sands.

A great many brassica transplants appear on sales benches. I think that's half the reason most gardeners believe cabbage, cauliflower, broccoli, and brussels sprouts *must* be raised from transplants. But if strong brassica seed is sown when weather conditions are favorable—not too early—and if their seedbed is loose and fertile, then direct-seeded brassicas produce more than transplanted crops.

Brassica seeds form in small, slender pods. Some pods split while still hanging on the stalk, scattering seeds that may sprout after an inadequate summer rain but then die when the soil inevitably dries out. And some pods protectively retain their seed, which delays germination until autumn, when soil conditions remain moist. Seedling clusters are also more likely than a single

seed to establish successfully. It is easy for a pest to knock over an isolated young seedling, just as one seedling fails to emerge through hard soil. If the gardener imitates nature, sowing four or five brassica seeds where each plant will ultimately grow and then thinning progressively as the cluster of seedlings becomes established, success is all but assured.

Seedlings of refined brassica varieties are delicate; they absolutely require airy, fertile soil during their first month. Few soils come that way; garden soils become that way. If yours isn't that good (yet), you can easily make a half-pint-size hole at every intended position, fill it with container growing medium, and sow a pinch of seeds in that.

There are two main garden brassica species. *Brassica oleracea* includes broccoli, cauliflower, cabbage, brussels sprouts, collards, kohlrabi, and Scottish kale (the type that grows opposed leaves up a central stalk). *Oleracea* in its first-year vegetative mode forms an unbranched stalk, although the stalk is not obvious in cauliflower and cabbage because the interstem has been hugely compressed. At seed-making time, side branches develop from every leaf notch and from the central growing point as well. Rutabagas and Siberian kale are another species, *B. napus*; for their first year *napus* grows a rosette habit, new stems emerging from a central growing point like lettuce does. Brassicas are bee pollinated. Fortunately for the seed saver, *napus* does not cross with *oleracea*. Some garden writers assert that home gardeners can get good enough purity with a half mile of isolation. For myself I'd want at least a clear mile. Having seen so many overlooked brassicas flowering in home gardens, if I lived in a city or its suburbs I'd consider brassica seed production a risky gamble.

Both *oleracea* and *napus* are biennial. Destroy any plant that makes seed in its first year; it is a highly undesirable off-type. Spring-sown Italian broccoli and ordinary cauliflower might actually be annuals; they do make seed in their first year, but in Cascadia may not have time to mature that seed. Most varieties of broccoli and cauliflower are not winter hardy in most of Cascadia. So commercial seed for these is produced in California. Seed for kale, brussels sprouts, late cabbage, kohlrabi, rutabaga, cabbage, and overwintering cauliflower are extensively produced in Cascadia.

To make your own brassica seed, with the first signs of spring, dig up and transplant true-to-type plants that survived winter. Put them in a part of the garden that you won't have to irrigate next summer. Involve at least six near-perfect plants—or better, several dozen plants so as to slow the inevitable loss of vigor due to inbreeding in successive generations. By April these plants will start putting out seedstalks that will soon be covered with yellow flowers. When the first seedpods start drying out, cease all irrigation. Eventually there'll be no more new flowers (or very few), and soon the majority of the pods will contain mature, dry, or nearly dry seed. A few pods will have released ripe seed. At this stage, cut off the huge sprays close to the ground. If the weather is dry and warm, and there is no dew expected, you may spread them on a tarp to dry in the field (the tarp catches shattering seed). It's safer to dry them under cover. Once the straw has become crisp, thresh, clean, and store the seed.

Each plant will produce over an ounce of seed, sometimes several times that amount.

But with refined brassicas, unless you have space to involve at least 100 plants in your seed productions, I suggest you do not continue into a second generation or you'll start seeing many nonproductive or weak plants. Still, with good storage the seeds from six plants will provide all the planting material that you, your family, and your friends can use for the next 20 years.

BROCCOLI *(Brassica oleracea* var. *italica)*

Ordinary broccoli varieties act like annuals when days are long. Spring sowings make large central flowers a few months after sowing and then form seed. Broccoli acts like a biennial when it is sown after August. However, having originated from less hardy Italian wild cabbage, it rarely survives winter in most of Cascadia. Purple Sprouting broccoli is strongly biennial and is about as frost hardy as kale; it usually survives winter and only makes flowers after overwintering. Even if you sow it in May, Purple Sprouting broccoli still grows through summer, autumn, and winter before blooming next spring.

Broccoli of either type is one of the easier brassicas to grow. Its seeds sprout vigorously. It can tolerate clay soils and moderate fertility, but to harvest really big heads with the best possible flavor, you must provide balanced fertility, lots of nitrogen, and airy, moist soil the whole way.

The cultural suggestions that follow serve as a prototype for growing the other large, fancy brassicas—cabbage, cauliflower, and brussels sprouts—and won't be repeated in detail.

SOW	HARVEST	TRANSPLANT
Earlies: mid-March to June Main crop: June to mid-July Purple sprouting: mid-July to mid-August	Earlies: mid-June to mid-August Main crop: mid-August to freeze out Purple sprouting: March to mid-May	N/A

BETWEEN ROWS	SEEDS	THIN
Earlies: 18 x 24 inches Main crop: 30 x 24 inches Purple Sprouting: 30 x 24 inches	Clusters of five	One plant per position, progressively

Culture

For harvest during summer and autumn, sow between March and mid-July. Sow early varieties in spring; they make medium-size flowers sooner but inevitably produce fewer, smaller side shoots. Sow longer-growing varieties in June/July. These grow taller before producing considerably larger main flowers and form more, larger side shoots over a longer period. If you sow late-maturing varieties in spring, they often make small heads with leaves emerging through them. They'll still be good eating, but not as choice as they could have been.

Broccoli is a medium- to high-demand crop. Sow clusters of four or five seeds, ½ inch deep. To harvest prizewinning flowers, prepare the bed for a low-demand crop and then make hills by digging a half cup of COF and a generous quart of your best compost into about a gallon of soil, forming a small, low mound of potting mix at each position. Complete thinning the seedling clusters to a single plant by the time they have grown four or five pairs of true leaves.

Crowd compact, early varieties into 18-by-24-inch centers. Arrange late varieties at least on 24-by-24-inch up to 30-by-24-inch centers. Push ordinary broccoli hard at first. Side-dress every three weeks in ever larger doughnuts around the plants, but spread no more COF after the plant begins forming its central flower because soon the bed will be filled up; crowded broccoli being force-fed too much nitrogen develops leaf diseases. If you want to experience how large the main broccoli flower can become and how long side-shoot production could be maintained, try positioning a late-maturing variety 36-by-30.

In the mild Central Valley of California late broccoli is sown late in summer for winter harvest and sown in autumn for spring harvest. Cascadians living among the redwoods and those near the southern Oregon coast should succeed with winter broccoli too. Purple Sprouting broccoli usually survives winter, but a cloche until early spring is good insurance. Consider Purple Sprouting a low-demand crop until it has overwintered. Sow Purple Sprouting between mid-July and mid-August on positions 24 by 24 to 30 by 24 inches. Sow a month later if you're using a cloche over the winter. Thin progressively. As soon as the first spring bulbs emerge remove the cloche, weed thoroughly, and side-dress abundantly to provoke the most rapid possible growth.

Garden planning

Cascadian gardeners can harvest broccoli most of the year. March-to-May harvests come after overwintering Purple Sprouting. Early June harvests come from transplants started indoors in February and set out mid-March under small hot caps, minicloches, or cold frames. This is the most difficult crop of the year, while raising transplants at best only gets you a few extra weeks of harvest. Outdoor conditions allow direct seeding between late March in the south of Cascadia to mid-April in the cooler districts and continuing into July. Mid-July sowings head up in October and make side shoots until the plants die (or nearly do). In mild areas where ordinary broccoli has a chance to survive winter, try sowing late-maturing varieties between late August and late September. They may bloom in winter, or in spring when Purple Sprouting does.

Hybrid varieties reduce harvesting costs by maturing all at once. But I want a single sowing to yield large, central flowers over as many weeks as possible, so when establishing a broccoli patch, I sow several hybrid varieties that have different growing times. (Cauliflower works the same way.)

If the patch yields big side shoots for a long while after the main heads have been cut, then I don't have to start new plants so often. When a broccoli plant can put new roots into fertile, unoccupied soil after forming its main flower, it continues forming *big* high-quality side shoots for at least another month. If broccoli doesn't have unoccupied growing room when the main flower forms, the first set of side shoots will be small and the second set becomes very small and fibrous. I prefer not to eat low-quality broccoli, so I start six to eight well-spread-out plants every five or six weeks from late March through mid-July.

Purple Sprouting broccoli flowers when there is little else to eat. I grow 12 plants.

Insects and diseases

Broccoli may only be slightly stunted by a population density of symphylans and root maggots that would ruin most cabbage and all cauliflower varieties. Early spring transplants must be fought for. Otherwise, direct seeding in fertile, balanced soil, sowing several more seeds in each position than are ultimately wanted, and then thinning progressively handles all insect problems except cabbage moth larvae. (See Chapter 8.)

Harvest

The main flower should be cut when the tiny beads begin to fatten slightly. After the main head forms, most varieties extend side branches from every leaf notch and soon secondary flowers develop. Side branches also branch and soon flower. Each successive set of side shoots will be smaller. Plants with room to grow often produce additional very large side branches from buds near the base. These usually form very large flowers.

Saving seed

Purple Sprouting and White Sprouting broccoli are covered in flowers by May and dependably mature seed in midsummer. Seed for ordinary broccoli varieties is best attempted by overwintering south of Yoncalla.

Varieties

Here's a review of open-pollinated varieties I have trialed in the last few years: *Umpqua* is a uniform late-season variety that makes a medium-size head of superior quality compared to the other open-pollinated sorts. *Nutri-Bud* uniformly produces rather small central heads with decent taste, medium-coarse beads, and far too few side shoots that form far too slowly. It might please someone with a small garden that used tight spacing. I regret to report that all the strains that I have grown of "heirloom" open-pollinated sorts—Waltham 29, DeCicco, and Italian Green Sprouting—yield smallish, highly variable heads, usually loose and coarsely beaded with below average to very unpleasant flavor. I find seed for these degenerated varieties on seed racks and from some catalog sellers of the sort I rarely buy from because I reckon any merchant selling junk seed like this is demonstrating dubious ethics. Johnny's, however, can be counted on; their photo of their DeCicco (Johnny's is the primary grower) looks great. Territorial has a new OP variety called "Thompson"; the catalog photo looks beautiful. I haven't grown it yet.

Use an early hybrid for spring sowings. Early varieties produce fewer side shoots and smaller main flowers. The best early I know of is the widely available Belstar.

We eat a lot of broccoli, so I never miss a chance to trial a new late variety. Considering the current assortment of popular and generally available hybrids, I prefer Windsor, Arcadia, Diplomat, Triathlon, Ironman, Shogun, and Marathon. Because starting a wide range of maturities at one go is so useful, be sure to check out Johnny's and Stokes's very broad offerings. Purple Sprouting probably originated from a kale to Italian broccoli cross. White Sprouting appears to be a cauliflower-kale cross. Sprouting broccoli is not as refined as Italian, and the flavor is stronger but much appreciated in spring. Lately, improved sprouting broccoli varieties, usually hybrids, have appeared in English seed catalogs.

Chinese broccoli, a.k.a. Gai Lan, is the latest "in" thing. It makes many small flowers with juicy, thick elongated stems. It may be grown on 18-by-18-inch centers. I've had excellent results (and best flavor) from Happy Rich and Green Lance, which are Gai Lan–Italian broccoli crosses. West Coast offers three types.

Dry gardening

Use Purple Sprouting; grow like kale. Start them late in May. Provide heaps of elbow room, about 5 by 5 feet, and just enough fertigation to get them through the summer. It won't matter if they get a bit gnarly or don't grow too big; after the rains start, they'll be restored. In Elkton, Oregon, mine got side-dressed early in autumn and again in early spring. They grew over 5 feet tall and 5 feet across by mid-spring.

Ordinary broccoli started early in spring and given growing room and mulched early in May may produce before the soil dries out too much.

BRUSSELS SPROUTS (*Brassica oleracea* var. *gemmifera*)

A Brussels sprout plant forms a miniature cabbage at every leaf notch along the main stem. Early maturing varieties are short, with the sprouts packed tight on the stem. Later-maturing varieties grow taller, providing space between sprouts, which prevents disease in winter by increasing air circulation. The genetic program of early varieties tells them to stop getting taller and switch to forming sprouts after growing a certain number of leaf pairs; sow earlies sooner and they'll mature earlier. Sprout formation on late varieties seems as much to be triggered by photoperiod. Sow a late-maturing variety too soon and it may grow so tall before starting to make sprouts that it must be tied to a stake; sown too late, they will form fewer leaf axials on less husky plants before sprouts start developing and hence yield fewer sprouts of smaller size.

The industrial vegetable business requires better appearance than a Cascadian winter allows; supermarket sprouts almost always come from California. Blustery weather punctuated by sharp frosts enhances sugar content, so Cascadian-grown sprouts taste much better.

SOW	HARVEST	TRANSPLANT
Late June to early July	October to early February	N/A
POSITIONS	**SEEDS**	**THIN TO**
30 x 24 inches	Clusters of five	One plant per position, progressively

Culture

Sprouts are a medium-demand crop. Position plants from 24-by-24-inch up to 30-by-24-inch centers and otherwise grow like broccoli. In the Willamette sow mid to late June so that you see the first sprouts form in October, not in September. I urge you not to try for an earlier harvest: who wants to fight for aphid-infested, loose, harsh-tasting brussels sprouts forming in September while there still are tomatoes and zucchini?

In England, this vegetable is usually grown on clay loam because on sandy soils the sprouts become loose and soft, while the tall plants can't anchor themselves well enough to stand up against winter's wind. I've never done a brussels sprout trial on light soil, but I betcha there are English varieties that'll tolerate sand and don't grow as tall.

Brussels sprouts need a steady supply of nutrients and moisture during summer. But providing too much nitrogen while they're forming sprouts makes the sprouts become loose and unpleasantly strong tasting, while overfed plants are also less resistant to harsh weather. So do not side-dress the crop after mid-August.

Garden planning

Aim to start eating brussels sprouts mid-October and hope to continue through February. Twelve plants barely supply my household. I use the ex–garlic bed for brussels sprouts because garlic is harvested just before brussels sprouts must be sown, because brassicas do well following alliums, and because my garlic crop occupied the amount of space our brussels sprouts need.

Insects and diseases

The spring flush of cabbage root maggots has already pupated by sowing time. You almost certainly will have to spray against cabbage worms. Aphids wreck early maturing varieties by covering half-formed sprouts. Colonies can be hosed off frequently, or killed with Safer's soap, but the easiest solution is evasion—choose varieties that don't form sprouts until cold weather eliminates the aphids.

Harvest

Brussels sprouts are snapped off the stalk with a strong thumb. The ones at the bottom of the stalk fatten first. Continue harvesting up the stalk as they enlarge. Commercial growers concentrate the harvest by breaking off the growing tip when the bottom sprouts start to fatten. This economically rational way of making all the sprouts size up at once is not a good idea in the garden. It is not easy to avoid breaking off healthy leaves as you harvest the sprouts. However, the plant does better with more leaves at work. On many varieties, lower leaves naturally turn yellow. Remove these to increase air circulation, and move them to the compost area to reduce slug habitat.

In March, brussels sprout flowers that have not yet opened make a delicious broccoli substitute.

Saving seed

Brussels sprouts are among the hardiest of the brassicas; they often overwinter successfully. Choose seed-making plants after having harvested their large, smooth, hard sprouts with uniform and attractive green color. Home gardeners also want a better taste, longer harvest period, and wider separation of sprouts forming on the stalk. Unfortunately, not many open-pollinated varieties remain in existence, and of those, only a few are still reasonably productive.

Varieties

When an seed supplier east of the Rocky Mountains says a variety is late, most likely in Cascadia that variety will start yielding mid-October, tapers off during November, and will be entirely over before Christmas. I especially like Diablo (JSS). There are European hybrids like Igor (TSS, WCO) whose harvest begins in January and continues into February.

Two American open-pollinated classics, Catskill and Long Island Improved, are worse disasters than Waltham 29 and DeCicco broccoli. Adaptive and West Coast sell a uniform and productive open-pollinated variety called Red Bull (or Red Ball). I found Red Bull's maturity to be in the very late slot, which is a good thing, but its flavor is too much on the wild side for me to enjoy. Maybe you'll respond differently. West Coast and Territorial sell a Roodnerf selection similar to Diablo but not as perfect. In 1980 there were dozens of commercial-quality open-pollinated Roodnerf strains that were specific for soil types, microclimates, and harvest slots between October and January. These were sold by small British seed companies that now have been gobbled up by bigger fish that only offer hybrids. Asian-bred hybrids like Jade Cross are productive, good eating, and offered in many garden seed catalogs. They are less pricey but also less cold hardy. Think of Jade Cross as an autumn variety, like Long Island Improved used to be when it produced useful food.

Dry gardening

Possible with late varieties. Direct-seed June 1 to 15, on positions 36 by 48 inches. Fertigate just enough to get it through summer's heat while growing slowly; probably a few gallons per plant every three to four weeks will do it.

CABBAGE (*Brassica oleracea* var. *capitata*)

Cabbage yields more delicious food per square foot than just about any other vegetable except root crops. One can just about live on them when the Weatherman sends us a cabbage year—a cloudy, cool, humid summer that wrecks the tomatoes but favors brassica crops.

SOW	HARVEST	TRANSPLANT
Earlies: April to late July Lates: late June Overwintered: early September	Earlies: June to October Lates: mid-September to early February Overwintered: March to late May	N/A

POSITIONS	SEEDS	THIN TO
Earlies: 18 x 18 inches Lates: up to 30 x 24 inches Overwintered: 18 x 18 inches	Clusters of five	One plant per position, progressively

Culture

Cabbage is a medium-demand crop.

There are three types: (1) early and "midseason," which is a larger, slightly slower-maturing early type, (2) late, and (3) overwintering (or "spring cabbage," as the British call this type).

Early cabbages are quick-maturing compact plants that form heads resembling those you find in the supermarket. Early and midseason varieties demand loose, moist fertile soil. Industrial crops are grown on something like 18-by-18-inch spacing. If most early varieties were grown on 24-by-24-inch centers, the heads would be too large for market requirements. Most earlies soon split open after heading up hard. Earlies aren't sufficiently winter tolerant in Cascadia. The cabbages that appear in supermarkets from November through July are earlies grown where winter is a mild, cool season. Small red cabbages are also early types.

Early cabbages can be transplanted out with the first broccoli seedlings, but being slightly less hardy than broccoli, they'll do better during this chilly month if hot caps or cloches are used. From April through the end of July, cabbage can be direct seeded, and should be. Directly seeded earlies mature only two weeks later than four- or five-week-old transplants put out on the same day seeds were sown. Directly seeded plants resist the cabbage maggot better.

Midseason varieties are like larger earlies that grow a few weeks longer before heading up. They're best spaced on 24-by-24-inch centers.

Sow autumn/winter varieties mid to late June. You can choose to harvest really big late cabbages by using 30-by-30-inch spacing or crowd them on 24-by-24-inch centers. English and Dutch very late varieties work well in Cascadia. These grow slowly and head up in November and December. The latest of them can hold in the garden until March while withstanding all the frost and rain this climate can usually dish out. Some resemble the usual supermarket cabbage protected by an unusually large number of loose outer-wrapper leaves. The best garden lates are savoyed, meaning they have crinkly, blistered leaves. Savoys make the tastiest salads.

Overwintering cabbage for spring harvest is a gamble that English (and Japanese) market gardeners often take. When I owned Territorial, I imported and sold spring cabbage seeds. I hope the situation soon improves, but these days no Cascadian company finds it economically rational to offer spring cabbage seeds. It requires considerable interaction with homeland insecurity minded bureaucrats before an American buyer is allowed to import seeds, although Canadian gardeners can still bring in less than 1 pound of seeds (combined weight of all packets in the shipment) without the bother of first obtaining an import permit. However, Agriculture and Agri-Food Canada is not entirely predictable about which species they pass unhindered and which packets they confiscate. I suggest Canadians contact Ag Canada about current rules and procedures prior to ordering from abroad.

Sow spring cabbage early in September. Initially, grow them on fertility remaining from the previous crop. Side-dress abundantly when spring regrowth begins. The strategy is to get the seedlings to their hardiest size—leaves spread 6 to 8 inches in diameter—before winter's chill and low light levels check further growth. Variations in autumn/winter weather can make big differences in growth rate—that's why most spring varieties are a gamble. If they're too small going into winter, they may freeze out in a cold snap; if they grow too big during winter, they'll make seed in spring without heading up first.

Spring cabbages are small, so spacing should be 18 x 18 inches. I had good luck overwintering them in frosty Lorane, by sowing during October on 9 by 9 inches in a cold frame, then digging and transplanting on 18 x 18 inches at about the end of February, side-dressing heavily at that time.

Garden planning

A Cascadian garden can supply cabbages nearly 12 months a year unless winter freezes them out. Begin next year's supply by sowing unprotected spring cabbage in September or else sow them in a cold frame in October. Take another gamble—around mid-March put out a few transplants of an early variety. Use hot caps or other small cloches. In warm springs these do fine; in harsh weather they'll be chewed to death or hopelessly stunted and prove a waste of effort. Early in April direct-seed more earlies. Include a few red heads in this patch to liven up early summer salads. Sow more earlies through May and into early June for harvest in summer. The main sowing for fall and winter harvest happens about mid-June. If you sow these too soon, the cabbages will burst by November—but if sown too late, the heads will be too small when they finally do form. If you sow lates way too early, they form pointy heads of lower quality.

Insects and diseases

In spring flea beetles can wreck transplants. Direct seeding and progressive thinning lessens the need to spray—most years. Root maggots especially trouble early varieties before mid-May, though they less frequently wreck direct-seeded plants. Cabbage worms must be controlled.

Harvest

Early varieties are tender because they make less fiber. That's why their heads burst shortly after getting hard, so harvest earlies promptly. Late types head up when low light levels and chill slow their growth, and they form more fiber, so lates usually hold through winter without bursting.

Saving seed

Cabbage stumps that survive winter often put up seedstalks in spring. Any mature cabbage that survives winter will make seed, but I do not recommend growing more than one generation of seed from only a few plants.

Varieties

Until hybrids were developed, Golden Acre was the most used open-pollinated early maturing small green cabbage variety. There were many Golden Acre strains and variants. The main commercial midseason varieties used to be Copenhagen Market, a Ballhead (West Coast still sells it), and Flat Dutch. The latest fashion in hybrid cabbage varieties changes so rapidly, there's not much point in listing and rating what's currently available. You can depend on varieties offered by the seed companies I recommend. When choosing an early or midseason variety, look for a promise to hold without bursting so that your kitchen doesn't have to deal with several splitting heads at one time.

Savoyed varieties have thin, crinkly inner leaves, make superior salads and slaws, and do as well as any other type when cooked or made into sauerkraut—all things considered, the Savoy is ideal for home gardening. When I was a new gardener, the traditional late (in the east of the rockies sense of late) open-pollinated savoy was Chieftain. Tim Peters was involved in its restoration and now Adaptive offers Chieftain. It should be excellent for fall harvest but won't be likely to withstand winter. Savoy King, a Japanese-bred hybrid, is similar to Chieftain. Another in the "King" family is Savoy Ace, sold exclusively by Stokes. This tender, tasty, and highly reliable mid-season variety is a week quicker to mature than King, but otherwise hard to distinguish from King. I depend upon Ace during summer and autumn. Ermosa (WCO) is this type.

In my trials Danish Ballhead (TSC) was never the best winter survivor. The English and Dutch have bred smaller, supermarket-sized lates that are so well protected by wrapper leaves that their inner heads retain good appearance after standing fully headed up in the field for several winter months. European Savoys are the most cold hardy of all. Japanese-bred Savoy King or Savoy Ace are thin-leaved, tender, sweeter, and better for salads, but they are more likely to freeze out. European varieties have much more fiber. The "late" Savoys from Stokes are actually midseason types in Europe. For really late Savoy cabbage, grow superhardy selections used in England and Holland for cutting after

New Year's. January King (WCO) is a traditional English half-savoyed winter garden variety. A newish and far more productive hybrid is called Deadon (WCO, JSS); it's right on! Territorial once sold a very late Savoy hybrid called Wivoy, now replaced by Tundra (TSC). Many times Wivoy was the only cabbage surviving a particularly harsh freeze. Wirosa (OSB) is similar.

American sauerkraut varieties are tough enough to withstand pressure canning after being sliced very thin and fermented—but canning is not necessary when making kraut at home. In my opinion, half-soured kraut made from any sort of cabbage that is taken from a still-working crock before it gets mushy is far superior. Few people realize that sauerkraut is an extremely healthy food when made without salt. All salt does is conveniently wilt the leaves and release the water they contain. If unsalted cabbage is pounded thoroughly before it is crocked and weighted, juice is rapidly released and the cabbage ferments well. Please try salt-free sauerkraut! If you want a bit of salt flavor, then add minimum salt immediately before eating it.

When I owned Territorial, I trialed many spring cabbage varieties. Most of them survived most Lorane winters, but most went to seed before making good heads. One variety, Spring Hero, proved entirely reliable. Spring Hero is so reluctant to make seed in spring that if the first head is cut carefully so that many base leaves remain attached to the stem, it'll start growing new shoots. Reduce these to one or two per plant, and you'll end up with additional heads before spring ends. Some mild, sunny springs I've harvested two additional sets of heads from Spring

Hero. When the summer solstice approaches, Spring Hero no longer forms round, tight cabbages and some of the plants will be putting up seedstalks. Time to yank the stump, but by that time the early cabbages are heading up. Canadian gardeners: I import Spring Hero from Tuckers in the United Kingdom.

Dry gardening

Easy enough with spring cabbages. Possible with early varieties if they are mulched in May and maybe fertigated in June.

CHINESE CABBAGE (*Brassica rapa* subsp. *pekinensis* and *chinensis*)

The cabbage root maggot makes this vegetable extremely difficult in Cascadia. It succeeded in Territorial Seed Company's trials, but at that time growing even the most challenging vegetables without using chemical pesticides was my job.

SOW	HARVEST	TRANSPLANT
Mid-June to mid-July	September to mid-October	N/A
POSITIONS	SEEDS	THIN TO
18 x 24 inches	Clusters of three	One plant per position, progressively

Culture

Chinese cabbage is a high-demand, fast-growing crop that requires abundant moisture at all times. The plant only grows to its full potential in light, open soil. You can produce loose, half-size heads on clayey soils if the bed is first improved by the traditional gardener's manner—dig in lots of compost and then abundantly provide COF.

Sow between mid-June and mid-July. Start clusters of three seeds, ½ inch deep on positions 18-by-24 inches apart. Push growth as much as possible. As soon as seedlings emerge, side-dress a ring of COF around the cluster. Thin to one seedling by the time they have reached 2 inches in diameter, which won't take long. *Permit no competition!* Do not use transplants; the seeds are big for a brassica, fresh seeds germinate fast and strong, and Chinese cabbage does better if its taproot remains intact. Because the plants grow so fast, side-dress a larger doughnut of COF every two weeks until the head begins to form. Like celery, keep their bed moist at all times.

Garden planning

There are hybrids for spring and early summer sowing. When I try one of these at 40 to 45 degrees latitude, at best the plant bolts just when the head begins to form. Autumn varieties can hold in the field for a few weeks after heading up if not invaded by root maggots. The best location for this crop is near the hose tap. My ex–leek seedling bed makes a good spot for two Chinese cabbages—the timing is right, the location is right, and brassicas do well following alliums.

Insects and diseases

Small gray slugs don't damage the heads, though they do like nestling in the outer leaves. In my variety trials, flea beetles showed an unusually strong attraction to Chinese cabbage seedlings and would have stunted the young plants had I not sprayed. Root maggots feed on Chinese cabbage in an extraordinarily destructive way. They tunnel across the bases of inner leaves, which immediately collapses it, soon causing the entire head to rot. Only one maggot ruins an entire head. Spinosad did not exist when I did this trial, but it probably would handle maggots if you got plenty into the forming head itself. However, I'm not sure I'd want to eat it after it was sprayed. This being a season of warm soil, I'd also try heavy soil inoculation with beneficial predatory nematodes a few weeks after the seeds are sown, but this is something I've never actually done because nematodes weren't available then either.

Maggots! Flea beetles! Instead of constantly dosing the crop, consider putting it under an insect-proof spun-polyester cloche as soon as the seedlings are thinned to their final spacing. I did this successfully on my Lorane trials ground; otherwise I never would have seen a mature head.

Harvest

Heads must be cut before they bolt. Bolting plants put up delicious flower stalks whose tender tips are excellent in stir-fries and winter salads if harvested before the yellow flowers open.

Saving seed

As far as I know, there are no longer any productive open-pollinated strains available, and in Cascadia the seed-making process starts too late to grow seed from true-to-type plants that have already headed—which is what must be done to maintain a high-quality variety. In short, forget about growing seed, or else consider Santoh (ADA), a primitive nonheading variant.

Varieties

Most hybrids originate from Asian seed companies. The varieties on offer change every few years, so there's little point in naming the ones in vogue now. Early varieties make small heads, if you're lucky. Stokes offers them. I recommend not wasting time and garden space on earlies. Late-maturing (main crop) types can make big yields. The broadest choice is in Osborne's catalog. Makes me wonder how and where the big boys in Cascadia grow this difficult crop; maybe it's done on the other side of the mountains.

Dry gardening

Impossible.

CAULIFLOWER *(Brassica oleracea* var. *botrytis)*

This vegetable must make continuous rapid growth or else it may fail to head properly, and by improper, I mean foul tasting and tiny. Most cauliflower varieties have weak root systems; letting their soil get dry checks growth even if there was no sign of wilting. If you buy transplants, make sure they aren't already pot-bound—a snarled root system has already checked growth. Preventing growth checks can be beyond your control. A few days of very hot weather in August may check the autumn crop. A severe spring frost may stun a soft transplant you just set out.

Because transplants are often both long on the tooth and soft, it is much easier to direct-seed cauliflower—in fact, when direct seeded, it becomes a fairly easy-to-grow vegetable.

SOW	HARVEST	TRANSPLANT
Earlies: April to mid-May	Earlies: June	N/A
Summer/autumn: early July	Summer/autumn: late September to December	
Overwintered: early August	Overwintered: March to mid-May	

SOW	POSITIONS	THIN TO
Clusters of five to six seeds	Earlies: 24 x 24 inches	One plant per position, progressively
	Autumn: 30 x 24 inches	

Culture

Cauliflower is a high-demand crop grown like broccoli. Sow or transplant the spring crop two weeks after the earliest broccoli, best in the first half of April, after spring settles. Cauliflower doesn't taste all that great when the curd forms in hot weather, and for sure there's no shortage of delicious veggies in the garden in midsummer, so I stopped trying to harvest cauliflowers during July/August. Sow for fall harvest in the first half of July.

Gardeners in the southern end of Cascadia where winter is less often frosty and more often sunny might try another sowing mid to late August (broccoli too). These mature during winter.

Position cauliflower plants 24-by-24 inches if they're spring sown. Space them 30-by-24 inches for autumn/winter harvest.

Like broccoli, if the plant gets large before flowering commences, the cauliflower will be large and delicious. So I *grow* cauliflower. I side-dress, the first time two weeks after germination, scantly (this time only) and tightly around the seedlings, followed by a larger application every three weeks. Stop pushing rapid growth when the new leaves begin to curl inward, which indicates the head will form within a month.

Overwintering cauliflower is much easier—if the crop doesn't freeze out. Except for varieties that mature in March, this crop has plenty of spring growing time to get really big before heading starts. Sow about August 1 and do not push the crop; grow it like Purple Sprouting broccoli. As soon as spring growth resumes, carefully eliminate all competing weeds and start *growing* the crop.

Garden planning

In most of Cascadia it is possible to harvest high-quality cauliflower during the hottest and coldest weather. The spring sowing is harvested in June. Commercial-quality cauliflower varieties mature uniformly. There isn't a wide range of maturity times among early varieties, so for a one-month-long supply, start a few plants every 10 days during April. Harvest autumn cauliflowers from October into December. I always start two plants from half a dozen different high-quality varieties with a range of maturities from 65 to 90 days.

Overwintered cauliflower produces when there's not much else to eat in the garden. I reckon the possibility of harvesting from late March into early June is worth the risk of the crop freezing out. Most overwintering varieties are bred for concentrated maturity. I suggest starting a few plants each from as many different overwintering varieties as you can obtain.

Insects and diseases

Cauliflowers form delicate, restricted root systems, so they require loose, open soil and must never cope with moisture stress. Crops started in spring must contend with maggots while sunlight is close to peak intensity. More than the slightest amount of root loss at that time causes catastrophic wilting. Early sowings are best protected from maggots by sawdust collars. Direct-seeded cauliflowers resist maggots better than transplanted ones. Sowings made June through August usually don't need maggot protection.

The usual leaf eaters require handling.

Harvest

If you intend to season cooked cauliflower with strong accents like cheese sauce, harvest when the curds begin to separate and you'll have a heavier cauliflower that tastes almost as good raw, but as the guru said, a difference that makes no difference is no difference. If you intend to eat them raw, harvest *before* there is any curd separation so that you'll have crisper nibbles.

In warm weather inspect a developing flower daily because it can progress from a nubbin to overblown in a week. Before self-wrapping varieties were developed, cauliflowers needed blanching, which meant tying the wrapper leaves around the forming curd to protect it from sun. (If the curd gets too much light, its color changes from white to yellowish.) All modern varieties form large inner leaves that naturally wrap the curd.

Saving seed

Unharvested cauliflowers soon turn into a mass of seedstalks covered with small yellow flowers. High-quality seed must be produced where the plants can form proper heads in the correct season and then get enough sunny, warm weather to ripen their seed. Early varieties might mature seed in Cascadia. Seed for overwintered cauliflower is produced commercially in the Skagit Valley.

Varieties

Every hybrid I've tried is productive and tastes great. After hybrids became industry standards, it became difficult to find productive, uniform open-pollinated seed. Serious gardeners (or market gardeners) wanting to harvest over the longest duration in autumn should invest in a broad assortment of cauliflower varieties. Get them from Johnny's, Stokes, or Osborne. For spring sowing, Snow Crown hybrid performs well and is widely available.

Certified organic now requires sowing organically grown seeds, while the mossback faction of the organic party still strongly disapproves of hybrids. These factors have created a market for commercial-quality certified organic varieties, open-pollinated and hybrid. But beware of degenerated open-pollinated varieties once used in industrial agriculture like Snowball X, or Y, or "123."

Winter heading and overwintering cauliflowers are extensively farmed in the United Kingdom and Holland. Traditional English winter varieties make huge heads in November, December, or January. They sometimes have a strong cabbagey back-taste I find unpleasant; I prefer the milder, sweeter-tasting Dutch autumn varieties. English garden seed catalogs offer a range of very long-growing varieties from both countries. The late-maturing English winter cauliflower varieties work in the less frosty parts of Cascadia.

Currently, Territorial Seed offers an overwintering blend that produces heads from March through late May, but not individual varieties. West Coast sells one variety for April harvest. Adaptive sells Leamington Winter Giant, which matures in May. Canadians can find a broad range at Tuckers in England (www.tuckers-seeds.com).

Purple cauliflower tastes like broccoli. I can't see any sense in growing a form of broccoli that doesn't make side shoots. Marina much appreciates Veronica, a Romanesco type that forms spirals looking like fractal Mayan temples. Her husband thinks he doesn't like cauliflower, but he does like Veronica.

Dry gardening

Possible with overwintered varieties. Start a dozen seedlings in a well-watered nursery bed early August, and transplant them out after the autumn rains start. Dry gardening might work with spring-sown varieties, if they're mulched after the soil warms up.

COLLARDS (*Brassica oleracea* var. *acephala*)

Collard greens are vigorous low-demand, non-heading cabbages as easy to grow as kale. Vates is hardier than Georgia. Johnny's has a new Vates selection called Champion. There is a new to North America variant called Beira Tronchuda, a modern version of the traditional Portuguese variety used to make *gallena* soup (JSS, WCO). Johnny's catalog says it is kale, but I say collards because it tastes like very sweet, tender cabbage. Start this one after the summer solstice or it goes to seed prematurely.

KALE *(Brassica oleracea* var. *acephala, B. napus* var. *pabularia)*

Of all the brassicas, kale is the easiest to grow and the most cold hardy. More than once kale was the only brassica in my garden that survived a spell of harsh freezing weather.

Kale is usually cooked, but half-grown leaves may be salad quality if they come from balanced soil, are very finely shredded, and don't dominate. Kale's palatability improves considerably after a few hard frosts. Kale is so cold hardy because it makes a lot of fiber. I think that's why fewer cabbage worms graze on it. Fiber also lets kale look good for a long while on the produce counter. Just-harvested kale is moderately chewy but gets a lot more so in only one day. If you find the supermarket stuff disgusting, I suggest getting over it. Give homegrown kale a chance during winter.

SOW	HARVEST	TRANSPLANT
Mid-July	Mid-October to mid-March	N/A
POSITIONS	SEEDS	THIN TO
24 x 24 inches	Clusters of five	Progressively

Culture

Kale may be sown in spring with the earliest broccoli and then grazed from early summer until it goes to seed the following spring. I prefer to consider kale an autumn/winter crop. This schedule avoids the unpleasantly strong taste kale develops in hot weather. Around mid-July sow five open-pollinated or three expensive hybrid seeds ½ inch deep on 24-by-24-inch centers, and thin progressively to a single plant per station. Or else thinly sprinkle open-pollinated seed in furrows a half inch deep, the furrows 24 inches apart, and thin progressively. Kale produces adequately when grown as a low-demand crop but produces more if you side-dress. Moderate moisture stress won't ruin a kale patch, but regular irrigation and careful weeding will provide an abundance.

Garden planning

Unless it's cooked to death, kale takes effort to chew; it has an intense flavor. For many years I disliked kale, but the garden slowly reeducated my palate. Bringing my soil into better balance improved the flavor. These days I mix finely shredded kale into green salads or coleslaw. I also cook a large volume of chopped raw kale, a small volume of quartered potatoes, and ½ inch of water in one pot and then mash them together with a big pat of butter; the Scots call this nutritious dish "colcannon."

Insects and diseases

I've had no serious problems. The roots are so vigorous that the maggot rarely causes damage, and symphylans don't prefer kale; the cabbage moth rarely lays eggs on kale plants that are sown in July. When I routinely spray Bt on all of my brassicas, I give the kale patch a light touch anyway.

Harvest

With *napa* varieties, cut or snap off some of the fully developed leaves as needed, but let the plant keep at least half its leaves. When the oldest leaves deteriorate, pick them off to enhance air circulation. Most gardeners harvest *oleracea* varieties by gradually picking large leaves without stripping the plant bare. However, enlarging new leaves are less fibrous and milder tasting, so I take half the young leaves. With *oleracea* kale, do not snap the growing point at the top of the stalk; doing that will stop the production of new leaves.

Kale grows slowly during winter. In spring *oleracea* varieties put out clusters of small, especially delicious side leaves resembling loose brussels sprouts. Flower stalks appear soon after. Kale flowers make an acceptable substitute for broccoli.

Saving seed

Grow seed as you would any other brassica. It is possible to retain reasonable vigor from much smaller plant populations than needed to maintain fancy brassicas—I suggest at least 12 plants.

Varieties

Open-pollinated *oleracea* varieties offered to gardeners are cheaply produced—often these working-class strains are called Blue or Green Curled Scotch. In the case of kale, lack of refinement doesn't matter much. Well-bred hybrids come from Euroland. I prefer Winterbor or Redbor, along with ordinary Siberian and Red Russian. There is a recently introduced open-pollinated Italian garden variety, Tuscano, which is an excellent choice for summer and autumn. It has long, strap-like leaves and a slightly more refined flavor than the curly leaf varieties but is not as winter hardy.

Dry gardening

If irrigation is scarce, sow kale midspring while there is still moisture in the topsoil. Make positions 3 to 4 feet apart in the row, with 4 to 5 feet between rows. Thin each position progressively. Get down to a single plant about the time they have four pairs of leaves. Weed the patch meticulously until the rains return. Fertigate generously if you want kale to eat in summer—or fertigate just enough to keep them from getting too gnarly—or on some soils fertigate not at all. In Elkton, I gave dry-gardened kale 5 gallons every four weeks through summer; each plant grew to 4 feet in diameter and 5 feet tall by November on Class I river-bottom silty clay loam.

KOHLRABI (*Brassica oleracea* var. *caulorapa*)

Kohlrabi is little known to Americans. It forms a crisp, sweet bulb located just above the soil where it is safe from the root maggot. Kohlrabi resembles an especially sweet inner core of cauliflower. It is excellent both raw and cooked.

Culture

Kohlrabi is a medium-demand vegetable. The faster it grows, the better it tastes. When growth slows, it becomes woody. In hot weather turning woody happens no matter what you do. Sow the spring crop in the first half of April so that you can finish harvesting before mid-June. For autumn harvest, sow in the first half of August.

I grow hybrids; their seeds germinate so strongly that I can sow only three seeds on each position in a tight cluster ½ inch deep, the positions 5 inches apart in rows 18 inches apart. Thin progressively so by the time the seedlings have four pairs of leaves, there is only one plant on every position. Then side-dress. Alternately you could position the clusters 3 inches apart, thin to one plant, and start harvesting at a smaller size by taking every other plant. Alternatively, you could sow open-pollinated varieties thinly in furrows, and thin and harvest progressively. Do not allow growth to slow because the patch has become crowded.

SOW	HARVEST	TRANSPLANT
Spring: early April Fall: early August	Spring: May/June Fall: October to mid-February	N/A
POSITIONS	SEEDS	THIN TO
5 x 18 inches	Clusters of three	One plant per position, progressively

Garden planning

In spring start no more than eight row feet. As soon as hot weather arrives, they turn woody; may as well yank immature or over the hill plants and use the space for something else. It's a happier story for the autumn crop. Fall crops retain excellent eating quality until Christmas some years. For fall I sow 50 square feet of

kohlrabi about August 1 and keep the patch growing by harvesting alternate plants.

Insects and diseases

In my trials some varieties outgrew maggot damage in spring. Fortunately, the autumn crop is rarely troubled. Kohlrabi leaves are not high on the cabbage grub's preferred list.

Harvest

Take alternate plants in the row; start when they're 3 inches in diameter. I love dipping raw cauliflower into curry-flavored mayonnaise. Kohlrabi chunks may be enjoyed the same way. It may also be grated and used for making a coleslaw variant good with either mayonnaise or vinaigrette dressing or else grated, crocked, and fermented into either sauerkraut or a kimchi variant. Koreans make kimchi out of many vegetables other than Chinese cabbage, including whole juvenile daikon radishes with leaves attached. Home-style kimchi often includes chunks of this or that.

To protect kohlrabi from freezing and then rotting, starting mid-November draw up soil against and over them (like hilling potatoes) until their crowns are several inches below the surface, hopefully with most of their leaves intact and sticking out. Also do this when growing seed crops.

Saving seed

Kohlrabi is not as freeze hardy as some brassicas, though it will overwinter without any protection in milder years. Hilling up a few inches of soil over the bulbs (but not covering the leaves) will usually get them through winter.

A kohlrabi variety can be maintained in a backyard. Start about 50 row feet for autumn harvest. Carefully select the best 25 specimens and mark them. Eat the rest. Get the seed formers over the winter without freezing. Each seed-forming plant ideally needs a root zone of about 2 by 2 feet.

The introduction of hybrid kohlrabi in the 1980s soon caused all productive open-pollinated varieties to disappear.

Varieties

Cheaply produced open-pollinated varieties throw a high percentage of plants that fail to make decent bulbs while most of the bulbs that do form are not highly desirable. They're often called Purple Vienna or White Vienna. Winner, Kolibri, and Kongo are productive hybrids. I know of no significant eating difference between purple- and green-skinned types, but then I'm not living in Europe. The new organically grown varieties, both hybrid and open-pollinated, should be of commercial quality.

Giant kohlrabi is a tastier version of the stock-feed varieties used in Europe. It grows slowly through the winter unless it freezes out. It can reach basketball size, so position seedlings as though you were growing medium-size cabbages. Territorial and West Coast import Superschmelz, an open-pollinated variety from a Swiss seed grower. Johnny's offers a hybrid giant variety that almost certainly is more refined than Superschmelz, but I have not yet had the chance to test it. Start giant varieties mid-July.

Dry gardening

Try this: sow a giant variety in mid-June, space each seedling cluster 2 feet apart in rows 4 feet apart. Spot-water each position just enough to sprout the seeds. From that point provide enough fertigation to keep them growing slowly. Thin each position to a single plant. Fertigate enough to keep it growing slowly through the summer. Superschmelz achieves the size of large cabbages and remains edible into the winter.

RUTABAGA *(Brassica napus* subsp. *rapifera)*

The rutabaga supports self-sufficiency. They're as easy to grow as kale. Harvest one anytime from late summer through winter. Their flesh does not get crossed with maggot tracks, at least not where I've grown them. Rutabagas produce very large yields of flavorful roots that seem half as starchy as the potato. If you previously did not like their stock-feed flavor, be advised that there are a few varieties with flavor so good I relish them.

SOW	HARVEST	TRANSPLANT
Early July	September to early March	N/A
BETWEEN ROWS	SEEDS	THIN TO
2 feet	One per inch	8 to 12 inches, progressively

Culture

Rutabagas are a low-demand crop. During the first half of July sow one seed per inch in furrows ½ inch deep. I make parallel furrows 24 inches apart arranged the long way down a 4-foot-wide raised bed. Competition strongly influences how big the rutabagas get, how frequently they need watering, and how many of them grow tops without useful bottoms. Thin the row progressively until the seedlings stand 8 to 12 inches apart.

Garden planning

Rutabagas can produce an enormous yield. You can count on them feeding you from September through February. I assign 100 square feet to rutabagas.

Insects and diseases

Root maggot traces are peeled away with the thick skin. Slugs sometimes dig cavities, as do mice. Then the bulbs rot. It helps to have a clean garden, with no mulch or decaying vegetation in the vicinity of the rutabaga patch.

Harvest

In my Douglas County, Oregon, garden, with no special handling whatsoever, the roots held in the field in acceptable condition through almost every winter. If winter turns freezing cold, even for only a few short days, exposed roots may freeze solid and then rot afterward. So during November draw up about 3 inches of soil over them.

Saving seed

Rutabagas cross with Siberian kale. Isolation of 1,500 feet is said to be enough for home-garden purity. A highly productive variety remains that way only if the seed is grown from near-perfect roots selected when they have achieved full size. During winter I fill a 100-square-foot bed with transplanted rutabagas arranged on 24 by 24 inches. They go in one by one as perfect roots are discovered while harvesting for the table. About 20 roots given this much space yield 5 pounds of seed (that I provide to a local seed company). I've grown five successive generations of a local variety this way without seeing any inbreeding depression of vigor, and each generation has become more productive and more uniform than the previous.

Varieties

Some varieties taste turnipy. Some taste like they were meant for stock feed. Varieties I prefer are sweet and satisfy almost like potatoes. If you think you don't like rutabagas, do a variety trial.

Dry gardening

Keep their intended row and a few feet to either side of it completely bare from late March. The surface will get dry, but much moisture should remain in the subsoil. Sow around mid-June. Put enough water on their rows to get the seed to germinate and initially help the fast-growing seedlings get roots below the topsoil. From then on, the crop may grow (slowly) on soil moisture if the soil is deep and naturally moisture retentive, if you thin plants to 24 inches apart in the row, make the between-row space 4 feet, and keep the patch entirely weed-free.

TURNIPS (Brassica rapa var. rapifera)

Turnips grow fast, like big radishes. To develop sweetly, they require the same careful thinning and moist soil that radishes need. In Cascadia turnip tops are much easier to grow than turnip bottoms. If you take every possible precaution, the cabbage root maggots may not ruin every one. (See Radishes in the Roots section, page 278.)

SOW	HARVEST	TRANSPLANT
April to August	Mid-May to late January	N/A
BETWEEN ROWS	**SEEDS**	**THIN**
18 inches	Thinly	Progressively

Culture

The edible part must develop rapidly if uninfested half-grown turnips are to be plucked from the cabbage root maggot's grasp. To grow fast, they absolutely require loose soil and plenty of moisture at all times. They are a low- to medium-demand crop.

Turnips can be started from April through August. Maggots do less damage to the summer harvest, but turnips forming in hot weather are strong tasting and have a tendency to develop woodiness. Sow the tiny seeds thinly, ½ inch deep, in rows 18 inches apart. When the seedlings are established, thin carefully to 3 inches apart in the row. Water frequently. In hot weather water even more frequently. The last sowing may start making bottoms when few cabbage flies are about.

Garden planning

For a continuous supply, start a short row every 10 days.

Insects and diseases

Chapter 8 discusses root maggot remedies for radishes. Do the same for turnips. If flea beetles slow growth, the maggots get more time to invade; spraying flea beetles may be in order if the leaves show much damage.

Harvest

In Cascadia unprotected turnips must be picked small to avoid the root maggot.

Saving seed

Because of root maggots, I suggest depending on rutabagas.

Varieties

Purple Top White Globe and its hybrid variants are slightly less attractive to the cabbage fly than milder, sweeter all-white Asian varieties. For greens, any variety makes edible leaves, but Shogoin was bred for this purpose. I suppose the difficulties with producing maggot-free turnips are why Cascadian seed companies are thin on the ground with respect to this vegetable. My favorite is Hakurei F1 (JSS, WCO), a Japanese variety I can munch on raw, like apples.

Roots

Many root vegetables are low-demand biennials that primarily feed in the subsoil, and yield a lot of food for the area involved. Consider the carrot. Soil conditions permitting, a carrot first drives a taproot 3 feet down, then spreads roots out into the subsoil and then, if soil conditions allow, gradually fills 3 more feet of soil depth with feeder roots by the time it is in full bloom after overwintering. One carrot plant can densely fill 50 gallons of soil with roots by the time it gets to making seed.

Root crops still produce when the subsoil is infertile, which is the usual case. It takes years of remineralizing a heavy topsoil before enough calcium (and other nutrients) leach into the subsoil to make carrots and beets taste much more interesting than most people imagine they could.

Root crops grow best on light (sandy) soils. They become difficult when the topsoil contains a lot of clay, and especially difficult when that clay gets so tight it won't allow the vegetable to swell.

Please consider the wild biennial's survival strategy. Its seeds dry down in Cascadia's low-humidity summer and sprout when the rains return. Biennials grow slowly over the winter, storing up sugar and plant nutrients. The following spring they draw down their savings account in order to rapidly outgrow competitors. Although wild biennials like Queen Anne's lace (wild carrot) thrive in infertile pastures, garden root crops provide the tastiest food only when their soil is friable, airy, and provides balanced fertility, and when moisture is always available. If the topsoil compacts, if the plants get crowded, or if the subsoil gets too dry, the leaves may still look okay, but the roots proceed to develop irregularly, get woody, and turn bitter. If the soil minerals are out of balance, but all other growth factors are okay, the root may achieve a large size and look okay, but it won't taste as great as it could.

I include potatoes and radishes (both annuals) with the biennial roots because they're equally sensitive to soil compaction, can succeed as low-demand crops, and, especially for radishes, are touchy about soil moisture.

To succeed in clay soil, root crops demand humusy beds but not too much nitrogen. If you dig in enough potent compost to loosen clay, you may see too much top and find too little bottom. Instead, an entire year before growing roots, dig in a layer of compost that is several inches thick and grow a high-demand crop. Next year use that bed for root crops. Yet another solution is to cover the clay 1 foot deep with imported loam. Make a few beds like that. Use loam for growing carrots, beets, parsley roots, and parsnips. After the root crop, rotate these beds into potatoes, celery, or melons. (Chapter 2 discusses the risks involved when buying topsoil.)

Timely, careful thinning (and first-class seed) leads to harvesting straight, smooth roots. A stable moisture supply grows higher-quality roots, but on deep, naturally moisture-retentive soils you can reduce the frequency of irrigation by separating plants far enough. I've grown tasty root crops entirely without irrigation in deep alluvial, silty-clay loam in Elkton. I predict roots can be dry gardened where there is a loam topsoil above a clay subsoil, which is the most common pattern found in temperate, humid climates. Getting the seed to sprout on natural soil moisture requires in sowing early May in the Willamette and mid to late April in southern Oregon. To help these deep feeders find adequate subsoil nutrition in a new garden, it's best to have already dug COF (and compost) into their prospective growing rows the previous autumn.

Arrange dry-gardened root crops in single rows 36 to 48 inches apart. Thin carefully: plants should stand 6 inches apart in the row by the time the tops are 4 to 5 inches tall. Keep them well weeded through the summer. During July harvest every other plant so that the remaining roots stand one foot apart. The roots may be good eating until next spring. Or they may become inedible before the rains return. Anyone exploring this possibility should do variety trials.

Hybrid beet and hybrid carrot varieties are available. Although hybridization doesn't hugely increase vigor in root crops, it does increase uniformity, and that makes the farmer more profit. Consequently, due to lack of plant breeder attention, many open-pollinated varieties have become less productive.

BEETS *(Beta vulgaris)*

Beets form perfect roots in deep loam soil, but do well enough in free-draining clay because the edible part forms mostly above the surface. Spells of cold weather or periods of heat-induced moisture stress result in "zoning"—white rings that don't affect the flavor much. Susceptibility to zoning depends on variety.

SOW	HARVEST	TRANSPLANT
April to August	June to February	N/A
BETWEEN ROWS	**SEEDS**	**THIN**
18 inches	Thinly	Progressively

Culture

Beets are a low-demand crop. Sow from April through July. Make early sowings ½ inch deep. In hot weather make the furrow ¾ inch deep and sow twice as many seeds. Each beet seed is actually a fruit containing several embryos, so seedlings emerge in clusters. Seedlings often disappear in the first two weeks after emergence, so it's best to sow two seeds per inch in rows 18 inches apart. Thin progressively; by the time the seedlings have grown to about 6 inches tall, they should stand far enough apart that at harvest the beets barely touch. If you do not thin this carefully, you'll still get decent beets, but the development of some will be suppressed by more vigorous individuals. Sometimes the weaker plants grow larger after these supergrowers are harvested, but you'll see the most handsome, productive result if you thin carefully in a timely manner. Baby beet varieties form perfectly round roots at a very small size; initially thin these to 1 inch apart, and when they bump, harvest every other plant. Thin regular canners (uniform vigorous selections bred for once-over harvest) to 3 or 4 inches apart before they start forming bottoms. Winter-storage varieties can grow very large and need in-the-row separation of about 8 inches.

Garden planning

Through summer my kitchen and a few lucky friends use the production of eight row feet of baby beets sown about once a month. I suggest this schedule for the Willamette Valley: Sow in April as early in the month as germination seems likely, again mid-May, and then again mid-June.

For winter harvesting, sow about 50 square feet of bed around July 15 and use a thick-skinned variety that can grow bigger.

Insects and diseases

Aboveground, early sowings interest flea beetles and *Diabrotica* (looks like a yellow ladybug with black spots, a.k.a. the Western spotted cucumber beetle). And slugs. The no-spray solution for these pests is to plant lots of seed, let the insects help you thin it, and next year wait two more weeks before starting the beet patch. Leaf miners attack beets; for organic handling, see Chapter 8. If most of your seedlings mysteriously disappear before they get well established, suspect symphylans.

Harvest

Slow-growing beets become woody and lose sweetness, so make growing room for them by harvesting the largest individuals. Most full-size round varieties develop a thicker, winter-resistant skin when they get large. Winter keepers develop especially strong skins and grow very large. All these sorts usually hold outdoors from October to March, although their flavor declines through winter.

Beets form on the surface. If they freeze, they'll rot immediately after thawing. Protect beets during winter with a straw mulch if you don't have too many mice nibbling on them, or else hill up some soil over them before the first severe frost.

I learned the easy way to cook beets from Tasmanians. Cut off the tops with about an inch of stalks still attached. Do not cut off the taproot. The skin reduces loss of nutrients during cooking. Boil until tender; the amount of time depends on variety but is usually around 20 minutes. Pour off the boiling water and immediately fill the pot with cold water. As soon as the beets have cooled enough to handle with minor discomfort, rub them, and the skin, stems, and root all fall away. They're still hot enough for the table. Most people only know pickled beets. I like beets hot—boiled, steamed, or roasted, with butter melting over them. Most people do not know that beets are good raw. Here's a recipe for beetroot salad. Grate a few raw beets, skin and all. Peel a navel orange and cut it into chunks. Add some sweet raw minced onion. Mix it all together. Generously add olive oil and black pepper. A small amount of lemon juice or vinegar may improve the flavor. Toss.

Swiss chard is a beet bred to form delicious leaves. The leaves of most table beet varieties make acceptable cooking greens when the plant is young.

Saving seed

Beet pollen is carried great distances by wind. To grow genetically pure seed, you need over 1 mile of isolation from any other blooming plants, including chard. Beet seed can last 10 years if stored properly dry in the least-heated room in your house. Starting in October, as you harvest full-grown roots for the table, choose the best ones for making seed. Select for narrow-diameter tight crowns, thin single taproots, smooth skin, perfect shape, and deep color. You may take a small slice off the side of the beet to inspect its internal color and also taste that slice (cooked or raw) before putting that root in your seed patch. Transplant selected roots in a part of the garden that need not be irrigated while the seed is drying down. Bury each beet with its crown far enough below the soil line that it is protected against frost. The amount and size of seedstalks a root puts up depend on its size. Position small beets 18 to 24 inches apart in all directions; space lunkers 3 feet apart. When perennial spring bulbs start emerging, the roots will put forth new leaves and then flower stalks will soon become huge, tangled sprays. The pollen has a strong, musky scent. Keep the patch free of weeds while you still can. Some seed will rot because it is lying on damp soil unless you work out a method of supporting the heavy flower stalks. The tangled stalks ripen their seed load irregularly over several weeks. Once half the seed has turned brown on a stalk, cut off that stalk and finish drying it under cover, spread out on a tarp. Strip the dry seed from the brittle stalks by hand, wearing gloves; winnow the dusty seed by dribbling it out of one bucket into another a few feet below in a mild breeze. Six plants will produce pounds of seed. The Organic Seed Alliance says 60 plants minimum are needed in each production to maintain vigor. I've gone two generations using a dozen parent plants without noticing obvious problems. Navazio says beets are strongly self-incompatible; it takes more than one blooming plant to make seed.

Temperatures over 80 degrees F while seed is maturing can reduce germination and vigor. That's why so much beet seed is produced in the Skagit Valley.

Varieties

If I had to use only one variety, I'd make it Early Wonder because it is productive and has tasty leaves, and this genuine heirloom comes from a time when people considered flavor before profit. Vigor in Early Wonder varies from plant to plant, so you can thin big beets out of a patch over a long time. Early Wonder makes better growth in cool weather than most canners, which are selected for uniform shape and size at maturity, little waste, and thin, smooth skins before they get too large. If I wanted high production for canning or pickling, I'd use Red Ace.

Baby varieties like Pablo (TSC) develop small, perfectly round roots weeks before canners do. My kitchen depends on Pablo in all seasons because it is especially delicious and retains excellent quality when it gets big.

Cylindrical varieties such as Formanova (or Cylindra) and Forono can be conveniently sliced into uniform-diameter rings. Cylinder beets are bred to be fast cooking, a characteristic that saves canneries time and money. Cylinder beets only develop properly in loose, sandy soil. Winter keepers (a.k.a. Lutz) are very large, long standing, irregularly shaped, and thick skinned. Sow about July 1 to mature in October. Feel free to experiment with any beet variety from any seed seller, including white, yellow, sugar beet crosses, and monogerm. All should grow well in Cascadia. Most manage winter.

Dry gardening

Very possible. (See introduction to the Roots section, page 260.)

CARROTS *(Daucus carota* var. *sativa)*

SOW	HARVEST	TRANSPLANT
April to mid-July Overwintered: late August to mid-September	June to early March Overwintered: mid-April to mid-May	N/A

BETWEEN ROWS	SEEDS	THIN
18 inches	Two to three per inch	Progressively

Culture

Carrots are a low-demand subsoil-feeding crop that is sown from April through July, with the possibility of an even later sowing of an over-wintering variety. Thoroughly blend in COF, a foot deep if possible. Place the small seeds ½ inch deep, two or three seeds per inch, in rows 18 inches apart. Carrot seed takes 12 to 14 days to emerge. Whatever it takes, the soil touching those seeds must remain moist until taproots have begun penetrating. Carrot shoots are weak; they cannot force their way through a crusted surface. You can help them germinate by raking a ¼-inch-thick layer of finely divided compost into the surface before making their furrow, or else fill the furrow with something that won't crust over or dry out quickly—like finely divided compost or the container growing medium recommended in Chapter 7.

During its first weeks, the carrot seedling concentrates on extending a hairlike taproot into the subsoil, and then it grows faster aboveground. If the root does not encounter impenetrable clods or zones of excessive fertility, such as might come from pieces of undecomposed fresh manure or dissolving chemical fertilizer granules, it grows straight without splitting (forking) or stubbing off. Carrot taproots do not react to the materials used to make COF. If the topsoil remains fairly soft and if the roots don't overly compete with each other or with weeds, the top inches of the taproot will swell up nicely.

Growing the most beautiful carrots requires giving each one enough space to fully develop without quite bumping the next carrot in the row at maturity. Thinning should be progressive and completed by the time the tops are 6 inches tall. Keep the bed weed-free. A sudden increase in soil moisture after moisture stress can cause salad varieties (tender because they form less fiber) to split.

When carrot seed is sprinkled into the furrow by hand, the almost inevitable result is a tangle of crowded seedlings. No matter how much patience it takes, precise thinning is well worth the trouble. (And there's a sowing shortcut explained in Progressive Thinning, page 130.)

Garden planning

Carrots enlarge steadily if they're not over-crowded; a patch can be harvested for months. Fifty square feet of carrot bed sown in spring supplies my household all summer if we're not making juice. If you prefer very tender varieties that split when large, like Mokum, it's best to start a new bed every month.

Do not prepare your spring carrot patch before the soil has dried enough to form a fine, loose seedbed. Yes, carrot seed will sometimes germinate in colder, wetter soil, but starting a month sooner usually means ending up with a lumpy seedbed. If the seeds do manage to sprout, they'll grow so slowly at first that you'll harvest only one week sooner, end up with less weight per square foot of bed, and have carrots of a lower quality.

I would start a larger patch the first half of July, at least 100 square feet. These carrots size up by late September and are consumed during autumn/winter. If I wanted to juice carrots during winter, I'd start several such beds.

If your topsoil goes into spring in reasonably loose condition despite being pounded by winter rains, you'll probably get a good result from Merida FI (TSC). This variety is bred for overwintering and spring harvest. Sow Merida in September, thin it progressively, and don't allow weeds to swallow the bed over winter. Merida has unusually frost-hardy tops. The roots fatten in April instead of going to seed with the other carrot varieties.

Insects and diseases

Carrot rust fly maggots and wireworms feed on carrots during autumn and winter. Both leave unappetizing trails behind. Chapter 8 discusses how to handle carrot maggots. Wireworm damage has always been minor in my garden. The rare track can be cut away before the carrot is eaten. If either sort of damage is severe, consider digging your carrots in October and storing them in an outbuilding where they won't freeze.

The colder storage conditions are, the longer they hold before resprouting. The traditional cellaring method for root crops is to fill a barrel with alternating layers of roots and damp, coarse sand. (Chapter 8 describes methods to keep flies out of carrot beds.)

Harvest

If the variety you grow will come out of the ground by tugging on its top (many don't), start the harvest by taking every other carrot; this helps the survivors grow faster. Otherwise, first loosen the row with a spade or digging fork. In my current garden carrots hold in the ground all winter without protection and without damage. In frosty Lorane, I covered them with straw to protect the crowns from freezing in the event of a severe cold snap. (If the crown freezes, they rot.) Covering the straw with a sheet of black plastic increases the protection by keeping the bed dry, but it also makes a haven for field mice that feed on carrots. Covering the crowns with an inch of soil also works and is much less inviting to mice.

Saving seed

Carrots need I mile of isolation to produce fairly pure seed. While harvesting in winter select near-perfect roots and immediately transplant them on 12 by 24 inches and let them proceed in spring. But there is a hitch—wild carrots, also called Queen Anne's lace, cross freely with garden carrots. The weed grows along roadside ditches and other neglected land. Their flowers carpet unused sunny land and infertile pastures. Wild carrot crosses result in dry, fibrous whitish roots with little sweetness. I opine this is the reason Adaptive does not sell carrot seed. Tim Peters says he grew small quantities of high-purity carrot seed near Myrtle Creek, Oregon, by covering the seed-making plants with a 5-foot-tall window-screened box that keeps out all flying insects. He also located the carrot seed patch close to an active anthill. The ants pollinate enough flowers for a decent seed yield.

Varieties

Some varieties may not suit your soil. The foot-long types you find at the supermarket require sand or sandy loam to develop to visual perfection and usually aren't the greatest-tasting varieties, but our weekly box customers adore Sugarsnax F_1. Shorter cylindrical, blunt-ended Nantes varieties are tender, good for raw munching and salads. Nantes types are best eaten by midautumn; they are tender because they have little fiber, so they tend to split as they enlarge. The best-tasting Nantes I know of is Nelson F_1. It is so superior I import seed—and get some Sugarsnax too while I'm at it. The type of carrot that was widely called Danvers when I was in the seed trade (Flakkee, the Europeans call it) makes pointed roots 6 to 7 inches long with higher fiber content than Nantes types. These are especially good for winter harvest and dry gardening. Some modern cylindrical types, especially Bolero FI, handle winter well too. Short, broad, chewy Chantenay varieties can develop in clayey soils. Autumn King varieties make enormous roots. The ones I've trialed have a coarse, horsey-treat flavor.

Territorial sells the aforementioned Merida FI; it is spendy seed.

Dry gardening

Sow midspring while enough soil moisture remains to sprout the seed. Arrange rows 4 feet apart; thin to 12 inches apart in the row by the time the plants are 6 inches tall. Use a variety with high fiber content.

PARSLEY and PARSLEY ROOT

(Petroselinum crispum)
Think of leaf parsley as a carrot grown for its edible leaves. The parsley patch is easy to direct-seed in cool weather. Most people unnecessarily buy transplants.

SOW	HARVEST	TRANSPLANT
April	July to mid-March	N/A

BETWEEN ROWS	SEEDS	THIN TO
18 inches	Two per inch	4 inches, Progressively

Culture

Parsley seed germinates best in moist, cool soil. It germinates slowly, even in warm soil. I suggest sowing mid-April. If you start it in May/June, the seeds must be watered almost daily for nearly three weeks.

Leaf parsley may be considered a low-demand crop or a medium-demand crop; it all depends on how much leaf you want to pick. Sow two seeds per inch, ½ inch deep, in rows 18 inches apart. Thin progressively to 6 inches apart in the row. If leaf production falters or seems insufficient, side-dress or irrigate.

Grow root parsley like carrots. Direct-seed, absolutely. Thin progressively so that plants stand

6 inches apart in the row; tight spacing makes for small, rough roots. Parsley root is widely said to be intolerant of clay soil. I can neither confirm nor deny this from personal experience.

Garden planning

Eight row feet of leaf parsley produce all the garnishes and seasonings my household can use. Unless the plants freeze out, harvesting goes from July until next spring when tomato seedlings go out. Parsley roots taste much like parsnip. Root parsley produces less than parsnips will for the space involved, but parsley may do better in difficult soil. Like the parsnip and carrot, root parsley holds in the ground all winter.

Insects and diseases

I have had no problems.

Harvest

Snip full-size leaves as needed, but don't take more than half the new growth. Remove any old yellowed leaves to improve air circulation. In mild winters leaf production continues slowly; the plants die back to the soil line in colder circumstances but resprout in spring for a brief round of cutting before going into bloom. However, if the crowns freeze, the roots rot. Mulch applied late in October helps get them through severe cold snaps.

Dig root parsley from September through February. In late October cover the crowns with a few inches of soil to ensure against freezing. If you want to find out what parsley root tastes like without the bother of growing it, dig a leaf parsley plant, wash the root, and then steam or

boil it. It'll not be easy to get all the soil out of all the forks and crevasses, but once cooked it'll taste just like root parsley.

Saving seed

Parsley is an insect-pollinated biennial; seed is produced like carrot.

Leaf varieties do not require digging, selection, and replanting because there is no reason to select for root qualities. Choose seed-making plants for productivity and the most winter-tolerant and attractive leaves. Protect the crowns from freezing over winter and the plants will form seed next spring.

Seed for root varieties should be grown only from carefully hand-selected roots, dug at full size in winter and replanted like carrots.

Varieties

I've done trials involving a great many leaf varieties; there are subtle flavor differences. Some varieties handle winter better than others. Some have longer, fatter stems; some are curlier, darker, lighter; some make slightly easier chewing. To me, none of these differences are important, but a gourmet chef might care. Flat-leaf types, often called "Italian" or "plain," have more intense flavor; they're better for drying and for cooking. The root varieties offered by ethical seed resellers are high-quality, uniform European selections (parsley root is a commercial crop in Euroland).

Dry gardening

Grows like carrots. Its root system is not nearly as extensive as the other root crops; parsley may fail without fertigation.

PARSNIPS

If well-formed, straight roots are to be produced, parsnips absolutely require deep, loose topsoil. If parsnips do poorly in a new garden, keep in mind that it takes years for an acidic, clayey subsoil to be recharged by plant nutrients you put into the topsoil. Here's a crop where double digging and working in an inch of compost and a dose of COF into the second foot might be a worthwhile effort.

SOW	HARVEST	TRANSPLANT
May to mid-July	July to mid-February	N/A
BETWEEN ROWS	**SEEDS**	**THIN TO**
18 inches	Three per inch	4 inches

Culture

This is a low-demand crop. Loosen the bed as deep as your spade or fork will go. If your soil gets hard again soon after digging or it fails to work up to a fine seedbed deeply and thoroughly mix in an inch-thick layer of finely divided, completely finished compost and COF one month before sowing and then dig the bed again just before sowing.

Sow parsnip from May through mid-July. May sowings germinate with less watering. Achieving good germination in hot weather requires almost-daily watering for two weeks. Parsnip seed sprouts slowly and scantly. Field emergence from decent seed is usually below 20 percent. The shoot is weak; it cannot push through a surface crust. Sow three or four seeds per inch in furrows ¾ inch deep and 18 inches apart. Especially in hot weather, cover the seeds with fine compost; this step helps to keep the seeds moist until they sprout. Thin the seedlings carefully and do it before there's any serious competition. I thin to four inches apart in the row, but if you're going to dig them small, 2 inches apart is enough. Wait too long to thin and you can't yank them out of the ground. Try, and the top breaks off; a few weeks later the root resprouts.

Garden planning

Spring sowings should be completely harvested by the end of September. July sowings are for use in autumn/winter.

Insects and diseases

I currently live on the edge of suburbia with several thousand acres of forest across a 20-acre field that has just been subdivided into (mostly still vacant) building blocks. Around the end of summer my property gets invaded by that year's crop of young mice and rats looking to establish their own territory. I know what I do to them is politically incorrect, but at that season we put out a couple of rodent-feeding stations and keep them stocked until all the mice and rats in the vicinity have lost their appetites. This step seems to prevent most winter gnawing on my carrots, parsnips, rutabagas, beets, etc. I do not recall any major problems with rats or mice when I was gardening in a Southern California suburb in the 1970s, but at that time we shared our backyard with two half-wild female calico cats.

If your soil carries a disease called "parsnip root rust," some or many parsnips will develop rusty brown patches. Parsnip root rust vanished from my garden after I did a soil test and remineralized. In trials I observed some varieties resist rust better.

Harvest

If the crown freezes, the root rots; so before winter arrives, spread a few inches of soil or a thick layer of grain straw over them. When parsnip roots prepare to resprout in spring, they become inedible. Parsnips must be dug. In frosty weather young parsnip leaves taste like tough celery, and in very small quantities, finely shredded, they are said to improve winter salads.

Saving seed

Every midsummer I harvest a few pounds of parsnip seed grown from transplanted, rigorously selected mature roots. Midsummer is also the best time to sow parsnip seeds for autumn harvest, so I immediately consign a bucket of fresh seed to the local garden center where people take home a generous scoop for a few dollars. The bucket sells out in a few weeks because unlike the old stuff in most seed rack packets, my fully ripe, gently handled seed grown on remineralized soil germinates strongly and makes perfectly configured roots with excellent flavor. Piece of cake!

Parsnip seed crops require 1 mile of isolation if you want near-perfect purity. Grow seed from at least 25 carefully chosen roots. During winter as I dig parsnips for the kitchen, whenever I spot a near-perfect root, I immediately replant it in a seed production bed. The root is always too long for convenient transplanting, so I cut off enough of the bottom to make the

part I transplant about 7 inches long. I position seed-making roots 18 inches apart in a pair of parallel rows that are about 2 feet apart along a 4-foot-wide raised bed. One seed-making bed of about 50 square feet holds enough genetic diversity to prevent loss of vigor and produces a few pounds of seed with a rather short storage potential—and that's why I offer the neighborhood a big bucketful every time I grow parsnip seed. Besides, income from that seed covers all my year's purchases from that garden center.

Ripe parsnip seeds shatter from the flower whenever there's enough breeze to carry them a few feet. So your task is to harvest flowers one at a time when the seeds in a particular flower have turned light brown but only a few seeds have been lost. I patrol the seed patch once a day and cut ripe flowers off with an inch of stem still attached. They finish drying spread on a tarp in the garage. Parsnip seed that starts out strong retains excellent vigor for two years; it will barely germinate in the fourth year. The strongest seeds are the big ones coming from the main ("king") flower.

Varieties

If you want every parsnip in the row to be smooth, straight, and easy to wash, either buy open-pollinated seed that was honestly raised from painstakingly hand-selected full-size roots, grow a hybrid variety, or grow your own seed from painstakingly hand-selected roots. If the variety you start with doesn't prove to be as uniformly perfect as the catalog copy led you to expect, it probably can be cleaned up by a few generations of careful selection, and then you'll always have fresh seed you can count on to be productive. However, to find two dozen near-perfect roots from a degenerated variety, you might have to dig 40 dozen. For a great many years the best North American variety was Harris Model (WCO). Hybrid varieties have replaced most of the old standards. Adaptive sells Halblange Weisse, a German half-long variety reselected for shape and vigor, perhaps better suited to heavier soils.

Dry gardening

Like carrots.

POTATOES *(Solanum tuberosum)*

Potatoes are solanums that prefer cool weather. Most of Cascadia provides plenty of that. You might not think that potatoes, being inexpensive, are worth your time and garden space. Think again. When spuds are provided with complete, balanced soil fertility, their flavor is noticeably better. Remarkably better! And there are noncommercial varieties with flavor that entirely outshines the profit-making types used in industrial agriculture. Plain home-garden potatoes can be a delicious health food that doesn't need to be deep-fried or slathered in butter, sour cream, vinegar, salt, pepper, or sugary ketchup. Proper potatoes won't leave a bitter aftertaste. Garden spuds are not treated with sprout-inhibiting chemicals.

Potatoes yield a great deal of high-quality nutrition from a given space and growing time. It takes a fertile half acre to produce 20 bushels of high-protein bread wheat, which is enough to supply the chickens and make the year's daily bread for a small family that considers wheat

and eggs their staffs of life. An irrigated eighth acre produces over 2 tons of potatoes. And in case you don't know it, leached soils don't grow high-protein wheat; the wheat crops you may have seen in the Willamette Valley contain about half the minimum amount of gluten needed to make bread. Cascadian wheat provides about 7 percent protein and is used to make instant-soup-packet noodles. Potatoes grown on remineralized soil provide as much as 11 percent protein. Potatoes, not starchy, soft white wheat, must form the core of a healthy self-sufficient Cascadian gardener's staff of life.

SOW	HARVEST	TRANSPLANT
Earlies: early May	Earlies: July to October	N/A
Main crop: early June	Main crop: early October	

BETWEEN ROWS	SEEDS	THIN TO
4 to 5 feet	One seed piece per foot	N/A

Culture

If your aim is to grow a nine-month supply of top-quality potatoes, you're about to discover a method that gives you back a great many very large potatoes for the least work. Achieving a high yield depends as much on providing loose soil as it does on providing soil nutrients and moisture. Industrial potatoes almost always grow in soil that naturally stays loose from planting to harvesting. Before high-tech farming, high yields of potatoes were produced on many types of soil. Farmers eliminated weeds by plowing them under in a manner that also flipped loose soil over the forming spuds. Those old-fashioned farming techniques can be imitated in your backyard with a common garden hoe.

If young potato vines experience even a light frost, they die back to the soil line. New shoots soon emerge, but this setback means the final yield will be lower. So exercise patience. Start the main storage crop well after frost danger has passed. There'll still be plenty of time for it to mature. I suggest June 1 for planting the main crop. Starting a few weeks after this date slightly reduces yield; starting earlier will make the crop finish before conditions cool down enough, and in consequence, you may dig already sprouting tubers that do not store as well.

Locate the potato row in the middle of a 4-foot-wide fertile strip or down the center of a raised bed. Four feet of root zone for a single row may seem wasteful, but I assure you the vines emerging from *certified* seed will completely cover the area and photosynthesize every possible erg of solar energy hitting that space to make starch with which to swell your potatoes. The yield will be enormous. Many of the spuds will be lunkers.

If you're using certified seed, spread a double dose of COF over the area and dig or roto-till it in. If the seed carries potato viruses, use half that amount of COF. I specify that much fertilizer at the beginning for three reasons: my method restricts side-dressing, you're not going to be germinating seeds, and more fertility makes a much higher yield. After the COF, spread a ¼-inch-thick layer of compost over the bed and roughly rake it into the surface. Doubling that quantity wouldn't hurt for this crop. The humusy surface inch you create will

soon get pulled up over the potatoes. Because of all that compost, it'll stay loose.

The very best seed potatoes are called "single drops," small potatoes weighing 2 to 3 ounces that you don't have to cut into segments. Larger seed potatoes should be cut into sections weighing 2 to 4 ounces; each piece should contain at least two or, at most, three eyes. Carol Deppe says it is unwise to plant a seed piece containing more than three eyes because every eye emits a shoot and too many shoots in one spot result in harvesting many small potatoes instead of fewer larger ones. Carol says this precaution especially applies to finger varieties that make small potatoes at best and normally form a great many eyes on each tuber. In my experience small spuds also occur because of stiff competition. Certified seed producers want to harvest single drops; they achieve this by tight spacing. If you want big ones, use my spacing suggestions. And lots of COF. And certified seed.

Many half-truths are in circulation about how and when to cut seed potatoes. Some say do it a few weeks before planting and hold the pieces in a cool place in bright, indirect light to let the cuts heal over and encourage the pieces to begin sprouting. When I tried this, my pieces dried out so much that many of them failed to sprout. Some people plant immediately after cutting the pieces but first treat the cuts with fungicide or natural rot suppressants. I think all this is unnecessary bother. I plant immediately after cutting pieces, but instead of fungicide, I cut up chitted potatoes.

Chitting seed potatoes means encouraging them to green up and start sprouting before they are cut into pieces. Chitted seed gets to growing before it can begin rotting. Commercial growers can't chit because already-sprouting seed potatoes need far gentler handling than machine planting allows. You, on the other hand, are going to plant gently, by hand. You should chit. Get your seed potatoes in hand well in advance. Four weeks before planting, spread them out in bright light (not direct sun) where it is cool but not cold (55 degrees F). After a few weeks in the light they'll green up and buds will form at the eyes; after only one month in the light these buds should not emit sprouts, or if they do, the sprouts will still be short. Cut the seed into pieces immediately before planting them. Do not break off any sprouts! Handle gently. If you start greening them up too soon, or if ambient conditions were too warm, there'll be a great many very delicate sprouts to avoid damaging.

Using a common garden hoe, make a bold, deep furrow lengthwise down the center of the potato bed and gently place seed pieces in it 1 foot apart. Take care that the majority of eyes face up, or at least not pointing down. Cover them.

Each action I am about to suggest works toward maintaining *very loose*, dryish soil around the forming tubers without stepping on the bed.

Potatoes rarely develop below the seed piece. They are attached to the vines a few inches *above* the seed piece. If you initially planted the seed piece deep enough that the spuds forming above it aren't exposed to light (say 8 inches under the surface), then the soil around and above the seed will resettle to its natural degree of compaction before tubers form. Instead, sow the seed

piece shallowly. As the vines grow, loose soil is gradually pulled in against them with a common garden hoe. The same action weeds the row. The loose soil you just scraped up surrounds the forming potatoes while the crop's rapidly expanding canopy prevents rain and irrigation from compacting it.

After the vines have grown about 6 inches tall, place your feet at least 18 inches to one side of the row to avoid compacting the root zone, reach over the vines with a common garden hoe, press the hoe blade lightly on the ground, and pull it toward you, scraping up soil against the vines. Do this from both sides of the row. Bend at the waist and lean over the row. Never stand any closer than absolutely necessary. Repeated hilling up gradually builds up a low mound over the bed's center. The first time, move about an inch of soil over the row leaving about 5 inches of vine still able to photosynthesize. Then, once a week, hill up again. After five or six times, hilling up becomes impossible without damaging the vines. By that time you should have created a long low mound of loose soil about 12 inches high and 18 inches wide that is filling with potatoes.

Hilling up eliminates weeds. By the time hilling up can no longer be done, it'll be high summer and there won't be many new weeds appearing. If an odd weed manages to appear, hand-pull it. It'll yank easily from the soft soil. Hilling up rows was how farmers grew weed-free potato crops before they started using herbicides. Before herbicides were widely used, farmers considered spuds to be the best-possible crop to grow when converting a pasture to row crops.

That loose soil will be protected by the leaf canopy, so when you irrigate or if it rains, this soil remains loose. Consequently the yield will be much larger. Synchronicity, eh? One more big advantage to my method: digging potatoes out of loose soil takes less effort.

At first the potato plant only grows leaves. Then flowers appear. The vines start setting tubers at the same time. Blooming goes on for some weeks and then ceases. At this point vines stop growing and no more potatoes are set. Then the plant concentrates on manufacturing starch. While the plant was growing new leaves, it needed lots of plant nutrients. During the time it fills its tubers with starch, it needs few nutrients because starch is a form of concentrated energy made from water and carbon dioxide gas. The abundant nutrient supply released by the heavy dose of COF you initially dug in is also fading away. More synchronicity, eh?

Eventually the sun weakens, and the vines begin to deteriorate. The crop will end up with tougher skins that store better if you'll stop irrigating from this point. Hope it doesn't rain. Then frost kills the vines, if they didn't already brown off on their own. It's time to dig spuds.

If you aim to dig some new potatoes as soon as possible, then plant chitted seed of an early maturing variety two weeks before the last usual frost date. The vines won't emerge for a few weeks. If a late frost blackens the young vines, they'll come up again but won't yield as much. No big deal if that happens; this isn't the crop that'll feed you through autumn and winter. Here's an occasion to use spun-fiber cloth for frost protection. Frost cloth also speeds up early

vine growth. You must take the fabric away to hill up, but I suggest you put it back over the row to accelerate growth. A few repeats and it'll be summer, the (probably tattered) fabric cloche will no longer be needed, and you'll soon be digging new potatoes.

If soil conditions permit and if the seed you planted was genuinely virus-free, the root system has the potential to extend 3 feet below and 2 feet to either side of the seed piece. If you want to achieve an even higher yield, facilitate root development by double digging the easy way. First step, excavate a ditch 18 inches wide and about one shovel's blade deep down the bed's center. Temporarily place the soil you remove along both sides of the ditch. Then dig a double dose of COF and an inch-thick layer of compost into the exposed 18-inch-wide band of subsoil. Mix them into the depth of another shovel's blade. If there's a lot of clay down there, the digging will be difficult and the mixing irregular— in that case, also dig in an extra dose of aglime as though starting a new garden. Then refill the trench and prepare the top foot of the entire bed as I suggest in the beginning of this section.

Garden planning

Grow spuds my way using certified seed on anything except clay soil and you'll find that a 100-foot-long row yields from 400 to 800 pounds. Immediately after harvest, plant the potato patch to garlic or shallots or else grow a green manure. Winters in the redwoods are mild enough to allow overwintering bulbing onions to be sown immediately after the spuds are dug.

Insects and diseases

Scabby, tough, corky patches on the skin are caused by a soil-dwelling bacteria. Scab decreases storage life. Many so-called experts say scab is promoted by soil pH over 6.0, so they prohibit liming the potato bed. Actually, the species has a high need for available calcium. The potatoes I grow using COF are entirely without scab, yet COF contains lime. I think scab has more to do with nutrient-deficient out-of-balance soil, which describes most farmland. I also grow spuds on a four-year-long rotation that reduces scab. However, the year after harvesting potatoes, there will inevitably be some coming up from tiny tubers that were overlooked. Be sure to kill every one of these volunteers, and do that well before *they* form small tubers. And during that four-year-long break do not grow other solanums like tomatoes, peppers, or eggplant. These can host the infection. And vigilantly yank nightshade, a wild solanum.

Virus diseases are a serious matter. They reduce plant vigor and lower yield. A lot. There are more than 20 common potato virus diseases. Potato viruses do not make their presence obvious to amateurs until harvest time. Someone familiar with how certified seed performs notices that fewer vines appear from each infected seed piece and that these vines are shorter. Starting a row with infected seed for some varieties and certified seed for others makes this difference obvious. Grown in very good soil, virus-riddled stock puts out vines (and roots) that might reach 18 inches to either side of the row center, while certified seed in the same row will cover a 5-foot-wide area (roots, too). If you grow heirloom varieties from uncertified seed, you may as well reduce the between-row space and amount of fertilizer accordingly. Potato viruses are spread by aphids. Once a plant is infected, the virus is carried on ever after in its tubers. Each additional year that you plant last year's potatoes, the number of virus diseases in the stock increases, and the yield decreases.

Harvest

Treat yourself to a few very new potatoes. Dig one plant at the sunniest end of the row two to three weeks after flowering starts. Although barely the size of hens' eggs at this stage, they'll be the most delicious potatoes of all. But try to restrain yourself; the spuds you haven't yet dug are growing a size larger every sunny day.

Dry topsoil at the finish helps toughen the skins, and that improves storage. September rain may thwart your hope. Ideally, dig the crop shortly after a hard frost makes the vines brown off. Early maturing varieties may have browned off by mid-September, but I suggest not digging these spuds until October because the temperature of the soil in the last half of September might be lower than it is in your shed and certainly will be more stable. Be gentle when harvesting. Do not bruise the skins. Do not wash them before storage; washing greatly shortens storage life. Instead, try to dig when the soil is dryish so less (or none) of it sticks to the potatoes, which means, don't put off harvesting!

Potatoes can remain where they grew and can be dug a few at a time as needed, but they probably won't keep as well that way. However, I always had a place to store mine where the temperatures remained in the necessary range. So don't just accept my evaluation; perform an experiment! Leave 10 row feet in the ground, and lift a nest every two weeks from November through March. Decide about this for yourself.

Green potatoes have become poisonous throughout. Peeling off the green outer flesh does not help. The green is not the poison; it is chlorophyll that formed because there was light present. That light also induces the manufacture of solanine, a toxic alkaloid that permeates the entire potato. Don't feed green spuds to livestock. Get rid of them—and not in the compost heap where they'll grow minitubers that spread throughout the garden and stop you from ever getting potato scab under control.

Potatoes store best in moderately humid conditions at a stable 40 degrees F with good air circulation. If the temperature goes much lower than this, the potatoes convert starch into sugar, degrading their taste. If they freeze, they're ruined. In Cascadia, providing humidity is never the problem.

Elkton had rather mild winters. There I stored our year's supply in a dozen cardboard apple boxes stacked tightly three boxes high and two wide. This forms a thermal mass that stabilizes storage temperature. Stacking also slows moisture loss yet allows enough air exchange through the exposed surfaces. The stack was kept in an insulated pump house, so it was enough to stabilize the temperature by covering the stack on top and sides with old blankets and tarps. At frosty Lorane I kept them in a very drafty dirt-floored corrugated metal shed where the potato boxes had to be buried

in a heap of loose grain straw more than a foot thick. These did not freeze during the harshest freeze I experienced at Lorane—four days of continuously sub-freezing weather that reached 3 degrees F one night. Books on root cellaring in general, and Carol Deppe's *The Resilient Gardner* in particular, have lots of information about this subject.

Any spuds that get cut or otherwise damaged while being dug should be eaten within a few weeks. Spuds showing diseased or rotting spots should be discarded. If stored, they will rot and then induce rotting in adjoining spuds. Sometimes a small discrete potato erupts from a larger tuber and remains connected to it by a thin tube that easily breaks. Sometimes the tuber heals that small wound and does not rot in storage. Sometimes. Those also go straight to the kitchen. Potatoes with scab store less well.

Saving seed

Although you can plant small potatoes from last year's harvest, you shouldn't unless you're passionate about growing heirlooms. And if you do preserve heirlooms, then Carol Deppe will instruct you on how to (maybe) limit virus infection in your own stock. Virus-free seed is not cheap, but still, I pound of certified seed potatoes makes five to eight seed pieces, and each expertly grown piece produces 5 to 10 pounds of spuds.

Varieties

There are two basic sorts: starchy and waxy. Starchy varieties are best for baking, frying, or roasting. The baked flesh of starchy spuds becomes flaky and dry, and with some sorts the skins get crunchy crisp all by themselves in a hot oven. Starchy types are best for mashed potatoes because they'll self-crumble. Starch is what fries to a tasty brown crispness, so chips and french fries are made from high-starch varieties. For making potato salads or putting firm (boiled or steamed) chunks on the plate, use a variety with a lower starch content that can hold its shape and firmness.

Varieties that make the most starch only do that in semiarid climates. The variety that made the Idaho potato industry, the Russet Burbank, fails to perform as expected if it is grown in humid Cascadia. Cascade (WCO) is a similar variety Canadians can use. I think the popular and highly productive Yellow Finn is delicious. In Oregon I deeply appreciated a Ronniger's variety called Red Gold, with flaky, rich yellow semicrumbly flesh inside a red wrapper, and we grew Caribe, a purple-skinned, white-fleshed, crumbly baker that usually makes huge yields and keeps well. The new owners of Ronniger Potato Farm (www.potatogarden.com) still offer these as well as Nooksack, a variety like the Russet Burbank that does well west of the Cascades. I hope they keep their promise to soon supply genuinely certified seed for every heirloom Ronniger offered for so many years. Territorial currently sells Purple Viking instead of Caribe. I can't obtain any seed for it because of the Tasmania quarantine, but Marina says Purple Viking is fantastic. Purple-fleshed spuds (as opposed to purple-skinned spuds with white flesh) definitely taste different! I don't like their earthy flavor and suggest you only plant a few seeds the

first time you grow this type. Down to Earth Distributors says German Butterball is their best seller. I know that variety well; it's a lot like Dutch Cream (and another similar one, Bintje). Kennebec is the main variety in our kitchen now. It's an excellent high-yielding all-purpose spud with fine flavor. Finger potatoes usually are waxy and often extraordinarily tasty. Nichols Garden Nursery offers certified stock for Makah Ozette, an excellent-tasting regional heirloom dating way back.

Canadians find many certified varieties in their local garden centers, including Warba (also known as Pinkeye), Bintje, and Dutch Cream. In my opinion, Dutch Cream is markedly better tasting than Bintje, but it may not store as well. I know Pinkeye quite well. Tasmanians grow it for new potatoes. Here, it's an incredibly delicious variety when smallish, but as summer progresses, Pinkeye forms irregular lumps and creases that are hard to wash clean or peel. Maybe Pinkeye behaves differently at 50 degrees latitude than it does at 40 degrees where I live.

Certified seed potatoes start out in a tissue culture lab. Individual cells are sliced from the absolute tip of a growing shoot. These cells have not yet been infected by whatever viruses are present in the tuber. These cells then float in small test tubes filled with nutrient/hormone solution and are kept in bright light until they have morphed to tiny seedlings. These are transplanted into fine, sterile potting soil and grown in an aphid-proof greenhouse or screen house where they produce minitubers, called "first-generation seed" in the trade. Minitubers are usually the size of quail eggs, but being entirely virus-free, when planted next year prove to be many times more productive than later-generation seed potatoes that are much larger.

Minitubers cost far too much to use for anything except to raise second-generation virus-free seed potatoes by planting them in isolated, higher-elevation fields that are virtually free of both aphids and potato virus diseases. Second-generation tubers are still too expensive to use as ordinary planting stock, so this second generation is again increased. The third generation is still nearly free of virus infection. To be officially certified, the seed potatoes must be proved to contain very little virus and be no more than four generations away from the tissue culture lab.

Before tissue culture, the only way to obtain virus-free potatoes was to plant the actual seeds from small green tomato-like fruit that form on the vine and hope one or more of those seeds would produce a useful variety. When a good variety was discovered it was increased in the same cool, higher-elevation districts that now grow certified seed. Before tissue culture, most new varieties remained productive for 10 years or so, and then lost so much productivity they were replaced by something newer.

Dry gardening

Potato cultivation began in the Andes, an arid, cool climate. Most potato varieties can still forage for water. A century ago spuds were dry farmed in southern Idaho with yearly rainfall of less than 15 inches. Now irrigation is routine for all commercial crops because it greatly boosts yield, although the flavor of unirrigated spuds can be much better. To dry garden main-season

varieties, make the rows 5 feet apart and space the seeds 18 inches apart in the row. *Eliminate all weeds*, and if at all possible prepare the bed the previous autumn using the double-digging technique described above and overwinter a legume green-manure that gets chopped in early, well before the soil starts drying down.

RADISHES *(Raphanus sativus)*

What seems like it should be a quick, simple crop is often ruined by the cabbage root maggot. Winter-storage radishes are slightly easier to succeed with.

SOW	HARVEST	TRANSPLANT
Salad: March to August Storage: August	Salad: April to mid-October Storage: mid-October to February	N/A

SOW	SEEDS	THIN
Salad: two per inch Storage: one seed every 2 inches	Salad: 2 inches Storage: 18 inches	Salad: to one per inch, promptly Storage: 2 to 6 inches

Culture

Radishes are a low-demand vegetable with a high need for moisture. A lot of water gets stored in the swollen root, so even young radish plants survive a few days to a week of moisture stress without much apparent effect. But salad radishes will only be sweet and tender when they've been growing fast, which means there has always been abundant, ever-present moisture. Most vegetable crops aren't seriously stressed until soil moisture goes below 60 percent of the soil's total capacity to hold water. Salad radishes need soil that at all times is above 70 percent; to grow really succulent radishes, make that 80 percent of capacity. So that's your first challenge: keeping the salad radish bed constantly moist. To assist with that, I suggest digging twice the usual quantity of compost into the radish bed instead of raking it in and locating the bed near a hose tap.

Sow salad radishes from March through August. In one way the earliest sowings are the easiest because the bed stays moist naturally. However, you'll not harvest appetizing radishes in cool spring weather unless you grab them before the root maggot does. Summer crops contend with fewer maggots, but in that heat you may get sharp-tasting, chewy radishes no matter how much you water. Suspending 50 percent shade cloth over the summer radish bed can make a huge improvement.

Sow two salad radish seeds to the inch, ½ inch deep, in rows only 12 inches apart. The husky seed usually has a high germination rate; carefully placing one seed at a time can be easier than thinning out an overseeded row. *Radishes will not bulb well when crowded.* By the time the seedlings are developing their first true leaves they should stand ¾ inch apart in the row.

Sow storage (or winter) radishes in August, in rows 18 inches apart. Thin the rows promptly so that at full size they will not quite touch; with Black Spanish, that's about 6 inches apart in the row. Hilling up 2 inches of soil over the crowns may help protect them against hard frost.

Garden planning

Salad radishes form within a month of sowing. Because of the root maggot, salad radishes must be harvested the instant they're barely large enough. Each sowing must be harvested over 10 days at best. Radishes can grow between rows of another crop sown at the same time; they'll soon be out of the way. Putting early spring radishes between rows of overwintered bulb onions may deter flea beetles, making for quicker bulbing, which lets me yank them from the jaws of hungry root maggots in the nick of time.

Insects and diseases

Flea beetles relish radish leaves; the holes they make slow growth. But radishes become hot and woody when they fail to swell up rapidly. Worse, the slower they develop, the more likely they are to become the prey of the root maggot. Both pests must be dealt with.

When beetles make leaves into pin cushions, spray pyrethrins every few days or use longer-lasting Spinosad. Tall-topped varieties tolerate flea beetles better. Commercial growers prefer short-topped varieties; these make higher yields for the area involved. Of course, industrial agriculturalists use potent long-lasting pesticides. (Handling root maggots is discussed in Chapter 8.)

Harvest

Harvest salad radishes promptly! Even if effectively protected from root maggots, they rapidly become pithy, split, or hot when allowed to grow too large.

In addition to the bulb, the leaves on young plants make acceptable stir-fry or soup greens, especially after an arctic winter blast has wrecked the winter garden. The seedpods have a crunchy, mild radishy flavor if picked before seed formation is too far along. They are excellent in salads.

Saving seed

Salad radishes are annuals. Growing low-quality seed is easy. Simply do not harvest a spring sowing; don't even bother to thin it much. The plants will bolt in less than two months and ripen seed midsummer. Harvest when most of the seedpods have browned off and the seed within them is ripe, then let the tangled branches dry fully under cover, thresh out the seeds, and winnow them until clean. Seed produced this way is good for sprouting, like mung bean seeds.

Growing seed that actually produces a high percentage of useful salad radishes is not quite so easy. It'll go much better by starting with the most uniform (expensive) open-pollinated variety obtainable. Select perfectly configured roots for seed production while you're harvesting for the table. Their skins should be smooth and thin with a single hairlike taproot; they should have a tight, small crown, with the variety's ideal shape (globe, egg, long) and skin color exactly right. Pinch off all the larger leaves in order to reduce moisture stress, and bury the bulbs to their crowns, 12 inches apart in rows 24 inches apart. Water once or twice until they're well established. A high-quality variety should provide you with plenty of near-perfect bulbs. If you start with cheap seed, you'll be lucky if most plants make a radish.

I've had very good results growing storage radish seed from carefully selected overwintering plants, proceeding much as I do when growing rutabaga seed.

Situate the radish seed patch in a section of the garden where water can be withheld while the seeds are drying down. Radish varieties cross freely; varieties must be isolated by a half mile. To maintain vigor, involve at least 50 plants in each seed production. Radish seed remains vigorous for up to seven years stored in a rarely heated room where the humidity is not excessive.

Varieties

Some salad varieties grow well from spring through late summer. Others do poorly when days are long. Some salad varieties are mild and juicy unless they grow slowly or finish in hot weather. Others are intended to be sharper tasting and chewier. The catalog usually doesn't tell you. Do your own trials. Generally, tall-topped varieties work better in home gardens.

Champion (and recent derivatives of that traditional variety) is a tall-topped variety best for early spring and late summer sowing because when days are shorter, it'll get large without becoming pithy. Champion will not bulb properly during the long days of summer. Easter Egg was bred from Champion and behaves like it.

Hybrids have come to dominate the radish market in recent years. Hybrids make perfectly uniform rows.

In half a dozen attempts over the years I have always found White Icicle to be unpleasantly hot and pithy. I suggest you avoid the large white Asian radishes. Slow to form, these become riddled with maggots unless grown under screening or spun-fabric row covers. However, I really love Black Spanish. It's a big, long-keeping, black-skinned, semipungent winter radish that I grate, season with fresh raw onion and black pepper, and slather with olive oil. I would fight for Black Spanish. Nero Tondo (JSS) is uniform and productive.

Dry gardening

It's possible to grow salad radishes in the month of April without irrigation. Take advantage when the soil gets damp late in August and stays moist through September. Then you can grow winter radishes without irrigation.

Cucurbits

Garden *Cucurbitaceae*—cucumbers, melons, pumpkins, and squashes—are annual fruiting vines. None of them withstand frost, and all are poorly adapted to cool, damp weather—some more so. Wild cucurbits are ground-covering desert vines appearing where there is subsoil moisture—many garden varieties still form taproots as well as a broad network of surface-feeding roots that mirror images the vine (with the exception of bush squash, where the roots will, if they can, extend farther than the tops). Cucurbits do better when directly seeded; they do not transplant easily in any case, while confinement to a container stops the taproot. When experiencing higher humidity, lower light intensity, and cold nights at the end of summer, cucurbits fall prey to powdery mildew, a disease that covers their leaves and prevents

photosynthesis. Powdery mildew disease (PMD) stops fruit from setting and soon kills the plant if frost doesn't.

I have a nutritional handling for PMD that works in my soil. It seems harmless even if it fails to make a difference for others. Cucurbits are big feeders on zinc; nutritionists recommend pumpkin seeds as a concentrated source of nutritional zinc. And when you get a cold, nutritionists often suggest zinc supplements to boost immune function. It is possible that cucurbits succumb to PMD at summer's end because they have already taken up and used all the available zinc in their root zone. When you first see PMD spreading over any cucurbit, try this: dissolve I heaping tablespoon of zinc sulfate in I gallon of water, and in the morning before the sun gets strong and while the leaf stomata are open, heavily spray that mixture until water drips off every leaf, top and bottom. The disease will vanish almost immediately because you sprayed a salt solution on it. Spraying bicarbonate of soda at I tablespoonful per gallon will also kill PMD, but with bicarb the disease returns the next day. If zinc shortage was the cause, the vine will remain PMD-free, at least for a few weeks (and then you may spray zinc again, if needed). If foliar zinc did not eliminate PMD, do not repeat it.

Squash handles cool, humid conditions best, then in declining order, cucumber, cantaloupe, and watermelon. Most summer squash varieties grow anywhere in the region, although some kinds of winter squash won't fully ripen north of the Columbia. Cucumbers (the right varieties) tolerate cool nights and grow well throughout Cascadia, but all cucumber varieties require warmer conditions than squash needs to germinate and make early seedling growth. Some cantaloupe varieties produce half-size delicious fruit in the Willamette Valley if encouraged like eggplant. The best of those produce a very small, average-tasting fruit in a warm summer north of the Columbia. Most summers only a few watermelon varieties barely produce a few small ones in the Willamette Valley, but these are reliable in southern Oregon.

Cucurbit seeds require warm soil to germinate. Don't even try to sprout squash seeds before the soil reaches 65 degrees F measured 2 inches below the surface. Cucurbit seeds are large; they should be placed deep enough that in most soils they won't need watering until after they emerge. In fact, you should hope it does not rain from the time you sow until the seedlings open their first pair of leaves. Emerging seedlings can get powdery mildew. To avoid that, it's essential that the root penetrates moist soil while the shoot comes up through loose, dryish soil. Rain or irrigation lowers soil temperature. Chilling slows sprouting speed, making the seedling even more vulnerable. Gardeners who try to help cucurbit seeds sprout by watering them frequently experience poor germination. At sowing time the soil should be damp but not at full capacity. Only sandy soils—which dry out very rapidly—may have to be watered more than once before seedlings emerge.

Sometimes the weather turns chilly and rainy while waiting for cucurbit seeds to emerge. The best thing to do in that case is to sow again as soon as the weather settles. Some springs I've had to make three sowings around the same position,

each made one week after the previous. Whichever sowing grows best takes over the area.

You'll get faster and more certain germination by presprouting or chitting cucurbit seed. In a good spring chitting won't make much difference; when summer arrives late chitting makes a huge difference. Cucurbit seeds are moisture shy, so they are chitted differently. Fold two separate squares of kitchen paper towel into quarters. Sandwich a few cucurbit seeds between them. Moisten the paper until water drips out, and then, holding the sheets between your palms, firmly press them together. Squeeze out as much water as will easily release; don't make the towels too dry because even 10 big seeds will suck up a lot of moisture. Then put the sandwich inside a small airtight container somewhere where the temperature stays close to 75 degrees F. You can stack several seed sandwiches in the same container and keep track with a small plastic label in each one. Start checking closely at the end of the second day because at that temperature roots should already be emerging from the most vigorous seeds. Sow them before the fast-developing very brittle roots get longer than the seed itself or form loops. If the root is long enough but you can't plant until the next day, overnight the container outdoors or in the warmest part of the fridge. At each final growing position carefully place two or three chitted seeds about 1 inch deep, the root pointing down. Cover with loose, damp soil. Do not break the root; this kills the seed.

Cucurbit vines must first grow a genetically predetermined number of leaves before flowers appear, often as many as 10 leaves in the first weeks. The first five to seven flowers along the vine will all be males, and then the vine starts making female blooms, usually alternating male and female but sometimes several males and then a female. Male flowers open at the end of a long thin stem, last for a day or so, and then fall off. Female flowers open from the tip of an ovary that resembles a miniature fruit. Of course, no fruit can be set until female flowers appear. From emergence to first female flower takes more than one month. In Cascadia's cooler districts, obtaining fully ripe winter squash before the growing season ends and—even more so—harvesting any ripe melons at all, requires getting fruit to set as early as possible. The gardener can give the young vines a head start by raising transplants or better, by sowing chitted seeds.

All garden cucurbits produce more when fertilized like high-demand crops. Side-dress them when the vine begins growing fast (old-timers say it starts running). I side-dress COF in wide bands over the soil their roots are going to invade during the next 10 days. The sprawling vines soon cover the side-dressing, and it is time to side-dress again. Each side-dressing uses more COF to cover a larger doughnut.

If cucurbits run out of unoccupied fertile growing room, the production of new fruit tapers off greatly. This is especially true of bush summer squash, whose compact aboveground appearance fools gardeners into thinking the root system has been similarly shortened. Suppose you've got a 4-by-12-foot bed assigned to produce zucchini. Gardeners often cram about 10 plants into that space. By mid-July the bed is overcrowded, production falls off to next to nothing, and these stressed zucchini plants more readily fall to powdery mildew. Suppose instead that only two zucchini plants were given that entire space. Before the end of July they would still cover the bed and would be producing far more high-quality fruit than 10 crowded plants. And production on this uncrowded bed would continue at a higher level until autumn weather arrived. Those two plants could run down the surrounding paths and into adjoining beds something like a restrained winter squash. If you want more early production from bush squash, start the bed out crowded and then as soon as the vines have produced a few fruit each, remove most of the plants and dig more COF into the gaps. The same principle holds true of *Cucurbita maxima* winter squash. I give each sprawling vine 150 square feet of root zone. Each plant produces about 15 very large squash.

Copycat garden writers say cucurbits naturally wilt during midafternoon heat and that this wilting is harmless. This is incorrect; temporary wilting is a major, yield-lowering stress the gardener can easily avoid by growing only one plant in each position and providing lots of root zone. Cucurbits usually wilt because there is too much root zone competition, not because the topsoil has become slightly dryish while sun is strong. Having two strongly competing plants growing out of each position while putting the positions rather close together seems entirely correct practice for eastern North America, where the squash vine borer can collapse an entire vine in an instant. The borer is most destructive early in the season, leaving plenty of time for surviving plants to fully take over the space. In Cascadia there are no vine borers and far too many how-to-garden books from the East.

Pollination is done by bees and, sometimes, other insects. When producing seeds, varieties that can cross must be separated by a mile or more. Fortunately, it is easy to keep bees out of cucurbit flowers while you hand-pollinate them. A few such intentional pollinations produce all the seeds a gardener could ever want. Every adult knows intuitively how to do it. Very early in the morning before the bees are at work, remove a freshly opened male flower and strip off its petals, leaving only an erect stamen with a dab of pollen on its tip, then locate a brand-new female bloom that first opened that morning, insert the stamen into the female flower, and gently brush the tip against the pollen receptors.

Then protect the hand-pollinated female bloom from bees for a few days. Squash, with their huge blossoms, are simple: shut the flower by twisting its tip, and secure it with a string or twist tie. The petals soon fall off. Cucumber and melon flowers are too small to manage like squash. One day before a female flower opens, put it into a small bag made of cheesecloth or spun polyester fabric. The fabric is tied to the stem behind the flower. The shield is removed to hand-pollinate the flower and immediately replaced. Remove the fabric a few days later to let the fruit develop.

Mark the intentionally pollinated ovary by loosely tying a brightly colored piece of yarn or strip of cloth to the stem, and permit this fruit to get fully ripe before picking it. Be sure to transfer pollen between several plants to prevent depression of vigor from inbreeding.

CUCUMBERS *(Cucumis sativus)*

Sun Tzu's classic book *The Art of War* defines patience as the ability to control the normal desire to end a conflict. When growing heat-loving crops in Cascadia, restraining the natural urge to get the garden planted is the key to success. With cucumbers, delay sowing until conditions are truly favorable. Most years in the Willamette Valley summer weather stabilizes around June 1. Occasionally it takes until mid-June. And some years summer doesn't ever seem summery. Cucumber seed germinates poorly before June in the Willamette; unprotected transplants don't grow when put out in average May weather and may get permanently stunted or diseased. Be patient. Cucumber vines develop incredibly rapidly in warm weather. In short-season Lorane I sowed mid-June and usually harvested cukes from late July until nearly the end of September.

SOW	HARVEST	TRANSPLANT
Early June	August to mid-September	N/A
POSITIONS	**SEEDS**	**THIN TO**
4 x 4 feet	Five per position	The best plant, progressively

Culture

Cucumbers are a medium-demand crop. Spread the usual amount of COF, and dig the bed. Spread compost too, and rake it in. Then prepare planting hills on 4-by-4-foot centers or else 4 feet apart down the center of a wide raised bed. At each position place a shovelful of compost and ½ cup of COF, and then deeply dig the spot, making a low fertile hill about 18 inches in diameter. More or less in the center of that hill, press down firmly enough with your fist to make a depression about 2 inches deep, thus assisting subsoil moisture to help keep that spot damp. Place four or five (best chitted) seeds on the firm bottom of that depression, laid flat, or with the emerging root pointing down, and cover them 1 inch deep with loose fine soil. If conditions stay warm, and it doesn't rain much, they'll sprout quickly.

I suggest gambling on the early arrival of warm weather. Sow chitted cucumber seeds when setting out tomato seedlings. If conditions turn cool or it rains, immediately start chitting more seeds and resow that hill as soon as the weather settles. Be resigned in advance to resow weekly until an attempt sprouts fast and grows rapidly from the start. To keep track, I make the initial sowing in the hill's center, a second sowing at three o'clock toward the outside of the hill, and a third sowing, if necessary, at six o'clock. When the seedlings have their first true leaf and are growing rapidly, progressively thin each hill to the single best plant from the best-performing sowing attempt.

Garden planning

Through August two healthy plants with unoccupied soil to grow into will yield at least half a bucket of prime cucumbers every two days. The vines lose productivity toward the end of August and fall apart after mid-September, making their bed available for a winter green manure.

Insects and diseases

I've seen no troubles except with powdery mildew disease (PMD). If frost doesn't get them first, the vines succumb to PMD. Although some varieties are said to be PMD resistant, what this means is that they'll grow a few days longer under bad conditions before breaking down. Resistance is not the same as immunity.

Harvest

Harvest promptly; seedy cucumbers are third-rate. Overlooked (oversized) cukes should be removed from the vine when spotted because while seeds develop few or no fruits set.

Saving seed

When the skin turns yellow, the seeds are ripe. Remove the pulp (somewhat like tomatoes), and ferment it in a kitchen mixing bowl. Stir daily. The pulp semiliquefies and separates from the seeds within a few days. Pour the contents into a sieve, wash the seeds until they are clean, and then spread them on newspaper to dry at room temperature.

Varieties

The best open-pollinated varieties for Cascadia have long been Marketmore strains (a super-market-style slicer) and Wisconsin SMR strains (a pickler).

Hybrids grow more vigorously and yield sooner. Unfortunately for the seed saver, any burpless or long, skinny heat-loving Asian variety that is early enough to produce much in Cascadia is almost certainly a hybrid—and needs to be.

Industrial agriculture uses gynoecious hybrids, meaning the variety only makes female flowers; pollination is accomplished by including a small percentage of seeds of a similar variety that does make male flowers. Since the first five or so flowers to form on normal varieties are male, having only female flowers on most of the plants means harvesting begins sooner. Gardeners should not *only* depend on a gynoecious variety because gardeners only grow a few plants—there may be no male flowers. Yes, bees will bring in pollen from nearby gardens, so you'll get some cucumbers but probably won't pick nearly as many.

The "greenhouse" type also produces only female flowers. However, these must not be pollinated or the fruit becomes an inedible gourd. That doesn't work outdoors.

Crystal Apple and Lemon Apple are similar heirlooms that make lemon-size fruit with a sweet, crisp texture. I've seen one plant aggressively cover over 50 square feet of bed with vines running up the paths and into other beds as well. Possessing so much vigor makes them an excellent choice for dry gardening and for difficult conditions.

In my opinion the best-of-all salad cucumber is variously named Lebanese, Middle Eastern, or Beit Alpha—these are intermediate in size between pickling and slicing cucumbers and are so thin skinned they do not need peeling. Middle Eastern varieties fail to produce much where nights are cool. When I owned Territorial, I sold a variety that worked, Amira F_1. Not only did Amira have flavor that was head and shoulders above anything else on offer in the States; at that time it was the only Beit Alpha variety capable of being highly productive in Cascadia. Because of seed industry concentration, Amira's primary grower was gobbled up by a bigger fish and some head office bean counter must have decided Amira was an inefficient allocation of resources. So the variety vanished. Then Alan Kapuler of Peace Seeds, Corvallis, who also appreciated Amira's extraordinary flavor, was moved to breed an open-pollinated variety from it that he calls "Mideast Peace." I've grown Alan's variety; it is not as early as Amira, but Mideast Peace tastes much the same. It's sold now by Adaptive Seeds. Marina says Mideast Peace did not fruit for her until almost September in a cool summer. She agrees that it is an especially delicious cucumber.

When Amira disappeared, I sought a replacement among the half dozen or so American-bred Middle Eastern varieties currently on offer in garden seed catalogs. I discovered that most of them now produce in cool conditions, but the breeders changed the flavor to match the usual North American supermarket cucumber. I'd probably like these new varieties better if I never had tasted the real thing.

Dry gardening

Cucumbers, being such a watery vegetable, seem unlikely dry-gardening candidates, but if hills are placed at least 5 feet apart in all directions and promptly thinned to one plant per hill, their entire root zone and then some are kept meticulously weed-free, and the vines are *fertigated when they're looking stressed*, they'll surprise you. Especially good for this is Lemon Apple.

MELONS (*Cucumis melo, Citrullus lantatus*)

Muskmelons and cantaloupes do not handle cool, humid conditions well. North of the Columbia and near the coast they rarely produce outside plastic tunnels. If the right variety is mollycoddled, it'll yield without a cloche in the Willamette. Watermelons are riskier—around the Willamette they'll only grow well in light, warm soil and may not produce much if anything at all in a poor summer. They're fairly dependable in southern Oregon. *Use only proven varieties, and best they be hybrids.*

SOW	HARVEST	TRANSPLANT
Early June	August to mid-September	N/A
POSITIONS	SEEDS	THIN TO
4 x 4 feet	Five per position	The best plant, progressively

Culture

Melon vines require loose, airy soils. Some heavy soils barely grow them if well loosened with organic matter. Melon vines won't grow until the soil warms to summertime temperatures, but they may acquire PMD while they're waiting; putting transplants out early is usually counterproductive.

Either start chitting melon seeds about June 10 for direct seeding into a bed covered with black plastic mulch or about June 1 start seedlings indoors (see Chapter 7). Either way, prepare their growing bed as though for cucumbers. Then spread a sheet of black plastic over the bed, and anchor the edges with soil or lengths of two-by-fours. Your goal is to warm the bed as much as possible, so keep the plastic clean so that it soaks up as much sun as possible. Just before putting chitted seeds into the ground or transplanting, cut out a 4-to-6-inch-diameter hole over each position. Spread a dozen slug pellets just under the plastic at each opening. If you don't do this, your seedlings may be catastrophically chewed away because the black plastic creates an ideal gastropod habitat. North of the Columbia, instead of black plastic try putting a 4-foot-wide tunnel cloche over the melon patch. If that doesn't make conditions warm enough, try spreading black plastic first and then putting a cloche over that. But be very careful if you use this solar-water-heater approach—until the vines completely cover the black plastic be sure to provide plenty of ventilation when the sun shines. Starting about August 1, remove all new female flowers to hasten the ripening of what is already on the vine.

Garden planning

I never harvested a fully ripe watermelon when I lived in chilly Lorane. I did harvest a few grapefruit-size cantaloupes in a good summer. Elkton, though, was melon paradise! In that banana belt a 100-square-foot bed of cantaloupes and honeydews overwhelmed us for about a month. Even watermelons produced. Because they go in rather late, melons fit in nicely after a cereal rye green manure. Rye makes the vines grow better because the soil is so finely fractured by decomposing roots.

Insects and diseases

By early September, lowered light intensity, cooler nights, and heavier dews combine to weaken even the most resistant varieties. Then the leaves mildew, all ripening ceases, and the immature fruit rots.

Harvest

When a cantaloupe or muskmelon is truly ripe it'll slip the vine (detach) when your thumb pushes gently on the stem where it connects to the fruit. Melons develop yellowish-orange tints as they vine ripen. Melons do not ripen after harvest! Supermarket cantaloupes were cleverly bred to show yellowish-orange tints sooner. They never equal the real deal. If held on the kitchen counter for a week or so, supermarket stuff may soften slightly, but it cannot become sweeter or tastier. Once I learned what a vine-ripened melon tastes like, I never bought another industrial cantaloupe.

Watermelons do not ripen after harvest and must be picked after knowledgeably tapping the side and listening to the hollow sound a firm tap makes. I regret I lack the vocabulary to explain better. You'll learn after you've thumped a half dozen watermelons and tried to enjoy eating the ones taken too soon.

Saving seed

When cantaloupes and muskmelons slip the vine, the seeds are mature. Remove the seeds and pulp, ferment them in a bowl for a few days, then pour into a sieve and wash the seeds clean. Spread them out to dry on newspaper several sheets thick. Seeds from fully ripe watermelons only require drying.

Cantaloupes have netted skins; they rarely or never (depends on the authority you consult) cross with muskmelons (honeydew), which have smooth skins; certainly neither crosses with watermelons. If I lived where summers were hot, I'd certainly know in which pollination group to assign all the exotic melons like Crenshaw and Santa Claus.

Varieties

Only a few open-pollinated varieties yield a few small melons in better summers. For cantaloupe, try Minnesota Midget (TSC). For watermelon, it is Sugar Baby or Moon and Stars (TSC). Adaptive Seeds has an interesting list of open-pollinated varieties; they must ripen at Sweet Home, Oregon. Nichols still offers one heirloom cantaloupe—Charentais. South of Drain, open-pollinated varieties do better.

When I go to the bother of growing melons, I intend to harvest plenty, so I grow hybrids. But most so-called early hybrids only yield sooner than regular hybrid varieties where nights are warm. And that's not Cascadia. Please only grow melon varieties offered by Cascadian suppliers. My favorite honeydew is Diplomat (WCO); it is far more reliable and far better tasting than Earli-Dew. Territorial and West Coast offer productive watermelon hybrids—especially Yellow Doll (WCO), but I expect Yellow Doll to soon disappear like Amira cucumber. I hope I'm wrong.

Dry gardening

Like cucumbers but less likely to succeed.

SQUASH and PUMPKINS

(various *Cucurbita* species)

All Cascadian districts produce summer squash abundantly. North of the Columbia and close to the Oregon coast, some winter squash varieties need every advantage to get fully ripe. My family eats a lot of squash in all its incarnations. We steam chunks of zucchini, mash them to pulp, add butter, and call it "splosh." I eat splosh like some people eat soup. I can eat volumes of it almost every day from the first zucchini to the last tiny ones we strip off the vine after it has been touched by frost. Native Americans relied upon winter squash. I think winter squash ranks right below potatoes for an independence-minded person.

SOW	HARVEST	TRANSPLANT
Late May	July to October	N/A
POSITIONS	SEEDS	THIN TO
Summer: 6 x 4 feet Winter: 100 sq. feet per plant	Five per position	The best plant, progressively

Culture

Prepare hills as for cucumbers but with more growing room. Best to position most summer squash varieties 6 feet apart down the center of a 4-foot-wide raised bed. Do not share the slightest bit of that huge empty space with any other crop; the squash plants will soon fill the entire area. Varieties bred for small spaces and containers can't use that much growing room.

Winter squash roots speed through loose, fertile, moist topsoil as far and as fast as the vines grow. You'll end up with more, larger squash by giving each *maxima* plant (see Saving Seed, page 291) at least 100 square feet of uncontested root zone; 150 square feet per plant is not too much for aggressive varieties. I am a show-off, so I dig up the long path between two beds and in that 10-by-25-foot space I start only two hills that soon support only one vine each. They get lots of side-dressing and soon cover the entire area with vines escaping down paths and over adjoining beds in every direction, proving that two beds' worth of root zone are not enough.

In the Willamette Valley *maxima* winter squash require every possible sunny day to fully ripen. Chitting the seeds before putting them in the ground provides a few more growing days with no risk of transplanting setback.

For both summer and winter varieties, place five seeds per position or hill, 1½ inches deep. Initially thin each position to two strong plants. As soon as winter squash vines start running, thin each position to one plant. Allow two open-pollinated summer squash plants per position until the first fruits form. Even high-quality, open-pollinated summer squash varieties occasionally throw off-type plants. So after you have harvested the first few fruit, remove the least-desirable plant by cutting it off at the base, leaving only one plant per hill or position. This radical surgery only makes production drop off for a week. Then you'll never know it happened. The result of that small sacrifice will be more to harvest later in the summer.

As the vines (or "bushes") expand, side-dress ever-larger COF doughnuts around them. Stop side-dressing when the crop runs out of growing room or at the latest, July 20.

Garden planning

Two uncrowded summer squash plants provide my household with a great excess most of the summer. Yield drops off around the end of August no matter what I do because the plants have become exhausted by heavy bearing. To harvest more during September, I suggest starting more plants about mid-July on closer spacing (3 by 4 feet) because they won't have the growing time to get large.

Winter squash grown two per position and with the usual amount of growing room experience fierce root-zone competition and produce around 50 pounds per hill. I prefer to give one plant 100 to 125 square feet of very fertile uncontested root zone; I harvest 150 pounds per plant. One year I *grew* a vine. I deeply dug and heavily fertilized new ground in 3-foot-wide doughnuts just ahead of the root system's expansion. The roots zoomed through this extremely loose, fertile soil. Two plants ended up covering about 500 square feet and produced 42 very large squash. Imagine what might have happened if I'd grown one of those giant jack-o'-lantern varieties with that much fertilizer and root zone and then only allowed one pumpkin to develop!

Insects and diseases

Seedlings that get infected with PMD often die, and if they seem to recover, don't grow fast. So be prepared to sow repeatedly in spring. Sowing again is cheap, effective insurance when it turns rainy and chilly while seeds are germinating. At summer's end, powdery mildew aggressively covers winter squash leaves.

Harvest

Summer squash are best eaten while they still have tender skins and haven't started forming seeds. Allowing seed to develop in even one fruit reduces the setting of new fruit. So harvest at less than half of full size and be vigilant: promptly remove overblown, overlooked squash.

Partly ripe winter squash have light-orange, less tasty flesh and thin seeds that sprout poorly, if at all. Really ripe squash have deep orange flesh, and the seeds will be fat and dense after drying. A completely ripe winter squash is attached to a shriveled brown stem that no longer transports nutrients. Only twice during nine Lorane summers did I achieve this degree of finish with *maxima* varieties. To encourage ripening, beginning about September 1, unburden the vine by removing every squash that isn't close to full size. These are unlikely to fully ripen in any case. And during the rest of September cut off all newly pollinated squash and remove all female flowers as soon as you notice them. The annoying side effect may be unwanted vines escaping down paths and over adjoining beds faster than would have happened had the vine been trying to ripen all those small fruit.

Allowing winter squash to remain unharvested after powdery mildew has covered most of the vine's leaves lowers storage potential. So does letting them go unharvested for more than a few days after the first frost has burned back the vine's leaf cover. To prevent rotting while in storage, I fill the kitchen sink with disinfecting-strength solution of laundry bleach and wash the just-harvested squash in it. Then I cure the skins by drying them at room temperature for a week or so. While curing, I rotate them every few days to make sure every bit of skin is exposed to good air circulation.

Winter squash stores best at a stable 55 degrees F, at low humidity, with air freely moving around them. I've had them keep fairly well when loosely stacked in a cool bedroom closet with the closet door open for more airflow. I've also had them keep poorly under the kitchen sink where humidity was high, air circulation poor, and temperatures warmer. The best choice between too warm (and low humidity) or cool and damp is warm and dry. The longest storage happens when no squash touches another and only one layer sits on a wood lattice that allows air circulation underneath them.

Saving seed

I know of four species: *Cucurbita pepo*, *C. maxima*, *C. mixta*, and *C. moschata*. Fortunately for the seed saver, *C. pepo*, the group that includes all summer squash, will not cross with *C. maxima*, the other main subfamily used in temperate climates.

C. pepo includes all the summer squashes of whatever shape and color, Halloween pumpkins, and small winter squashes including Acorn, Delicata, Sweet Dumpling, and Vegetable Spaghetti. There's also Gem (or Rôlet), a delicious globe-shaped summer squash with a vining habit originating from South Africa that stores and eats like a winter squash if you let it get fully mature.

Pepo varieties can usually make smaller seeds that don't make good eating.

The Willamette Valley summer provides around 140 frost-free days. To fully ripen its seeds, *pepo* requires that about 90 of these days be warm and sunny. Ripening *pepo* is a sure thing. In the cooler parts of Cascadia, *pepo* winter squash may be the reliable choice. Unfortunately, *pepo* varieties rarely keep for more than a few months.

Large, hard-skinned, longer-keeping winter squash such as Sweet Meat, Buttercup, Delicious, numerous Hubbards, and Japanese hybrids are *C. maxima*. Compared to *pepo*, *maxima* seeds are recognizably larger, require slightly more heat to sprout, and often make excellent nibbles. *C. maxima* varieties require about 120 warm, sunny growing days to completely ripen. Most summers the Willamette Valley enjoys just about 120 such days.

Butternut, *C. moschata*, needs 120 to 130 sunny, warm growing days for full maturity of fruit and seed. Except in the southern banana belts, most years Cascadian gardeners don't achieve fully ripe Butternuts.

After harvest, allow the squash to cure for at least a few weeks in a warm place while the seed finishes ripening, and then extract the seeds. Wash them free of pulp by rubbing in water, and then spread clean seed out on a screen or newspaper to dry. Fat, well-filled seeds will stay strong for more than seven years given dry, cool storage.

Carol Deppe says squash varieties can be propagated indefinitely from two to four plants with little risk of inbreeding depression of vigor.

Varieties

Hybrid vigor inevitably grows slightly faster, sets fruit sooner, yields more, and every hybrid plant makes perfect fruit. In consequence, open-pollinated summer squash varieties get less plant-breeder attention and now throw more than the occasional off-type.

The original Early Yellow Crookneck (EYCN—Territorial says they sell it) is the summer squash English settlers obtained from Native American gardeners. It makes a uniquely rich-tasting splosh compared to ordinary zucchini, green or yellow. I think that's because the genuine heirloom has a thick, warty, very oily skin. It is difficult to harvest EYCN without snapping necks off, and the variety is so leafy that the pale yellow squash are hard to spot. The heirloom grows so aggressively that it is the best candidate for I know dry gardening. Like almost every other garden seed supplier these days, Johnny's sells an "improved" version: uniform, attractive-looking darker yellow squash that are far easier to find in the more open bush but that lack both the thick, extremely rough skin and the original flavor.

In my opinion, most summer squash of whatever shape or color have an uninspiring flavor—except Gem and the sort variously named Lebanese, Middle Eastern, or Gray (Magda, JSS; Cavili, TSC). Costata Romanesco makes a larger-than-usual aggressively growing bush that makes the richest-tasting green zucchini I know of. Given the opportunity, Costata will occupy half again more space than a typical bush summer squash, if not double. Its ovaries start out twice the size of other varieties, and its male flowers are equally huge. Most zucchini varieties require harvesting before they're 10 inches long because at this size they start developing seeds and tough skins. Costata can get 16 inches long before it starts to toughen up.

In my opinion Delicata and its variants like Sweet Dumpling have the richest flavor of all the *pepo* winter varieties. They're better keepers than the popular Acorns but still don't store nearly as long as *C. maxima* varieties.

In trials at short-season Lorane, nearly every *maxima* variety matured *in a good summer*. In a cool summer you'll wish you'd grown the strain of Sweet Meat that was restored and improved by Carol Deppe. She intended it to be the most productive, delicious, and reliable winter squash for Cascadia. Nichols sells it.

My hat's off to Nichols for selling Queensland Blue (QB) and Triamble—Australian "pumpkins." Down Under vocabulary seems upside down to Americans. Aussies say "pumpkin" when Americans say "winter squash." Aussies hardly know what to call that strange thing Americans cut faces into. The flesh of Aussie pumpkins is firmer, drier, and less sweet than American winter squash. It is entirely delicious when you roast it. It also makes savory pumpkin soup as well as sweet. QB develops such hard, gnawing-kangaroo-proof skin that it keeps for nine months. QB loves the mainland's heat but fails to fully ripen some years on Tasmania. Tasmanian gardeners don't grow Triamble; it better suits scorching Western Australia. Be cautious with these: I'm sure they'll perform in southern Cascadia. I wish Nichols offered Sweet Gray, Tasmania's equivalent of Sweet Meat.

Dry gardening

Make hills for summer squash 8 by 8 feet apart; dry garden winter squash on at least a 10-by-10-foot grid. Fertigate at least four times—the first time a small amount shortly after emergence, then a gallon when the vines begin running, and at least two more fertigations of about 5 gallons each every few weeks through the end of August. Locate the fertigation bucket as close to the plant's center as possible. The original Yellow Crookneck and Costata Romanesco are the best survival summer squash varieties. Most winter squash varieties, *pepo* or *maxima*, are likely candidates but avoid those with a bush habit.

Alliums

Leeks, shallots, scallions, onions, and garlic are alliums. All of these vegetables are frost-hardy biennials; all of them except a few onion varieties grow vegetatively until change of day length triggers reproduction, bulbing, or seed formation. Once reproduction begins, no new leaves develop. A variety flips into reproductive mode on roughly the same date every year. With bulbing alliums, the size the top has achieved when bulbing starts determines the ultimate size. So in order to harvest big onions or garlic, you must encourage vegetative growth while it is still possible.

Alliums require abundant nutrients and airy, moist soil to grow fast. Think of them in vegetative growth mode as a high-demand crop with a weak root system. Once bulbing starts, alliums have little use for soil nutrients but still need moisture. In the final weeks of bulbing the plant withdraws nutrients from its leaves, making the tops weaken and fall over. I make the last side-dressing about one month before the stems begin to swell into bulbs. Alliums store moisture in thick-walled juicy leaves. Consequently, once they've gained a bit of size, alliums can slide through a week of moisture stress while giving hardly a sign of difficulty other than making little or no growth. Gardeners usually don't notice this happening until the yield turns out disappointingly small. So keep their soil damp. And fertile. And before sowing, do whatever is necessary to make sure it stays loose while the crop grows. A young seedling's roots do not penetrate any deeper than the slow-growing tops reach. So in addition to irrigating the entire garden, I am prepared to hand-water allium crops a few times between germination and when they're about 6 inches tall.

The allium's root system does not thrive in tight soil. Prepare clay by first digging in an inch-thick layer of compost in addition to the usual COF. On heavy soil, if onions were thinned properly but failed to bump in the row at harvest, or if garlic heads are small, try tighter interplant spacing next year and you'll probably end up with more medium-size onions or more small heads of garlic from the same space. If your soil is loamy or sandy, but your onions or garlic are small, then irrigate more often and/or feed them more.

Starting from seeds results in harvesting the longest-storing bulb onions and is the most economical way. Allium seeds will germinate in chilly soil, but their delicate shoots can't emerge through crust or hard soil. If "crusty" or "hard" describes your soil, there's some useful techniques to coax better germination out of it in Chapter 6. Allium seed doesn't store for many years, so there's a lot of weak stuff sold. Consequently, many gardeners raise big onions by planting little ones, even though the storage potential of onions grown from sets never equals that of onions from seeds.

Allium seedlings with shafts ³⁄₁₆ inch in diameter or larger transplant easily with naked roots. Transplants for leeks and overwintering onions are easiest to grow to this husky size in outdoor nursery beds, a procedure I describe in detail under "Leeks."

Insects rarely cause problems. There is a common yield-reducing onion pest, thrips. Commercial growers find it profitable to reduce their population with pesticides. Home gardeners rarely notice thrips. (See Chapter 8.)

Diseases attack allium leaves when humidity is high and especially when the plants have poor air circulation. If there is a windier part of the winter garden, this is where to concentrate alliums. (Allium leaves have an aerodynamic shape that is not easily damaged by wind.) Industrial onion and garlic crops require fungicides because they grow on soils that are not fully remineralized. If you use COF, follow my spacing suggestions, and have free-draining soil, you may never see any disease. Allium crops have a high need for sulfur and often grow much better when fed some. The gypsum in COF provides abundant sulfur. If you don't use COF, at least spread the amount of gypsum in COF on the allium beds.

Brassicas grow well after alliums.

Allium flowers are insect pollinated; varieties in the same species have to be isolated by 1,500 feet for fair purity (commercial seed fields are separated by a mile). Commercially grown allium seed usually is short lived—expect it to last no more than three years at normal household temperature and humidity. Your own seeds grown in fully remineralized soil can easily last five years under those conditions. To reduce inbreeding depression of vigor, involve at least 25 plants in a seed production. The Organic Seed Alliance specifies a minimum population of between 80 and 200 plants, depending on the allium species.

Bulbing onions, shallots, and garlic store best at 50 degrees F with enough air circulation and exchange to maintain low humidity. If you store them in mesh bags, they should be hung with air on all sides. The very best storage comes from plaiting onions or garlics and hanging the braids. I even braid shallots. As with pumpkins, if you have to choose between cool but too damp conditions or dry but too warm, choose warm and dry.

GARLIC *(Allium sativum)* ## and SHALLOTS *(A. cepa)*

Garlic and shallot crops start growing in autumn and are harvested early next summer. They store much better if they mature in dryish soil. Most garlic varieties finish late May to early June. If it rains much within 10 days of the garlic harvest, or if you should irrigate at that time, you may harvest some (or many) rotting bulbs. Shallots finish weeks later than garlic, so they almost always cure in ideal weather. In an unusually rainy year, rather than lose many heads to rot, the garlic crop can be lifted up to one week prematurely. But if you harvest too early, the cloves don't form properly and you'll end up with nothing.

SOW	HARVEST	TRANSPLANT
Late September to mid-October	June to early July	N/A
BETWEEN ROWS	SEEDS	THIN TO
Garlic: 18 inches	Garlic: 1 clove every 4 inches	N/A
Shallots: 12 inches	Shallot: 1 bulb every 12 inches	

Culture

Garlic bulbs form just below the soil's surface. For them to swell up large, the soil must remain loose through the entire spring after having been pounded on by winter rains for months. So when growing garlic in clayey soils, first dig in an inch-thick layer of compost. After that, if garlic still doesn't produce well in your heavy ground, consider trying shallots. They form bulbs on the surface and aren't quite so fussy about soil conditions. And keep using COF; it is designed to gradually loosen tight soils.

Each garlic clove you plant becomes a head containing many cloves. Shallots are small bulbing onions that multiply; plant one and harvest a cluster. In both cases I only plant the largest cloves or shallots because these grow noticeably larger plants. Prepare the bed with the usual COF and compost. Plant both garlic and shallot late September through mid-October, one clove or bulb per position with the top of the clove or bulb 1 inch below the surface, root side (flattened end) down. Position garlic cloves 4 to 6 inches apart in the row, and make the rows 18 inches apart. With shallots, depending on soil fertility, past performance, and the variety, arrange positions 12 to 14 inches apart in rows 12 to 14 inches apart. If shallots are arranged in a near perfect hexagonal grid, then hoeing weeds will prove much easier.

Garlic and shallot have the potential to make useful growth in winter. Shortly after sprouting, side-dress COF close to the row. To end up with really large garlic or shallot bulbs, when the daffodils emerge, thoroughly weed the bed and side-dress. This is enough side-dressing for early finishing garlic varieties. Late-to-mature garlic varieties and shallots make more vegetative growth if given yet another side-dressing mid-April.

Garden planning

Depending on variety, garlic is harvested from late May through June. Shallots are lifted late June to early July. Each garlic clove you plant becomes a bulb containing 7 to 15 cloves. How many cloves depends on the variety; how large they will be depends on the grower's skill and the soil. One shallot yields from 5 to 12 depending on the variety and growing conditions. Our household consumes most of the production from 75 square feet of garlic and about half that in shallots.

The amounts of space we assign to brussels sprouts and garlic are about equal. I have already mentioned this crop rotation: In year one, main crop storage potatoes; immediately after digging spuds, plant garlic and shallots. In year two, shortly after harvesting garlic, sow brussels sprouts. Following shallots, plant autumn brassicas.

Insects and diseases

Leaf diseases strike when air circulation is poor and humidity is high. If you use COF and the generous interplant spacing my book recommends and still see leaf diseases, try increasing interplant spacing even more. Also read *The Intelligent Gardener*, get a soil test, and fully balance the soil.

Like potato viruses, garlic viruses and—even worse—garlic diseases can reside in the cloves. Viruses reduce yield. Extension service literature gives a long, scary list of seed-transmitted microbial and fungal diseases that can prevent you from growing garlic for a great many years. Best start with reputable seed.

Root rot happens during winter if the soil becomes too compacted and airless. Balancing the soil's calcium to magnesium ratio is the most hopeful remedy because it improves drainage and increases the air supply. Regular use of COF should gradually accomplish that. Digging in an inch-thick layer of compost before planting also helps.

Harvest

Hardneck garlic varieties put up a seedstalk at the same time bulb formation begins. The seeds on top actually are a cluster of tiny garlic cloves, often called "bulblets." The best practice is to pinch off the emerging seed head as soon as it can be distinguished. Do this and harvest bigger

bottoms; some assert they'll be one-third larger and heavier. When hardneck garlic dries down, a hard, seedstalk remains in the core. Hardnecks do not store as long as softnecks but often are more potent. Occasionally one bulb in a cluster of shallot bulbs will emit a flower stalk that would form seed like any other onion. I pinch these off the moment they are spotted.

To increase hardneck planting stock in a great hurry, start with top bulblets. But by planting a bulblet you'll only harvest a "rondelle," a single, much larger than usual, round, unsegmented clove. In northern Europe special dishes are prepared using rondelles. If rondelles are planted, they produce a regular-size segmented head. With some varieties it takes more than two years to go from bulblet to a segmented head. Growing from bulblets does not eliminate virus diseases.

The longest-storing garlic is lifted from dryish soil *a few days after* the heads have fully segmented and formed internal skins that have begun to dry. At this point the leaves are browning off; how withered they look depends on the variety. As harvest approaches, I check for maturity every few days by digging one bulb for the kitchen. You won't waste anything by doing this. An immature garlic that has not yet fully segmented is still useful when minced like a big onion. Do not delay harvesting! If hardneck garlic is allowed to remain in the ground too long, even one week after it should have been dug, the bulbs split open around the stem, soil enters, and storage life is reduced. If this garlic was intended to be a homestead cash crop, it now is worth much less. If the crop experiences rain or irrigation within one week of harvest, it may adsorb so much moisture that it rots after harvest. Cascadian weather is usually trustworthy at harvest time, but if rain threatens, the uncertainty can be agonizing.

After drying for a few days under cover (we use the garage floor), the dirty wrappers strip away easily if you pull the outside leaves down and off. But delay too many days and the outer leaves become too brittle to peel. The clean heads must continue to dry/cure until the tops have withered enough to plait or be cut off. Delay plaiting and the leaves get too brittle. Even hardneck varieties can be braided if you have strong hands. Or else hang bundles with stalks attached, or after the necks have *thoroughly* dried, clip tops and hang the bulbs in mesh onion sacks.

Many gardeners have great success growing garlic and see income potential in it. Anyone thinking of growing garlic for sale should first consider manifesting the temporary labor force needed to peel and process the harvest. Growing several varieties gives the possibility of spreading the harvest workload over as much as a month and reduces the risk that one unseasonable rain at harvest time will ruin the entire crop. And please consider that industrial crops are grown around Gilroy, California, on light soils in the perfect winter climate and where spring can be counted on to be dry.

Shallot leaves wither like bulbing onions. Shallots should be harvested when all the bulbs have gone the shallot equivalent of tops down—the leaves have wilted and are starting to brown off. Separate the clusters into individual bulbs, spread them out on a tarp, under cover, and let them finish drying thoroughly or they'll soon rot at the neck. We have tried various ways to prevent shallots from rotting in storage; the best is to make long, hanging braids before the leaves have become too brittle to plait. It might seem a ridiculous amount of work to braid shallots, but because the leaves are soft and thin, they plait rapidly. Also, since shallots are lightweight, the braids can be long.

Saving seed

Every head of garlic I've ever broken apart contains a mixture of clove sizes. To harvest the largest bulbs, plant only the larger cloves from the finest-looking heads. In my garden, garlic started from big cloves ends up 25 percent larger than those grown from small cloves. Shallots coming from one cluster also vary in size. Always plant the largest, finest shallots from the previous crop.

Hardneck garlic does not routinely make viable seeds. As far as I know, softnecks never make seeds. Some types of shallots do make seed, though these are still best propagated from bulbs. Ted Meredith's *The Complete Book of Garlic: A Guide for Gardeners, Growers, and Serious Cooks* (Timber Press, 2008) may be the best book available on garlic. Among other things it explains how to induce hardneck garlic to produce true seed. This allows the breeding of new virus-free varieties because virus diseases are not transmitted by seeds.

Varieties

In the 1980s supermarket garlic was grown near Gilroy; those varieties grow okay in Cascadia. In those days the source of unusual varieties was Italian, Greek, and Korean grocery stores.

These days American supermarkets offer semi-tropical varieties imported from China that do not grow well in Tasmania—the same latitude as Cascadia. Fortunately, these days Territorial and Adaptive offer many varieties. Territorial also has several shallot varieties, some started from actual seeds.

Elephant garlic is an easier-to-grow garlic look-alike. It is really a leek. The elephant garlic plant is several times larger than true garlic; the cloves are enormous. If you choose to grow elephant, arrange the bed with 8 inches between plants in the row, rows 24 inches apart. Unlike the real thing, elephant garlic makes viable seed that forms in flowering globes larger than those made by onions. Elephant has a serious downside. Like gladiolus, it forms tiny, loosely attached corms that detach during harvest and come up later. The seeds, too, can naturalize. And the flavor is only similar to real garlic. Gourmets shun elephant garlic, but Marina, who shuns ordinary garlic, loves eating it.

Dry gardening

Cascadian garlic grows fine without irrigation. Increase interplant spacing; make it 6 to 8 inches apart in rows 2 feet apart. It's okay if you have to delay planting until rain moistens the ground, but the harvest will be larger if the crop is started sooner. Garlic matures on natural moisture if given careful weeding, and perhaps mulch spread on sandy ground in April. Remove the mulch when harvest time approaches to allow the topsoil to dry. Shallots mature later than garlic does, so they may run out of soil moisture before bulbing initiates; the result will be small bulbs.

LEEKS (*Allium porrum*)

My domestic goddess says her kitchen requires plenty of onions. She also opines that alliums are nature's health food, while the only unsprayed, nutrient-dense onions available to us at any price come from my garden. So I keep my precious DG well supplied all year. What to use during winter? In my opinion, the easiest and most certain crop is leeks.

Locally grown onions don't always store well. Leeks eliminate this problem. Leeks are dug as needed from October until April. They rarely freeze out. In very heavy soil where a bulbing onion would barely grow, leeks do okay. Chefs say leeks are superior for cooking. I find leeks far milder in winter salads than storage onions.

SOW	HARVEST	TRANSPLANT
Late April	September to late March	Mid-July, 4 to 24 inches
BETWEEN ROWS	**SEEDS**	**THIN TO**
12 inches	16 per inch in a nursery bed	8 seedling per inch

Culture

Leeks grow to supermarket size when they're treated like a medium-demand crop. Leeks grow even larger when fertilized like a high-demand crop and given enough growing room. Like all alliums, leeks do best in light, loamy soil. When they must be grown on clayey soil, first loosen up their root zone by blending in a heavy dose of compost.

Leeks are slow growing. Transplants need nearly three months after germination to achieve the diameter of a lead pencil. Transplanting the spindly seedlings found on garden center sales benches is painstaking and not always successful. It's far more effective and a lot less work to raise husky leek transplants in an outdoor nursery bed. Leek seedlings take a long time to get roots down deep, so they only grow (relatively) fast when they get irrigated more often than most crops. For this reason I locate my nursery bed close to a hose tap.

Sow leek seeds the last half of April. Four row feet provide enough transplants to fill a bed that supplies our kitchen all winter. A 4-by-4-foot nursery holding three such rows can become enough leeks to equal several hundred pounds of storage onions and to gift much-appreciated transplant bundles to friends and neighbors. Leek seedling bundles could also be a profitable homestead cash crop.

Start the leek nursery by turning the top 4 inches of a 4-by-4-foot area into potting mix. Using a common garden hoe, vigorously and deeply chop in a 1-inch-thick layer of well-aged compost and a quart of COF. You could substitute, or better, also include an inch of sphagnum moss or even better, coir (coco peat). On clayey soils spread compost 2 inches thick and chop it in deeply. All this organic matter later lets you lift the transplants with more roots still attached. Then rake out a level seedbed, make 3-inch-deep furrows 12 inches apart, and sow about 16 seeds per inch. Cover with loose soil. Thin any seedling clusters; try to end up with a fairly uniformly spaced eight seedlings per inch—that's extremely tight and soon going to be very crowded, but you want the seedlings to compete so that they grow slender and tall.

Leeks turn out to be better to eat when the transplants are leggy, because the blanched (white) stem forming below the soil line is the tastiest part. The deeper the transplant can be buried, the longer the white part will be. Even more of the stem gets blanched if you pull soil up against it as it grows. Harvest the longest white stems by transplanting into a trench that is gradually filled in as the leeks grow, after which even more soil is drawn up against them.

Dig the transplants when the largest have achieved pencil thickness. This will be around mid-July. Gently shake them apart; avoid damaging the roots more than absolutely necessary. If the nursery soil has become too compact to crumble away from the roots without causing massive damage, blast the soil off with a moderately strong water jet from hose and nozzle. Then make handful-size seedling bundles with bases carefully aligned, and then with a sharp knife cut off about one-third of the leaves. Surgery reduces transplanting shock; they'll resume growing a lot quicker if you do this. Temporarily store the clipped seedlings in a bucket, roots down. I put a quarter inch of water in the bottom of the bucket to keep the roots moist before transplanting, but not so much as to put them underwater. You'll shock the seedlings less if you can transplant on a cloudy day. Best to transplant immediately, although putting an airtight bag of clipped seedlings into the fridge for a day or two won't do them any major harm.

Two parallel long rows of mature leeks barely fit a 4-foot-wide raised bed. If the bed is less than 4 feet wide, put a single row down the bed's center. Spread a double dose of COF and some compost. Dig in or till in these amendments. Go deep. Then, using a common garden hoe, make a very deep furrow (try for more than 4 inches) down the entire length of the bed, or if the bed is wide enough, a parallel pair of them at least 24 inches apart.

Then place seedlings 4 inches apart in the furrow. One by one spread out the roots as best you can and cover them an inch deep while holding the seedling upright. Gently compress enough soil over the roots and around the stem to keep them upright. Do the entire length of the row. Immediately side-dress more COF in a band extending no more than 6 inches to either side of the row of transplants. Side-dress generously. Then gently refill the furrow, and while doing that try not to get any soil trapped in the leaf notches.

Finally, hand-water the seedlings. If the weather turns particularly hot during the next week, water every few days. After that water them whenever the rest of the garden needs moisture.

I suggest feeding so much fertilizer because leeks will respond by getting much larger sooner, and because once you begin hilling up, the actively feeding root zone ends up too far below the surface to benefit much from side-dressing.

Does accomplishing all that sound like a lot of work? Preparing and growing the nursery bed, preparing 100 square feet that'll produce 50 row feet of mature leeks, digging and transplanting seedlings into it: the whole thing combined takes me around four hours. In exchange we harvest many more leeks than we can use all winter.

Ongoing, eliminate the weeds while drawing soil up against the stems much like hilling potatoes. Take care not to get soil into the leaf notches, and do not cover the stem above the bottom leaf notch. As the leeks' height increases, continue to scrape up soil against them with a common hoe. If you squeeze two parallel long rows down a 4-foot-wide raised bed, then sometime in September the leaves will have spread so far you won't be able to hill up any more soil. If the rows are farther apart (or there is a single long row on a bed), you should be able to keep hilling up until winter and end up with even longer white stalks.

If you want to harvest the largest-possible leeks with even longer white shafts, start out by superfertilizing the subsoil before you fertilize the topsoil. (See Potatoes, page 271.) And then set them 6 inches apart into a furrow at least 6 inches deep.

Garden planning

Cascadian home gardeners shouldn't hope varieties bred for late summer/early autumn harvest can supply the kitchen in winter. Summer/autumn leeks grow faster but lack hardiness. I usually grow 50 row feet of leeks: 10 row feet of autumn leeks, the rest for winter and early spring. I transplant leek seedlings into a bed where I recently harvested peas.

I start digging leeks in October, working my way down the row as the kitchen demands them. Most varieties go to seed in April.

Insects and diseases

I've grown leeks for 40 years and have had no insect or leaf disease trouble. In microclimates with especially rainy winters, as a precaution I'd space them 6 inches apart in the row for better air circulation.

Harvest

Leeks must be dug. Many people waste the leafy tops, but these are as useful as any other onion when making soup stock. Once flowering initiates, the core of the leek becomes too woody to use, but for a few more weeks some useful food still comes from the outer half of the shaft.

Saving seed

Leeks do not cross with other alliums. Provide isolation of about 1,500 feet. Choose seed-making plants as you dig leeks for the table. Except for short, fat heirlooms, select individuals with a lot of distance between the base and the first **leaf joint** and without bulbous bottoms (an undesirable trait). Transplant selected leeks into a bed that will not have to be watered with the rest of the garden when the flowers start drying down. Set the stem's base about 6 inches deep, plants 1 foot apart in the row, the rows 2 feet apart. You may transplant straight back into the bed they were dug from. The experts say there should be at least 80 plants in each seed production—I've grown my variety, Durabel, from only 20 to 25 plants for three generations without experiencing any inbreeding depression of vigor that I can notice.

The seed patch requires irrigation through summer. Around September, the balloon-shaped flowers will, irregularly, one at a time, show the still-moist black seeds they contain, suggesting it may be time to harvest that particular flower. It also indicates it's time to stop watering and hope it doesn't rain. To check if a seedstalk is ready to harvest, try to gently draw it out of the soil. If it pulls out easily, it was ready. If it resists, there still are active roots; tug it again in a few days.

Seeds continue ripening for weeks after you harvest the stalk. Hang the stalks upside down over a tarp or spread them over a tarp and wait. After the entire stalk has browned off and dried out, the seed heads themselves still won't be completely dry. One particularly humid autumn I had to cut the flower balls off their dried-out stems and bring them into the house to get really dry. When the flowers are crisp through and through, crush and rub them between your (gloved) hands. I keep the resulting mixture of seeds and chaff in a woven plastic feed/fertilizer sack over the winter and winnow it on a warm, sunny day next spring. Frankly, it's not easy to sow allium seed thinly enough; having the seeds mixed with chaff is only good when it gets distributed by hand.

Varieties

High-quality leek seed originates from northern Europe. Hybrids are marginally more vigorous and perfectly uniform. Well-maintained OP varieties can be uniform enough and productive. All the seed sellers I recommend offer a broad range of excellent varieties.

Autumn leeks are faster growing, more tender, and less pungent than winter varieties. In exchange they are unlikely to survive Cascadian winter.

North American seed sellers often call these "summer" leeks. *Winter leeks* are bred for ultimate hardiness, so they're tougher and more pungent than autumn leeks.

Dry gardening

I've never done it, but I think it is possible. Start an irrigated nursery bed at the end of May; choose a winter variety. Do not start the nursery with a double dose of COF. Do not try to make them grow especially fast. Make the nursery rows 18 inches apart, sow less seed, and thin progressively to ½ inch apart in the row. Give the nursery just enough water to keep it healthy over the summer. Do not side-dress. Transplant in October or sooner in the rare year there's significant rain in September. You'll harvest December through March. Position them closer in the row: they'll be like giant scallions at harvest.

ONIONS AND SCALLIONS *(Allium cepa)*

Bulbing onions can be started with seeds, transplants, or sets. I discourage the use of sets because onions started that way frequently go to seed prematurely or else make poor-keeping double bulbs. Sets do avoid one obstacle many gardeners find overwhelming—getting onion seed to sprout and become established. Yet I've never experienced an in-the-field germination failure with onion seed that would sprout well in a germ lab.

North America grows three types of bulbing onions and three sorts of scallions. If you choose a type incorrect for your location, or for the time of year you are sowing it, your crop produces less, or nothing. I could simply instruct "buy from a Cascadian seed seller and you'll have no problems," but it's best if you are empowered. Please read on; you'll soon know your onions.

Short-day bulbing onions grow vegetatively during winter's short days and form bulbs in spring. They are sown at the end of summer, make slow progress through winter, resume growing rapidly when the daffodils first emerge, get large in spring, and bulb in May/June. Short-day varieties usually are soft and lack pungency; some are so mild I eat them like apples. They don't store many months. I've grown half-pungent varieties that kept until mid-November.

Intermediate-day-length varieties are grown in central California. Before hybrids took over, intermediate-day-length varieties were called "Sweet Spanish." I wouldn't mention intermediate-day onion varieties at all, but many garden seed catalogs offer them without distinguishing their ecological niche. They don't suit Cascadia very well.

Long-day varieties fit latitudes between 40 to 55 degrees F—the north United States and southern Canada. They're usually bred for long storage. Onions must be pungent to keep a long time. Storage is enhanced by thin, hard-fleshed rings and thick, many-layered scales wrapping the bulb. Long-day varieties are spring sown, and finish in August and September. Only early long-day varieties work in Cascadia because in August they cure before conditions turn humid. A few long-day varieties are salad quality—mild, sweet, and tender—but they can't be stored for many months.

Early varieties don't produce the largest onions. If you want to harvest long-day lunkers, start early-maturing varieties indoors late in February and transplant them out after the weather has settled.

Scallions (all varieties) form thin, tender, translucent outer skins. Some are late-maturing bulbing varieties that are used as scallions before bulbing starts. If sown in spring, they'll reach useful size by summer and still be useful in September. Lisbon can be sown anytime from spring through midsummer. When spring sown, it makes very poor bulbs in summer that fail to go tops down; instead the plants produce more scallions. Midsummer sowings produce nicer-looking scallions in autumn and winter. Lisbon goes to seed in spring. Welsh onions are a different species (*A. fistulosum*) that is spring or summer sown, multiplies over winter, and then goes to seed in spring. They do not bulb. *Fistulosum* are pungent, rather coarse textured, and far hardier than Lisbon.

SOW	HARVEST	TRANSPLANT
Storage: late March Overwintered: August Scallions: mid-March to mid-July	Storage: mid-August to mid-September Overwintered: late May to mid-June Scallions: mid-May to mid-March	N/A

BETWEEN ROWS	SEEDS	THIN TO
18 inches	All types: three per inch	Storage: 2 inches Overwintered: 1 inch before winter Scallions: thin by harvesting

Culture

Onions of all sorts grow large when you treat them as high-demand crops that have an especially high need for moisture when they are small.

Sweet Spanish varieties can be made productive in Cascadia by starting them indoors very early in spring and transplanting out substantial seedlings. Set out transplants 3 to 4 inches apart in rows at least 18 inches apart. They may be very late to finish; they may not keep long.

Storage onions can't grow much in the Willamette during March, even though the seed may germinate. I think you'll end up harvesting more by sowing late March/early April. Starting later than this produces noticeably smaller bulbs.

Sow the seed ½ inch deep, three seeds per inch, in rows 18 inches apart. Side-dress soon after they sprout. Thin the row progressively so that the plants end up about 2 inches apart in the row.

Overwintered onions. Discovering the correct sowing date for your location is essential. Sow too late and they don't get large enough to survive winter. But *don't sow too early* because when shaft diameter exceeds pencil thickness during in winter, they go to seed in spring rather than forming bulbs. If you sow on the cusp of "too early," some plants will go to seed in spring. In frosty Lorane, I sowed on August 1; in Elkton, where I got more growth during winter, I found September 1 to be best. The first time you grow overwintering onions, I suggest testing three sowing dates: August 1 and 15, and September 1.

Start overwintering onions as a low-demand crop because you must prevent them from getting too large during winter and because they may be hardier if not pushed. Arrange the bed as for storage onions, but sow more seed because some young plants vanish during winter. Have them standing 1 inch apart in the row as the crop goes into winter.

When spring regrowth begins (usually the crocuses come up at the same time), treat overwintering onions like a high-demand crop. Thoroughly weed the bed, thin the surviving onions to 2 inches apart in the row, and side-dress generously. If your soil has not gotten too compact over the winter, excess onion seedlings can be gently tugged out with plenty of roots still attached. These can be transplanted into any gaps, used to establish new beds, or given to friends. Thinnings may also be replanted densely for use as scallions over the next few months. Side-dress again mid-March. Bulbing begins in May, so there's no net benefit from side-dressing in April because too much nitrogen in the soil while bulbs form lowers quality.

Scallions. Lisbon and Welsh onions may be sown from April through July. They will over-winter on tight spacing; thin these by harvesting. Sweet Spanish varieties are sown March/April. When well established, thin to about ¼ inch apart in the row. They'll be done by October.

Garden planning

With bulbing onions, one row foot yields 2 to 4 pounds. Long-day storage varieties usually keep until next spring. How long into spring depends on the variety, how well they cured, and the storage conditions. Nonpungent varieties don't last that long.

Later-to-finish overwintering varieties keep from July until Christmas but aren't so sweet and mild. Nonpungent varieties like Walla Walla finish in June; these are so soft they inevitably resprout within a few months of harvest.

It hardly takes four row feet of scallions to supply my kitchen in summer, but as good as Lisbon scallions are in salads, sweet and tender short-day onions are better.

Insects and diseases

I've had no problems with thrips, probably because I never bothered to look closely enough to spot them. And perhaps I never noticed thrips because I was not, like onion farmers must, pre-cisely measuring my enormous yield.

I don't ignore onion leaf diseases; they can devastate a bed. The best garden preventives I know of are better air circulation achieved by wider interplant spacing and growing the crop in fully remineralized soil.

Harvest

Bulbing onions. Newbies, the second time you grow bulbing onions, stop watering a week before the tops go down and ask that it doesn't rain until the bulbs have cured. Bulbs that split into distinct parts (called "doublers" by onion growers) do not keep long. Eat them first. Onions that start bulbing and then put up a seedstalk (bolters) do not form proper bulbs. This plant should be pulled and eaten as a giant scallion at the first sign of a flower stalk.

When half the tops have naturally fallen over, push over the tops that are still standing, wait a week, and then lift the onions. Brush off any large bits of soil clinging to their roots. Then spread them out under cover to finish drying. Commercial growers dry onions in the field, but **I think slow, uniform drying makes a longer-keeping onion.** Mine cure excellently spread out on the garage floor with the door fully open during the day and mostly closed at night.

To store onions, I braid them when their leaves have pretty much dried down but have not yet become brittle. I only put about 10 pounds of onions in each braid so that it won't break while hanging.

Alternatively, after the leaves have fully dried (especially the neck of the onion must have fully dried), clip the tops and store the bulbs in recycled onion sacks. Onions put into sacks with wet necks may rot. Either way, braids or sacks, it's best to hang them in a dimly lit, well-ventilated **place with low humidity and stable, cool conditions: 50 to 55 degrees F is perfect.** Warmer and dry is better than colder and damp, but anywhere with good air circulation that doesn't go below 40 degrees F in winter will serve.

Scallions. Harvest them by thinning the row. Either gently tug the plant out of the ground or, if your soil is hard, cut its roots off below the soil line with a sharp knife. Lisbons multiply; they're capable of refilling their row as fast as you thin. During winter scallions may appear badly weather damaged, but you'll be amazed at how good they look once the tops are cut back to about two-thirds their length and the outer skins and damaged leaves have been removed.

Saving seed

Plant near-perfect bulbs that are sprouting, or soon will be. Bury them shallowly; barely cover the neck. Space them 12 to 16 inches apart in rows 24 inches apart. The bulbs resprout, grow tops (sometimes overwinter), flower, and form seed in summer. Sometimes the flower stalks require support to keep them erect. The seed is harvested and processed much like leek seed, but it finishes much faster. The stalks mature over a few weeks' time. Cut them off close to the ground when black seeds begin showing but before too many fall out.

Open-pollinated varieties are out of vogue and often throw less productive offtype plants. However, by starting with a large population and selecting from it only near-perfect bulbs to make seed with, in a few generations a degenerated variety can be restored.

Overwintered onions. If you sow short-day varieties too early, you'll end up with seedstalks next spring instead of bulbs. Even if you want to grow seed, you shouldn't produce it this way because the main breeding effort on all overwintering varieties has been to suppress seed making the first winter. Also, there is no way to eliminate plants that would have made imperfect bulbs because you never see finished bulbs. Grow seed from carefully selected near-perfectly configured bulbs replanted immediately *after* they resprout, usually in September/October. They'll overwinter like giant scallions and make seed that dries down next summer. Onions that haven't sprouted in storage by late October could be planted out anyway because cold, wet conditions induce sprouting. Selecting in that direction leads to longer storage potential and more pungency.

Storage onion seed is grown from true-to-type bulbs that are planted back out when they resprout in spring. Reject early sprouters. If your variety has not yet resprouted by the end of April, plant some bulbs anyway; outdoor conditions will induce sprouting. Select for configuration (round, or flattened, or whatever) and narrow necks (usually keep better). It has been my experience that globe-shaped storage onions keep better and are more pungent than those with flattened tops.

Scallions. Welsh and Lisbon onions go to seed after overwintering. I've never bothered to make individual plant selections; I collect seed from the bed I was eating from last winter. Welsh onions do not cross with *Allium cepa* varieties.

Varieties

Long- and intermediate-day-length. Milestone (TSC) is a mild, sweet, early maturing variety with decent storage potential. So is Candy (WCO, JSS). Alisa Craig is the traditional mild salad variety but doesn't keep as long. Osborne's offering may confuse: in addition to what grows great west of the Cascades, they sell hybrid Sweet Spanish storage onion crosses to farmers east of the Cascades. Cascadians should only use Osborne's earliest-maturing varieties. Adaptive offers a useful open-pollinated storage variety, Newburg, bred by Alan Kapuler. Stokes, as always, has the largest assortment involving all types.

Red onions usually are storage types that happen to make red skins, but I have grown short-day red varieties that were as mild and sweet as the yellow- or brown-skinned ones. Pickling onions usually are early maturing bulbing onions bred for thin, tender, translucent skins that don't require peeling. Picklers are grown on very close spacing.

Overwintered varieties. There are several strains of Walla Walla. All local seed companies (except Adaptive) sell this poor-keeping, very mild, and tender variety. Osborne sells a Walla Walla strain for early fresh market sales that matures a few weeks earlier but makes thick necks (low storage potential); Osborne also offers a later-maturing longer-storing Walla Walla strain. Avoid overwintering varieties bred for southern latitudes, often called Grano or Granex. If they do survive winter in Cascadia, they bulb before they get large enough. Incidentally, northern overwintering varieties can be started indoors early in spring and transplanted out. They'll top down a few weeks later than usual and will end up somewhat smaller but will still be quite sweet.

Scallions with Japanese names are almost certainly Welsh onions. Some Lisbon varieties act like intermediate-day onions; they start to bulb in summer but fail to go completely dormant and immediately resprout, multiplying in the process much like shallots do. Some Lisbon strains act like short-day onions and bulb (or make seed; some varieties do both at once and multiply as well) in spring after overwintering. Whatever, I've always had good luck with Lisbons. Territorial no longer sells Lisbon; perhaps that's because the majority of their customers are no longer Cascadians, but the West Coast has great interest in Lisbon and its modern descendants. White Gem hybrid from Stokes is a sweet Spanish scallion.

Dry gardening

I speculate that overwintering onions can be dry gardened because most of their growth happens in spring. Start them at the usual time in a well-watered nursery bed, overwinter them in the nursery, and transplant very early in spring. Spread mulch at the first sign of bulbing.

MISCELLANEOUS ONIONS (*Allium cepa* var. *proliferum, A. cepa* var. *aggregatum*)

Top-setting onions are perennial scallions that make aggressively self-sowing bulblets atop the stalks instead of seed. They'll survive the worst winter freeze. Catawissa and Egyptian Walking are not very different. Both varieties walk when the tall leaves, overweighted with maturing tip bulblets, fall away from the plant's center and then self-sow. I classify walking onions with other menaces, like horseradish and comfrey.

Potato onions, also known as multiplier onions, are a sort of easy-to-raise survivalist's shallot. The local sort I've grown also produced tops that tasted good enough to be used as scallions.

Unrelated Vegetables

ASPARAGUS (*Asparagus officinalis*)

Asparagus is a wonderful treat that can be especially important after a severe winter. Asparagus is perennial. Its dormant crowns can survive being frozen solid for months, but they die if the soil fills with water for days at a time. Washington gardeners on fast-draining glacial sand can produce excellent asparagus if they *grow* it. I had a neighbor in Lorane who lived on low ground that often got waterlogged, so he grew asparagus in a 4-foot-high and 8-foot-square aboveground box made from four full sheets of marine plywood entirely filled with fast-draining sandy soil. And asparagus grew beautifully for me on Malabon silty clay loam along the Umpqua. Where soil conditions permit, asparagus puts roots down 4 or more feet. If asparagus is started in shallow topsoil over a clay subsoil that doesn't drain well, the bed probably will fail.

Asparagus is sexy; the edible part even looks phallic. Like spinach and cannabis, male asparagus plants make pollen. Females make seeds. An all-male asparagus bed produces fatter spears over twice as many years as a mixed-sex bed because making pollen burdens males far less than forming seed, and without females you avoid severe overcompetition from self-sown plants. Asparagus ferns die back when hard frosts arrive. In spring the crowns shoot up new stalks that grow 4 or more inches a day and soon resemble 7-foot-tall ferns. All summer asparagus stores up food in a fleshy root system while the crowns multiply and spread. Asparagus demands balanced humusy soil and plenty of moisture in this year's growing season in order to store enough food so that next spring the spears will be fat, tender, and abundant. Intense competition forces asparagus to make smaller spears that don't taste as great. Hoeing weeds in an asparagus bed may damage the crowns. That means if you want big, tender asparagus, you'll do plenty of painstaking by-hand weeding.

Culture

Treat asparagus as a high-demand crop during its first years. When the bed produces more than you can eat, consider it a low-demand crop. Many assert that planting 2-year-old crowns brings the first harvest years sooner than had you sown seeds. The truth is, what the garden centers and catalog sellers call 2-year-old crowns are now *entering* their second growing season. The truth is that starting from crowns brings about the first harvest no sooner than starting from seed because digging and transplanting those crowns constitutes a huge setback that destroyed far more than half the root system and costs the plant at least half a year's progress. There are advantages from starting a bed by direct seeding: you can afford to destroy female crowns; there are extraproductive hybrid and hybrid all-male varieties you can't buy crowns for; and you will save money.

Prepare a 4-foot-wide bed as though growing a low-demand crop. Sow about the time the apple trees are blooming, while the soil is reasonably warm but won't dry out too rapidly. It's essential that you soak asparagus seeds at room temperature overnight before sowing them (the soak time not to exceed 12 hours). Drain, and then remove surface moisture by blotting the seeds because slightly damp seeds are easier to handle than slippery-wet ones. Then immediately sow.

If you're sowing an ordinary variety, be precise about this next step! Place one seed precisely every 4 inches in a ¾-inch-deep furrow down the center of that extra fertile band of soil you just created. *Do not drop more than one seed at a time* because if there is more than one plant at a position, it will be impossible to eliminate only one of them. Make absolutely certain that the seeds stay moist until they sprout more than two weeks later. In a cold spring, emergence can take three weeks.

Complete thinning the row to 12 inches apart by August. Asparagus crowns effectively resist death, even when young. It may be necessary to thin with a small trowel or sharp peeling knife so that you entirely remove/destroy the cluster of growing points you're weeding out. Be thorough about this; by the end of summer those young plants will already have divided several times. Ending up with plants that are *at least 1 foot apart in the row* is essential if you hope to establish an all-male bed. If plants are closer than 1 foot, you probably will fail to eliminate all the females without severely damaging adjoining males in the process. If it is an all-male hybrid, sow one seed per foot. In either case, do not fret if a year later you end up with a few 3-foot-wide gaps in the row. It won't matter.

The thick, fleshy roots store a lot of moisture; asparagus can survive moisture stress. But to have a hope of tasting a few spears next spring, keep the row growing fast all summer. Water it abundantly; side-dress more COF a few weeks after germination and again mid-July. Keep the bed thoroughly weeded. Always! Continue that practice in coming years too. Especially go after grasses. Weeding with dull fingers will be required.

Around midsummer in the bed's first year, *a small percentage* of the females might make seeds. Male flowers release pollen and then fall off.

Female flowers become small, juicy red berries when ripe. Male flowers cannot be easily distinguished from female flowers until the plant either makes seedballs or the remnants of that flower fall off. Absolutely, *before any even half-ripe seedballs drop on the bed*, dig up and destroy female crowns; thoroughly remove their seed-covered ferns to the compost-making area, because these seeds still may ripen enough to sprout.

Most directly seeded female plants start forming seedballs during their second summer, by which time the crowns have spread out to the size of teacup saucers. And that is why it is crucial to have the plants separated enough that you can completely destroy one cluster without damaging its neighbor's root system (very much). There is more to consider than gender when thinning the row. Open-pollinated varieties are variable. Most plants, male or female, will make 6 to 12 substantial ferns in their second spring. A few off-type plants may form a great many thin, spindly spears that you wouldn't prefer to eat. Even if these nonproductive plants are males, they should be dug out and destroyed as soon as they're spotted, even if that makes gaps.

By the end of the bed's second summer, you will have destroyed almost all the females; my current asparagus bed revealed its last few females in its third summer. If you started with an "all-male" hybrid, there will only be a few females to dig out. Maybe none. If you started with an open-pollinated variety or a regular hybrid, it'll be half and half; the remaining males, on average, will be 24 inches apart. Asparagus crowns primarily spread by division, but when digging up females, I've found underground runners (like strawberries do) extending as much as 6 inches from the parent crown; so over time, gaps in the row will fill themselves in. If, after purging the bed of females, there should be any gaps more than 3 feet wide, dig up one of the more productive clusters of male crowns during the winter, tease that cluster apart into individual crowns, and transplant these into any gaps.

In autumn the ferns turn brown; cut them off an inch or two above the ground, and compost them. During winter cover the bed with a thin layer of compost, and when the spears start emerging, spread the usual dose of COF. And side-dress once or twice. And keep it weeded—religiously. After a few years, a large bed could produce far more asparagus than you can eat; the harvest will go on for at least two months; then give up side-dressing it.

One other thing you might do: mix a measured half cup of sea salt into the amount of COF for 100 square feet of bed. This much salt will do no harm. All the nineteenth-century market gardeners spread salt on asparagus and spread a lot more than ½ cup per 100 square feet. The presence of more sodium in my soil adds flavor.

Garden planning

An all-male bed should produce heavily for 20 years or more. In my current bed's fourth spring, 75 feet of row generously covered two dinner plates every two days for two months. When initially choosing the bed's position, keep in mind that by its third year asparagus ferns will grow 7 feet tall. These ferns shade adjoining beds if restrained in an upright position. If not supported, they fall over on adjoining paths and beds and end up occupying a space over 12 feet wide. I have always supported asparagus ferns. I can't imagine how I'd weed a bed during the growing season if the ferns were spread over the ground.

Insects and diseases

Root diseases do not happen in well-drained soil. Asparagus beetles strip the ferns that feed the crowns that store the food that makes the shoot that you eat next spring. If they're taking more than 10 percent of the foliage, control them with pyrethrins or Spinosad. Neem oil might work.

Harvest

There can be no harvesting in the first year that crowns are transplanted. In its second year a bed started with crowns will produce a few extraordinarily fat spears that you can sample. If a directly seeded row grows well in its first summer, it'll also produce a few superfat spears that you can taste in its second spring. Harvest only those spears at least as large in diameter as your index finger, and take only one spear per cluster. I'm sure they'll be incredibly delicious, but instead of self-indulgence allow the crowns to create more foliage, thus developing a larger food reserve.

By the bed's third spring the larger spears may be taken until the size of most of the shoots begins to decrease. Probably you'll enjoy three to four weeks of harvesting. Beds in their fourth year provide fat spears for two months. I suggest never harvesting any spear thinner than your ring finger.

Harvest this way: when a spear stands about a foot tall, grasp it about 4 inches below the tip and pull it sideways and down until the shaft snaps wherever it will. Below the point it snaps, the stalk will be too woody to eat; above that point it'll be tender. By June the flavor is getting strong. Time to stop harvesting; let the plant grow without interference.

Saving seed

Asparagus is wind pollinated and needs considerable isolation if genetically pure seed is to be produced. I suspect purity may not matter much for gardening because undesirable plants can be eliminated during the bed's first three years. Each seedball contains a few black seeds. Let the berry get overripe. Crush them in a bowl or small bucket, mix the crushed pulp with water, stir well, and the seeds immediately settle to the bottom. Pour off the pulp, repeat to remove almost all the pulp; then wash the seeds in a sieve until they're clean and, finally, spread the seeds out on newspaper to fully dry.

Varieties

Hybrids are more productive, and that's why major garden seed suppliers no longer sell the old OP varieties. You'd have to search the Internet to find them on offer. All-male hybrids produce predominantly male plants, in the 90 percents but not 100 percent males. Hybrid seed seems quite expensive but still works out to be far cheaper than purchasing crowns. Annie and I make side money by growing a thousand or so crowns every year for a few local garden centers. Because hybrid seed is very spendy, I also grow traditional open-pollinated varieties. When we dig first-year plants in autumn, hybrids like

Jersey Knight make crowns twice the size OP varieties make, and the garden center pays us a premium for them. Mary Washington is one of the oldest OP varieties. It makes small crowns with short roots and probably isn't highly productive. UC 157 F2 is two-thirds as vigorous as Jersey Knight. My 75-foot-long bed is UC 157. About 10 percent of the plants were not productive. With UC 157, there's a great deal of difference from plant to plant about when the first spears appear, giving the home gardener a less concentrated harvest period. All the crowns make delicious spears, and many of them make smaller numbers of very fat spears, something I consider highly desirable.

Dry gardening

I am speculating here. Unwatered asparagus should survive in naturally moisture-retentive deep, open soil and produce adequately *if kept well weeded and mulched*. A new bed started from either seed or crowns probably requires minimal irrigation on a 1-foot-wide strip the first year.

CORN (*Zea mays*)

Corn produces in almost any soil type. It will produce acceptably if fertilized like a low-demand crop; it will produce much more if also side-dressed when it is about 6 inches high. Varieties that are early in places where summer is hot may fail to ripen before frost in most of Cascadia because the amount of time corn grows vegetatively before it starts making ears is not determined by how large the plant gets, nor how long it has grown. Nor usually is seed making influenced by day length (a few day-length-sensitive

corn varieties were bred for the Canadian prairies). Corn grows vegetatively until the plant has received and recorded enough heat; then reproduction begins. Here's an extreme example: in Lorane I once sowed a 67-day "early" variety called Truckers Favorite White from Park Seed Company (South Carolina) on June 1 and watched it grow 12 feet tall before tassels appeared in mid-September. Since tassling happens several weeks before harvest, I deduced that as much heat accumulates in less than 50 days of South Carolina summer as happens in about 110 days in Lorane.

Breeders use a measurement called the "heat unit" to accurately describe how much warmth each variety must register before seed formation is triggered. Heat units are computed this (intentionally oversimplified) way: starting from the date of the last usual frost, add up the number of hours during each 24-hour period that the temperature is above 50 degrees F and multiply this figure by the number of degrees the temperature is above 50 degrees F.

Some primary sweet corn seed growers state the number of heat units (HU) their varieties require, not days to maturity. The earliest varieties need about 1,300 HU to ripen; late types require more than 2,200. The Willamette Valley receives, on average, 2,000 HU over the summer. Jubilee is one of the tastiest varieties that suit the Willamette; Jubilee needs 1,750 HU. Jubilee took 84 days at Stokes's trials ground when Stokes sold that variety, 87 days at Johnny's (they too no longer sell Jubilee), and 90 to 105 days in Cottage Grove (TSC). I conclude that summer is a bit warmer in Ontario than in Maine and warmer at Johnny's trials ground than in Cottage Grove. Jubilee barely ripens around Puget Sound. Jubilee might get harvested after growing less than 80 days in the Rogue Valley.

SOW	HARVEST	TRANSPLANT
Mid-May to July	August to October	N/A
BETWEEN ROWS	**SEEDS**	**THIN TO**
3 feet	4 inches apart	12 inches

Culture

Corn grows best when it is fed like a medium-demand crop.

Corn is wind pollinated; each strand of silk connects a pollen grain to what will become a kernel. The ear fills completely if all the silks receive a pollen grain. Corn pollen is dense; it falls down from the tassles as much as it blows away. To achieve thorough pollination, corn is planted in blocks, not single long rows. Rain or irrigation happening while pollen is dropping can make blank spots in the ear. That's one reason I don't crowd the corn patch; I prefer a plant density that can go through an entire week of hot weather (while releasing pollen) without being irrigated. The minimum patch size that can be counted on to fully pollinate is 10 by 10 feet holding three parallel rows that are 30 to 36 inches apart. Sow a single short row of corn and you'll be lucky if most of the kernels swell up.

Sow the seeds 1½ inches deep. Either drop about three seeds per foot of furrow and gradually thin the rows so that the seedlings average 12 inches apart, or else pinch two seeds between thumb, and first finger and then every 12 inches along the row, jab them into soft soil 1½ inches deep. I do that. There's an old-fashioned device called a "jab planter" that does the same thing while the operator stands up. If both seeds germinate, thin the position to a single plant when they are about 6 inches tall. Occasionally no seedlings emerge from a pair of seeds; in that case, allow two plants to grow to maturity in an adjoining position in the row or even in the next row. Corn seed does not germinate well when the soil is below 60 degrees F. Corn is sensitive to frost. The earliest a sowing should be risked is one week before the last anticipated frost date. I get better germination, faster initial growth, and harvest larger ears on nearly the same day by sowing corn on the day I put out unprotected tomato seedlings.

Side-dress heavily; distribute a second full batch of COF between the isles when the seedlings are about 6 inches tall. Keep the weeds thoroughly hoed until the corn has formed a leaf canopy whose shade suppresses weeds, and then stay out of the patch until harvest time in order to avoid compacting the soil.

Garden planning

All the main ears on a hybrid variety go from barely ripe to getting too starchy in about 10 days. Simultaneously sowing three different hybrids that mature 10 days apart creates a month- to six-week-long harvest period.

Corn is in the grass family. Like other grasses, it makes the soil hospitable to succeeding crops. South of Drain, there might be time to start autumn vegetables after the earliest corn has been harvested. The ex—corn patch always grows a fine winter stand of favas, clover, or cereal rye. If your rototiller is up to chopping up and turning under standing cornstalks, thickly scatter green-manure seed late in September and shallowly till everything under. Alternatively, cut off the stalks just above ground level, remove them to the composting area for use as a crisscrossed base layer of your next heap, leave the stubble in the ground, and hoe in or shallowly rototill in green-manure seeds.

Insects and diseases

Earworms are common in California. I saw a few in Elkton, but the climate may be changing. They are close relatives of the cabbage worm and can be handled with Bt or Spinosad, spot-sprayed directly (and heavily) on the silks when the tassels first drop pollen, and again about 10 days later.

Harvest

Each variety shows different indicators as the kernels ripen. The ears may be ready to take when the wrappers have browned off slightly; sometimes the ears will lean out and plump up when ready for picking. When I haven't yet learned to read a variety at a glance, I gently strip the wrappers of one ear back an inch from the end to peak inside and determine readiness.

Saving seed (and growing field corn)

Corn pollen doesn't travel far. Five hundred feet of isolation from another patch located downwind will serve for home-garden-quality seed, as long as the usual direction of the prevailing wind actually prevails while pollen is being released. For assured purity, you need 1 mile of isolation in all directions. If a multicolored corn variety and a nearby patch of yellow corn should release pollen at the same time, every ear of yellow corn will have occasional kernels of different colors, textures, and flavors.

Garden seed companies offer only a few open-pollinated varieties. That is an especially unfortunate circumstance regarding field corn because there is much solid evidence showing that hybrid cereal corn varieties are not as nutritious as the old open-pollinated ones. There shouldn't be nearly as much nutritional difference between regular hybrid (not sugar boosted) and open-pollinated sweet corn varieties.

A convenient home-garden method for maintaining or improving open-pollinated sweet corn is to provide each plant with half again more in-the-row spacing so that each plant receives enough light at the base to encourage tillering (produce secondary stalks that make smaller ears). When you harvest a main ear for the table, immediately strip its wrappers and give it a close inspection; if it is a highly desirable ear, allow the secondary ears to continue developing. Use these for seed.

Ideally, harvest corn seed after it has dried in the field. Practically, late summer rains and heavy dews probably will arrive before the crop has fully dried. Cut the plants close to the ground, tie them in bunches of five or so, bring them under cover, and hang the bunches upside down to finish drying. Save seed from at least 20 and, better, from 50 plants. The Organic Seed Alliance says it takes a gene pool of at least 200 plants to prevent inbreeding depression of vigor.

Varieties

If you're interested in open-pollinated sweet corn, New Mama (ADA) looks promising. Territorial's Hooker's Sweet Indian yields small ears that taste great. In my Oregon trials I scored Hooker's at only 7.5 out of 10 because of low yield. Johnny's produces Double Standard, an OP bicolor.

Golden Jubilee hybrid has long been the most popular main-season variety in the Willamette Valley. I consider Jubilee to be Cascadia's quality standard. In my trials, Jubilee always scored 9.75 out of 10. North of the Columbia, choose a quicker variety for the main crop. Earlier corns can't be as high yielding as Jubilee while still tasting great because earlies don't have as much growing time to store up food reserves. Before tassling, the corn plant banks sugar in the pith of its stalk. Once corn pollinates, it quickly translocates this sugar into the fast-developing ear. For a demonstration of this, chew on the sugary pith of a cornstalk just before tassels emerge. If you wanted to make homestead corn syrup, you'd boil down juice squeezed from the pith. After the ear has filled the stalk is no longer the slightest bit sweet. Many early sweet corn varieties form large ears. But there ain't no free lunch. With less growing time to store nutrients the kernels on a big-eared early variety must of necessity be shallow and mainly composed of a fibrous skin holding slightly sugary water lacking "complexed" minerals and proteins. That's profitable. I prefer midmaturity varieties that make moderately sized ears with nutrition in them. The best trials score I've ever given any variety of any type that matured more than a few days earlier than Jubilee has been 8.5.

White corn varieties usually mature late. Territorial offers several that must mature in the Willamette. As I'd expect, West Coast does not sell white sweet corn.

I like eating bicolor sweet corn; it is no more difficult to produce than yellow varieties. I currently grow Honey & Cream (TSC, WCO). It is my choice because it tastes like corn used to taste.

I am disappointed at the general direction sweet corn breeding has taken in the last decades. The plant has to balance sweetness against nutrient density and flavor. Varieties tagged SE (Sugar Enhanced) are a bit sweeter, but not over the top. They still taste like corn. I can enjoy eating them. But I find SH2 and "supersweet" varieties excessively sugary with little corn flavor. If supersweet varieties are pollinated by regular or SH2 varieties, the crossed seeds will be **starchy and tough**. The new Synergistic varieties are also supersweet but with fewer liabilities; they germinate better in cold soil and don't require isolation from regular types. They still are too sweet.

Dry gardening

Sweet corn has always been bred to grow in garden soil although some varieties cope without irrigation. Field corn is usually far better adapted to unirrigated conditions and less fertile soil. Johnny's offers a broad choice. Uprising does too. Nichols provides Carol Deppe's Cascade Ruby-Gold Flint, a diverse variety Carol says is the ultimate Cascadian survival corn. To grow field corn without irrigation (the only way it makes sense to me to grow a basic survival staple), you need deep, open soil and you must be prepared to accept a lower yield than people get in the Midwest. Make fertile hills on a 4-by-4-foot grid. Instead of Squanto's fish, each hill gets a cup of COF deeply dug into it. Best do this a month before sowing. Then sow a few seeds in each hill when the tomatoes usually go out. Progressively thin each hill to one plant. Given such wide spacing, most varieties tiller aggressively (form many ear-bearing stalks); if the soil provides enough moisture, you'll find the corn patch on 4-by-4 feet ends up with fewer gaps than you'd expect. By the way, you can eat many types of immature field corn as sweet corn. It usually has a lot of flavor. If eaten within a few hours of picking, it won't be overly chewy and will seem sufficiently sweet. Sweet corn varieties were selected to be slower to convert the sugar in their seeds into starch after being picked. Uprising says their Amish Butter makes very good sweet corn and—when fully mature—good grinding corn.

HORSERADISH (*Armoracia rusticana*)

Left to its own devices, horseradish quickly becomes a horribly invasive, hard-to-eliminate weed that makes roots so small and twisted, it is not easy to use them as food. By "horribly," I mean the ability (in soft garden soil) to spread 10 feet each year. By "hard to eliminate," I mean that any fragment of horseradish root is capable of resting semidormant for months before putting up leaves. But with a bit of forethought you can grow easy-cleaning, easy-peeling roots *and*

keep the plant from spreading. Here is how to get all the benefits without the liabilities.

Culture

Start your patch with a piece of root. Almost any bit of root will grow, but starting with a crown or part of a crown is slightly better. Anyone who has horseradish in his veggie plot will have hundreds of pieces he'd be delighted for you to take away. Your aim for the first growing year is to (1) grow some long, fairly straight pieces of small-diameter root and to (2) keep the wildly spreading plant under control.

First thing: forcibly confine your horseradish. *Surround it with compact, infertile soil growing regularly mowed grass that extends on all sides at least 6 feet from the edge of the patch. Better, 10 feet on all sides.* It need not be a large area; a 4-by-4-foot bed located in the middle of your lawn will grow all the horseradish a family could ever use. And the large, long

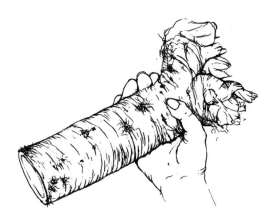

leaves look vaguely ornamental. Also concerning containment, if the plant puts up any seedstalks, cut them off well before any seed forms.

Horseradish is a low-demand crop that needs loose soil to develop well. The bed should be deeply dug while working in an inch-thick layer of compost and a full dose of COF. In subsequent years, the usual COF and a thin layer of compost once a year will maintain the bed.

Position the initial root piece horizontally about an inch below the surface in the bed's center. Do this in spring. Keep the bed weed-free all summer. Irrigate deeply, but no more than what it takes to keep the plant growing.

In October dig the bed thoroughly, deeply, and gently, meticulously searching for and removing every root and fragment of root you find, each and every one. Dig in such a way that any long, relatively straight pieces come out intact, not having been broken or cut by the spade. Your goal here is to find a few reasonably straight pencil-thick pieces that are at least 12 inches and up to 18 inches long.

Upon discovering a long, straight root piece, take the end that was closest to the crown and cut it off square. At the farther end, clip the root at a 45-degree angle. That way, next spring there'll be no doubt about which end grows the top and which end grows the root system. Tie these in a loose bundle using ordinary twine, with all the square cuts at one end and the angle cuts on the other. Bury that bundle in the horseradish bed under 2 inches of soil—deep enough that if there happens to be a few days of continuously subfreezing weather, the roots won't freeze. Let the bundle rest over winter.

Civilized horseradish roots. Now you're ready to grow something you may have seen at the supermarket but that few gardeners know how to produce—clean, straight, easy-to-wash-and-peel horseradish roots larger than the hugest carrot you ever saw.

In the month of March dig up the bundle of root pieces. Spread compost and COF, and dig them in. If you find any more root fragments during this digging, remove and destroy them—and not in the compost heap. Burn 'em! If your bed is as I suggested only 4-by-4 feet, plan on growing only two big roots. Two will be plenty to provision your kitchen. Make two parallel furrows as long as the root pieces, centered in the bed about 18 inches apart and 1½ inches deep. Place a root in each furrow, making note of which end the square cuts are. Cover them with soil. Destroy the others—burn 'em!

In the first month a great many leaves will emerge along the entire length of each root piece. Then comes step one: gently and gradually uncover the root, starting with the end you cut off square. Permit the last 2 inches (the end you cut off at 45 degrees) to remain underground, undisturbed; that's where you want the feeder roots to develop. You'll discover fine new roots emerging all over. Starting at the square-cut end, lift the flexible root gently out of the earth just far enough to slide a finger underneath and break off all feeder roots—but do not disturb the roots coming out the last 2 inches at the angle-cut end. And break off all emerging leaf clusters, except for the leaves emerging from the last inch at the square-cut end. Now scratch out that furrow again, and rebury the root piece.

Step two: there probably will be dozens of little horseradish plants emerging from bits of overlooked root. Treat these as the nastiest weeds imaginable. If you repeatedly cut them off before they can start to produce and store more food, they *will* die, eventually.

Then once a month, in May, June, July, and August, repeat step one. The root will grow fatter; you may have to scrape up a bit of soil over them to make sure they stay covered until the next manicure. Repeat step two every time you see a new horseradish weed.

In early October the root should be at least 2 inches in diameter and under at least an inch of soil. Harvest it by cutting off the feeder roots. The leaves will be clustered at the other end. Cut or break them off too. Gently wash the root without making scratches on the skin. Let it dry. Then put it into a tight plastic bag; keep that in the fridge to be grated and used at your convenience. It might keep through winter.

Thoroughly dig the bed immediately after harvest, extract a few long, straight root pieces to hold over for next year's crop. Also remove and destroy every other bit of root you can find to reduce the weeding next summer.

I warn you: if you didn't allow a large enough barrier of infertile, compacted soil around the patch, you'll never want to grow horseradish again. I once grew horseradish inside the garden fence using this method. The roots I harvested were magnificent, but it took me several years of persistent hoeing as far as 20 feet away from the spot to finally eliminate the plant.

OKRA (*Hibiscus esculentus*)

When I lived in Southern California, I grew okra bushes 5 feet tall. The pods were so tender and sweet raw, I ate them for breakfast in the cool of the morning while doing garden tasks. That's why frozen or canned okra disgusts me. Okra on the supermarket produce counter has gotten way too old for me to enjoy. After many attempts to grow okra since I left California in 1978, I can state with fair certainty that okra is not practical in most Cascadian gardens. Maybe it'll produce in and around the Rogue Valley. Or in a greenhouse open to bee pollination. I have tried black plastic mulch; I have trialed every readily available okra variety, including the so-called early hybrids. I have direct-seeded okra and also raised large seedlings and transplanted them out. My best result happened in an unusually hot summer when I grew a patch of weak, stressed-looking plants about 2 feet tall: some plants yielded a few minuscule pods; some plants yielded nothing. In cool summers the inevitable result was no yield at all.

Chapter Ten

ORNAMENTALS AND HERBS

By MARINA McSHANE

When the world wearies and society ceases to satisfy, there is always the garden.

—Minnie Aumonier

MANY FOOD GARDENERS wonder if flowers and herbs should be integrated into veggie areas or if they are best grown separately. There are practical considerations to direct your placements. Annuals perform their entire life cycle in one year, usually from spring to hard frost. These are easily included in the veggie areas if you want to put them there, because they allow vegetable crop rotation. Many flowering perennials perform better in their second and subsequent years, so I plant them out of the way of veggie crop rotation schemes, but if they attract beneficial insects, you may want them nearby.

Seed packets or plant tags should state if a plant is perennial, annual, or biennial, but Cascadia is on a bit of a crossover point—some flowering plants can be perennial or annual depending on the winter temperatures, drainage, and degree of shelter they receive. California poppies, bachelor buttons, or sweet alyssum may fool a casual gardener (one not looking too closely) because they show up every year, but actually are self-sown progeny and not the original plants. Some perennials may be fully deciduous like mums (die back entirely to the ground), or be semi-evergreen like daisies, or be fully evergreen like hellebores. Dahlias, lilies, alliums, and others grow from bulbs or tubers, which are usually perennial, or behave as such in the Pacific Northwest. There are some notable biennial ornamentals as well, which typically flower in their second season, like Sweet William or many foxgloves.

Due to space limitations, this chapter focuses on general cultural directions, simple propagation tips, and discussion of more popular and easily grown ornamentals and herbs, which vegetable gardeners may want to incorporate into their gardening work. Carol and Norman Hall's *Timber Press Guide to Gardening in the Pacific Northwest* (Timber Press, 2008) is an excellent resource for gardeners who want in-depth information about cultivating the full scope of ornamentals from tiny groundcovers to garden-worthy trees.

Most vegetable-seed growers carry some flowers and herbs, and their catalogs usually offer basic cultural directions. Stokes has particularly helpful online resources about how to grow them well.

Soil and Fertility

Your answer to this essential question guides soil preparation: Are you wanting the leaves of a particular plant, or is it the flowers you're after? If you want flowers, prepare the soil as though you are growing tomatoes—initially provide a balanced food to grow the plant to a good size, then lean toward more phosphorus during the flowering stage. If you use COF or have embarked on a long-term plan to remineralize your garden soil, you'll be building phosphorus levels that eventually act as a reserve. Use the three levels of COF—the same as for veggies; the basic amount serves as a foundation (as for low-demand crops), which is sufficient for most annuals. Then add fertigation or side-dressing for more demanding situations. Top dressing is the most practical option for perennials or bulbs, usually applied when the plant starts back into growth in early to mid-spring. I like to lightly scratch it in with a hand fork or rake.

Keep in mind that many popular annuals, especially those grown for cut flowers, are really warm-weather plants. The cool weather we often get in May and June delays their development just as it does peppers or eggplants. Once the sun shines regularly, growth will commence in earnest. A second feeding isn't really necessary for most ornamentals, but if I want to give a plant a boost, fertigation or foliar feeding acts quickly. For heavy feeders, I suggest side-dressing with COF, boosted with a double dose of bonemeal during the flowering stage. Deadheading regularly (picking off spent blooms) is usually a better method to keep the flowers coming, assuming you got the plants off to a good start in suitably fertile soil.

There is an ever-expanding group of flowering plants that are marketed as "specialty annuals." These usually are sold individually in 4-inch or larger pots. Many specialty annuals are sterile hybrid clones propagated by tissue culture in Central America. Wholesale growers in the United States pot them up and sell them to nurseries and retail outlets. These clones will produce little or no seed, and if they do form seed, it won't be vigorous or true to type. The payoff is exceptionally heavy flowering lasting for months. Many of these newer varieties are self-cleaning as well, eliminating the need for deadheading. Because of their extreme vigor, these specialty annuals will benefit from extra feedings. Many experts recommend using half-strength liquid fertilizer with every other watering. Side-dressed COF works about as well. Extra feeding for containerized plants is recommended—remember, they are captives and cannot send roots out into fresh soil in search of nutrients.

With most flowering annuals, feeding too much nitrogen produces excess foliage at the expense of flower formation and can cause plants to fall over when irrigated overhead. Conversely, nitrogen may be just the thing if you want to grow giant cannas or an ornamental banana plant. With aromatic herbs like basil, there are two schools of thought. We grow basil for its leaves; I use a high nitrogen regimen (and plenty of water) to make big plants. But some gardeners think that minimal water and fertilizer make more concentrated flavor and fragrance.

Lean soil fertility better suits "subshrubs," like rosemary and lavender, because they have a woody structure that does not die back like deciduous plants. Richly fed and copiously watered woody perennial herbs are prone to winterkill. Cascadia is sometimes likened to a Mediterranean climate where many of these herbs grow wild, but the comparison falls short. Sure, we have dry summers and wet winters like many parts of the Mediterranean, but Cascadia has much less winter sunshine and the soil can naturally be so acidic that the comparison is meaningless. Herbs such as rosemary and lavender typically thrive in our region if their soil drains well, but a wet winter can be disastrous in heavy soil. If your rosemary, santolina, lavenders, thymes, salvia (sages), or other woody herbs are not thriving, try planting them with a generous shovelful of pumice or fine gravel underneath the root zones, and give them as much sun as possible. If you can, harden off perennial herbs before winter by withholding irrigation from September on (but not to the point of wilting).

Early fall is a good time to take cuttings from woody perennials—pull off side branches with a piece of heel attached (a bit of the bark from the main stem), and put a group of as many as a dozen into a 4-inch pot of gritty coir/sand/pearlite mixture, about 2 inches deep, and firm them into the pot. Cover with a plastic bag, ventilate occasionally, and keep in bright shade. If things go well, they will have struck some roots before the weather turns cold; but rather than move them into individual pots right away, it's best to leave them be until spring. Keep the soil barely moist but not soggy. A cold frame or bright, unheated indoor spot is best over winter. By spring, cuttings that have rooted will kick into obvious growth. Rooting hormone and bottom heat will increase your success rate, but if you use bottom heat, you have to check the moisture level more often.

Layering is another way to propagate a hardy woody herb: choose a side branch of this year's wood that is still attached to the parent plant and pull it down to the soil or into a pot you've positioned for this purpose. Give it something inviting to root into (gritty coir/sand/compost). Strip some leaves from the few inches where the stem touches the soil, cover lightly with the soil mix, and peg it down firmly. A piece of wire bent like a giant hairpin or a smallish stone should do the trick. With luck it will root with no further care and give you an identical plant. Separate the new rooted plant in the spring. This method can be faster than growing plants from seed if you only want one or a few more plants.

Avoid feeding nitrogen to perennials from August onward. Most years they will pull through, but losses are likely if we get one of our real arctic blasts, and more so if they go into winter "soft." I plant mine in decently fertile soil, water moderately, and hope for a gradual transition from fall into winter without any extreme cold snaps. We had two recent winters when a mild October ended with low temperatures of 18 degrees F around Halloween, and many people lost woody plants that would have been perfectly hardy had a more gradual decline prepared them with their own biological "antifreeze."

Transplants

In order to enjoy heat-loving flowering annuals earlier in the summer, start transplants indoors just as you would tomatoes or peppers. Herb and flower starts will need potting on and hardening off as described in Chapter 7. The growing directions some seed suppliers provide online (Stokes and Johnny's, for example) will help you figure out approximately how long they'll require to reach blooming size, but expect your own seedlings to take a bit longer without the fully controlled growing conditions that commercial seedling raisers provide. A dedicated amateur flower grower will likely be adding soil-heating cables and a powerful grow light to her wish lists because these two items make it possible to grow sturdy plants of some hard-to-get-going species such as begonias, heliotrope, or impatiens.

Some species require vernalization—a period of winter chill—to get their seeds to germinate. This can be managed easily by refrigerating seeds for a specified period of time or by leaving the seeded containers outdoors under the shelter of overhead trees, under the eaves, or in a cold frame. Some professional flower growers like to sow seeds as shallowly as possible and top the soil surface with small/medium-size chicken grit. This accomplishes two things: it keeps the seeds from being washed away by watering or rains and gives the newly emerged seedlings a firm base to plant their first roots into.

You'll find species or cultivars offered in seed catalogs that are difficult to find as transplants and aren't found on any local seed racks. Don't be deterred if you don't have an elaborate transplant-raising setup—many annuals are extremely easy to start in pots with no special treatment other than a bit of extra heat until the seeds sprout and then a simple cold frame for growing on. Lacking that, you can always direct-seed after the soil has warmed up enough.

Self-Sowing Annuals

Self-sowing annuals naturalize best in loose, humusy soil; they come up by themselves when conditions are right, usually in spring. Some perennials also self-sow. These self-sowers take very little care after you first get them established. You may have to make some provision to maintain soil fertility—surface scatterings of COF will help a lot.

Careful and early thinning is key to getting the most from self-sown volunteers. Do as you would in a veggie bed you have seeded too thickly—get them off each other's backs right away, and progressively thin.

On a neighborhood walk one late July, I noticed someone had let a clump of cosmos go unthinned, and about 20 stunted plants covered an area of about 2 square feet. I could almost hear them crying out for help as I passed by. A few plants managed to form tiny flowers at their very tips; none of them had developed side branches.

Individual spacing is not always the rule, though. Some species are grown in small clumps, such as lobelia, linaria, and nemesia. Usually these are weak-stemmed smallish plants that gain support from being in a bit of a tangle and whose individual flowers are too small to make an impact unless they are grouped. For larger-seeded self-sowers like calendula or sunflowers, you can relocate volunteers as soon as the seedlings have two or four true leaves. Usually this coincides with the season of frequent rain showers, but if not, do remember to water those you've moved if a dry spell occurs. An old kitchen fork makes a good transplanting tool. They'll be set back a little bit by the disturbance, but that's not all bad, because you'll have some coming into their prime while the first ones may be tapering off.

Plant Placement

The usual cultural practices for vegetables generally apply to flowers and herbs, but there are aesthetic considerations that may influence how you arrange your plantings. Unless you are growing cutting flowers or plan to harvest a batch of basil or other herbs for a big single harvest, you probably have a blended planting in mind where several species mix and mingle. Personal taste will dictate what you choose to plant and influence how best to arrange the bed, but you should follow basic horticultural principles and locate plants so that they can achieve their potential.

Plants with similar needs should be grouped together and their eventual heights kept in mind so as to avoid shading sun lovers. Many flowering plants manage okay with less than full sun, but most of the semiwoody herbs such as sage, rosemary, santolina, and similar will not grow well without it. "Full sun" means a minimum of six continuous hours a day, including midday, and it creates compact, strong-growing plants and triggers better flower production. Insufficient sun makes plants stretchy and weak, with fewer flowers. Most herbs do well in decent garden soil. Some herbs do fine in heavy soil—typically these species have lush foliage and strong roots that can break up clay. Examples are comfrey, burdock, bergamot, and many mints.

If you are mixing perennials and annuals, it makes sense to position your perennials according to the size they'll achieve in a few years, and then fill in the gaps with annuals. Some people like each plant to own space distinct from its neighbor, and others prefer a more mingled look—suit yourself in that regard.

Managing Flower Production and Display Attributes

Most gardeners grow flowers to cut for bouquets and to perfume and decorate the garden. Most flowering plants contribute to both aims, but some are definitely at one end of the spectrum or another. Alyssum, for example, is so short in stature that it's not much use for bouquets. Dutch iris are not very interesting before bloom and decline rapidly after bloom, so you wouldn't want to feature them in a prominent display area.

The main reasons to deadhead are to tidy the plant and prevent it from using its energy to form seed; instead, they can continue to bloom or make stronger blooms next year. Some perennials bloom once and then are done for the year: these include daffodils, peonies, iris, and certain poppies. You will not get more flowers from these by deadheading. So cut them for bouquets or enjoy on the plant—either way it won't matter in terms of more bloom.

Many perennials, especially the newest cultivars, will send up more blossoms when deadheaded. Among this group are *Achillea* (yarrow), aconite (monkshood), columbines, lavenders, *Leucanthemum* (daisies), *Penstemon*, salvias, *Dianthus*, and *Viola*. Cultivars that like rich soil benefit from a little side-dressing when you deadhead them. However, one disadvantage of providing rich soil is that the spring growth or the regrowth can be so lush that the plants need staking or some kind of support, and we often don't anticipate it in time for it to be discreet—remedial staking never looks as nice as when done in advance. I like to use old tomato cages (and rusty ones visually disappear better than shiny new ones) put in place early or bamboo stakes and twine for tying up the stems needing support. You may have some around that you've found inadequate for a well-grown tomato. They can be shortened with a wire cutter to a better height for a particular species; cut down, they are great to keep peonies, daisies, some dahlias, and others from flopping, especially when overhead watering weighs down the plants.

Pinching and cutting back are effective ways to control plant size, flower size, timing of blooms, and stability for many annual species and some perennials—mums are the most familiar example. When only the growing tip of a shoot is removed, it is called "pinching"; if more length is removed, it is called "cutting back." In either case, this removal stimulates the formation of more branches, and since branches terminate in flowers, you get more flowers—often smaller flowers than had you not pinched, but not always. Many people think the multiplied smaller flowers look more natural than fewer larger flowers, though the latter may be desirable for cut flowers.

Cutting back creates a shorter plant that is stockier and self-supporting, eliminating the need for staking. At the same time you will be slightly delaying bloom, but it is usually worth it. Some annuals have better self-branching habits than others—often an improved cultivar can be worth the extra money. If your plant is gaining height but not developing many side branches, pinch it a time or two.

You can lengthen the blooming period of perennials like phlox and asters by pinching some but not all of the stems. The unpinched stems will bloom first, followed by the pinched. Leaving the center unpinched works well, for it will be taller; then the shorter, later-blooming outside stems support the center and hide the "bare legs," which sometimes develop in the center of a plant.

Cutting back can renew the whole plant at once. You can either clip one stem at a time, making the cut right above the forking lower branches, or you can grasp a bunch of stems and cut them off as a group. Though the one-stem-at-a-time method is optimum, I confess that as a very busy gardener with a whole lot of plants to care for, I often resort to the grasp-and-cut method. For a detailed explanation of these techniques and many useful lists as to which plants benefit from which treatments, see Tracy DiSabato-Aust's book *The Well-Tended Perennial Garden* (Timber Press, revised 2006). Although it is focused on perennials, many of the shaping and staging techniques apply equally well to annuals.

Following are some guidelines for growing some popular flowers and herbs that are relatively easy to start from seed, and a few that may be best established from a purchased plant but are highly recommended for the region.

Flowers: Alyssum to Zinnias

More flower possibilities have been omitted than are discussed here; some flowers, like petunias and begonias, need controlled greenhouse conditions for likely success, and the rest are simply too numerous to cover here.

Annuals are usually easiest to start from seed; perennials may be easy from seed too, but because they often don't flower in year one or attain enough presence their first year to have much of an impact, you may want to get a start (plant division) from a nursery or a gardening friend. Perennials that bloom their first year from seed are usually so designated in catalogs. Be aware of the self-sowing conundrum: many of the easiest-to-grow annuals are enthusiastic in perpetuating themselves and can become a bit of a nuisance. I always say forget-me-nots should be called forget-me-can'ts.

Cool season annuals are at their best in cool weather; they may peter out during midsummer heat. Warm weather annuals don't grow or flower well until temperatures are higher—just like the difference between spinach and eggplants.

Note: Assume a preference for sun and irrigation unless otherwise mentioned. Drought-tolerant plants are just that—tolerant. Many grow better with regular water, unless otherwise noted.

ALYSSUM (*Lobularia maritima*)

Cool season annual, direct-sow or start indoors. Will grow in part sun. Thin progressively; okay to be a bit crowded in small clusters. Blooms in six weeks. White/pink/purple color range on short carpeting plants, but white is most fragrant. Bee plant. Self-sows. Shear with scissors for rebloom.

AMARANTH (*Amaranthus*)

Also called love-lies-bleeding. Decorative types of amaranth have various flower forms from plumes to rope-like flower heads in many colors. Fast-growing large to very large back-of-border plants bloom in late summer; many produce edible seed. Food plant for some butterflies; dye plant, dries well. Easy to direct-sow; full sun. Can become a nuisance with self-sowing but easily weeded out.

BACHELOR'S BUTTON (*Centaurea cyanus*)

Direct-seed into cool soil; will later self-sow. One of the best true blues in the flower kingdom. Great cut flowers and dries easily; good in potpourri for color. Dwarf varieties available, but tall (24 inches) are better for cut flowers, though they may topple if grown in rich soil. Easily grown; declines without constant dead-heading. Plant near cosmos or similar plant that sizes up when Bachelor's Buttons are

slowing down, or cut back by half for renewal, or pull out.

BELLS OF IRELAND (*Moluccella laevis*)

Clusters of apple-green flower calyxes cover the upright stalks, good fresh or dried. Grows to 3 feet; pinch when young for multiple but shorter stems. They need room to develop well—good candidates for row culture.

CALENDULA (*Calendula officinalis*)

Easily grown cool-season annual; direct-sow or start indoors. Three-inch flowers in shades of orange from apricot to near red. Edible but sharp-tasting flowers, also used as a dye and food coloring. Many medicinal uses, especially for skin inflammations when used in salves and tinctures. Pinch early for better branching, and watch out for slugs during seedling stage. Bloom slows down in summer heat but resumes when weather cools; tolerates mild frosts and self-sows.

CHINA ASTER (*Callistephus chinensis*)

Warm-weather annual. Fantastic cut flowers in many colors, heights, and flower forms but sadly prone to aster yellows, a disease spread by leafhoppers. Try them once and see how they do—the problem may not visit your garden, at least for a few years. Fairly easy from seed, but needs a head start—sow indoors.

COSMOS (*Cosmos bipinnatus*)

Cosmos is the most common form grown as a warm-season annual. Single and now double forms offer different shadings and petal shapes on 18- to 40-inch-tall varieties, most in the white-pink-rose-red range. Related perennial species are sulfur yellow and orange. Foliage is finely divided, and plants have a willowy charm. Often self-sows.

DAHLIA *(Dahlia variabilis)*

Most often grown from a tuber to get a particular form but actually easy from seed, usually available as a mix of colors. Plants range 12 to 60 inches tall, grow quickly in warm weather, and come in every imaginable flower form and all colors except true blue. Taller types benefit from staking; brittle stems can snap with overhead watering or weight of flowers. Avoid high-nitrogen fertilizers. Gardeners in most of the States dig and store tubers over winter, but in Cascadia they are usually fine in the ground if drainage is decent. Slugs are attracted to the emerging shoots, so bait or scout early in the season.

DELPHINIUM *(Delphinium)*

Annual and perennial species. Annual larkspur seeds (now reclassified as *Consolida*) are easy directly sown in fall or early spring; thin to 10 inches apart. They look best in masses, and excellent true blues are the hallmark of the species, though shades of pink, purple, and white are available. Seen with a child's eye, there is a bunny head in each flower. Perennial *Delphinium elatum* is a classic cottage-garden plant, which makes impressive spires of clustered flowers in the same color range as larkspurs, but each flower is complex and spectacularly formed, and can appear almost opalescent. Newer reselected European types have replaced the older strains, but they usually require staking, rich soil, slug

patrol, and luck that it won't be constantly raining or blazing hot when they do bloom. A second bloom is possible if the flowered stems are promptly removed down to basal foliage and the plant fed again; somehow this second flowering seems even more welcome in late summer than in the heady days of June. The belladonna types (*D. bellamosum*) offer the same intense blues but on a shorter, bushier plant, also requiring rich, moist soil.

ECHINACEA *(Echinacea purpurea)*

Also called Prairie or Purple Coneflower—a tough perennial with coarse but cheerful-looking purple or white flowers. It can handle clay soils and is not difficult to grow from seed, though it blooms a year after sowing. This species is the source of medicinal *Echinacea*, made from the root parts of mature plants. A quantity of plants would be required for herbal use, but as an ornamental plant it is easily grown, fairly long blooming, and a great butterfly nectar source. Plant breeders have crossed *E. purpurea* with *E. paradoxa* and have now marketed plants with orange, yellow, and red shades as well as doubles, pompoms, and skinny ray petals. These plants are produced from tissue culture, and their vigor in the garden is variable. Reports of diminished heat tolerance compared to the tough original prairie species would probably not trouble most gardeners in the Pacific Northwest. If you want to try these fancy types, you'll have to get them from a nursery, as they are not seed grown.

FLOWERING TOBACCO (*Nicotiana* spp.)

A personal favorite because it self-sows reliably, attracts hummingbirds and (in the evening) hummingbird moths, and perfumes the evening too, if you stick with the fragrant kinds. Some of the shorter hybrids don't have much fragrance, but easy-to-find *N. alata*, Jasmine Tobacco, has wonderful fragrance from star-shaped white blossoms on airy 3-foot plants. Lime Green is also fragrant and a very pretty mixer with any partners. My hands-down favorite flower fragrance (like a blend of lily and carnation) is from *N. sylvestris*, which grows to 5 feet and has large, sticky, and somewhat rank-smelling foliage, an excellent back-of-border plant. Sow *Nicotiana* indoors in March or direct-sow in late April—after that you'll likely have volunteers. Species freely interbreed, so you can reselect the plants you like best in subsequent years. An additional plus is that *Nicotiana* grows fine in half sun.

FOXGLOVE (*Digitalis purpurea*)

Biennial or occasionally perennial. Widely naturalized, variable, and usually easy. Fall or spring sowings in most cases bloom the following year. First-year-blooming strains are available. They bloom for a longer period but are sterile hybrids and won't resow. Thrives in partial shade. Space young plants at least 18 inches apart so that they can grow a large frame to support the flowering stalks. Leaves at the base of the plant that touch the ground may look ratty by the second spring; trim these off and fertilize in early spring for best bloom. May send up second batch of blooming stalks if cut back soon after bloom. Copious reseeder, but extras can be transplanted or hoed. Choose your first variety wisely because you'll have them a long time. The improved flower forms are generally superior to the basic species, which has naturalized widely.

FUCHSIA (*Fuchsia* spp.)

I heartily recommend hardy fuchsias. The Northwest Fuchsia Society maintains a website with descriptions of hardy varieties and full cultural directions, and hardy varieties are now easy to find. The larger-flowered hybrids, both single and double, are more showy than the basic *magellanica* species. Cultivars with white or light colors show up better from a distance. Take advantage of this species; it attains near perfection here, growing into a small to medium shrub and blooming from midsummer to frost, long after many other flowers are finished. Hummingbirds love them. Avoid plants propagated in California—a devastating outbreak of fuchsia gall mites is out of control there, but so far not much of a threat here.

GAURA (*Gaura lindheimeri*)

One of the lowest-maintenance and longest-blooming perennials around. Mounding plants spill their slender stems toward the sun, offering a plethora of small four-petaled blooms in white to pinks that fall away cleanly—no deadheading. Called Wand Flower or Butterfly Flower because of the shape of the dainty blooms. Drought tolerant; Award of Garden Merit winner. Will bloom first year from seed with an early start, 10 weeks before last frost when sown indoors. Several good cultivars in nurseries.

HELLEBORE *(Helleborus × hybridus)*

These very early and long-blooming perennials are long lived and easy to maintain, tolerant of many soil types, and happy in full sun (with irrigation) to part/light shade. They can be grown from seed but take three or so years to bloom. Gardeners already growing them likely have some self-sown seedlings under their plants, which transplant easily. Ernie and Marietta O' Byrne from Northwest Garden Nursery in Oregon have hybridized spectacular strains that take an already-excellent plant to new heights of dazzling beauty. Tough evergreen plants hold their place all winter; cut the weathered foliage off in late winter to highlight the flowers that pop up in February and turn their faces to the sky. Individual flowers look good for months as they hold their shape while fading slowly.

HYSSOP *(Agastache)*

Annual and perennial species; grows 12 to 48 inches tall. Fragrant foliage, upright habit, spikes of tubular flowers with colorful calyxes. Cold hardy but must have good drainage to overwinter. Fairly drought tolerant, low maintenance, deer resistant, rewarding, hummingbird magnet. Propagate from seed or by division.

LOBELIA *(Lobelia erinus)*

Used for edging borders or trailing out of containers, this small cool-season annual gives months of tiny flowers in every shade of blue as well as some pinks, purples, and whites. When happy, it self-sows; if you've grown several types, it will hybridize in your garden and you'll have your own strain. Seeds are tiny—if you want to save seed, pull up a few plants and shake them over a bowl, then strain what fell through a very fine sieve. Sow in February or March; dust thinly on the surface of a light seed starting mix. I like to mix the seed first into a few spoonfuls of sand and put that into an old saltshaker to aid in distributing it. If you plant a flat of it, once the seedlings are up and growing about an inch tall, slice the flat into squares like brownies and lift each one (I use an old fork) into its own 4-inch pot. Each section will be a clump of seedlings, which is desirable. If you buy seed, it may be in multiseed pellets; in which case plant them according to supplied instructions. Fancy, often sterile lobelias are vegetatively produced; these keep blooming longer without shearing in midsummer and have larger flowers. They have to be purchased each spring.

MARIGOLD *(Tagetes)*

One of the most easily grown and universally recognized annual flowers, these come in the yellow-orange-red spectrum, with bicolors, pinwheels, flecking, singles, doubles, and variation of heights from 8 to 24 inches. These make a great first flower to plant with kids because they germinate so easily and flower quickly, offering a memorable if not pretty scent. Sow under lights six weeks before frost, or direct-sow when weather has settled. Gardening lore says that marigolds act as insect repellent and nematode control, but this is the subject of some debate—some tests have shown that marigolds can attract insects, especially spider mites. Washington State University Extension reported that extracts of marigold plants had a protective effect against cabbage root maggots and certain nematodes when applied to soils in controlled experiments, a very different scenario than marigolds grown as a companion plant.

NASTURTIUM (*Tropaeolum* spp.)

Nasturtiums are familiar to many for their showy, edible flowers in "hot" colors; pretty, rounded foliage; and a peppery smell and taste. Flowers are good tossed into stir-fries and salads. Plant habit can be mounded or trailing. Some strains have creamy flowers over bluish-green foliage, an elegant change from the bright orange usually associated with nasturtiums. This is one flower that does well in poor and dry soils—rich garden soil can produce lush foliage with little bloom. Easy to direct-seed. An overnight soak speeds germination. If you want to get a head start and sow indoors, transplant quickly before plants become root-bound. For something different and just as easy, try *Tropaeolum peregrinum*, Canary Bird Vine, which has lobed foliage and masses of small light-yellow flowers, which do resemble birds.

PANSY AND VIOLA (*Viola*)

Garden pansies grow fairly well in Cascadia, but take a long time to reach the size of the plants you can buy everywhere in the spring if you are starting from seed. If you want flowering plants in the spring, you'll need to sow them in the fall and overwinter them in a cold frame. Various leaf spots and other diseases can be a nuisance, as can predations by earwigs, slugs, etc. My advice is to buy some plants in the spring and plant them in fertile soil, in bright light or part shade but not hot sun, deadhead early in the season, and then let them set and drop some seed. By midsummer your focus will have likely moved on, and you can pull the plants out and later be pleasantly surprised by a nice crop of seedlings in the fall or spring, having let nature do the work. They hybridize freely, so expect variation in type. Violas, being a smaller near-wild pansy, naturalize quite successfully for many gardeners and are a lot less trouble than the fancy pansy.

POPPY (*Papaver* spp.)

Several kinds of annual poppies are easily grown from seed, and most will reseed reliably. The flamboyant opium poppy, *Papaver somniferum*, has been rebranded in the trade as breadseed poppy, but it is one and the same plant. This hardy annual comes in a wide assortment of colors from white to red to almost-black purple, many with blotches and streaks. Double-flowered forms and even superfrilly pompom forms are available from seed suppliers and gardeners who save seed. Sow on the surface, lightly raked, in early spring where they are to bloom, in full sun and well-drained ground. They do not need rich soil. When conditions are right, they will germinate and grow quickly, blooming in early summer. Early thinning is recommended—plants can grow quite large and tall. Alas, the show is over pretty quickly, so unless you want to grow a bunch for seed, in which case you'll have to let the plants stand till the pods are ripe and dry, you can pull most of the plants and use the space for something else, leaving a plant or two for seed for next year's flowers. The plants are an eyesore while drying down, so you may want to enjoy other people's poppies and give your space to something without this major drawback. California poppies, *Eschscholzia*, are a different annual species, which is direct-sown also in the fall or early spring on lean soils. Like other poppies, they resent transplanting, but once established will usually reseed. Their common appearance along roadsides is a clue that they need sharp drainage, tolerate dry soil, and revel in heat. Lovely ferny foliage in light bluish green is a perfect foil for the single or double forms, which breeders have developed. Light orange and yellow are the original wild colors, but now one can get many streaked, ruffled, and shaded tones including reds and creams. Toss some seed at the edge of your driveway or another suitable spot for a few months of dazzling color for very little effort.

SUNFLOWER *(Helianthus)*

From dwarf to giant, creamy white to burgundy red and all the yellows and oranges in between, sunflowers are more popular than ever, and most seed catalogs offer several kinds. For cut flowers, choose pollen-free varieties. It's easiest to direct-sow once the soil is warm and night temps are above 50 degrees F, usually late May or early June. The shorter types can be started indoors too, but they need to be transplanted before they outgrow the pots. Full sun and rich soil are essential for success. Sterile, seedless hybrids will not attract birds, and the lighter flowers are less likely to break the stems, which can be a problem with the large-headed seeded types. Stokes, Johnny's, and Territorial all have great selections. Because all but the smallest types grow fairly big, sunflowers are a good candidate for row culture—they need space around each plant to look and grow their best.

SWEET PEA *(Lathyrus odoratus)*

Sweet peas are making a comeback as part of the heirloom resurgence in gardens. We in Cascadia have the advantage of being well situated to get a good crop, because they like the long period of cool weather our early summers usually provide. Most require support. Dwarf and shorter bush varieties, which don't require trellising, are available but less common. As their variety designations indicate, some kinds are larger and showier, and the best-smelling ones are somewhat smaller in their flower size but still lovely in their color and form. All kinds need rich, moist soil and a location where they will not be blasted by the hot sun. Plant in fall or early spring, or both times for an extended harvest. I often put in seeds at the edges of my snap pea plantings—they are not the same species as garden peas and need a bit more nitrogen, but it's easy to scratch in some extra COF where the sweet peas are. The timing is perfect to enjoy their blossoms while you're out picking peas. The fragrance is wonderful as is their lasting performance in a vase. Seed is easily collected if you leave some flowers to form pods and allow them to dry. Sweet peas can also be started indoors in February; if you do this, it helps speed things up to pregerminate the seeds or at least soak them overnight, as they have a hard seed coat. Ideal is to nick the seeds with a nail clipper, just to break into the hard shell, but do not cut the seed through. If you do this, there's no need for the overnight soak.

They can take a month or more to germinate in cold soil outdoors and are attractive to slugs too, so be prepared to replant if yours somehow don't show up.

ZINNIA

Hot weather annuals in short to tall varieties, with rather coarse, rough foliage but strong stems excellent for cut flowers. Blooms come in every color but blue. From small button flowers to very large fancy shapes, all offer the flat landing-pad surface and central discs that butterflies seek. Gardeners in the warmer areas of Cascadia will have an easier time with zinnias because they need warm soil to germinate and size up, though they can be started indoors about the same time as your peppers. Plants languish in cool weather when viral diseases and slug damage can cause problems; powdery mildew may strike when the temperatures are up. They do best with good air circulation around each plant, so consider growing them in a row or section, rather than in a closely packed jumble.

Herbs

Some herbs are simple to raise from seed, and if you anticipate harvesting large amounts, it might be practical to grow some as a crop—basil is an excellent example, or lavender if you want to harvest a quantity of flowers for drying. But most herbs are wanted in smaller quantities, and one or a few plants will likely provide plenty for fresh use and drying.

In that case it may be simpler to buy starters or get a piece from another gardener.

Interestingly, many herbs are in the mint family (*Lamiaceae*, which has over 7,000 species). All the mints such as peppermint, spearmint, and pennyroyal obviously belong, but so do lavender, oregano, horehound, basil, sage, and lemon balm, to name a few. Those which form mats of laterally spreading stolons can be propagated by pulling off a few bits of these surface rooting stems and potting them up, or transplanting right away if the pieces are sturdy and the weather not extreme. This would include the mints, marjoram, oregano, lemon balm, bee balm, germander, and hyssop. Rosemary, sages, and lavenders have a different growth habit and are best started from seed or vegetatively propagated from cuttings at the nursery, if you want to get a particular cultivar.

Here's a brief summary of some of the most popular herbs.

BASIL (*Ocimum basilicum*)

Direct-seed into warm soil from late May on, or raise seedlings under lights. Basil seems more vigorous when direct seeded. I like to preheat my intended basil area by erecting a simple minigreenhouse—a piece of field fencing bent into a wide *U* shape and covered with clear plastic. I do this in April and let any weeds sprout and be eliminated while the soil warms, then I plant the seed mid-May into warmer, drier soil than the uncovered outdoors. Even a few square feet is enough to get some early plants going, and then you can put your main crop in later. But transplants are okay too—just a bit more susceptible to shock than most veggies (harden them off well). Some people like to grow it thickly, but I prefer to give each plant reasonable space. Staggered plantings are good because once flowering begins, the leaf quality diminishes. Many specialty types are available with cinnamon, anise, licorice, or other flavor tones, as well as varying degrees of intensity and leaf color. Most companies would rather sell you multiple packets rather than a mix, but at the time of this printing I was able to find a good mix from Bountiful Gardens. Basil loses flavor when dried, but an easy way to keep it is to mince finely, cover with olive oil, and freeze into cubes in an ice cube tray or small pleated paper sauce cups. Make multiple batches, store frozen in a ziplock, and use as needed.

BORAGE (Borago officinalis)

Borage leaves have a decided cucumber flavor, good in salads, as a garnish, and used in some southern Europe cuisines. It is also a significant medicinal herb. Bees are attracted to the small intense blue flowers, which have a sweet cucumber taste too and are charming frozen into ice cubes to decorate a drink. Sow seed shallowly midspring to midsummer in part sun. Borage is a prolific self-seeder, but unwanted plants are not hard to hoe out.

CHIVES (Allium tuberosum)

The mild onion flavor of chives is very welcome in the kitchen. A good plant to grow in a pot nearby so that you can run out and snip some at a moment's notice. Most people will only need one plant; cut it frequently even if you're not using all you cut. Once it starts to flower, tenderness of the leaves declines, and tiny chive seedlings are

hard to remove where they are not wanted. Either from a pot or in the ground, divide and replant fresh sections of the clustered root mass in the spring into rich soil.

CILANTRO/CORIANDER
(Coriandrum sativum)

Also known as Chinese parsley. The fresh leaves are called cilantro, and the dried seed is the spice called coriander. Many find cilantro an essential ingredient in salsas and a version of pesto; although some, myself included, are in the approximately 12 percent of people who cannot abide by the perceived soapy taste, apparently the result of a genetic component of the olfactory mechanisms. Growing advice is found on page 222.

DILL (Anethum graveolens)

A bright taste of summer and easy to direct-sow, as well as a prolific self-sower. Dill gets fairly tall and can be grown in a thicket closely spaced or as fewer larger plants in ordinary, not too rich soil. As with cilantro, some varieties are slower to go to seed, so select the cultivar to suit your preference for leaves or seed; all will eventually flower by late summer.

FENNEL (Foeniculum vulgare)

Two forms are grown, one for the flavorful seed and the other for the delicious enlarged bulbing base. In the latter form, it is called Florence fennel, Azoricum group, or finocchio in Italian. The swollen leaf bases have a sweet anise flavor and are eaten raw and lightly cooked. These must be grown in rich soil with no dry spells, which can send the plants into bolt mode. Wait to sow until June to permit rapid growth, which gives the most tender bulbs; hilling up soil around the bases of the plant will help too.

Unharvested plants will bolt, but their flowers are a phenomenal draw to myriad small, beneficial pollinators, and the pollen grains of fennel flowers are a superb flavoring ingredient to sprinkle on fish, pastas, stir-fries, and the like. No special treatment is needed to produce seed, but try to harvest in dry weather.

LAVENDER (*Lavandula* spp.)

There are several forms of lavender—Spanish, French, English, and so forth—but distinctions may be blurred. Height, flower color, fragrance, bloom time, stem length, essential oil content, and hardiness vary tremendously. If you want some particular quality, check the herb seed companies listed and order seed, or make a short list of varieties to look for locally. There are a few cultivars that will bloom in the first year from seed, but a cutting from a grown plant is faster to reach a decent size. Generally speaking, *L. stoechas* and *L. dentata* are less hardy than others—check your zones and follow hints about drainage given earlier. Most lavender plants decline with age; though they benefit from trimming back in early spring, after several years they should be replaced.

MARJORAM and OREGANO (*Origanum* spp.)

These two perennials are related, but oregano has the more intense aroma/flavor, while marjoram is sweeter. To confuse the issue, there is also another marjoram species and a different species called oregano too, but the *Origanums* are grown similarly, in fairly lean soil with lots of sun, moderate water, and good drainage in winter. Both benefit from shearing back to promote leafiness. Discard the woody centers every few years, replanting pieces from the outside of the clump into fresh soil.

ROSEMARY (*Rosmarinus officinalis*)

The two basic types are shrubby and trailing (prostrate), with many cultivars to chose from. Hardiness varies; site your plants for maximum warmth in winter, and avoid cold air traps. Follow cultural directions as described earlier for woody subshrubs. Clip regularly for dense growth.

SAGE (*Salvia* spp.)

Many species in this wonderful family. The culinary sages, *Salvia officinalis*, have three common forms of foliage (plain, tricolor, and variegated), but like lavenders, fine points abound in variety selection. Refer to seed companies for variety details and growing directions for woody subshrubs. Other salvias are great for flavoring teas, fruit salads, scenting potpourri, and medicinal uses. Many are borderline hardy, such as pineapple sage (*Salvia elegans*), but they can grow large enough in one season to be rewarding, and given a warm winter may reemerge in the spring. The shape of salvia flowers is very attractive to hummingbirds. Blue *S. guaranitica* is a show-stopping 4-foot magnet that blooms from mid-summer to frost.

THYME *(Thymus* spp.*)*

A valuable herb for the kitchen with powerful medicinal uses as well. Culinary thyme is available in many varieties besides the plain. There are orange, lemon, balsam, and many other cultivars. Most are similar in growth habit, typically mat-forming low mounds with tiny leaves and very small flowers on short stems. If you want to harvest lots of the leaves, shear to prevent flowering. Usually perennial in Cascadia. Like the oreganos and marjorums, the center of older plants can get woody—grow from newer edge pieces pulled off and replanted in spring. Follow the woody herb mantra: sun, good drainage, especially in winter, some water and COF but not too wet or too rich.

Additional Reading

Desire always precedes action; coming to understand "why-to" is more important than knowing how-to. After reading some—or better, all—of the books listed below, you'll thoroughly appreciate why it makes sense to do whatever it takes to grow nutrient-dense food for your own kitchen. At the date of this book's publication, every title in this list is available for free download from the Soil and Health Library: www.soilandhealth.org. Steve Solomon created the library in 1997, and it was largely his project until 2014. Now it is owned by a New South Wales registered charitable association; Steve sits on the committee.

Albrecht, William. *Soil Fertility & Animal Health.* Webster City, IA: Fred Hahne Printing, 1958.

Albrecht published hundreds of scientific papers, journal articles, and even a many-years-long series of monthly health magazine articles. This, his only book, encapsulates his major messages. A reprint of Albrecht's book is currently sold as *The Albrecht Papers, Vol. II* by Acres (2005). (There are many Albrecht papers and articles in the Soil and Health Library.)

Dale, Tom, and Vernon Gill Carter. *Topsoil and Civilization.* Norman: University of Oklahoma Press, 1955.

A summary of world history that explains how every previous civilization fell because they degraded their agricultural resource base, and asks—quite pointedly—how long ours is going to endure.

Elliot, Robert H. *The Clifton Park System of Farming.* London: Faber & Faber, 1943.

Originally published in 1898 as *Agricultural Changes.* Elliot developed a system of laying down land to grass, dependent on no input except a complex mixture of deep-rooting pasture seeds. The pastures would be plowed under after four to eight years, cash crops would grown until the humus levels declined, and then the field would be restored by again growing grass/clover/herbal mixtures.

Howard, Albert. *Farming and Gardening for Health or Disease.* London: Faber & Faber, 1945.

Albert Howard founded the organic farming and gardening movement. *Farming and Gardening for Health or Disease* was republished as *The Soil and Health* in 1947 by Rodale Press.

Howard, Albert, and Yeshwant D. Wad. *The Waste Products of Agriculture: Their Utilization as Humus.* London: Oxford University Press, 1931.

This is Howard's most important scientific publication, detailing the nature, practice, and significance of composting as he learned to do it at Indore research farm.

Jenny, Hans. *Factors in Soil Formation: A System of Quantitative Pedology.* New York: Dover, 1994.

One of the most important books about soil ever written about soil fertility. This is a scientific text that can be understood without high-level mathematics; however, a well-grasped secondary school chemistry class and a touch of geology will go a long way toward making this book fully comprehensible. Dover publishes a paperback reproduction of the 1941 edition.

King, F. H. *Farmers of Forty Centuries, or Permanent Agriculture in China, Korea and Japan.* N.p.: 1911.

King was a masterful observer of farming and keenly aware of the massive ecological destruction happening a century ago. This is, if nothing else, a great travel book.

Krasil'nikov, N. A. *Soil Microorganisms and Higher Plants.* Moscow: Academy of Sciences of the USSR, 1958.

Translated in Israel by Dr. Y. Halperin. Published for the National Science Foundation, Washington, DC, and the Department of Agriculture, USA, by the Israel Program for Scientific Translations (1961). This is the ultimate study of the microbial process in soil. It has been little known since its publication. In the Soviet Union of the 1930s, '40s, and '50s, industrial production was scanty. So Krasil'nikov focused on the biological and found ways to improve plant growth with special composts and microbial ferments of the sort that could be produced by the farmer in an old barrel. All these "primitive" solutions are based on a very high-level understanding of the microbial process in soil and the interactions between soil microbes with each other, of how crop species interact with each other via long-lasting soil residues (root exudates), and of how plants and microbes interact with each other.

Parnes, Robert. *Fertile Soil: A Grower's Guide to Organic & Inorganic Fertilizers.* Davis, CA: Agaccess, 1990.

This extremely useful but scarce paperback book is very expensive if you can find a used copy.

Price, Weston, D.D.S. *Nutrition and Physical Degeneration.* New York: Paul B. Hoeber, 1939.

In the 1930s Dr. Price journeyed to extremely isolated regions, finding people who, because of their remoteness, enjoyed excellent nutrition, and from that, general good health, long life, and virtual immunity to dental disease. Price visited Scotland, Switzerland, Canada, Alaska, Peru, Africa, Down Under, and Melanesia, etc., and in each region found extraordinarily healthy (and extraordinarily isolated) peoples who did not partake of the industrial food system because they could not. Contains remarkable photographs that show the differences between what healthy bodies and physically degenerated bodies look like far better than words ever could. No one who spends time studying these pictures will ever view the health and appearance of their friends, their neighbors, or their own face in the mirror in the same way.

Solomon, Steve, and Erica Reinheimer. *The Intelligent Gardener: Growing Nutrient-Dense Food.* Gabriola Island, BC: New Society Publishers, 2013.

Explains how to interpret a soil test and using that information, bring soil into the kind of balance that produces nutrient-dense food. The book can be comprehended by anyone that genuinely learned primary school arithmetic.

Smith, J. Russell. *Tree Crops: A Permanent Agriculture.* New York: Harcourt & Brace, 1929.

Any plowed field sloping more than 3 percent cannot be prevented from eroding away over the course of a few centuries (sometimes a lot quicker). Smith's solution, the one leading to a permanent civilization, is the use of food-producing tree crops on sloping lands. Smith shows us photos of places where people mostly eat food from trees and shows the possibilities for tree cropping in North America.

Tiedjens, Victor A. *More Food from Soil Science: The Natural Chemistry of Lime in Agriculture.* New York: Exposition Press, 1965.

Tiedjens is right up there with Albrecht on the list of those who most advanced the science of growing nutrient-dense food.

Tiedjens, Victor A. *Olena Farm, USA: An Agricultural Success Story.* New York: Exposition Press, 1969.

Tiedjens chronicles how he restored an exhausted Ohio farm mainly by the use of agricultural lime.

Weaver, John E. *Root Development of Vegetable Crops.* New York: McGraw Hill, 1927.

A classic study filled with species-by-species illustrations, each one worth tens of thousands of words. You can't understand what's going on above the soil line unless you appreciate what the plant is trying to accomplish belowground.

Widtsoe, John A. *Dry-Farming: A System of Agriculture for Countries under a Low Rainfall.* New York: MacMillan, 1911.

Hidden between the paragraphs of this book one can see how lack of ethics and greed led farmers to ignore Widtsoe's warnings, making the Great Plains dust bowl inevitable. This book provided insight that allowed me to develop dry gardening.

Wrench, G. T., *The Wheel of Health.* London: C. W. Daniel Company, 1938.

In this book Dr. Wrench considers the Hunza, a mountain people renowned for their longevity and vigor. It should rest at the very foundations of one's personal explorations of health and its roots. In this book you will encounter a summary of the life works of two other renowned health explorers, Sir Robert McCarrison and Sir Albert Howard. Their writings are also available in the Soil and Health Library. You will also have the opportunity to meet Dr. Wrench, an individual possessed of the most admirable intelligence.

INDEX

Note: Illustrations are indicated by *italics*.

Z

ABOUT THE AUTHORS

STEVE SOLOMON spent much of his adult life in rural Oregon, where he started Territory Seed Company, a mail-order vegetable seed business, which he sold in 1986. Although he retired from the seed company at age forty-four, he continued to research, practice, and refine methods of organic gardening.

Now an active seventy-three-year-old, he currently grows vegetables and vegetable seeds on an entire quarter-acre residential house block. His surplus veggies go into regular weekly food boxes that help a few local families. He makes presentations about gardening and health-related topics and moderates an active Yahoo e-mail chat group called "soilandhealth." He serves the community as a neighborhood soil analyst with a rapidly expanding list of clients.

Photograph by Jemimah Duncan

In 1980 **MARINA McSHANE** came across the first Territorial Seed Company catalog, and noticed the founder Steve Solomon lived fairly close by. She visited the seed company's trial grounds and discovered that Steve willingly shared his knowledge and offered her advice on her own struggling vegetable plot. He had a sincere desire to help other people achieve their aims. Soon after, she went to work at Territorial's seed room and helped out in the trial gardens, which provided intensive learning.

For several years Marina operated a micro-nursery—growing perennials, shrubs, and trees. She currently lives with her husband and dogs near Eugene, Oregon, where she grows vegetables and ornamentals.

Photograph by Paul Lanz